1991

John Dewey

The Later Works, 1925–1953

Volume 15: 1942–1948

EDITED BY JO ANN BOYDSTON

TEXTUAL EDITOR,

PATRICIA BAYSINGER

ASSISTANT TEXTUAL EDITOR,

RICHARD W. FIELD

With an Introduction by Lewis S. Feuer

Southern Illinois University Press

Carbondale and Edwardsville

COMMITTEE ON
SCHOLARLY EDITIONS

AN APPROVED TEXT

MODERN LANGUAGE
ASSOCIATION OF AMERICA

The text of this reprinting is a photo-offset reproduction of the original cloth
edition that contains the full apparatus for the volume awarded the seal of the
Committee on Scholarly Editions of the Modern Language Association.
Editorial expenses were met in part by a grant from the Editions Program of the
National Endowment for the Humanities, an independent Federal agency.

The paperbound edition has been made possible by a special subvention from
the John Dewey Foundation.

The Library of Congress catalogued the first printing of this work (in cloth) as
follows:

Dewey, John, 1859–1952.
    The later works, 1925–1953.

    Vol. 15 has introd. by Lewis S. Feuer.
    Continues The middle works, 1899–1924.
    Includes bibliographies and indexes.

    CONTENTS: v. 1. 1925—v. 2. 1925–1927.—[etc.]—v. 15. 1942–1948.
    1. Philosophy—Collected works.   I. Boydston, Jo Ann, 1924–.   II. Title.
B945.D41   1981   191   80-27285
ISBN 0-8093-1535-1 (V. 15)

ISBN 0-8093-1681-1 (paperback)

Contents

Introduction
By Lewis S. Feuer

The years 1942–1948 were for John Dewey probably the most intellectually isolated of his life. He had opposed as late as the spring of 1941 America's getting involved in the war against Nazi Germany, for he feared that in such a war, America would sacrifice its own democratic liberties. After the Japanese attacked Pearl Harbor, however, and Hitler formally declared war against the United States, Dewey fully supported America's unparalleled exertions to achieve a victory. As a philosopher and social scientist, however, Dewey criticized bravely and wisely the outpouring of propaganda that began to rewrite Soviet history and to apologize for the cruel suppressions on the part of Stalin's dictatorship and secret police. With his experience on the Trotsky Inquiry Commission fresh in his mind, Dewey watched with consternation how the former American Ambassador to the Soviet Union, Joseph E. Davies, assured millions of Americans that the "Moscow trials" had been the means whereby Stalin had gotten rid of his "Fifth Columnists," such as Trotsky, Bukharin, and Marshal Tukhachevsky, who were purportedly waiting to betray the Soviet Union to the Nazis when war came. Davies's book *Mission to Moscow* was a best seller; its film version, with honest-faced, craggy-lined Walter Huston acting as the ambassador, captivated Americans with its comforting portrayals of Stalin and his party apparatus.

No writing of Dewey's ever was as laden with blunt, telling blows as the review and the letters that he wrote concerning Davies's *Mission to Moscow*. He compared sardonically Davies's "Miraculous Revelation" three years after he had left Moscow to the conversion on the road to Damascus of St. Paul: "In the case of Ex-Ambassador Davies, the holder of the Moscow Mission became a missionary." He suggested that if Davies were to read Koestler's *Darkness at Noon,* "he might conceivably receive another flash of revelation." Above all, Dewey warned that "a false idealization of Russia" would complicate the negotiating of our terms of peace, and that we would have "to pay a high price for building up Stalinites and fellow travelers."

Dewey admonished wisely in the *New York Times* that one might "rejoice in Russian victories over the common enemy without idealizing Stalin's regime of terror," that during our own Civil War, we had been grateful for "aid from autocratic Russia" without therefore undertaking to eulogize the czarist regime, and that Stalin was accepting all our aid to him without for a moment altering his belief that "totalitarianism and democracy will not mix." Availing himself of the recently published book of the former Soviet intelligence officer Walter Krivitsky, Dewey dared suggest that "Stalin's liquidation of the Old Bolsheviki" had been part of his "price of success in his dealings with Hitler," with whom he had been "trying very hard to reach an agreement." Dewey argued that it was dangerous for any public official "to present the totalitarian despotism of Stalin in any but its true light." In his interchange with the educator John L. Childs, Dewey warned presciently that negotiations already in progress envisaged "the sacrifice of the Baltic states and of Poland," and that the crucial time for wresting concessions from Stalin for a democratic evolution was being lost: "When Stalin needs our help is the time to start setting up these conditions."

Dewey did little further writing on the war. Other public issues, however, continued to engage his philosophic writing. He was troubled especially by what he took to be the growing, deleterious influence of anti-naturalism, especially as represented by the Roman Catholic church. Dewey had been deeply affected by the significant role that the church had played in preventing the appointment of Bertrand Russell as professor of philosophy in 1940 at the College of the City of New York. For much as he disliked Russell personally,[1] Dewey had written and given of his

---

1. To his friend Boyd H. Bode, Dewey wrote on April 3, 1948: "I've not [gotten] over being sorry that I let B. Russell down so easily as I did. I have never been able to take him seriously enough intellectually to do him justice. If any evidence of the dam low estate of philosophy at present were needed, his inflated rep would be enough—he may or may not be an authority on the formalization of mathematics. I'm suspicious about that on the authority of A. F. Bentley, but even so it is pitiful that should give him a rep in philosophy" (*Letters from John Dewey*, University Microfilms, Ann Arbor).

time to organizational efforts to defend Russell's appointment against the lawsuit instituted by a Catholic mother on behalf of her daughter, and the ensuing decision rendered by a Catholic Tammany judge, under the pressure of clergymen. Dewey's essay "Anti-Naturalism in Extremis" had a sharp tone that he would never have employed against theological philosophy in his earlier years; even such a Catholic liberal as Jacques Maritain was not exempted from Dewey's thrusts, for Dewey held categorically that inherent in every variety of anti-naturalist philosophy was a base "and degrading view of nature."

Was naturalistic philosophy however a certifiable guide to nobler conceptions? Under the aegis of the Soviet Union with its historical materialist standpoint, a contempt for human life had been nurtured that underwrote the killing of millions in labor and prison camps,—"class enemies," Kropotkinites, Mensheviks, Trotskyists, Bukharinists, peasants, critical workers, bourgeois, Zionists, Baptists. The Marxist naturalistic view that there were no universal ethical principles but only shifting rules that reflected changing class interests could be no less potentially degrading to the moral sense than any theological dogma. Dewey remarked pointedly that "some of the bloodiest and most cruel wars" were "waged in the name of . . . supernaturalism and of the ecclesiastic institution," that when St. Thomas Aquinas said "Love thy neighbor as thyself," that was consistent operationally with torturing one's fellowman physically in order to save his soul from hell's eternities, and that anti-naturalism had blocked the path of scientific progress in social problems. To Dewey as a prophet of science, it was clear that naturalism alone provided the basis for "the worth and dignity of men and women," for it found the source for human values in human nature itself, in its natural social relationships. Was it true, however, that anti-naturalists perforce resisted the rise of scientific methods? The leaders in the scientific revolution had included such men as Descartes, Leibniz, Spinoza, Newton, Locke—all of them, in Dewey's sense, "anti-naturalists"; was it Leibniz, indeed, who first used the word "naturalism" when he wrote in criticism: "Spinoza begins where Descartes ended, *in Naturalism*"?[2] making it clear

2. George Martin Duncan, trans., *The Philosophical Works of Leibnitz,* 2d ed. (New Haven: Tuttle, Morehouse and Taylor Co., 1908), p. 269.

that he was numbered among the anti-naturalists. In any case, naturalists such as Freud and Nietzsche, reporting that human nature, with its innate aggressive drives,[3] was the irremediable source of war, hatred, envies, had a small regard for the worth and dignity of man. Was naturalism then a sufficient basis for a humanistic ethics?

To be sure, Dewey argued that the supernaturalist standpoint had nurtured a pessimistic conception of human nature, and that a hope for mankind truly emerged only when such naturalistic liberal philosophers as Thomas Jefferson appeared. It does seem, however, that naturalism, humanism, optimism, are all what Arthur Lovejoy called "unit-ideas," that is, each of them is independent of the others, and one can consistently hold to all possible combinations of these tenets and their contraries; one can be a naturalist without being, for instance, either a humanist or optimist. From Lucretius to Hobbes and Santayana, naturalists have held to a pessimistic conception of human nature. Lucretius looked out upon his social world as in decline: "they amass wealth by civil bloodshed and greedily double their riches piling up murder on murder, . . ." "Yes and even now the age is enfeebled and the earth exhausted. . . . And now the aged ploughman shakes his head . . . that the labors of his hands have come to nothing. . . . The sorrowful planter . . . impeaches the march of time. . . ."[4] Thomas Hobbes, born to fear as his pregnant mother "was big with such fear" at the approach of the Spanish Armada, "bringing the day of doom to our race," always regarded human beings as prone to brutish deeds, and therefore needing to be curbed by an absolute sovereign;[5] Dewey had once written a detailed study of Hobbes's political philosophy, and the relation of its psychological theory of man to the restless warring of Hobbes's time; Dewey knew the basis for a naturalistic pessimism. And indeed, the chief proponents of the American Constitution, James Madison and Alexander Hamilton, were likewise

3. Sigmund Freud, "I have found little that is 'good' about human beings on the whole. In my experience most of them are trash, . . ." (*Psychoanalysis and Faith: The Letters of Sigmund Freud & Oskar Pfister*, ed. Heinrich Meng and Ernst L. Freud, trans. Eric Mosbacher [New York: Basic Books, 1963], p. 61).
4. Lucretius, *On the Nature of Things*, trans. H. A. J. Munro (London: G. Bell and Sons, 1929), pp. 85, 81.
5. "The Autobiography of Thomas Hobbes," trans. Benjamin Farrington, *The Rationalist Annual, 1958* (London: Watts and Co., 1957), p. 24.

naturalistic pessimists in their conception of the human character. The authors of *The Federalist Papers* did not rest their case on human benevolence, public spiritedness, or disinterestedness; Madison wrote that "the spirit of faction" pervaded men.[6] The authors of the Constitution fashioned a system of checks and balances because they wished to impede the propensity toward selfish interest on the part alike of democratic assemblies, oligarchical chambers, and elected executive officers.

Dewey, moreover, surely knew that even humanistic naturalism seemed to impose upon its greatest advocates a pessimistic burden. Thomas Hardy, whose *Tess of the D'Urbervilles* Dewey esteemed in 1936 as the most influential novel of his last fifty years, apart from Bellamy's *Looking Backward,* ended his story with a symbolic protest against "the President of the Immortals," and looked forward himself to "the close of the human show."[7] Thomas Henry Huxley, whose textbook of physiology had a tremendous effect on Dewey as an undergraduate, wrote that the consciousness of the "great truth" of physical determinism "weighs like a nightmare . . . upon many of the best minds of these days," and this naturalistic nightmare itself evidently affected Huxley with recurrent depressions. A favorite pupil of Dewey's, Clarence Ayres, had narrated the story vividly in his biography of Huxley.[8] Even Herbert Spencer, the high naturalistic philosopher of progress for the first half of Dewey's life, avowed most of his years a basic doubt that his life was worth living.[9] Nonetheless, Dewey held to a kind of secular faith in a preestablished harmony between the naturalistic philosophy and its efficacy against "escapism and humanistic defeatism."

Apart from his sociological critique of anti-naturalism, Dewey, however, wished as a philosopher to establish naturalism on philosophical grounds as a theory superior to all the varieties of

6. Arthur O. Lovejoy, *Reflections on Human Nature* (Baltimore: Johns Hopkins Press, 1961), pp. 46, 51–52.
7. See Edward Weeks, "Fifty Influential Books," *Publishers' Weekly,* March 23, 1935, pp. 1227–29, also p. 1230. "Savants Select Most Influential Volumes," *English Journal 25* (June 1936): 497–98. Carl J. Weber, *Hardy in America: A Study of Thomas Hardy and His American Readers* (Waterville, Maine: Colby College Press, 1946), p. 261.
8. Clarence Ayres, *Huxley* (New York: W. W. Norton and Co., 1932), pp. 115–16.
9. Hugh Elliot, *Herbert Spencer* (New York: Henry Holt and Co., 1917), pp. 46–47.

anti-naturalism. His opportunity to do so came in 1945 when his former students, Sidney Hook and Ernest Nagel, asked that he join them as co-author of an article entitled "Are Naturalists Materialists?" Dewey cheerfully agreed to do so. Except for the opening paragraph, Dewey contributed little to the essay, which was mainly written by Nagel; he obviously was pleased, however, to stand with these men more than forty years younger than himself in defense of the book *Naturalism and the Human Spirit* to which they had contributed. The critic whom they were rebutting, W. H. Sheldon, a distinguished professor of philosophy at Yale, idealistic in standpoint, was respected for his careful, many-sided considerations. Sheldon charged their naturalism with being "just materialism over again under a softer name," since they held that conscious or mental events were "*wholly* at the beck and call" of physical processes. According to Sheldon, the reasoning of the naturalists was circular; Nature, for them, was defined as whatever can be studied by scientific method; hence, if angels, private thoughts, and God could not be studied by scientific method, it was assumed that they were not part of Nature and, therefore, nonexistent.

The answer of Dewey, Hook, and Nagel was forthright. To begin with, they noted they were not "reductive materialists," that is, they did not maintain that mental states, emotions, joys, apprehensions of meaning, were subsumable under the heading of physical entities or events; nevertheless, they held that these mental occurrences were adjectival to physical ones and were in this sense analogous to such properties as temperature and solubility, which were not themselves physical entities, inasmuch as for instance, they had neither volume nor shape. Mental occurrences, moreover, they argued, were caused by physical ones; they depended on certain organizations of physical things, without, however, being themselves additional physical entities. This second type of "materialism" Dewey and his associates called "naturalism"; it was akin to what C. D. Broad in his exhaustive, classificatory *The Mind and Its Place in Nature* called "emergent materialism."

How cogent was this reply of Dewey and his friends to the dualistic theory of mind? The analogy of mental events to such physical properties as temperature was hardly well taken. For in what is known as the theory of dimensions, the three dimensions of mass, length, and time are the base into which all the definitions of physical concepts are fitted. Temperature, of course, has its appropriate physical dimensions, and this theory indeed was first developed by Joseph Fourier in his famed *Theory of Heat*.[10] Now there are no analogous dimensional definitions for reflections, dreams, memories; they stand outside the dimensions of mass and length; a person may observe our public physical states while we privately dream, but that correlation lacks the logical structure of the operational physical definitions of temperature or solubility. It is noteworthy that the greatest physiologist of reflex action, Sir Charles Sherrington, called the "supreme philosopher of the nervous system" and the "man who almost single-handedly crystallized the special field of neurophysiology," remained all his life a dualist with regard to the relation of mind and body. His years of life (1857–1952) spanned those of Dewey; the same biological and psychological evidence was available to both of them, yet Sherrington, in contrast to Dewey's perhaps emotive discomfort with any "separation," any dualism, wrote: "the physical is never anything but physical, or the psychical anything but psychical," yet the two systems "are largely complemental and life brings them co-operatively together at innumerable points." The mental and the physical, Sherrington said, constituted a dualistic "liaison": "That our being should consist of *two* fundamental entities offers I suppose no greater inherent probability than that it should rest on one only." Sherrington, for all his vast physiological knowledge, thought in 1947 that the issue "remains where Aristotle left it 2,000 years ago."[11] "The two seem incommensurable."[12]

According to Dewey, such a dualistic conception as Sherrington's should have greatly impeded his investigations into reflex action and constituted a metaphysical burden. Far from it, Sher-

10. W. Stanley Jevons, *The Principles of Science: A Treatise on Logic and Scientific Method*, 2d ed. reprinted with corrections (London and New York: Macmillan and Co., 1892), p. 325ff. P. W. Bridgman, *Dimensional Analysis* (New Haven: Yale University Press, 1922), p. 24.
11. Judith P. Swazey, "Charles Scott Sherrington," *Dictionary of Scientific Biography*, vol. 12 (New York: Charles Scribner's Sons, 1975), p. 401. John C. Eccles and William C. Gibson, *Sherrington: His Life and Thought* (Berlin: Springer International, 1979), pp. 111, 128ff., 232–34.
12. Sir Charles Sherrington, *Man on His Nature*, 2d ed. (Cambridge: Cambridge University Press, 1951), p. 247.

rington's scientific investigations flourished, though he felt to the end there was an utterly inexplicable gap between the physio-chemical sequence of events and the mental ones. Émile Meyerson, the historico-logical student of scientific method whom Einstein most admired, likewise felt that the relationship between physical and mental events remained irrational, that the pattern of conservation (or identity) that was essential to scientific explanation could not be fulfilled in the case of mental-physical interaction. To Dewey and his co-workers, however, such "psychophysical dualism" seemed to open the way toward an idealistic absolute, with all manner of anti-scientific resistances to free inquiry. A dualistic philosophy, Dewey held, imperils the investigation into the causes and consequences of human values. Perhaps there remained in Dewey an oversystemic tendency to link together the various philosophic ideas that he opposed. Arthur Lovejoy, who was perhaps the most trenchant critic of the ambiguities in Dewey's pragmatism, was also the most vigorous and searching proponent of dualism in American philosophy. Though Lovejoy's *Revolt against Dualism* did not stem the anti-dualistic trend, its author was profoundly aware that nonlogical drives largely control the directions of intellectual movements. Lovejoy himself never evolved from dualism toward absolute idealism, or anti-scientific supernaturalism; he remained a probing critic of "eternalistic" idealism, calling himself a "temporalist," and his allegiance to science was certainly as unswerving as Dewey's. It is noteworthy that Lovejoy and Dewey were founders, and first secretary and first president respectively, of the American Association of University Professors. One would have thought on the basis of the close connection that Dewey drew between philosophy and politics, and especially the dangers latent in dualistic separations, that his collaboration with Lovejoy would have been improbable or, at best, the fortunate outcome of an inconsistency on Lovejoy's part. It is harder to imagine the painstaking Lovejoy as ever having been in his life inconsistent.

At most, Dewey was prepared to concede to the dualist as, for example, in his discussion with Philip Blair Rice, that personal events such as a toothache are "*centered* in particular organic bodies"; he denied, however, that they constituted a privately felt, nonpublic knowledge. So resolute was Dewey to eliminate any dualism between public and private knowledge that he advanced

the physiological speculation that "a certain grafting of the proprioceptor nerve-tissues of two organisms could be successfully
effected" so that different observers would experience alike the
same allegedly "private" event that was thus rendered "public."
Dewey, strangely enough, did not consider that this bold claim
was at odds with the principle he often reiterated—that the experimental arrangement to enquire concerning a given existential
object itself interacts with and reconstructs that object. The in-
sertion of wiring, or the cultivation of additional tissue, to join
one person's nerves with another would therefore itself differentiate the qualitative character of the second experience, not to
mention altering that of the first. Thus, the private, qualitative
experience could never be altogether duplicated publicly.

Dewey's naturalism was meant to provide a basis for studying
and hopefully solving ethical and moral problems through scientific methods; ethics, in effect, was to become an applied social science, enabling decisions to be made not by appealing to transcendental intuitions or religious imperatives but on the basis of the
best available scientific information. In 1944, however, Charles L.
Stevenson's book *Ethics and Language* was published, which despite its acknowledgment to Dewey, essentially challenged his
conception of a scientific ethics. Drawing on the linguistic analyses of Ogden, Richards, and Wittgenstein, Stevenson argued that
ethical terms such as "good" or "duty" have an emotive rather
than a scientific, or descriptive, meaning; they were partially
akin to such emotively expressive sounds as sighs, groans, or interjections. Such words as "good" or "duty" therefore served "a
quasi-imperative function"; they helped parents, teachers, pro-
pagandists, and political leaders to alter, redirect, or reinforce
people's attitudes or commitments in a given direction. If, however, a basic disagreement in attitude arose, that is, one such that
no adducing of further information could alter either person's
given attitude, and if each remained impervious to his critics'
emotive imperatives or persuasions, such disagreement as to attitudes or values could in no way be resolved scientifically. Presumably a convinced Nazi, confirmed in his emotive attitudes,
was ethically beyond the scientific criticism of any humanistic
liberal who found the Holocaust horrifying.

Now Dewey had encountered such "ethical relativity" while
he was teaching at Columbia University in New York. Lovers,

poets, and artists in Greenwich Village had in the early twenties invoked Einstein's theory of relativity to justify their view that "all is relative."[13] Moreover, at Columbia University, brilliant young anthropologists, such as Ruth Benedict, combining a devotion to Franz Boas's field methods with an acceptance of Dewey's conception of a plastic human nature, had emerged with a philosophy of cultural relativity; they affirmed that all cultures were equally valid patterns of living that had evolved under diverse historical and material conditions.[14] It followed, of course, that every culture had its institutional means for inculcating in the growing child its values as to what was "good"—the circumpressure of family, teachers, and linguistic devices. Curiously, a dualism was at the outset involved in the child's conception of "good"; on the one hand, "good" was the child's spontaneous expression of pleasure in some activity, as when it tasted a food that it liked, but "good," even "duty," provided the mother with her linguistic means for encouraging the child in its toilet training; the child's obedient behavior brought the reward of reassurance of the mother's love. The latter sense of "good" has an emotive-persuasive significance, a conditioning function in helping to form in the child's unconscious its guilt-engendering conscience.

According to Stevenson, however, if two men confronted one another with a presumably ultimate disagreement in attitude, all they could do would be to engage in emotive-persuasional contests with the word "good"; if the emotive devices of one were more potent than the other, or the other were psychologically vulnerable, a conversion might ensue, but their procedure was in no way that of scientific experiment testing some hypothesis.

Dewey, however, always questioned whether any value was "ultimate"; every statement as to what was good or valuable or desirable was from his standpoint more than an observational report of a "liking," or a consummatory experience: it included as

13. Maxwell Bodenheim, *My Life and Loves in Greenwich Village*, 2d ed. (New York: Belmont Books, 1961), p. 123. Also, pp. 50, 54, 111, 123. Doubt has been cast as to whether Bodenheim was indeed the author of this book. See Jack B. Moore, *Maxwell Bodenheim* (New York: Twayne Publishers, 1970), p. 184. The descriptive detail, however, seems authentic, and the inauthenticity of its authorship would confirm that the "relativist" ethic ascribed to the Greenwich Village of an earlier period still persisted.
14. Margaret Mead, *An Anthropologist at Work: Writings of Ruth Benedict* (New York: Atherton Press, 1966), p. 4.

well some judgment, some reflection and conclusion, as to the relative place of the item of experience in relation to the rest of our experience. If Freud believed that one could undermine the fixation of the "ultimate" values of a sadist or masochist by exploring their origins, Dewey endorsed not only the genetic method but the consequential; his pragmatism in scientific ethics relied not only on inquiry into origins and causes (conscious and unconscious) but also into the consequences of values and attitudes; scientific questioning and reconstruction of our value judgments were always possible. A "liking" doesn't enter into ethical knowledge unless it is considered in a scientific way, just as some physical observation doesn't take its place in science until it has been studied in the light of relevant hypotheses and further tests, confirmations or contraventions. As Dewey wrote in interchange with Philip Blair Rice: "the satisfaction, liking, enjoyment . . . is not itself a *value* save in a figurative way. . . . [It] is not a *judgment* of the value of what is enjoyed." If this seems a quarrel about words, Dewey's genetic-consequential method has nonetheless shown its heuristic power. The Puritan ethic of asceticism was, for instance, scientifically criticized by showing that its self-punitive notions of "good" derived from an era of scarcity when ascetic attitudes contributed toward the survival of one's family against the threat of famine; such attitudes, however, in an era of abundance perhaps were obsolete. Similarly, even if some aggressive ingredient always seemed present among human drives, it was expressed in such diverse forms as wars, baseball, scientific research, invention, and economic competition; "pure aggression," as such, was an abstraction never encountered in direct experience, even as in physical science, energy always takes a specific form—such as mechanical, electrical, magnetic, or heat.

Thus, Dewey pleads for rationality in human ethical judgment; in a courtroom trial, he notes, we try finally to discount the lawyers' emotive "intonations, facial expressions, gestures, etc.," as not being a *part* of legal propositions *qua* legal, and look to the actual evidence adduced. Therefore, Dewey concludes: "If moral theory has any distinctive province and any important function it is, I would say, to criticize the language of the *mores* prevalent at a given time, or in given groups, so as to eliminate if possible this factor [the anti-ethical and pseudo-ethical] as a component of their subject-matter." Moreover, the very usage that Stevenson took as the typically ethical, that is, the "quasi-imperative" function, "Do this!" seemed to Dewey to incorporate a situation of superior addressing the inferior; the analyst of ethical language thus took as his controlling (perhaps unconscious) norm the "ultimate" attitudes of traditional class systems rather than the standpoint of a common scientific enterprise conveyed by the ethical language of a democratic, egalitarian society. As Dewey wrote in his essay on "William James as Empiricist," one school of philosophy "that claims to represent the exclusively scientific point of view" holds that all values are "either mere ejaculations or else commands issued to inferiors, . . . something close to virtual endorsement of the use by totalitarian nations of science as a weapon . . . for achieving despotic power."

The influence of William James on Dewey deepened with the years, and in 1942, the centenary of James's birth provided occasions for Dewey to explain James's greatness. In Dewey's early manhood, it was James's conception of psychology as a natural science, free from metaphysical admixture, that had most affected him. In his last years, however, Dewey drew support from James for a conception of philosophy more humanistic, richer, and more speculative than that which logicians and linguists were providing. James's "will to believe," according to Dewey, had been grossly caricatured into an endorsement of wishful thinking. For James, as Dewey read him, was concerned not with "the truth of scientific propositions" but rather with "the significance, . . . the weight, the momentousness, the *raison d'être* of philosophic systems and principles." What then of the rejoinder by scientific philosophers that meaningless statements remained meaningless despite their having emotional-practical consequences? Dewey boldly replied that "things which are false or even meaningless" may nonetheless "acquire another import when they are interpreted in the context of their bearing upon human and social predicaments and activities," making use of "the most authentic science" but going beyond it.

Curiously, Dewey's conception of philosophy had veered toward an astonishing dualism, one between truth and significance. He had come near placing a limitation upon his experimental logic, for he was prepared to allow philosophers to engage legitimately in the making of experimentally meaningless propositions provided that the latter had worthwhile emotive-practical significances—an ultimate dualism between experimental logic and humanistic significance or meaning. Although the new generation of "scientific" and positivist philosophers invoked Dewey's name as a forerunner, Dewey evidently felt keenly in them the absence of those profound human concerns that had given meaning and significance to his own life; by this broad criterion of pragmatic empiricism, he felt that their new style of logical empiricism was constraining to the spirit. On the other hand, William James perdured for Dewey as the great example of one whose empirical philosophy was built on an "intimate union of emotion and knowledge." James was perhaps above all the philosopher who had outraged his contemporaries by daring to suggest that our trust in God's existence may actually strengthen the finite struggling God, and who had even speculated that the varieties of religious experience pointed in the direction of a possible plurality of supernatural powers. Was Dewey in his latter years occasionally restive with his own naturalism?

Meanwhile, the world's work demanded to be done, an imperative to which Dewey responded. Shared experience was, in Dewey's evaluation, the most rewarding there was; hence, he continued to indite and inscribe a long series of blurbs, introductions, forewords to books, personal appreciations, and such prefatory pages as those for his two co-workers in the peace movement, Salmon O. Levinson and Jane Addams. He introduced a book on a progressive children's school by his friend Agnes de Lima, and one on education in the British West Indies by the future first prime minister of Trinidad and Tobago, Eric Williams, and a third by Earl C. Kelley, a professor of secondary education, in which was emphasized the importance of the experiments on perception by Adelbert Ames; also a message to the teachers of Peru. Noteworthy were Dewey's personal tributes to two of his long-time philosophical co-workers, James H. Tufts, and Boyd H. Bode, with whom he maintained a correspondence almost to the end; and he wrote cheerfully a blurb for E. S. Cowles's *Don't Be Afraid!* in the field of psychological medicine, of which Dewey, like James, was periodically a proponent, and introductory words for a book *The Work of Herbert Bayer* and another volume on *The Unfolding of Artistic Activity.* Dewey wrote the paragraph cited in an advertisement in the *Partisan Review* that expressed the hope that the book by Sidney Hook, *Education for Modern Man,* would become "a guide-book for public understanding and public active effort." Then too, Dewey intervened for a rehearing of the case of a black sharecropper, Odell Waller, convicted on the basis of evidence that Dewey regarded as weak, of having murdered his landlord.

Most poignant for Dewey was the murder on January 11, 1943, of his good friend Carlo Tresca, with whom he had spent evenings of cheer and discussion.[15] Tresca was the staunchest, doughtiest, and physically most courageous fighter in the Italian labor movement. An editor of a syndicalist newspaper, *Il Martello,* and always wearing a big black five-and-a-half-gallon hat, he had been a force in the great strikes of the Lawrence and Paterson textile workers in 1912 and 1913, and he had stirred the miners in the Mesabi Iron Range Strike of 1916. "There is hardly a major industrial conflict, a genuine revolt of workers, in the first quarter of the century in which Carlo Tresca did not join the vanguard and stand in the front line under fire," wrote Max Eastman.[16] Tresca was feared by Fascists and Communists alike. He and his henchmen could outfight the totalitarian disruptionists at any meeting to preserve freedom of speech.[17] Even his romantic exploits were renowned, especially his many years' romance with Elizabeth Gurley Flynn, the heroine of the I.W.W. who deteriorated, before his eyes, into a frozen featured member of the American Communist party. He had once served four months in prison for publishing an advertisement of four lines for a book by Margaret Sanger on birth control. Finally, on an evening at the crossing on Fifteenth Street and Fifth Avenue, while he waited for the traffic light to change, a man stepped up, fired four shots, and escaped in a waiting car. Tresca died on the pavement. The labor, liberal, and Italian communities mourned; opinion was divided as to whether the deed was done by the Fas-

15. *New York Times,* January 12, 1943.
16. Max Eastman, *Heroes I Have Known: Twelve Who Lived Great Lives* (New York: Simon and Schuster, 1942), p. 22.
17. Jerre Mangione, *An Ethnic at Large: A Memoir of America in the Thirties and Forties* (New York: G. P. Putnam's Sons, 1978), p. 164. Also, see Rudolph J. Vecoli, "Carlo Tresca," *Dictionary of American Biography: Supplement Three 1941–1945* (New York: Charles Scribner's Sons, 1973), pp. 776–78.

cists or Communists. Dewey grieved for his friend, and in homage and remembrance wrote from a New York hospital where he was recovering from an operation: "We have all lost a wonderful lover of all mankind. But the world is much richer because of his life," and a letter of Dewey's addressed to "Dear Carl" was reproduced in facsimile in Tresca's journal.[18] Sidney Hook wrote a similar tribute to a man with a "simple faith in human beings," who lived without dogma, doctrine, defeatism, or disillusionment. Carlo Tresca was for them "a kind of Renaissance figure, passionately interested in ideas, people, and freedom. His passions flowed from an enormous appetite for life. . . . One felt that a lost cause always had a chance, that it was never a dead cause if Carlo was part of it." [19]

When the search for Tresca's assassin lagged, and it seemed indeed that the district attorney's investigator had Fascist associations himself, John Dewey joined with a group of well-known liberals, including Roger N. Baldwin of the American Civil Liberties Union, Norman Thomas, the Socialist leader, Edmund Wilson, the foremost literary critic, and the grizzled veteran of legal battles, Morris Ernst, to demand his removal from the case. Their demand was met, but the assassin was never brought to justice. Against the background of such a demonstration of how totalitarian power could strike down the defenders of freedom, Dewey felt all the more that letters such as those he wrote to the *New York Times* setting forth the misrepresentations in the film *Mission to Moscow* were necessary to help intellectuals themselves from yielding to what has been called the "totalitarian temptation."

During the 1940s, furthermore, Dewey, having previously resigned as a contributing editor to the *New Republic* found new journals arising whose standpoint was closer to his own. He became a valued writer for *Commentary,* the newly founded organ of the young war and postwar generation of highly gifted Jewish intellectuals; grounded in the social sciences, and having outgrown their youthful Marxist attachments, their knowledge and experience had prepared them to become the most informed critics of both Marxist ideology and Communist reality. They wel-

18. "Omaggio Alla Memoria Imperitura di Carlo Tresca," *Il Martello* (New York), March 28, 1943, p. 48.
19. Ibid., p. 44.

comed Dewey to their pages, and though several of them had strong religious existentialist feelings, their political philosophy coincided with Dewey's pragmatism. For their readership Dewey once again rewrote the central themes of his philosophy. "Liberating the Social Scientist" called again for sociologists and economists to free themselves from the constraints of the status quo, from the fixed frameworks it imposed even prior to their inquiries. Perhaps Dewey exaggerated the extent to which American social science had been constrained by the status quo; at Chicago and Columbia in Dewey's time, his sociological friends, W. I. Thomas, George Herbert Mead, Thorstein Veblen, Franklin Giddings, Vladimir Simkhovitch, had expressed their heterodox opinions freely and vigorously. In any case, during the post–World War II era, Dewey's program for social science inquiry was largely fulfilled. Beginning with the Truman administration, a large number of studies were generated by the series of governmental undertakings at home and abroad in the domains of civil rights, housing, employment, the alleviation and eradication of poverty, the economic development of backward peoples, democratic reforms in electoral procedures, the extension of governmental assistance from the kindergarten to the university, the extension of social security, the enlarged role of scientists in government. Also the continuous conflict with the Soviet totalitarian expansion and the heightened participation of university professors as cabinet secretaries, officials, and legislators combined to evoke fresh analyses in political sociology. The new political developments helped sustain an unprecedented growth in university departments of sociology, economics, and political science, as governmental and foundation funds were poured into the myriad of research projects designed to answer newly engendered questions. Rare was the graduate student or university teacher who had not been stimulated to inquiry by some such research grant. Whether this "liberating" of social scientists brought as much understanding as Dewey hoped remains doubtful. Problems—novel, unexpected, and awesome—multiplied in the wake of every situation resolved. The indeterminacies in social causal lines far exceeded the rather simple indeterminacy of the "problematic situation" that had so fascinated Dewey with its challenge of uncertainty.

It deserves a special note, however, that in one case Dewey

proved himself a far more astute observer than such noted Columbia political sociologists as Paul Lazarsfeld and his alert enterprising pupils. Dewey predicted the reelection in 1948 of Harry Truman as president of the United States and refused in 1947 to believe that Henry Wallace's third-party candidacy would assure the success of the Republican candidate.

As usual, European philosophical critics continued to indulge their hobbyhorse of depicting American pragmatism as a vulgarly motivated ideology. One such critic, the French author Julien Benda, was admonished by Dewey for his persistent willful misunderstanding of American philosophy. According to Benda, William James's writings showed that he was a philosopher of imperialism, who approved of the American campaign in Cuba in much the same terms that Cecil Rhodes used to justify British imperial advances in the Boer War. Benda claimed that American pragmatic philosophy was, like Russian Bolshevist doctrine, undermining the morality of the Western world. Whatever one's view of the role of imperialism in human history, Dewey made it clear that William James had been an eloquent, forthright critic of any American design to occupy either Cuba or the Philippines; James indeed had analyzed the American declaration of war against Spain as a case study in the psychology of crowds and had scolded Americans for their self-flattering belief that we are "a better nation morally than the rest. . . . Dreams! Human Nature is everywhere the same; and at the least temptation all the old military passions rise and sweep everything before them." Dewey cited too James's classic protest "against bigness and greatness in all forms . . . against all big organizations as such . . . all big successes." In a spirit of magnificent admiration for William James, Dewey declared that passage from James "comes as close to the spirit of pragmatism as M. Benda's account is remote from it."

To Dewey, pragmatism was finally synonymous with "the logic and ethics of scientific inquiry." As such, he took it as inherently opposed to "absolutism of any kind." He felt that social intolerance, even political "purges" "follow when absolutism becomes a dominant philosophy." One wonders whether some additional ingredient or motive must be superposed to transform absolutism into such a virulent doctrine. After all, Thomas Jefferson, whom Dewey much cherished, wrote in the Declaration of Independence of truths that were "self-evident." And perhaps James's own conception of the eternal truth of an "open universe" itself partook of an ultimate intuition?

At times a tendency on Dewey's part to become overpolemical became pronounced. He feared that every absolutism, because it tried to define a "superior reality," would set up at least a dualistic hierarchy of social superiors and inferiors, and would become anti-experimental because a dualism between "mind" and "matter" would inevitably lead to the conferring upon mind of the privilege of unchallengeable intuition. He argued that the rise of science and the empiricist-experimentalist outlook leading to a new technology was the primary cause for the end of feudalism and the growth of democratic, industrial society. In all fairness, however, one must observe that such rationalistic intuitionists as Descartes, Leibniz, and Spinoza were more involved with technology than any of the empiricist philosophers. Leibniz spent years trying to develop a windmill technology as a source of power for the Harz Mountain mines, and Spinoza, as a lens grinder, was earning his livelihood as a craftsman of the new instruments, microscopes and telescopes.[20] The rationalistic temper is as much a part of the scientific spirit as the experimental or the technological; the desire for world systems, for deriving explanations from a few simple, almost logical, laws has, as the examples of Newton, Einstein, and Darwin suggest, been part of the intellectual drive of science.

Dewey's vocabulary, however, tended to describe scientific theory as a practicalistic activity. He wrote in *Problems of Men* that ideas are "plans of action"; of course, if "action" is taken as equivalent to some experimentally obtained or observed consequence, then Dewey's assertion is identical with the condition for scientific meaningfulness; on the other hand, the word "action" does have a moral, political, or practical hortatory flavor, suggesting that every scientific idea must contribute to the human struggle with the physical and social environment. Perhaps primitive human ideas had such an orientation to evolutionary sur-

20. L. S. Feuer, *Spinoza and the Rise of Liberalism* (Boston: Beacon Press, 1958), pp. 236–38. E. J. Aiton, *Leibniz: A Biography* (Bristol: A. Hilger, 1985), pp. 87ff., 107–14. Georges Canguilhem, "Descartes et la technique," *Travaux du IXe Congrès International de Philosophie*, vol. 2, *Études Cartésiennes*, 11ème Partie (Paris: Hermann et Cie, 1937), pp. 77–85.

vival. Yet, the history of ideas suggests that its own emerging evolution has been from its function for biological survival to that of the pure satisfaction of intellectual understanding. Although the roots of "pure curiosity" may lie in childhood motivations to alleviate insecurities in a strange world, in aesthetic-sexual longings, and desires for mastery and power, nonetheless, the delight in scientific knowledge may perhaps become an autonomous factor, with an adventitious relation to action.

To the end, Dewey railed at Kant's formal, dualistic absolutism as a philosophy implicit with a commitment to the status quo. Perhaps some personal drama of self-liberation from Kant moved Dewey, for that philosophy, taught by his professors Torrey and Morris, had been the station for his intellectual departure. During Dewey's own lifetime, however, such a Kantian as Hermann Cohen in Germany applied that philosophy to provide the basis for a liberal socialism, and Jean Jaurès had done so much the same in France;[21] Eduard Bernstein inaugurated revisionist socialism with a call for "Back to Kant!" perceiving that only a reverence for human beings as ends in themselves would safeguard socialist society from degenerating into a dictatorship using people as means only, and Kurt Eisner, an ardent Kantian, led the revolution in 1918 that overthrew the Bavarian monarchy. In New York City, the achievements of Felix Adler rivaled in education and social reform those of Dewey; Adler made the Kantian outlook central to his philosophy of Ethical Culture. Nonetheless, Dewey, despite some reservations, sent his own children to the school that Adler founded. "If they have teachers like that," Dewey is reported to have said, "I guess the ethics classes can't do much harm."[22] Dewey as a father was more pragmatic in his judgment of Kantian ideas than was Dewey the philosopher.

The central teaching of the innumerable articles and statements that Dewey published in magazines, popular and professional, was a return to the oldest conception of philosophy, the search for wisdom. His last word in the introduction to *Problems of Men* explains that search for wisdom as one "for the ends and values that give direction to our collective human activ-

21. Harvey Goldberg, *The Life of Jean Jaurès* (Madison: University of Wisconsin Press, 1962), pp. 17, 83.
22. Horace L. Friess, *Felix Adler and Ethical Culture: Memories and Studies*, ed. Fannia Weingartner (New York: Columbia University Press, 1981), p. 127.

ities" and, in particular, "the projection of liberal hypotheses as to ways in which the required social change may be brought about." This movement is called, says Dewey, "by the names of pragmatism, experimentalism, instrumentalism." Dewey thus placed himself in that tradition which from Thales and the Seven Hellenic Sages to Benjamin Franklin has indeed been concerned more with the problems of men's everyday and social existence rather than with the ultimate nature of existence generally.

Dewey does indeed have much in common with his forebears in wisdom. From Thales to Franklin, the wise men were not only lovers of science but much occupied with its technological aspect; Franklin judged shrewdly that ordinary men could be persuaded to support the advancement of science only if its fruits as, in his own time, the lightning conductor, contributed to improving their lot. The wise men were naturally pragmatists; Thales, when asked "What is most pleasant?" replied "Success," and Franklin's Poor Richard instilled in all subsequent American generations the conviction that "Early to bed and early to rise makes a man healthy, wealthy, and wise," and his almanac became the most translated American book into foreign languages (including Russian).

Nonetheless, in several significant regards, Dewey has ventured far beyond traditional wisdom. For one, the men of wisdom heretofore, like Dewey's older contemporary, Justice Oliver Wendell Holmes, Jr., have not had a high respect for human nature and have not fostered Dewey's hope that its significant elevation was possible under changed social conditions. Few documents of such disillusionment with humankind have been written in America as that by Franklin to his fellow scientist Joseph Priestley in 1782: "Men I find to be a sort of Beings very badly constructed, ... more disposed to do Mischief to each other than to make Reparation, . . . and having more Pride and even Pleasure in killing than in begetting one another." He added that he had begun "to doubt" whether "the Species were really worth producing or preserving," a view that Justice Holmes shared. The sages' conception of social reform therefore was not that of the bold social experimentation that Dewey envisaged; they advocated constitutional reforms, as Solon did, primarily to assure social stability rather than to realize ideals of justice; Franklin would have preferred the maintenance of union with Great Britain and felt the

colonies had secured ample concessions from the mother country; as a committee man together with Thomas Jefferson, he judi-
ciously deleted the word "sacred" from Jefferson's adjectives for
human rights in the draft for a Declaration of Independence.[23]
Justice Holmes, after his youthful abolitionist fervor and Civil
War experiences, never attached himself to any "cause" or "moral
campaign." In short, a propensity for "liberal hypotheses" (in
Dewey's phrase) has rarely been a trait of the past men of wisdom; given their conservative temperament, they might have regarded him as not altogether one of their company. Thales, who
cornered the Milesian market for olive oil, and Franklin, the
prosperous printer, would probably have rejected Dewey's critique of capitalist enterprise. Dewey called upon philosophy to
consider "why it is that man is now so alienated from man" and
said its role must be to engage in "the act of midwifery" for the
world as yet unborn. The men of wisdom, however, might have
refrained from an impetuous midwifery that risked a stillborn or
defective offspring. Thales and Franklin alike did propose specific practicable measures for political reform; Thales advocated
a federation of the Ionian towns, even as Franklin more than two
thousand years later sought a federation of the American colonies. Would any of them, however, have been tempted to endorse
the Soviet Communist project for social planning or, even on a
homelier level, such dubious projects as that of Black Mountain
College?[24]

Lastly, the historic men of wisdom felt that a religious ingredient was essential to their philosophy; though none of them
were theologians, all found an intellectual ballast in traditional
religious beliefs. Franklin was explicit in his religious faith in a
benevolent God. Dewey held, however, that any supernaturalism

23. Carl Becker, *The Declaration of Independence: A Study in the History of
    Political Ideas* (1922; reprint ed., New York: A. A. Knopf, 1942), p. 142.
24. Martin Duberman, *Black Mountain: An Exploration in Community* (New
    York: E. P. Dutton and Co., 1972), pp. 40, 102. Dewey wrote in 1940: "The
    work and life of the College . . . is a living example of democracy in action."
    Duberman, op. cit., p. 446, from a letter of John Dewey to Theodore Dreier,
    July 18, 1940. Likewise, the president of Black Mountain regarded Dewey
    "as the only man I have ever known who was completely fit and fitted to live
    in a democracy." This compliment may not bode well for the future of de-
    mocracy. Dewey, at Black Mountain, much enjoyed its convivial life. See
    John Andrew Rice, *I Came Out of the Eighteenth Century,* 2d ed. (New
    York: Harper and Bros., 1942), pp. 331–32.

made finally for what he called a "penning up" of science, that is, a restriction as to which problems were to be opened to scientific method. Besides, any belief in a supernatural God signified for Dewey another "dualism."

The sources of Dewey's emotional antipathy to dualism, as he himself indicated in his first autobiographical writing, lay deep in what he regarded as the repressive aspects of the Northern New England culture in which he spent his formative years.[25] From the purely logical standpoint, his anti-dualism does not seem a necessary component of the pragmatic philosophy; it constitutes a separate, independent unit-idea. It would be a separate question to be decided on scientific grounds whether psychical events are altogether "adjectival" to physical ones, or whether they might have an autonomous causal efficacy. That "man is a part of the world" (in Dewey's words) does not entail that his psychical events would estrange him from it. Lovejoy, in a series of notable essays, argued strongly that their duality was both consistent with and most appropriate to a pragmatic philosophy that held that human ideas could make a difference in shaping the world. The dualistic standpoint does seem to be a universal mode of thought found in the most diverse social settings. The scientific revolution in the seventeenth century was a dualistic one, based on the distinction between primary and secondary qualities to which Galileo, Locke, and Newton subscribed, and upon which Einstein enlarged. Freud, for all his psychoanalytical aversion to metaphysics, drew a distinction between the "reality-principle" and the "pleasure-principle" that assumed the basic dualism between psychical experiences and the physical world. It is doubtful that any connection exists between dualism and an anti-democratic division of classes such as Dewey alleged. One would probably find as high a percentage of commonsense dualists on Israeli communal settlements as in capitalistic Hong Kong. Again, Dewey seems to have blended independent unit-ideas into a loosely integrated mixture. If he urged the role of so-

25. John Dewey, "From Absolutism to Experimentalism," *The Later Works of John Dewey, 1925–1953*, ed. Jo Ann Boydston, vol. 5 (Carbondale and Edwardsville: Southern Illinois University Press, 1984), p. 153; first published in *Contemporary American Philosophy: Personal Statements*, ed. George P. Adams and William Pepperell Montague, vol. 2 (London: George Allen and Unwin; New York: Macmillan Co., 1930), p. 19.

cial midwifery upon philosophers, one wonders whether the vehement anti-American "activism" of Bertrand Russell and Jean-Paul Sartre in their latter years was assisting the birth of a higher civilization.

Dewey reiterated his basic themes to diverse audiences—from the professional one in the *Journal of Philosophy* to the popular secularist the *Humanist* to memorial addresses for the university public on William James. For Dewey always remained in the New England tradition of Ralph Waldo Emerson, the preacher turned lecturer, who, feeling the call to educate the citizenry in democratic virtues, journeyed the far length of the land to do so. The sermon was the canonical literary form that Dewey as a youngster had imbibed in the First Congregational Church in Burlington, Vermont, and from his teacher at the University of Vermont, Henry A. P. Torrey. Despite the long distance he traversed in his formal philosophizing, Dewey's longing for the community one finds in a church with "a common faith" never abated. Once, at Columbia University, Dewey happened to be "entertaining a visiting humanist from England." To the surprise of his assembled "horrified" students, "who were more doctrinaire than the master," Dewey "joined with this gentleman in proposing to establish some sort of humanist church in the United States." [26] That was why Dewey kept writing what his admired Thomas Henry Huxley called "lay sermons." Rather than polish and do the research for a long, precise philosophic masterpiece, he preferred instead, as a religious democrat, to diffuse his ideas among teachers, churchgoers, and magazine readers whom philosophical technical specialists dualistically regarded as "inferior."

Dewey's abiding greatness lies more in what we might call "the method of character" rather than in the "method of intelligence" and "the logic of inquiry" to which he gave his scientific energies. For underlying the use of intelligence is the thinker's emotional balance. And that balance one can learn not from textbooks but either as a co-worker, whether in the laboratory or in life's conflicts themselves with a man in whose spirit that balance is exemplified, or perhaps fortunately by the grace of God or one's genes.

26. The story was told by Robert E. Fitch, a student of Dewey's at Columbia University and later Dean of the Pacific School of Religion at Berkeley, California, in "John Dewey—The Last Protestant," *Pacific Spectator* 7 (1953): 227.

Is the thinker's honesty, we finally enquire, such that he is pre-pared to consider dispassionately all the evidence relevant to a problem even when that evidence contravenes his own emotive preferences? All those who have known Dewey or his writings have experienced that balance of character in Dewey; he lived spontaneously by the axiom that his thinking was a moment in the common aspiring, often weary, sometimes discouraged, struggle of the human race for its self-enlightenment.

Essays

William James and the World Today

James refers in one of his writings to "the contemptuous shrug" with which were received his pluralism and his attack upon the absolutism of a block-universe. It is hardly too much to say that at the time his early ventures into the philosophical field appeared, the most favorable response they called out was an acknowledgement of the pre-eminence of James in Psychology with an expression of regret that he should trespass in a field for which he lacked proper preparation. It was not that most other philosophers of the time explicitly professed monism and absolutism, but that the general feeling was that it was the business of serious philosophers to move in that direction as far as possible. Scientists might be preoccupied with the temporal and changing, but philosophy was the guardian of absolute and immutable truths that provided underpinning for the relativities (and hence uncertainties) of actual experience.

It is a sign of change in the "climate of opinion" that today it is no longer considered queer or odd to profess pluralism or some form of temporal relationism. There were many persons during the years in which James taught who denied or doubted the tenability of absolutism. They were especially numerous outside the guild of university teachers of philosophy. But James shows, upon the whole, no more sympathy with them than with the members of the idealistic school then dominant in the professional circles of philosophy. It is not difficult to see why this was so. These others rested their case finally upon some weakness in human intelligence or some opaqueness in human experience which prevented access to the absolute and fixed truths and reali-

[First published in *William James, the Man and the Thinker. Addresses Delivered at the University of Wisconsin in Celebration of the Centenary of His Birth* (Madison: University of Wisconsin Press, 1942), pp. 91–97. Read in Dewey's absence by Carl Boegholt on 10 January 1942.]

ties which somehow undeniably existed beneath the things of relativity and mere experience. They were relativists and pluralists because they were first agnostics and "phenomenalists." They were, with less developed technical resources, the precursors of present-day logical positivists.

The peculiar significance of the pluralism of James is that it rests upon a positive instead of a negative foundation. He admitted the legitimacy of monism as a hypothesis. But pluralism was equally legitimate as a hypothesis. It had more empirical evidence on its side, and it possessed distinctively *moral* advantages. There is an entry in his diary which reads as follows: "Can one with full knowledge and sincerity ever bring himself so to sympathize with the *total process* of the universe as heartily to assent to the evils that seem inherent in its details? . . . If so, optimism is possible." Or the evils may be so outstanding that he becomes a pessimist. But there is a third possibility. "If a *divided* universe be a conception possible for his intellect to rest in, and at the same time he have vigor of will to look the universal death in the face, without blinking, he can live the life of meliorism."

It has been said more than once that the emphasis of James upon variety, spontaneity, and novelty were intellectual registrations of the pioneer adventuring frontier spirit of America— passing away even while James wrote. I have said something of the kind myself upon occasion. But when James's teaching is viewed in the perspective which is determined by the present world crisis, the pluralism and temporal relationism of James assume a much deeper significance. We may justly find in them a forefeeling for the conditions which have culminated in the life-and-death struggle for supremacy of democratic and totalitarian faiths. The source and the spirit of his pluralism assuredly become more understandable when his arguments in its behalf are placed in the context that is made so vivid and so engrossing by the present crisis.

The emphasis James places upon the individual quality of human beings and all things is, of course, central in his pluralism. But the adjective "individual" is often converted into a noun, and then human beings and all objects and events are treated as if they were individual and nothing but individual. The result is that identification of human beings with something supposed to be completely isolated which is the curse of the so-called individualistic movement in economics, politics, and psychology. I find the actual position of James to be well represented in a remark he quotes from a carpenter of his acquaintance: "There is very little difference between one man and another; but what little there is, *is very important.*" It is this element which is precious because it is that which nobody and nothing else can contribute, and which is the source of all creativity. Generic properties on the other hand are replaceable, and express the routines of nature.

James's own statement is so adequate that its citation is as pertinent to the present world situation as it is to an understanding of James. In his *Pluralistic Universe* James contrasts, as you will recall, the All-form and the Each-form. Of them he says: "The all-form allows of no taking up and dropping of connexions. . . . In the each-form, on the contrary, a thing may be connected, by intermediary things, with a thing with which it has no immediate or essential connexion. It is thus at all times in many possible connexions which are not necessarily actualized at the moment. They depend upon which actual path of intermediation it may functionally run into. We still have a coherent world." And so, on the psychological side, he speaks of *confluence*—"the confluence of every passing moment of concretely felt experience with its immediately next neighbor."

"And" is a fundamental category of the philosophical pluralism of James; it goes with "next," which is also next to its neighbor and so on. But because of multiple and indefinite intermediates, "or" "stands for a reality." In one place he compares the structure of the world to a "federal republic" as against a kingdom or empire. He speaks of a distributive, a disseminated world. "Something," he says, "ever goes indissolubly with something else." Again, "nature is a name for excess. Every point in her opens out and runs into the more."

I have cited these representative passages because they completely refute the idea that James stood for an atomic individualism in the sense in which physical science has now abandoned its old doctrine of complete isolation. The fact is that in James's view connections are of a much more intimate type than they are according to theories that reduce them to logical or "thought" relations. I have quoted them, however, for another and more urgent reason:—for their direct pertinency to problems of the present that philosophers must face unless they adopt one or another of the many current means of evading responsibility. The charge that can justly be brought against democratic practices and popular democratic ideas is that they have so far failed to cultivate the intermediaries by which we are tied together, and yet are not bound hand and foot as in totalitarianism, which is the social version of absolutism and the "All-form." Philosophy has not created this practical weakness of democracy. But neither has it done much to provide in advance for filling the vacua, the empty spaces which have been barriers to intercommunication and friendly intercourse. Given these blanks and holes in human association, we have no great right to be surprised that totalitarianism has intervened and claimed to express the only way in which vacua can be filled, and human beings brought into close union.

Neither James nor those who have followed him have accomplished much in the way of indicating concrete intermediaries by means of which a series of intimate associations from group to group would extend through the full scope of human relations. We have not even asked very seriously what kinds of social connection will secure and enlarge the freedom of human beings to contribute whatever their individual qualities make possible, and what kinds of social connections restrict their freedom, thereby depriving others of what might enrich their lives. We have greeted with applause the expression "liberty and union, one and inseparable." But we have not seriously tried to discover the kinds of union which express and enforce liberty. We have been satisfied with repeating generalities, which even as generalities are products of conditions of life and civilization that no longer exist. In consequence there is no mature, no well-developed, philosophy of democracy with which to confront totalitarian ideologies. Today, more than ever before, James both points the way and issues a challenge.

I quoted earlier a passage in which James spoke of a philosophy in which "the intellect can rest" in conjunction with a will which both faces evils and resolves to bring about a better state of things. Because James, as he somewhere says, hated "desiccation" above all things, and because he was unable to separate philosophy from life, he is outstanding not only among the philosophers of his own day but of all periods in his deliberate attempt to effect a union in philosophy of the demands of our emotional and desiring nature with the claims of our intelligence and scientific knowledge. When he asserted the right of the former to be taken into account when philosophies are framed, he sometimes failed to make it clear that he was thinking of philosophy, not of conclusions which fall within the scope of matters of fact. In consequence, he occasionally used expressions which left upon the reader the impression that he believed the emotions had rights in determining conclusions in those cases where evidence alone is relevant. But the context shows that James was thinking of philosophy not of science.

And right here is the point at which philosophy today, in my judgment, has most to learn from James. Science, yes by all means. James was himself trained as a scientist more than other American philosophers of his day, save Peirce. In matters where scientific knowledge is lacking or defective, the work of science is to be promoted and the conclusions reached are to receive our utmost loyalty. But these very statements are not themselves conclusions of science. They are expressions of a faith which is rooted in hope and desire; they manifest a resolve. They illustrate the fact that even with possession of the most extensive scientific knowledge there remains the question of the human ends to which it is to be devoted. That question involves in the most profound and urgent way our desires and our purposes—all the things of the emotional and volitional make-up of human nature.

The rapid advance of the physical sciences has for a long time been putting to philosophy the question of the bearing of the method and conclusions of science upon the conduct of human life. The present world crisis proposes in the most stark way the question whether science is to be used for destruction or for creation. To take the ground that philosophy has nothing to do or to say about this question is to promote the belief that it can be settled only by a clash of forces in which science is used to attain superiority in armed conflict. To take the ground that the chief business of philosophy, its most *distinctive* function, is to show how desire and ideas, purpose and knowledge, emotion and science, can cooperate fruitfully in behalf of human good, is to take our stand where James stood a generation ago.

It is also to set philosophy upon the only road on which philosophy does not either set itself up as a rival of science in matters where the latter has rightful jurisdiction, or else devote itself to playing a game with the mere formalities of knowledge; an operation which at its best is but sharpening of a technique and at its worst a sterile evasion of the reasons philosophy has for existing. The teaching of James is a challenge to philosophy to make a place for itself in a world in which a split between emotion and intelligence has played an active part in setting human beings at odds with themselves and so with one another. If it meets this challenge, philosophy will at least play a humble part in creating conditions for the existence of a more humane and friendly world.

William James as Empiricist

I shall make no attempt to present anything in the nature of a rounded appraisal of the work and the influence of that many-sided man and thinker whose centenary anniversary we celebrate. I shall confine myself to an informal statement of some reflections which have occurred to me concerning his significance for present-day philosophy. There are three loosely connected matters of which I shall speak.

William James, as we all know, was a teacher of philosophy during the time he produced his works, in fact a professor. One of the most striking characteristics of his work, however, is the absence of qualities usually associated with professorial and professional productions. It seems to me that this absence, together with the presence of an opposite kind of quality, has an intimate connection with the conditions of his own education, and that this connection has a lesson for those of us who are now teachers of philosophy.

For I think we are all the richer—the world in general and the group of philosophers in particular—because of the kind of education William James experienced. I believe we are all to be congratulated because of the non-academic character of that education. We cannot expect to repeat the positive aspects of that education in contact with our own students. We cannot supply his contact with his father and his father's friends, or the years he spent abroad, with their wide range of artistic and human experiences. But William James also escaped the academic conditions that too often have a benumbing effect. He had too much intensity of intellectual eagerness and too sturdy a moral indepen-

[First published in *In Commemoration of William James 1842–1942* (New York: Columbia University Press, 1942), pp. 48–57, from a paper presented at the Conference on Methods in Philosophy and the Sciences, New School for Social Research, New York City, 23 November 1941.]

dence for even the deadliest of academic atmospheres to have
suffocated or suppressed his native gifts. Nevertheless, the special
qualities of his work seem to me to give us as teachers of philosophy occasion for reflection upon our too frequently used methods of initiating students into philosophy.

I do not think that excessive regard for scholarship is the danger which threatens us professionally, and which actually arises
when scholarship is made an end in itself and becomes an oppressive load upon originality. What I have in mind is, rather, our
tendency to exaggerate the phase of technique, of formal skill, in
quasi-prescribed lines of thinking. We may recal how Bergson
compared "intellect" to the blinders of a horse keeping his vision
limited to the road ahead so that he does not tend to stray towards more attractive and greener fields. I do not believe intelligence is a limitation of this sort. But I am not sure that our professional attitude in teaching philosophy does not act to narrow
vision because of the stress that it puts upon attainment of a particular kind of technical competency. Attention is fastened upon
roads that were laid out in the past. Students learn, indeed, that a
good deal of re-grading has still to be done; that unnecessary
curves are to be eliminated; and that points of junction with
other roads, let us say those leading into science, art, or religion,
have to be rendered more accessible. But there hardly seems to be
a corresponding attention to green fields which may yield new
sources of nourishment, or to the peaks which the existing road
has chosen to go around rather than try to conquer. The work of
William James and also the reception it met from most professional teachers at its first appearance seem to me to hold a continuing lesson for us who teach and write philosophy.

My next reflection may perhaps best be introduced by a remark which verbally is somewhat opposite to what I have just
said. The virtual revolution effected by James in traditional beliefs about experience has provided those who would base the
conclusions of philosophy upon the analysis of experience with a
new and effective intellectual strategy and set of tactics. We find
even today European critics of empiricism engaging in elaborate
refutation of empiricism upon the basis of identification of empiricism with outmoded sensationalism. In our own country,
critics who have presumably read James, still criticise empirical
doctrines, even those of James himself, as if an empiricist must

hold that ideas are copies or compounds of sensations, and hence all lacking in original and productive significance.

I take it for granted that the *Principles of Psychology* is the greatest among the great works of James. I do not find it important to decide whether or not that work is adjudged to be "psychological science" on the basis of what is doing in that field today—though it is more than probable that even the authors of the most scientific work being done today could learn something from James. What I do hold important is that the *Principles* contain an exposition of the nature of experience which renders both sensationalistic empiricism and rationalistic criticisms of empiricism wholly out of date. The work of James replaces a dialectic analysis of experience with one based upon scientific knowledge that is now available, but was not formerly accessible. Thereby, I repeat, James has provided those who would use empirical and experimental method with a new equipment of intellectual weapons and instrumentalities. Fundamentally, he has accomplished this task by showing that experience is intimately connected with nature instead of existing in a separate world.

I mention a few considerations found in the *Principles* that justify for me this sweeping statement, and disclose the nature of pragmatic empiricism better than do the popular lectures on *Pragmatism*. Consider, for example, the importance of *analysis* in the procedures of knowing, and then note how James brought out the way in which discrimination and disassociation are directed by human interests, so that genuine distinctions in ideas and beliefs are what *make* a difference in behavior, in a literal sense of "making." If we turn to unifying functions in knowledge, we find that reasoning, general ideas, definition and classification are treated as "teleological weapons"; as means of attack upon the brute facts of existence in spite of the indifference of the facts in themselves to our "higher" interests, even (as is much more generally recognized now than when James wrote) to our concern for scientific knowledge.

That the intellectual life in all its phases may be employed to render experience in all its aspects and phases richer and freer is, to my mind, the central theme of James's account of the processes and operations by which knowledge is attained. I know of nothing more inept in philosophical criticism than arguments which assume that because James gives a reasonable account of all which is summed up in "reason," he therefore had slight regard for reasonableness. To connect "reason" intimately and intrinsically with experience is, indeed, a denial of the traditional account which puts reason in opposition to experience. But this fact is no excuse for those interpretations which are made of James by those who feel lost without the support they think they derive from the traditional view of an outside "Reason." Still less is there any excuse for those who distort the doctrine that interest and purpose are capable of directing knowing and the fruits of knowing to enrichment of our common experience into a glorification of "will" at the expense of "reason." No genuine empiricist, and certainly not James, ever thought in terms of such vague and unanalyzed notions.

The last chapter of the second volume of the *Principles* is relevant to this topic. James's account of the origin and test of those principles which have such organizing power in experience that they have been called necessary and *a priori,* anticipates in its special field the factor of evolution now called "mutation" in the wider biological field. There are, James holds, variations that amount to systematic re-arrangements of structures of the organism. They start as "sports," but they may be of decisive import for the course of subsequent experience, racial as well as ontogenetic. They are important in a way that no changes in experience wrought by accretion of sensible impressions or sense-data can possibly be. He goes so far as to say that "every scientific conception is in the first instance a 'spontaneous variation' in some one's brain." Many of these sports come to nothing. All have to be tested for acceptability by interaction with the environment. They are expressed in actions and their worth for further life-processes depends upon consequences in whose production the environment has a decisive say. What is said in the talks on *Pragmatism* about consequences as tests of ideas and beliefs may well be associated with what is involved in this topic. For the consequences are such as can be taken up into the continuing development of life. Those that occur at any given time are not final. The criterion of the finality for which many persons yearn is found in an ever-enlarging growth wherein experience becomes richer and freer.

James remarks in one place that substitution of consequences for antecedents, of last things for first things, as standards, would work nothing less than a revolution in the seat of authority. I believe we can say with equal truth that the development of the idea of experience to which James more than pointed, which he initiated for us, constitutes a revolutionary change in traditional empiricism. He speaks of *Pragmatism* as a new name for old ways of thinking. Anyone who reads British thought from Bacon, through Hobbes, Locke, Hume, and even John Stuart Mill, will find much more of the strictly pragmatic in them than is recognized in conventional histories. But James had scientific resources to draw upon that were not available to his predecessors. He used these resources to give support and body to ideas which had been not much more than hunches in the empirical strain of English thought.

One of these scientific resources is, of course, the advance which had taken place in biological science. The physiological and medical training of James provided his psychology, his theory of experience, with a background and an outlook lacking in the case of his predecessors. One almost hesitates to mention this factor because critics, with that zeal for reduction that seems to haunt them, have often implied that to make use of biological considerations in psychology and philosophy is to reduce experience to the *merely* biological. One does not have to go far below the surface in reading James to see that at his hands reference to biological considerations is a means of breaking down artificial barriers and compartmentalizations from which philosophy was suffering. Previous empiricists had, for example, treated experience as something set over against nature, separated from it by a gulf. This fatal barrier to development of a genuinely empirical philosophy was broken down by James. The biological aspect of experience is far from being the whole of experience. But recognition of its existence cuts under, once for all, every theory of experience which rests, consciously or unconsciously, upon the postulate that experience is set over against the natural world, and can be profitably studied in independence of our knowledge of that world.

He also used the biological connection as a means of breaking down divisions within experience that previous psychology had built up:—the division into separate compartments of knowledge, emotion, and action or "will." Experience as something done and undergone by a living creature cannot be split up in that way. Any such division in life would be immediately fatal to its very continuance. That the brain is at least an organ of a living being would seem to be a proposition having elementary truth. But even after James pointed out the consequences of that fact for any theory of ideas and knowing that has scientific support, the truth is still far from receiving common acknowledgment. For if the brain is an organ of life, it would seem to be a truism that the experiences which are mediated by it, namely ideas and knowing, have something intrinsic to do with carrying on of life-processes. The problem isn't so much whether they do or not, as it is discovery of the definite ways in which they perform this function. And in that matter James himself, and we who come after him, have hardly done more than make a start.

There are of course those who will say that after all the work of James concerns psychology, and psychology alone, that it has no bearing upon philosophy in its sacred and sublime aloneness. I do not enter upon the question of the relations of philosophy and psychology to each other. I content myself with citing a few facts. For empiricists, at all events, whatever throws light upon the nature of experience and provides us with better methods for its analysis is of basic importance, no matter what name be given to the source of that light. And it is important for thinkers of all schools not to go on repeating things about experience and empirical method that have been proved factually false. The self-stultifying quality of this procedure, especially for those who assert that they represent the high values of "reason," is not done away with by pronouncing the word "psychology" in a contemptuous tone of voice. And were this the proper occasion, I think it could be shown that two contemporary schools, now exercising considerable influence, the British analytic school and the school of logical positivism, suffer greatly because of their dependence upon pre-Jamesian psychology.

As human beings, philosophers, like all other human beings, are influenced by attitudes, dispositions, habits, that have come to them from education and environment. These are of a psychological nature; many of them come to us from a time when psychology was in a relatively unscientific state. Present-day biological, anthropological and psychological knowledge is required in order to purge the minds of philosophers of antiquated notions—whatever be the direct function of this knowledge in philosophy. So I return to the theme of the significance of James for those who take their stand in philosophy upon experience. He pointed to a new way of analyzing and reporting it. And he did more than point. He opened up paths of access to nothing less than a revolutionary change in traditional empiricism. During the thirty years which have elapsed since his death we have been able only to enlarge openings which James made, and to do something, not very much, toward getting rid of points of view and postulates which the earlier course of philosophic thinking has bred in us and which hamper us tremendously in seeing and using the resources present-day science and culture offer us.

The third respect in which I think the work of James is of vital importance for those who today are concerned with philosophy, I shall present only in outline. I venture to suggest that perhaps the part of his teaching which is most precious for us today is connected with that aspect of his teaching which superficially is most open to legitimate criticism, and has been most a stumbling-block to many who are otherwise sympathetic with the tenor of his work. I refer to those ideas to which he gave the name of the "will to believe," and which led him to insist upon taking emotional-practical consequences along with evidential consequences as a constituent of the test for the truth of ideas. James threw out his conceptions in a bold form, trusting unduly to the imagination of his readers to supply the qualifications he neglected to state in his challenge of conventional beliefs. But in fact, he does introduce enough qualifications so that it is a caricature to present his view as an endorsement of wishful thinking. As his statements stand, however, some of them seem to point to the conclusion that something beside evidence, namely, something in the way of personal predilections and their satisfaction, may in some cases be part of the test of truth.

Now I submit that a careful reading will show beyond doubt that what James was actually concerned with was not the truth of scientific propositions but the significance, that is the weight, the momentousness, the *raison d'être*, of philosophic systems and principles. He undeniably made statements that do not harmonize with this remark. There are passages in which he takes Peirce's statement of the way of arriving at the meaning of scientific conceptions as if it were intended to be a way of determining their truth; a confusion fostered by the ambiguity of the word "significance," which sometimes is used as a synonym for "meaning" in its logical sense, and sometimes as a synonym for "importance." If we free what James said from these confusions, and interpret what he said in the light of his vital concern that philosophy have vital significance for human living instead of being scholastic and academic, we shall, I think, be able to grasp the lesson he wanted to enforce.

Recognition that a sense for the bearing of philosophic issues and problems upon life has always actuated philosophers is a valuable clue to grasping the significance of what they have said. For things which are false or even meaningless if they are taken to be what they purport to be, statements about the ultimate structure of the universe and absolute truth, acquire another import when they are interpreted in the context of their bearing upon human and social predicaments and activities. Philosophers may surrender the presumptuous claim that they are engaged in producing and exhibiting truths of a scientific nature of a deeper, more comprehensive, and more ultimate sort than scientists as scientists can possibly discover. Their function is rather to inquire into the connection between the conclusions reached by the most authentic science available and those issues which do involve emotion and desire along with verified ideas. For all those issues having to do with guidance of human behavior involve desire and interest as well as known facts.

One of the most marked features of recent culture has been the growing perception of the immense role played in human affairs by vital factors, by impulses, desires, active tendencies, to which collectively the name "unconscious" has been popularly given—however ineptly. This recognition has seemed to many persons to afford confirmation of Hume's statement that "reason is and must be the slave of passion," "passion" being his word for the pre-rational and a-rational factors in human life. That what purports to be rational is often secreted and excreted in virtual slavery to impulse and desire—to "passion"—I do not doubt. That the relation must be one of slavery, that it cannot be one of cooperation, is a very different sort of proposition. The philosophy of James, instead of being a glorification of non-rational activity, is in effect a plea that philosophy devote itself to instituting a co-operative interaction of knowledge and the factors that move men to act.

Today the outstanding problem of philosophical inquiry is the relation of all that goes by the name "fact" to all that goes by the name "value." It is not difficult to find in what James said a sensitive anticipation of the pressing nature of this problem, and also an indication of the direction in which alone it can be adequately dealt with. When it is said, as it is today by one school of philosophy that claims to represent the exclusively scientific point of view, that all words and all aspects of experience that contain an emotive quality, all values, are either mere ejaculations or else commands issued to inferiors, we are faced with an impressive lesson as to the logical consequences of complete separation of science and emotion, ideas and desires. We are presented with a formulation which relegates all issues of conduct, personal and collective, all problems of our industrial, political, and international relations, to decision by superior force. Given the actual part played by physical knowledge in the present state of affairs, we have something close to virtual endorsement of the use by totalitarian nations of science as a weapon in a struggle for achieving despotic power.

When James's position is liberated from entangling associations, I find in it, accordingly, an anticipation of the most pressing problem of philosophy today and an anticipation of the need that empirical philosophy build upon foundations which recognize that experience is an intimate union of emotion and knowledge. James was a pioneer in his perception of their actual union. He was also a pioneer in perception of the fact of what this union signifies for the office and task of philosophy. Our best commemoration of what the present anniversary signifies for us as philosophers may consist in giving ourselves to the vocation which James in effect assigned to philosophers. When philosophy renounces ambition to lay bare the structure of ultimate reality and absolute truth, it may be able to devote itself to the humane if humbler office of indicating the light which present scientific knowledge throws upon the dark abyss of impulse and desire; of showing how scientific knowledge enables us to break through the imprisoning crust of outworn traditions and customs; of illuminating the path ahead by means of projection, upon the basis of our best attainable knowledge, of objects and ends that are neither expressions of sheer power nor yet shimmering will-o-the-wisps.

The *Principles*

Of William James it can be said more truly than of any other modern writer that nothing human was foreign to him. There was nothing compartmentalized in his attitude. His range of interest was broad; it was free from the professional and technical limitations that affect most scholars. This fact emboldens me to say something about his *Principles of Psychology*; for whatever be thought about its contents from the standpoint of present-day psychology, the book takes rank as a permanent classic, like Locke's *Essay* and Hume's *Treatise*. It does not lend itself to a pigeon-hole type of classification. Like them it is addressed to the general public, and every page shows the concern of its author that the public understand the bearings of the topics with which the book dealt upon everyday attitudes and affairs.

I do not mean that the book should be regarded as a philosophical treatise rather than as a psychological one. I mean that, as in the case of Locke and Hume, these conventional appellations do not signify. The primary fact is that James began as a student of medicine and physiology, and was deeply concerned to point out the bearings of new knowledge in these subjects upon understanding the make-up and workings of human nature. It is our good fortune that this preparation and mode of approach coincided with the catholic range and the freedom of James' interests, so that he brought his special training to bear upon almost every phase of human concern. Welding of scientific method with eager interest in every aspect of human nature was the result. It is this union which, in my opinion, renders James' *Principles of Psychology* a classic for all time no matter what changes occur in treatment of special themes.

[First published in *Psychological Review* 50 (January 1943): 121.]

William James' Morals and Julien Benda's

It Is Not Pragmatism That Is Opportunist

In his article, "The Attack on Western Morality" (*Commentary*, November 1947), M. Julien Benda chose to include what he regards as pragmatic philosophy as a leading figure in that attack. In fact, he assigns to it, along with and by the side of Russian Bolshevist philosophy, a place in the very front rank of the intellectual forces engaged in undermining the morality of the Western world. This is a serious charge; none the less serious because those who call themselves pragmatists will be highly surprised to learn that the philosophy they profess has had any such extensive influence either for good or evil. One's first impression is that M. Benda is using the term "pragmatic" loosely to stand for all movements that tend to put immediate and narrow expediency—in the sense of profit, whether financial, political, or personal—above all other considerations. Since "pragmatism" is a specific philosophical term having a definite meaning that has nothing in common with the usage just mentioned, this loose use would indicate also a loose sense of intellectual responsibility. But M. Benda cannot claim even this protection, slight as it is.

For after saying in his main sectional heading, "The Socratic-Christian Morality Was the Only One Honored a Few Years Ago," and giving to his next main section the caption "Deliberate Assaults Against this Morality at the End of the 19th Century—the Preaching of Pragmatic Morals," he proceeds to make a specific identification of these "pragmatic morals" with the doctrines of William James—who published, toward the "end of the 19th century," his book entitled *Pragmatism*.

Here is what M. Benda writes—and I quote it because it is the

[First published in *Commentary* 5 (January 1948): 46–50. For Julien Benda's article to which this is a reply, see Appendix 1.]

one and only textual reference by which he even suggests the evidence for the specific charge leveled against pragmatic philosophy: "Cecil Rhodes had already declared at the time of the Boer War: 'This war is just because it is useful to my country.' To be sure, he was only a business man; but an intellectual, Kipling, took a similar attitude. Dare I say that it was close, almost violently close, *to that of William James* at the time the island of Cuba was grabbed by his compatriots?"

The italics are inserted by me in order to make clear beyond doubt just what M. Benda intended by reference to pragmatic philosophy and morality. As authority for his statement about James, he expressly refers to "his *Letters,* II, pp. 73–74." What James *actually* said we shall soon see. By a curious coincidence, James refers in a later letter to Kipling's attitude to American seizure of the Philippines, and what he says on that point will also be quoted.

Here is what James actually wrote in a letter to a French philosopher-friend, François Pillon, on June 15, 1898. (The treaty of peace in which the "compatriots" of M. Benda's account grabbed the Philippines and Porto Rico—but *not* Cuba—was not signed until six months after the date of the letter to which M. Benda refers as his authority.) "We now have the Cuban War. A curious episode of history, showing how a nation's ideals can be changed in the twinkling of an eye, by a succession of outward events partly accidental." After referring to the "persuasion on the part of the people that the cruelty and misrule of Spain in Cuba call for her expulsion," and after mentioning the explosion of the Maine as the "partly accidental outward event" that suddenly changed the nation's ideals, he proceeds as follows: "The actual declaration of war by Congress, however, was a case of *psychologie des foules,* a genuine hysteric stampede at the last moment. . . . The European nations of the Continent cannot believe that our pretense of humanity, and our disclaiming of all ideas of conquest is sincere. It has been *absolutely* sincere." The force of the "has been" in this sentence comes out clearly in a passage that follows: "But here comes in the psychological factor; once the excitement of action gets loosed . . . the old human instincts will get into play with all their old strength, and the ambition and sense of mastery which our nation has will set up new demands. It shall never take Cuba; I imagine that to be very certain. . . . But Porto Rico, and even the Philippines, are not so sure. We had supposed ourselves (with all our crudity and barbarity in certain ways) a better nation morally than the rest, safe at home, etc. . . . Dreams! Human Nature is everywhere the same; and at the least temptation all the old military passions rise and sweep everything before them." [1]

I do not quote this passage in defense of William James; he does not need it. Nor do I quote it for a reason which would be wholly relevant in another context: namely, an exhibition of the realistic quality of his vision based on a degree of intellectual integrity and clarity that unfortunately is not ordinary. I quote the passage as Exhibit "A" with respect to the quality of M. Benda's intellectual responsibility. It may well be that James believed that the undeniable "cruelty and misrule" in Cuba, if not ended by the action of Spain itself, would in the end justify resort to war in order to free Cuba. That, however, is a speculative surmise. The *actual war*, as it took place, he attributes to what was, relatively, an external accident resulting in a manifestation of the "psychology of crowds," in which deep-seated instincts temporarily overthrew control by intelligence. A few years later, returning to the theme, he wrote: "I think that the manner in which the McKinley administration railroaded the country into its policy of conquest was abominable, and the way the country pucked [sic] up its ancient soul at the first touch of temptation, and followed, was sickening." (*Letters*, Vol. II, p. 289.)

James was not an absolute pacifist; possibly M. Benda himself did not carry his absolutism to the point of finding evil in the fact that the United States joined in the last war. But in any case, all

---

1. James' psychological doctrines were notable for assigning an importance to subrational vital conditions which he called "instincts," a position that is now a psychological commonplace but was then a startling novelty. That he glorified these instincts simply is not true. He treated them as facts of such weight that any policy for human improvement which ignores them is doomed to failure. It is pertinent to the understanding of the passage just quoted to refer to his more extended statements in "Remarks at a Peace Banquet" (1904), and "The Moral Equivalent of War," both published in his *Memories and Studies*. They are too long to quote here; but the opening sentence of the "Moral Equivalent" essay is: "I devoutly believe in the reign of peace and in the gradual advent of some sort of a socialistic equilibrium." The essay then states the necessity for a social order in which there must be a discipline in subordinating egoism and personal advantage to large and generous ideals if a peaceful regime is not to become a soft pleasure-economy.

this is merely introductory to the matter of the irresponsibility of M. Benda's account of James' position—his account of "pragmatic morality" as a philosophy of cheap and base expediency.

For it is not merely that what James wrote was written six months before the treaty in which we grabbed the Philippines. It is not merely that James was as right in his *prediction* that we would not take Cuba, as M. Benda is wrong in his report, fifty years later, that we *did* take it. These things are of minor importance, compared with the fact that William James was one of the first, one of the most indignant, and one of the most persistent of the Americans who protested against our seizure of the Philippines—an episode now happily terminated. Nor did William James wait till the seizure was legally completed. The very letter to which M. Benda refers in support of his statement about James, contains the following statement: "I am going to a great popular meeting in Boston today where a lot of my friends are to protest against the new 'Imperialism.'" (James was the vice-president of the Anti-Imperialist League.)

It is not for me to try to tell which horn of the dilemma M. Benda may prefer: either he had not read the letter, or he had read it and chose to suppress both it and the attempt to learn about the public and well-known record of James with reference to the war and to the taking of the Philippines. It is enough that he transforms a "grab" of the Philippines which James opposed, into a grab of Cuba—which did not take place; he then makes this transformation the main—because the one and only—textual reference for what he goes on to make of pragmatic morality. Comment on M. Benda's moral standard of responsibility in intellectual matters does not seem to be needed beyond noting that this is an emphatic and more genuine instance of "the treason of the intellectuals" than any he himself has fumed against.

M. Benda's association of James with Kipling is a secondary matter. But it is possible to quote from the same volume of James' letters the facts on this point. In a letter written in February of the year following the letter just dealt with, we find this passage about Kipling: "I wish he would hearken a bit more to his deeper human self and a bit less to his shallower jingo self. If the Anglo-Saxon race would drop its sniveling cant, it would have a good deal less of a 'burden' to carry." And then comes the passage with respect to the Philippines: "Kipling knows perfectly well that our camps in the tropics are not college settlements or our armies bands of philanthropists slumming it; and I think it is a shame he should represent us to ourselves in that light."

I doubt if it is mere coincidence that it was only a few short months after his reflections on the outbreak of the primitive in Americans, as in other men, that James wrote: "As for me, my bed is made: I am against bigness and greatness in all forms, and with the invisible molecular moral forces that work from individual to individual, stealing in through the crannies of the world like so many soft rootlets, or like the capillary oozing of water, and yet rending the hardest monuments of man's pride if you give them time. . . . So I am against all big organizations as such . . . all big successes . . . and in favor of the eternal forces of truth which always work in the individual and immediately unsuccessful way."

This quotation from the man who is presented by M. Benda as teaching a gospel of immediate "practical" success suffices, I believe, to show how "violently" M. Benda "dares" in his account of the pragmatism of William James. It is a typical specimen of how far he "dares" in his whole account of pragmatism. Although I am far from claiming that all of us who are named pragmatists measure up to either the intellectual or the moral stature of William James, I definitely do claim that the passage just quoted from him comes as close to the spirit of pragmatism as M. Benda's account is remote from it.

The culmination of what M. Benda "dares" is found in passages in which he affiliates pragmatism with the philosophy held and practiced by those in control of the Soviet Union. One of these passages is in the heading that reads: "Two Forms of Pragmatic Ethics Particularly Triumphant at Present," the second of the "two forms" being explicitly identified with the philosophy of Bolshevist Communism. This identity he "dares" to assert in the sentence reading "[pragmatism] tends to recognize no moral values—justice, truth, reason—except as determined by practical considerations—or, more exactly, by economic interest"— i.e., in the case of the triumphant Bolshevist version. Were I to say that M. Benda's account of the latter philosophy is no more accurate than his version of pragmatic philosophy and leave the matter there, he might use that remark as evidence of an attempt to defend Russian official philosophy. So I will say that Macaulay's schoolboy might well be aware of the fact that no practical considerations of any sort, not even those of "economic interest," are determining factors of Bolshevistic philosophy. On the contrary, it is as absolutistic as the philosophy with which M. Benda has allied himself, although the absolutism is that of "dialectical materialism" instead of what is presumably in the case of M. Benda a "spiritualist," possibly supernatural, variety. In any case the conflict of the two philosophies with one another is that of rival absolutisms. It is curious to observe that the absolutistic state philosophy of Bolshevist Russia interprets American pragmatism in pretty much the same fashion as the absolutistic M. Benda.[2] Neither can "dare" to report pragmatism in its own terms as the systematic elaboration of the *logic and ethics of scientific inquiry.*

The ideological amalgam expressed in M. Benda's phrase, "Socratic-Christian," is, to say the least, perplexing. Socrates was put to death on the ground that his questioning of accepted moral and civic doctrines was subversive. According to all accounts, the one thing for which he stood, the one thing that caused his death at the hands of established and recognized authorities, was that he placed the right and authority of continued systematic inquiry in the search for truth above all other authorities that claimed the right to regulate the course of life. M. Benda presumably has reasons he does not disclose for substituting "Socratic-Christian" for the usual phrase, "Judeo-Christian." But as long as these reasons are kept occult, one can only say that it looks a good deal like an attempt to eat the cake of supernatural absolutism and at the same time keep some of it under the pretense of questioning absolute claims. In any case, it is pertinent to state that, on the face of known facts, those who still assert the rights and authority of *critical* systematic examination of all *received* teachings and belief from any source—among whom pragmatists are numbered in the first rank—have the prior claim to the title "followers of Socrates."

If M. Benda should decide to write a responsible account of pragmatic philosophy, including its bearings on morality (for the phrase "pragmatic morality" *taken by itself* is meaningless), the

2. For the most recent effusion from the Soviet Union on American philosophy, particularly pragmatism, served up with *sauce Vishinskyeuse,* cf. "Contemporary Bourgeois Philosophy in the U.S." by M. Dynnik, in the November 1947 issue of *Modern Review,* with a critical comment by Sidney Hook.

account might well take its point of departure from the one and only correct statement in his recent article: the profound aversion of pragmatic philosophy to absolutisms of any sort, whether of the reactionary Right or the reactionary Left. An account that started from that point might be led to consider the grounds on which this aversion is based. These grounds are as simple as they are sufficient. By its own nature, absolutism of any kind tends toward a dogmatic assurance that regards all questioning of its tenets as morally subversive, morally destructive, and hence to be suppressed. The course of history from Socrates and Galileo to the present day of Bolshevist Communism, shows that this outcome has been an actual consequence *in fact,* not merely an implication of absolutist theories. The intolerance which follows in theory and practice alike from the dogmatism accompanying absolutism in belief invites, indeed demands, the elimination of dissenters as morally and politically dangerous. Purges did not begin with Nazism or Bolshevism. They follow when absolutism becomes a dominant philosophy.

But even this persecution of dissenters by imprisonment and death is not its only serious moral consequence. The less overt and less obvious suppression and perversion of inquiry may be an equally damaging result. The most effective means of smothering free inquiry proceeds from creation of an intellectual and moral atmosphere of matter-of-course conformity to ways of belief and behavior which are given the status of "eternal truths" through the backing by institutions whose prestige rests upon the supposed possession of these truths fortified by the weight of sheer historic success. It is absolutism, not pragmatism, which rationalizes the success of the status quo by identifying the real with the rational and existence with the real. It is still absolutism, and not pragmatism, which makes success in accomplishing a specially devised result its ultimate and all-sanctifying goal at the price of any means. It is not pragmatism but the system of M. Benda, insofar as it is absolutistic, which has something deeply in common with Bolshevist Communism.

In this connection the words already quoted from William James are of deep significance. He does not speak of "eternal truths" but of "the eternal forces of truth which always work," although *immediately* without success, as rootlets of plants work because they are *alive*—not because of external authority. The worst thing morally that can be said about the claim to be already in possession of eternal and absolute truth is that it can choke the life which otherwise would everlastingly be active in discovery of those temporal, even quotidian, truths by which life itself develops, disclosing as it develops still more truths that are alive because they are not closed and finished—as every "truth" which claims absoluteness is bound to be.

As for the moral and intellectual responsibility of the account given by M. Benda of the pragmatism he attributes to James, I can hardly do better than cite a statement by the authentic William James of what he regarded as the chief vice of American life: "That extraordinary idealization of 'success' in the mere outward sense of 'getting there,' and getting there on as big a scale as we can, which characterizes our present generation." It is probable that one of his best known phrases is "that bitch-goddess Success." This man who everywhere and all the time attacked what M. Benda presents as "pragmatic morality" is the man the latter "dares" to align with the Cecil Rhodes who (allegedly) said that something was just because it was useful to his nation! I should almost be grateful to M. Benda if I could believe that the very distortion of his account might serve to recall the attention of the present generation to all we still need to learn from the spirit that animates our legacy from William James.

What that spirit is can best be grasped not by isolated passages but from the whole of his writings, which reveal his profound love of variation, freshness, and spontaneity, his pluralistic conception of an open universe and man's creative role in it, his experimental theory of meaning and truth, his unwavering hospitality to new insights, and his imaginative fertility. To lump James with men who have called themselves "pragmatists," many of whom show no familiarity with his writings, who make absolutes of their doctrines, and who substitute the authority of uncritical tradition or violence for the authority of continuous scientific inquiry, is to be victimized by words. All the large words and abstractions of our time have been abused. After all, Hitler called himself a "socialist," Stalin calls himself a "democrat," clerical authoritarians call themselves "humanists," and Franco calls himself a "Christian."

To look behind the words to the substance of a man's vision is the sign of the free and sensitive intelligence.

How Is Mind to Be Known?

All interested in philosophy will agree that the question "What is mind and the mental?" is an important one. They will agree notwithstanding the great difference in conclusions that are arrived at. Some recent discussions of the topic have suggested to me that perhaps it is desirable, if only as a temporary expedient, to raise the question of how the problem of the nature of mind is to be approached—the question, that is, of the way in which the nature of the mental can be *known*. In offering this suggestion I do not intend to suggest anything of the nature of *epistemological* inquiry into the possibility of knowledge, but simply the general question of the method to be used, as one might raise the question of the most effective method of inquiry with respect to any subject-matter.

Asking about the question of method of knowing may serve to explain some of the differences now existing in the views that are held as to the nature of the mental. For it is evident that certain doctrines about the nature of the mental rest upon a virtual assumption that the only method that is at all appropriate is that of *introspection;* and of introspection in the sense in which that word has a signification radically different from the meaning borne by *observation* in connection with everything except the "mental."

The existence of another possible method and something about the character of that other method is suggested by the earlier meaning of the word "introspection." For it was originally used as a synonym for inspection, examination, looking into something, usually with the understanding that the thing looked into was one's own conduct from a moral point of view. It is doubtless true that the fact that one's own conduct was the thing looked into, played a part in development of the later sense of the word

[First published in *Journal of Philosophy* 39 (15 January 1942): 29–35.]

in which "introspection" came to stand for an alleged act of immediate and intuitive knowledge of mind or of consciousness. But nevertheless the earlier and later significations are in sharp contrast. The careful thoroughgoing investigation of the moral character of acts performed, which is what is designated by earlier usage, implies in a definite way that the moral nature of those acts is *not* properly known at the time they are committed, but is something demanding reflective examination.[1]

It was the accepted postulate of ancient and medieval knowledge that *certainty* is an essential property of anything entitled to be called knowledge in its full sense, so that inferred or discursive conclusions depend for their status as knowledge on being derived by inherently necessary true procedures from premises that are immediately and self-evidently known to be true. Modern physical science destroyed the grounds upon which rested the special propositions that had previously been taken to be ultimate first truths and to be the premises upon which the proof of truth of all other scientific truths depended. Nevertheless, the postulate of inherent connection of certainty with knowledge remained. It is a commonplace of the history of modern thought that immediate facts of consciousness, or "mental facts," were appealed to to provide the supposedly required unshakable and indubitable first truths without which there is no possibility of inferring other true propositions. One interesting illustration may be cited. Early modern philosophy retained the belief in the self-evident truth of mathematical definitions and axioms which was common to Greek and medieval philosophy. But the change in physical science furnished no logical warrant that truths which are self-evident *qua* mathematical are validly applicable to *physical* phenomena. Hence the necessity (exemplified alike in Descartes and Kant in spite of their other differences) of finding something completely certain in "consciousness" or "mind" that gives solid warrant to the application.

Persons who are fond of quoting Santayana's remark about the difference between knowing a thing and being it by taking com-

1. It is perhaps worth noting that a somewhat similar change took place in the significations of *conscience* and *consciousness*. *Con-scious,* and *conscire,* originally meant *to know with another,* and *conscire alii* and *conscire sibi* were both legitimate expressions. "To know with one's self" meant, without doubt, private or unshared knowledge. But it did *not* mean knowledge of something intrinsically private.

plete possession of it, as if knowing were a kind of eating, and those who accept that principle irrespective of Santayana's endorsement, will be aware of the existence of the radical contrast existing in methods employed in knowing the "mental." For the epistemological doctrine lying back of belief in immediate and certain knowledge of the mental is that in the case of the mental *to be and to be known* are one and the same thing. Indirect approach through more or less prolonged inquiry, with use of formation of hypothesis and by experimental observation, may be required for knowing everything else. But in the case of the mental, so it is assumed, the objects or events to be known are self-revealing, self-disclosing. To have them is to know them.

There are dialectical difficulties in the position. How do we know, apart from comparison and contrast with other subject-matters, that the particular objects or events in question are *mental*? What possible meaning does the word "mental," or even the word "consciousness," have in case the events they are supposed to designate are so unique that no identification with or discrimination from anything else is involved? I am not concerned to follow up this dialectical difficulty. I mention it as a way of calling emphatic attention to the fact that knowledge of *everything else* involves institution of *connections* through operations of comparison and discrimination by means of which connections are discovered. This is the contrasted method of knowing the nature of mind and the mental which is so frequently ignored as to justify raising the question to which this article is devoted.

The statement, often made, to the effect that the particular, individual, unique, can not be known is ambiguous until further qualified. It may mean that it can not be known in its capacity of being particular, or that it can not be known in any way or fashion. The first of these two meanings is consistent with the view that knowledge involves description in terms of traits of connection constituting a kind. In this sense, the immediate qualities that are *had* and which knowledge of the "mental" is *about* or is *of*, are like the immediate qualities of any event in its particularity of occurrence.[2] For the events which when known are

2. It is obvious that "mental" and "mind" designate *kinds*. I pass over the dialectical difficulty involved in the inconsistency of this trait with their alleged uniqueness, since it is probably another form of that previously mentioned—the difficulty of knowing something to be mental without comparison with and discrimination from other things.

called, say, fire, fever, fight, or by another common noun, are particular in their immediacy of occurrence. In the latter capacity they have no characteristics in common with other occurrences in *their* particularity. If awareness were conferred upon an event, as a Leibnizian monad, it could be said that the qualities of which the event is aware, are *private;* the word "private" being here a strict synonym for "particular." If the same logical method were employed as in the case of the doctrine of the immediate and intuitive self-knowledge of the "mental," an event could then be said to have knowledge of its own qualities, and to be the only existence able to know its "own" states and processes.

This fanciful endowment of events is indulged in as a way of calling attention to that difference between having and knowing (and being known) which characterizes every event in its particularity of occurrence. When, for example, it is said that my toothache is private, is immediately known by me, and is completely inaccessible to every one else, there is just one element in the statement capable of empirical verification. And that element has nothing to do with "knowing." It is a verifiable fact that your *having* a toothache is quite a different event from *my* having it. It does not follow that you know that *what* you have is a toothache any differently from the way in which any one else knows it. As a matter of fact, the dentist probably knows the nature of toothache, the special location and other characteristics of *this* toothache, much better than does the one who *has* it. And the "privacy" of what is had seems to depend upon physical conditions rather than upon anything intrinsic to its nature. There is good ground for believing that were our techniques further advanced, nerve-graftings might enable me to feel or have a toothache whose immediate locus is in the jaw of your head—just as by means of radio we hear a sound originating indefinitely far away.

There are, in short, such things as enjoyments and sufferings which are "private" in occurrence. That they are *known* in any way different from the way in which we know sounds, colors, etc., seems to be a dictum resting upon an epistemological theory, not upon any evidence specifically relevant to the case. Moreover, the privacy of enjoyments and sufferings in their occurrence seems to describe a *social* fact—as much so as in the case of a miser who has and gloats over a "private" store of gold. I ran across the following in a book I read recently: "The private individual privately setting forth his will by marking a private ballot." It needs no argument to show that ability to cast a private or secret ballot is a publicly determined matter, and an arrangement believed to be socially desirable. The "private individual" who is mentioned in the sentence quoted is able to cast a ballot only when publicly determined conditions of age, citizenship, registration, etc., have been satisfied. Similarly, emphasis upon "private initiative" in business as a mark of a certain *social* regime, is urged by those who support it as a social policy because of alleged social benefits. One can even go so far as to say that the *significance* of the recognition that enjoyments and suffering are privately *had*, is a matter of social morals. For it is an accompaniment of the rather recent development of humanitarianism and of philanthropy which goes beyond racial and creedal limits. The currency of the doctrine which mistakenly converts the event of having into a unique mode of knowing can be said to be a confused product of an "individualistic" *social* movement in politics and economics.

One retort to what I am saying is that it completely overlooks the primary mode of knowledge called *acquaintance*. My argument, however, is far from ignoring the fact of acquaintance. I shall not repeat here what I have said elsewhere about the intimate connection of acquaintance with knowing *how* to make appropriate active responses to an event, as in having a speaking acquaintance with a foreign language, or being acquainted with John F. Exbury. It suffices here to point out the difference between acquaintance-knowledge and any knowledge that makes scientific or philosophical claims for itself. Human beings were well acquainted with torrid heat and frigid cold, with various diseases, with stones, plants, and animals, long before they had anything approaching what now alone passes for scientific knowledge. As the case of Greek and medieval "science" proves, the belief that scientific knowledge is of the same order as acquaintance kept actual science in leading-strings for centuries. Personally, I doubt whether one could even be acquainted with the things he enjoys and undergoes, any more than with milk, oak trees, or neighbors, unless he got beyond what he *has* by means of operations of comparison and discrimination, which result in giving the things in question a general or public status. But the point I am making as to the difference between acquaintance and the kind of knowledge of the mental that could be entitled to recognition in philosophy or psychology is independent of this belief of mine.

Any theory of the nature of the mental which depends for its validity upon postulation of a special mode of knowing, one applying to that particular object and to nothing else, would, I believe, be regarded with highly suspicious eye were it not for the currency of a special type of epistemology. Given that currency, the case for antecedent suspicion is countered by what, upon examination, turns out to be a special case of reasoning in a closed circle. It is said in effect that the peculiar, the extraordinarily peculiar, nature of mind requires an equally peculiar, unique procedure by which to know it. Since, however, the doctrine of the completely unique nature of the mental rests upon an assumption of the way in which it is known, the argument is not exactly convincing.

If the nature of the phenomena termed mental is to be known in the way in which other immediately present unique qualities, such as this *hot,* this *cold,* this *red,* are known then the "mental" stands pretty well at the opposite pole from things that are known with a slight amount of mediation. To know scientifically what red color is, an extensive field of knowledge, factual and theoretical, is a necessary condition. Carefully tested ideas of the nature of light had to be attained, and they were found to involve a tested theory about electro-magnetism. I need not go into further detail to illustrate the point about the indirect character of knowledge of a particular quality immediately *had* in experience. While I am not here concerned to try to tell what are the distinctive characteristics that describe the mental, I am suggesting that in order to discover the nature of the mental, we might have to begin with the best conclusions that have been reached about behavior from the standpoint of biology, and then utilize all that is known about the modifications produced in such behavior by the complex of conditions constituting culture, including communication or language.

C. I. Lewis, in his article "Some Logical Considerations concerning the Mental" [3] uses at least nine times the phrase "behavioral [behavioristic] and [or] brain states." He thus identifies,

---

3. *Journal of Philosophy,* Vol. XXXVIII (1941), pp. 225–233.

without argument, the behavioral account of the mental with description in terms of the brain. Hence it is probably well to state that *behavior,* as I use the word in the previous paragraph, even on the biological level (without reference to behavior as it is culturally constituted), includes a great deal more than "brain events." Indeed, I have difficulty in seeing how any one can give an intelligible account of cerebral behavior unless that limited mode of behavior is itself descriptively determined in connection with the whole scheme of what is known about behavior in its widest biological sense—a sense in which interaction with environmental conditions is included. There is one passage, as against nine of the kind just mentioned, in which Mr. Lewis speaks of "brain facts or facts of physical behavior." Even if "or" is here used to express an alternative instead of a synonym, the adjective "physical" constitutes a limitation of the behavioral approach which will be accepted only by "behaviorists" who subordinate their account of behavior to epistemological considerations.

The last paragraphs are introduced only to illustrate the fact that to *know* mind, in distinction from just *having* qualities that are "mental," one has to go to things that are *not* mind nor mental and to translate qualities that immediately occur into a set of connections between events. The idea of method which they are intended to illustrate is one which stands, as has been indicated, at the opposite pole to the method of complete and indubitable immediate knowledge—a method that eliminates, once for all, the need for reflection and inquiry. Since it is the question of method I am raising, I shall not say anything here about the conclusions as to the nature of mind to which use of the method of systematic investigation might lead us. It is, however, pertinent to say that much more in the way of positive results has already been attained than is indicated anywhere in this article.

Inquiry and Indeterminateness
of Situations

I am indebted to Mr. Mackay for the opportunity to correct some wrong impressions about my theory of inquiry, especially as to the meaning of "indeterminate" in connection with it.[1] While I hope I may be able to say something of a clarifying kind, study of his paper has led me to believe, for reasons that will appear later, that the difference between us goes much deeper than the special difficulties he points out. If I am correct in this belief, my reply to Mr. Mackay's questions and criticisms would have to take up issues more fundamental than those he brings up, and my article would be different from the one his paper evokes.

Two questions are raised by Mr. Mackay. Since he says that his second question, that concerning an alleged material flaw in my analysis, is probably the ground for his first charge, that of vagueness, and since I agree with him that such is the case, I begin with the second, "the more serious difficulty." Mr. Mackay introduces his discussion by asking the following question: "What does it mean to say that *the existential conditions* in a problematic situation are indeterminate?" That the crux of Mr. Mackay's difficulty and criticism has to do with the use of the word "existential" is shown not only by his use of italics but is explicitly stated in the next sentences. "Assuming that the situation is indeterminate, proleptically, with respect to its eventual issue, Mr. Dewey seems to suppose that the antecedent conditions must also be existentially indeterminate on the ground that the issue is itself an existential and not a merely intellectual affair. *But the issue, while still pending and in the future, is an ideal or intellec-*

1. D. S. Mackay, "What Does Mr. Dewey Mean by an 'Indeterminate Situation'?" the *Journal of Philosophy*, Vol. XXXIX (1942), pp. 141–148.

[First published in *Journal of Philosophy* 39 (21 May 1942): 290–96. For Donald S. Mackay's article to which this is a reply, see Appendix 2.

tual affair, an affair of meanings, an anticipated possibility" (p. 145, italics not in original text). Consequently he charges me, apparently on the ground of a statement made by me in another book in discussing another topic, of "conversion of eventual functions into antecedent existence"; of "reading the *indeterminate* character of an eventual function, *before* its fulfilment, back into a causal antecedent reality." He makes the same criticism in other language when he says that I confuse an experienced quality of indeterminateness which is purely *cognitive* (that of the eventual issue *before* accomplishment) with the *practical* and *operational* indeterminateness of the experienced quality of the original antecedent situation.

The sentence stating that an eventual issue before fulfilment is reached, or while still future, is ideal or intellectual, and hence a non-existential affair, is, then, the crux of Mr. Mackay's position. It is the only ground adduced for the charge brought against me. This fact makes it the more extraordinary that Mr. Mackay offers no argument or evidence in support of the proposition. Usually such a course signifies that the writer regards the statement as self-evident, or at least as obvious beyond reasonable doubt. But if this is the case here, Mr. Mackay believes, and believes it to be self-evident as a general proposition, that whatever is in the future is merely intellectual and non-existential. I hesitate to ascribe to Mr. Mackay the idealistic metaphysics according to which the future and future events, even when they are so bound up with what is going on at a given date as to be the issue or outcome of the latter, are merely ideal and non-existential. But in case that is his view, I must say it is the opposite of mine, and there is no ground whatever for interpreting what I have said in terms of his belief.

There is another possible explanation, one which, upon the whole, seems the more probable. Mr. Mackay may suppose that *my theory as a whole* commits me logically to acceptance of the proposition he makes, so that it expresses my actual position, which, however, I have in my confusion covered up and virtually denied. Even so, it seems to me astonishing that no evidence is given and no passages of my logical theory are alluded to in support of ascription to me of such a view.

Usually it would be extremely difficult to reply to or even discuss a thesis left in such a vague state. But in this particular case it happens to be a simple matter to point out that the view in question—the premise, be it recalled, of which the charge of basic confusion is the conclusion—goes contrary to my whole theory of inquiry; and to such an extent, moreover, as to make nonsense of the theory. I should have supposed that the general tenor of my theory of inquiry would have been made clear by the definition of inquiry which Mr. Mackay himself quotes in his article. An eventual situation which is the "controlled or directed transformation" of an original indeterminate situation would, I should have supposed, be seen to possess, necessarily, the *existential* nature of the original situation. If, however, the fact that such is the nature of my position does not appear from this definition of inquiry, the doctrine that the original indeterminate situation and the eventual resolved one are precisely *initial and terminal phases* of one and the same existential situation, is involved in every chapter of my *Logic* in treating every problem taken up.[2]

Proof of the statement I have just made would, in order to be completely adequate, obviously involve giving a resumé of the entire text of my *Logic*. Since this course is out of the question and in view of the fact that Mr. Mackay cites no specific evidence in support of the view he ascribes to me, I confine my remarks on the view I actually hold to one general and one special point—a point, however, which is a special case of the general theory. As to my general position, I believe the following passage, in its context and as a sample of many other passages to the same effect, shows that my view treats the original and the eventual situation as the two existential ends, initial and terminal, of one and the same existential situation: "The transformation [accomplished in inquiry] is existential and hence temporal. The pre-cognitive unsettled situation can be settled only by modification of its constituents. . . . The temporal quality of inquiry means, then, some-

2. In the course of his article Mr. Mackay makes, also without supporting evidence or reference, the following statement about the resolved final stage of the situation under inquiry: "Its determinateness belongs to the context and not to the content of the knowledge, or warranted assertibility, to which the inquiry leads." In my view the determinateness of the final phase of the situation undergoing inquiry is not only the *content* of knowledge, but it provides the *definition* of knowledge, as far as that determinateness is the outcome or "issue" of the operations constituting the inquiry.

thing quite other than that the process of inquiry takes time. It means that the objective subject-matter of inquiry undergoes modification." [3]

The existentiality of the situation from beginning to end is, indeed, so directly and so intimately bound up with every part of my discussion of inquiry that I almost hesitate to quote a special passage. To learn that my treatment is capable of being understood in precisely an opposite sense is a discouraging experience. But this completely contrary interpretation is contained in the sole reference made by Mr. Mackay to my fundamental "doctrine of the continuum of inquiry," when, instead of treating it as a temporal existential continuum, he says "it succeeds only in confusing the two kinds of indeterminateness without bridging the gap between them"—one kind being, of course, the nonexistential indeterminateness *he* attributes to the eventual resolved situation, and the other kind the "practical, operational" indeterminateness he supposes I give to the original situation— depending, moreover, as is shown later, upon its indeterminateness being taken by him in a merely privative sense. In this connection, Mr. Mackay's reference to "*causal* antecedent situation" makes it pertinent to mention that one chapter of my *Logic* contains a detailed criticism of the "antecedent-consequent" interpretation of the causal relation, and an exposition of the view that it functions in inquiry as the means of instituting temporal "historic" continuity.

The more special point to which I call attention is a particular case of the general proposition set forth. The idea that the eventual situation is ideational (instead of being the existential issue or outcome of the existential transformation of the situation which in its first phase was indeterminate) makes nonsense of the very theory developed in my *Logic* regarding the nature of *ideational*. An *anticipation* of the eventual issue *is* an *idea;* such anticipation of a *possible* outcome defines being an *idea;* and (according to my view) such anticipations are necessary factors in effecting the *existential* transformation which it is the business of

3. *Logic: The Theory of Inquiry,* p. 118 [*Later Works* 12:121–22]. Emphasis upon the necessity of experiment for competent inquiry and denial of the *mentalistic* nature of "thinking," because of the necessity or performance of overt operation, are mentioned in the context of this passage.

inquiry to accomplish: these propositions are indeed parts of my theory. But it is equally a part of my theory that the idea, or anticipation of *possible* outcome, must, in order to satisfy the requirements of controlled inquiry, be such as to indicate an operation to be *existentially* performed, or is a means (called *procedural*) of effecting the existential transformation without which a problematic situation can not be resolved. Moreover, in my account of ideas it is expressly stated, at some length, that the *validity* of the idea, as an anticipation of eventual resolved existential situation, is *tested* by the contribution which performance of the operation prescribed by it makes to the institution of the final determinate phase. Exactly the same kind of interpretation is also given of the logical import of observed *data,* as the *material* means of effecting the needed existential transformation. That Mr. Mackay might object to my actual theory even more strenuously than he does to the one he thinks I hold, I can well understand. But that fact does not affect the irrelevancy of the view ascribed to me as the ground of the criticisms he actually sets forth.

II

In dealing with the difficulty due to *vagueness* in my idea of indeterminateness, I wish first to state that in one point mentioned by Mr. Mackay I was guilty of a loose use of language of a kind that readily leads to misunderstanding. I am glad of the occasion given me by Mr. Mackay's paper to correct my mistake. In a passage cited by Mr. Mackay I used the term "*doubtful*" in connection with the pre-inquiry situation, and used it as if it were a synonym for the indeterminateness I attribute to that pre-inquiry situation. Doubting is, obviously, correlative with inquiring. The fact that my misuse in this particular case did not bear at all upon the particular issue then under discussion may have been a factor in producing my carelessness but is no excuse for it.

Mr. Mackay's discussion of the second point makes it clear that he regards the *indeterminateness* of the antecedent situation as purely *privative.* He speaks of it as signifying "a felt *lack* of knowledge"; as the "*absence* of certain characteristics that are to be *eventually* determined by means of *further* inquiry" (italics not in original text). His belief in the merely privative character of *indeterminate* in this connection is shown also in his quotation from James of the *toto coelo* difference between feeling of an absence and absence of a feeling. This view is also involved in his treatment of the indeterminateness of the original situation as "practical" and "operational." In this matter again Mr. Mackay's treatment does not enable a reader to judge whether he thinks his interpretation is "self-evident," in the nature of the case, or is a necessary logical implication of my theory. As far as his discussion is concerned, the statement is an *ipse dixit*. Accordingly, I can only say that as far as my own view is concerned, assertion of the negative or privative character of the original situation inverts my position. According to me, it is positive and intrinsic and in *that* capacity it evokes and directs the inquiry that attempts to effect existential transformation into an eventual determinate situation. What is said about "situation" applies in full force to the situation which is *indeterminate* in quality. "A situation is a whole in virtue of its immediately pervasive quality. . . . The pervasively qualitative is also unique; it constitutes each situation an *individual* situation, indivisible and unduplicable. . . . Without its controlling presence, there is no way to determine the relevancy, weight or coherence of any designated distinction or relation."[4] The "controlling presence" of the *uniquely* pervasive indeterminate quality of the situation provides the direction which Mr. Mackay's criticism finds to be absent—and which, of course, *is* absent if the indeterminateness in question is a mere lack or absence, a deprivation. If, however, Mr. Mackay holds that the original situation is indeterminate in a purely negative sense, it is *he* who seems committed to the view that sheer ignorance, if felt, is capable of evoking effective inquiry. It is my denial of that view, my belief that only intrinsic, positive indeterminateness of a unique character is capable of bringing inquiry into existence, which provides the ground for my assertion that doubting and doubts which are not formulations of an initial distinctive existential indeterminateness are pathological, to the extent at least of being captious, arbitrary, self-made.

Mr. Mackay suggests that it is possible that my use of a num-

4. *Op. cit.*, p. 68 [*Later Works* 12:73–74].

ber of words as synonyms of "indeterminate," as applied to the initial antecedent situation, increases rather than lessens the vagueness of that term. As for myself, I wish that I had enough poetic or dramatic capacity to multiply the words used still further. For no word can describe or convey a *quality*. This statement is, of course, as true of the quality *indeterminate* as it is of the qualities *red, hard, tragic,* or *amusing*. The words used can at best only serve to produce in hearer or reader an experience in which the quality mentioned is directly had or experienced. There was enough novelty in the view developed in my *Theory of Inquiry* to cause me to appreciate the difficulty that would take place in the having of the kind of situation that would give the word "indeterminate" realized meaning in the sense in which I used it. Accordingly, I spoke of some situations (those which evoke and direct inquiry) as perplexed, troubled, unsettled, open, imbalanced, in the hope that some adjective might induce readers to call up for themselves the kind of situation to which the word "indeterminate" is applied in connection with inquiry. I might also have used, possibly I have at times used, such words as insecure, precarious, even *uncertain,* not indeed in its cognitive sense but in the sense in which it is said that a man's footing is unsure. How far the "vagueness" involved in use of a name that designates a quality is, in a given case, a matter of lack of proper skill of evocation on the part of the one who uses the word, and how far it is a matter of declining to have a situation which would give the designation its intended import—a refusal due as a rule to habits previously formed—can not be decided on general principles. But I hope the variety of words I have used and suggested will at least protect the quality involved from being taken to be negative and privative.[5]

III

Were it not for the light shed upon the matter by Mr. Mackay's interpretation of *indeterminate* as sheer lack and ab-

5. On pages 68–70 of *Logic: The Theory of Inquiry* [*Later Works* 12:73–76], in connection with the word "situation" I have said something about the fact that in certain cases words, and discourse generally, can serve only as *invitations* to a reader or hearer which the latter may accept or refuse. What is there said is peculiarly applicable to the "indeterminate" under discussion.

pointing to a possible alternative definition in order to indicate the necessity for explicit formulation and explicit justification of a certain view of "intrinsic good," so as to make sure that it does not ultimately rest upon an ambiguity of the word "intrinsic" in connection with a metaphysical position which is left unstated.

Anti-Naturalism in Extremis

Philosophical naturalism has a more distinguished ancestry than is usually recognized; there are, for example, the names of Aristotle and Spinoza. However, the Aristotle who has exercised the greatest influence upon modern philosophy was one whose naturalism did not prevent him from regarding the physical as the lowest stratum in the hierarchical order of Being and from holding that pure intellect, "pure" because free from contamination by any trace of matter, is at the apex. It is to be doubted, however, whether the work of Aristotle would have inured, as it has done, to the credit of anti-naturalism if he had not been adopted as the official philosopher of the Church, and if his writings had not found their way into modern culture through the transformation undergone in the medieval period.

For in this period, the out-and-out supernaturalism of the Roman Catholic Church was injected whenever possible into interpretation of Aristotle. The naturalistic elements in his teaching were overlaid, covered up, with supernatural beliefs; or, if that was not possible, were slurred over as the views of a pagan not enlightened by the Hebraic-Christian revelation from on high. The supernaturalism thus read into Aristotle united with elements in him which are genuinely non-naturalistic from the standpoint of present science. It resulted in his being held up by many modern writers as the founder, in conjunction with Plato, of spiritualistic anti-naturalistic philosophy.

However, when it is a question of moral theory, the naturalism of Aristotle lies so clearly on the face of what he said that medieval Christian theological philosophy was compelled to give it a radically different turn. How different was this turn may be inferred from words of Cardinal Newman which express the or-

[First published in *Partisan Review* 10 (January–February 1943): 24–39.]

thodox view: "The pattern-man, the just, the upright, the generous, the honourable, the conscientious, if he is all this not from a
supernatural power, but from *mere natural virtue*" "has the
prospect of heaven closed and refused him."[1] When such measure is meted out to such virtues as honor, uprightness, justice,
and generosity, one readily gathers how conduct proceeding
from appetite and desire will be judged. For the latter are even
more deeply dyed with the Pauline and Augustinian view of the
total corruption of the body and the carnal lusts of flesh. The historic source of the doctrine of the corruption of nature and the
fallen estate of man may be relegated to the background. But the
Western world was reared under the influence of the doctrines
and sacraments of the Church. Contrast between the old Adam
which is "natural" and a higher self which is "spiritual" remained the assumption of philosophers who avowedly repudiated supernaturalism—as in the striking case of Kant. The
Church never forgot to remind its adherents of the lost condition
that was due to their fallen estate. For otherwise there would
have been no need for the work of redemption supernaturally entrusted to it. Similarly, the professedly non-supernatural philosopher who was anti-naturalist never ceased to dwell upon the
merely sensuous and self-seeking character of the natural man
and upon the morally seductive character of natural impulse and
desire. For otherwise there would be no place for the doctrine
that the truly moral factors in human relations are superimposed
by a spiritual non-natural source and authority.

It is needful to use such terms as non-naturalist and anti-
naturalist. For in addition to frank supernaturalism, there are
philosophers who claim to rest their extra- if not super-natu-
ralism upon a higher faculty of Reason or Intuition, or whatever,
not upon special divine revelation. While I am personally convinced that their philosophy can be understood only as an historical heritage from frank supernaturalism, I shall not urge that
view. I wish rather to call attention to a point of agreement and
practical cooperation between the members of the two anti-
naturalistic schools. Both of them identify naturalism with "materialism." They then employ the identification to charge naturalists with reduction of all distinctive human values, moral,

---

1. The word *mere* plays a large role in anti-naturalistic writings.

esthetic, logical, to blind mechanical conjunctions of material entities—a reduction which is in effect their complete destruction. This identification thus permits anti-naturalists to substitute name-calling for a discussion of specific issues in their proper terms in connection with concrete evidence.

Regarding the identification in question, it suffices here to note that the naturalist is one who of necessity has respect for the conclusions of natural science. Hence he is quite aware that "matter" has in modern science none of the low, base, inert properties assigned to it in classic Greek and medieval philosophy:—properties that were the ground for setting it in stark opposition to all that is higher, and to which eulogistic adjectives may be applied. In consequence he is aware that since "matter" and "materialism" acquired their significance in contrast with something called "spirit" and "spiritualism," the fact that naturalism has no place for the latter deprives the former base epithets of philosophic significance. It would be difficult to find a greater distance between any two terms than that which separates "matter" in the Greek-medieval tradition and the technical signification, suitably expressed only in mathematical symbols, the word bears in science today.

Reference to science reminds us that nobody save perhaps the most dogmatic supernaturalist will deny that modern methods of experimental observation have wrought a profound transformation in the subject matters of astronomy, physics, chemistry and biology, or that the change wrought in them has exercised the deepest influence upon human relations. The naturalist adds to recognition of this fact, a further fact of fateful significance. He sees how anti-naturalism has operated to prevent the application of scientific methods in the whole field of human and social subject matter. It has thereby prevented science from completing its career and fulfilling its constructive potentialities, since it has held the human is extra-natural and hence reserved for organs and methods which are radically different from those that have given man the command he now possesses in all affairs, issues, and questions acknowledged to be natural. It is beyond human imagination to estimate the extent to which undesirable features of the present human situation are connected with the split, the division, confusion and conflict that is embodied in this half-way, mixed, unintegrated situation in respect to knowledge and attainment of truth. Democracy cannot obtain either adequate recognition of its own meaning or coherent practical realization as long as anti-naturalism operates to delay and frustrate the use of methods by which alone understanding of, and consequent ability to guide, social relationships can be attained.

In this connection, it is appropriate to say something which is more or less apart from the main topic of this paper. Philosophic naturalism still has a work to do in a field that so far it has hardly done more than touch. Because of the influence of supernatural religion, first Catholic and then Protestant, it is not just "matter" which continues to reflect the beliefs of a pre-scientific and pre-democratic period. Such words as mind, subject, self, person, *the* individual, to say nothing of "value," are more than tinged in their current usage—which affects willy-nilly philosophical formulations—with significations they absorbed from beliefs of an extra-natural character. There is almost no word employed in psychological and societal analysis and description that does not reflect this influence.

Hence comes the conclusion that the most pressing problem and the most urgent task of naturalism at the present time is to work out, on the basis of available evidence, a naturalistic interpretation of the things and events designated by the words that now exert almost complete control of psychological and societal inquiry and report. For example, no issue is more basic for naturalistic theory than the nature of observation. A survey of contemporary literature will, nevertheless, disclose that it is rarely discussed in its own terms:—that is of procedures employed by inquirers in astronomical observatories; in chemical, physical and biological laboratories; in the examinations conducted by physicians, and in what is done in field excursions of botanists and zoologists. Instead, it appears to be obligatory to substitute for observation of observation its reduction to terms of sensations, sensa, sense-data (the exact word is of little import), which are affected by an inheritance of non-naturalism.

The current discussion of language—also a topic of basic importance—affords another example. Students of this subject, from a logical and a social point of view, who regard themselves as anti-metaphysical scientific positivists, write as if words consisted of an "inner," private, mentalistic core or substance and an "outer" physical shell by means of which a subjective intrinsically incommunicable somewhat gets conveyed "trans-subjectively"! And they appear quite unaware of the extra-natural origin and status of their postulate. Until naturalists have applied their principles and methods to formulation of such topics as mind, consciousness, self, etc., they will be at a serious disadvantage. For writers of the "rational" philosophical variety of anti-naturalism almost always draw their premises from alleged facts of and about mind, consciousness, etc. They suppose the "facts" are accepted by naturalists. When they do not find the conclusions *they* draw, they accuse naturalists of holding an inconsistent and truncated position.

II

Since this topic is too large for discussion here, the rest of this paper is occupied with the contrast existing between charges brought against naturalism (because of its alleged identity with "materialism") and the facts of the case. At the present time there is a veritable eruption of such accusations. Many of them seem to regard the present tragic situation of the world as a heaven-sent occasion for accusing naturalism of responsibility for the manifold evils from which we are suffering. I begin with citing some specimen cases.

"Determinists, materialists, agnostics, behaviorists and their ilk can be sincere defenders of democracy only by being inconsistent; for their theories, whether they wish it or not, lead inevitably to justifying government by brute force and to denying all those rights and freedoms which we term inalienable." Naturalists are not included by name in the foregoing list. But a miscellaneous roll of writers that follows shows they fall within the "ilk" in question: "Kant and Carlyle, William James and Herbert Spencer, William McDougall and Henri Bergson, Gobineau and Chamberlain—all of them would be horrified at the complete product of Nazism—made such a philosophy [as that of government by brute force] not only possible but almost inevitable by their denial of one or more of the fundamentals on which any free and humanitarian and Christian concept of society must be built."[2]

2. Thomas P. Neill, in the *Catholic World*, May 1942, p. 151.

The grouping together of men whose philosophies have nothing, or next to nothing, in common beyond denial or neglect of
the dogmas of that Roman Catholic theological philosophy,
which is held up by the adherents of this faith as the sole basis of
a "free" and ordered society, is a commentary on the intellectual
criteria employed by the writer. It is kind of gross carelessness
that a naturalist would not dare to engage in. Only the confidence of one who thinks he is speaking for a divinely founded
and divinely directed institution could lump together men of
such contrary beliefs. Even more to the point is the fact that
among those who are regarded as causes of the present social disorder is Kant—one who is a philosophical anti-naturalist, and
who among other things formulated the doctrine that every human person is an end in himself, possessed of freedom because of
membership in a realm above the natural world:—the Kant who
regarded it as the function of history and the gradual improvement of social institutions to usher in republican government as
the only one that conformed to the philosophical principles he
laid down.

   In view of the fact that Bergson is included in the list, it is interesting that the next quotation is from a writer, held up to Prot-
estants as a specimen of the liberalism of the Catholic Church,
who has publicly expressed peculiar indebtedness to this very
Bergson: "What the world and civilization have needed in modern times in the intellectual order, what the temporal good of
man has needed for four centuries, is Christian Philosophy. In
their place arose a separate philosophy and an inhuman Humanism, a Humanism destructive of man because it wanted to be
centered upon man and not upon God. We have drained the cup;
we now see before our eyes that bloody anti-Humanism, that ferocious irrationalism and trend to slavery in which rationalist
Humanism finally winds up."[3]

   A "mere" naturalist would hesitate, even if he counted upon
the ignorance or short memory of his audience, to assume that
the world was in a state of blissful order and peace, free from
blood and ferocity, before the rise of rationalism, naturalism and
humanism. Even the ordinary reader might recall that some of
the bloodiest and most cruel wars in human history were waged

3. From J. Maritain's "Contemporary Renewals in Religious Thought," p. 14,
   contained in *Religion and the Modern World*.

in the name of and with the explicit sanction of supernaturalism and of the ecclesiastic institution which dominated European culture until the last "four centuries," so significantly mentioned.

If, however, the reader is familiar with the articles of supernatural medieval philosophy, he will also recall that bloody and ferocious persecutions and oppressions are very different when carried on in the interests of the Church. For in this latter case they are intended to save from eternal damnation the souls of believers in heresies; or if that is not possible at least to protect others from being contaminated by literally "damnable" heresies. The interpretation put by St. Thomas Aquinas (now the official philosopher of *the* Church) upon the Biblical injunction "Love thy neighbor as thyself" is proof for the orthodox that since the love in question is love of an immortal soul which can be saved only by acceptance of the creed of the Church and by sharing in its sacraments, that injunction of Jesus is far from having the meaning that would naturally be assigned to it. For it is an express authorization of any and all means that will tend to save that soul from the tortures of hell. For what are peace, earthly and natural contentment, and a reasonable degree of happiness for a mere three score years and ten in comparison with supernatural eternity? Hence, the proper course to be taken by genuine "love"!

I come now to a statement which, if I mistake not, has both supernatural and philosophical anti-naturalists among its sponsors. "Men who hold to this naturalistic view in democratic countries are unaware of the dangers in their position. Influenced by the last remnants of philosophical Idealism, romantic Transcendentalism, or religious Theism in our day, they act as if they believed in the spiritual conception which they have intellectually repudiated. They try to maintain their feeling for the dignity of man, while paying homage to an essentially materialistic philosophy according to which man is simply (sic!) a highly developed animal. They are living off the spiritual capital which has come down to them from their classical and religious heritage. . . . Since this contradiction will prove to be intellectually intolerable, scholars and teachers *must* (!) recover and reaffirm the spiritual conception of man and his good which we have derived from Greek and Hebraic-Christian sources. If they fail to do this, not only religious reverence and moral responsibility, but also the scholarly activities with which they are directly concerned, will be greatly endangered. Already under totalitarian regimes and to a lesser extent in the democracies, these activities are being undermined."[4]

It is probable that the signers of this statement belong to both the supernatural and the rationalistic varieties of anti-naturalism. Reference to our classic *and* religious heritage, to Greek *and* Hebraic-Christian sources, indicates that such is the case. They agree for purposes of attack. But cross-examination would disclose a fundamental incompatibility. For example, philosophical anti-naturalists are obliged to confine themselves to dire prediction of terrible things to happen because of naturalism. Their companions of the supernatural variety are aware, however, of active and forcible means that were once employed to stay the spread of heresies like naturalism so as to prevent the frightful consequences from happening. If they are literate in their faith, they know that such methods are still required, but are prevented from now being put into execution by the spread of naturalistic liberalism in civilized countries. When members of this group think of the pains that were taken when the Church had the power to protect the faithful from "science falsely socalled," and from dangerous thoughts in scholarship, they might well smile at the innocence of their colleagues who imply that inquiry, scholarship, and teaching are completely unhampered where naturalism has not obtained a foothold. And they might certainly say of their merely philosophical confreres, that *they* are living off a capital derived from a supernatural heritage. A mere naturalist will content himself with wondering whether ignorance of history, or complacency or provincialism with respect to the non-Christian part of the world, or sheer rhetorical dogmatism is the outstanding trait of the pronunciamento. A historian of ideas would be able to contribute some interesting information as to the beliefs of the persons who have done the most to make democracy and freedom of mind a reality in the modern world, and

4. From a statement signed by a group of Princeton professors, published in Vol. II of the *Proceedings of the Conference on Science, Philosophy and Religion*. Although "science" appears in the title, the meetings and discussions of this Conference have been chiefly devoted to asserting some aspect of anti-naturalism; literary writers, being innocent of the philosophical issues involved, serving as cement of the amalgam.

as to the beliefs of the persons who withstood their efforts at every turn until the march of events forced them to desist from that particular line of obscurantic obstructionism.

I conclude these citations with a passage written somewhat before the crisis had reached its present intensity. In a book G. K. Chesterton wrote after a visit to this country, he spoke as follows of the prospects of democracy in this country. "As far as that democracy becomes or remains Catholic and Christian, that democracy will remain democratic. . . . Men will more and more realise that there is no meaning in democracy if there is no meaning in anything; and that there is no meaning in anything if the universe has not a centre of significance and an authority that is the basis of our rights."

I should not have supposed that advance was to have been expected in greater realization of the truism that if there is no meaning in anything, there is no meaning in democracy. The nub of the passage clearly resides in assertion that the rights and freedom which constitute democracy have no validity or significance save as they are referable to some centre and authority entirely outside nature and outside men's connections with one another in society. This intrinsically sceptical, even cynical and pessimistic, view of human nature is at the bottom of all the asseverations that naturalism is destructive of the values associated with democracy, including belief in the dignity of man and the worth of human life. This disparaging view (to put it mildly) is the basis upon which rests the whole enterprise of condemning naturalism, no matter in what fine philosophical language the condemnation is set forth. The fact of the case is that naturalism finds the values in question, the worth and dignity of men and women, founded in human nature itself, in the connections, actual and potential, of human beings with one another in their natural social relationships. Not only that, but it is ready at any time to maintain the thesis that a foundation within man and nature is a much sounder one than is one alleged to exist outside the constitution of man and nature.

I do not suppose it is a matter of just expediency or policy in winning adherents that keeps in the dim background the historic origin of the view that human nature is inherently too depraved to be trusted. But it is well to recall that its source is the Pauline (and Augustinian) interpretation of an ancient Hebrew legend about Adam and Eve in the Paradise of Eden. Adherents of the Christian faith who have been influenced by geology, history, anthropology, and literary criticism prefer, quite understandably, to relegate the story to the field of symbolism. But the view that all nature was somehow thoroughly corrupted and that mankind is collectively and individually in a fallen estate, is the only ground upon which there can be urged the necessity of redemption by extra-natural means. And the diluted philosophic version of historic supernaturalism which goes by the name of rationalistic metaphysical spiritualism or idealism has no basis upon which to erect its "higher" non-natural organs and faculties, and the supernatural truths they are said to reveal, without a corresponding thoroughly pessimistic view of human nature.

III

I now come to the question of the moral and social consequences that flow from the base and degrading view of nature in general and of human nature in particular that inheres in every variety of anti-naturalistic philosophy. I begin with the fact that the whole tendency of this view has been to put a heavy discount upon resources that are potentially available for betterment of human life. In the case of any candid clear-eyed person, it is enough to ask one simple question: What is the inevitable effect of holding that anything remotely approaching a basic and serious amelioration of the human estate must be based upon means and methods that lie outside the natural and social world, while human capacities are so low that reliance upon them only makes things worse? Science cannot help; industry and commerce cannot help; political and jural arrangements cannot help; ordinary human affections, sympathies and friendships cannot help. Place these natural resources under the terrible handicap put upon them by every mode of anti-naturalism, and what is the outcome? Not that these things have not accomplished anything in fact, but that their operation has always been weakened and hampered in just the degree in which supernaturalism has prevailed.

Take the case of science as a case of "natural" knowledge obtained by "natural" means and methods; together with the fact that after all, from the extra-naturalistic point of view, science is *mere* natural knowledge which must be put in stark opposition to a higher realm of truths accessible to extra-natural organs. Does any one believe that where this climate of opinion prevails, scientific method and the conclusions reached by its use can do what they are capable of? Denial of reasonable freedom and attendant responsibility to any group produces conditions which can then be cited as reasons why such group cannot be entrusted with freedom or given responsibility. Similarly, the low estimate put upon science, the idea that because it is occupied with the natural world, it is incapacitated from exercising influence upon values to which the adjectives "ideal" and "higher," (or any adjectives of eulogistic connotation) can be applied, restricts its influence. *The fruit of anti-naturalism is then made the ground of attack upon naturalism.*

If I stated that this low opinion of science in its natural state tended to lower the intellectual standards of anti-naturalists, to dull their sense of the importance of evidence, to blunt their sensitivity to the need of accuracy of statement, to encourage emotional rhetoric at the expense of analysis and discrimination, I might seem to be following too closely the model set by the aspersions (such as have been quoted) of anti-naturalists. It may be said, however, that while some writers of the anti-naturalistic school say a good deal, following Aristotle, about the "intellectual virtues," I fail to find any evidence that they have a perception of the way in which the rise of scientific methods has enlarged the range and sharpened the edge of these virtues. How could they, when it is a necessary part of their scheme to depreciate scientific method, in behalf of higher methods and organs of attaining extra-natural truths said to be of infinitely greater import?

Aside from displaying systematic disrespect for scientific method, supernaturalists deny the findings of science when the latter conflict with a dogma of their creed. The story of the conflict of theology and science is the result. It is played down at the present time. But, as already indicated, it throws a flood of light on the charge, brought in the manifesto previously quoted, that it is the naturalists who are endangering free scholarship. Philosophic anti-naturalists are ambiguous in their treatment of certain scientific issues. For example, competent scientific workers in the biological field are agreed in acceptance of some form of genetic development of all species of plants and animals, mankind included. This conclusion puts man definitely and squarely within the natural world. What, it may be asked, is the attitude of non-theological anti-naturalists toward this conclusion? Do those, for example, who sign a statement saying that naturalists regard man as "simply a highly developed animal" mean to deny the scientific biological conclusion? Do they wish to hold that philosophical naturalism and not scientific inquiry originated and upholds the doctrine of development? Or, do they wish to take advantage of the word "animal" to present naturalistic philosophers in a bad light?

Since the latter accept without discount and qualification facts that are authenticated by careful and thorough inquiry, they recognize in their full force observed facts that disclose the differences existing between man and other animals, as well as the strands of continuity that are discovered in scientific investigation. The idea that there is anything in naturalism that prevents acknowledgment of differential traits in their full significance, or that compels their "reduction" to traits characteristic of worms, clams, cats, or monkeys has no foundation. Lack of foundation is probably the reason why anti-naturalist critics find it advisable to represent naturalism as simply a variety of materialism. For the view attributed to naturalism is simply another instance of a too common procedure in philosophical controversy: Namely, representation of the position of an opponent in the terms it would have *if* the critic held it; that is, the meaning it has not in its own terms but after translation into the terms of an opposed theory. Upon the whole, the non-supernatural anti-naturalists are in such a dilemma that we should extend sympathetic pity to them. If they presented the naturalistic position in its own terms, they would have to take serious account of scientific method and its conclusions.

But if they should do that, they would inevitably be imbued with some of the ideas of the very philosophy they are attacking. Under these circumstances, the ambivalence of their own attitude is readily understood.

Lack of respect for scientific method, which after all is but systematic, extensive and carefully controlled use of alert and unprejudiced observation and experimentation in collecting, arranging and testing facts to serve as evidence, is attended by a tendency toward finalism and dogmatism. Non-theological anti-naturalists would probably deny that their views are marked by that quality of fanaticism which has marked the supernatural brand. And they have not displayed it in anything like the same intensity. But from the standpoint of logic, it must be said that their failure to do so is more creditable to their hearts than to their heads. For it is an essential part of their doctrine that above the inquiring, patient, ever-learning and tentative method of science there exists some organ or faculty which reveals ultimate and immutable truths, and that apart from the truths thus obtained there is no sure foundation for morals and for a humane order of society. As one critic of naturalism remarked (somewhat naively indeed), without these absolute and final truths, there would be in morals only the kind of certainty that exists in physics and chemistry.

Non-theological anti-naturalists write and speak as if there were complete agreement on the part of all absolutists as to standards, rules, and ideals with respect to the specific content of ultimate truths. Supernaturalists know better. They are aware of the conflict that exists; they are aware that conflict between truths claiming ultimate and complete authority is the most fundamental kind of discord that can exist. Hence, their claim to supernatural guidance; and hence fanaticism in carrying on a campaign to wipe out heresies which are dangerous in the degree they claim to rest on possession of ultimate truths. The non-supernatural variety in the more humane attitude it usually takes is living upon a capital which is inherited from the modern liberal developments professedly repudiated. Were its adherents to yield to the demands of logic, they would see how much more secure is the position of those who hold that given a body of ultimate and immutable truths, without which there is only moral and social confusion and conflict, a special institution is demanded which will make known and enforce these truths.

During periods in which social customs were static, and isolation of groups from one another was the rule, it was comparatively easy for men to live in complacent assurance as to the finality of their own practices and beliefs. That time has gone. The problem of attaining mutual understanding and a reasonable degree of amicable cooperation among different peoples, races, classes, is bound up with the problem of reaching by peaceful and democratic means some workable adjustment of the values, standards, and ends which are now in a state of conflict. Dependence upon the absolutist and totalitarian element involved in every form of anti-naturalism adds to the difficulty of this already extremely difficult undertaking.

To represent naturalistic morals as if they involved denial of the existence and the legitimacy of any sort of regulative end and standard is but another case of translation of a position into the terms of the position of its opponents. The idea that unless standards and rules are eternal and immutable they are not rules and criteria at all is childish. If there is anything confirmed by observation it is that human beings naturally cherish certain things and relationships, they naturally institute values. Having desires and having to guide themselves by aims and purposes, no other course is possible. It is also an abundantly confirmed fact of observation that standards and ends grew up and obtained their effectiveness over human behavior in all sorts of relatively accidental ways. Many of them reflect conditions of geographical isolation, social segregation, and absence of scientific methods. These conditions no longer obtaining, it requires a good deal of pessimism to assume that vastly improved knowledge of nature, human nature included, cannot be employed or will not be employed to render human relationships more humane, just and liberal. The notion that such knowledge and such application, the things for which naturalism stands, will increase misunderstanding and conflict is an extraordinary "reversed charge" of results produced by dogmatic absolutism in appeal to extra-natural authority.

Reference to the pessimism which is involved reminds one of the chorus of voices now proclaiming that naturalism is committed to a dangerously romantic, optimistic, utopian view of human nature. This claim might be looked at as a welcome variation of the charge that naturalism looks upon everything human as "merely" animal. But it happens also to be aside from the mark. It is probably "natural" for those who engage in sweeping rationalistic generalizations to match their own pessimism by attributing an equally unrestrained optimism to their opponents. But since naturalists are committed to basing conclusions upon evidence, they give equal weight to observed facts that point in the direction of both non-social behavior and that of amity and cooperation. In neither case, however, are facts now existing taken to be final and fixed. They are treated as indications of things to be done.

Naturalism is certainly hopeful enough to reject the view expressed by Cardinal Newman when he said "She (the Church) regards this world and all that is in it, as dust and ashes, compared with the value of a single soul. . . . She considers the action of this world and the action of the soul simply incommensurate." Naturalism rejects this view because the "soul and its action" as supernatural are put in opposition to a natural world and its action, the latter being regarded as thoroughly corrupt. But naturalism does not fly to the opposite extreme. It holds to the possibility of discovering by natural means the conditions in human nature and in the environment which work in detail toward the production of concrete forms of both social health and social disease—as the possibility of knowledge and corresponding control in action by adequate knowledge is in process of actual demonstration in the case of medicine. The chief difficulty in the road is that in social and moral matters we are twenty-five hundred years behind the discovery of Hippocrates as to the natural quality of the cause of disease and health. We are also behind his dictum that all events are equally sacred and equally natural.

I mention one further instance of the contrast between the relative bearings of anti-naturalism and naturalism in connection with social problems. Because of the influence of a low view of human nature and of matter a sharp line has been drawn and become generally current between what is called *economic* and what is called *moral:*—and this in spite of facts which demonstrate that at present industry and commerce have more influence upon the actual relation of human groups to one another than any other single factor. The "economic" was marked off as a separate compartment because on the one hand it was supposed to spring from and to satisfy appetites and desires that are bodily and carnal, and on the other hand economic activities have to do with mere "matter."

Whether or not Karl Marx originated the idea that economic factors are the only ultimate causative factors in production of social changes, he did not originate the notion that such factors are "materialistic." He accepted that notion from the current and classic Greek-medieval-Christian tradition. I know of no way to judge how much of the remediable harshness and brutal inhumanity of existing social relationships is connected with denial of intrinsic moral significance to the activities by means of which men live. I do not mean that anti-naturalism is the original source of the evils that exist. But I do mean that the belief that whatever is natural is sub-normal and in tendency is anti-moral, has a great deal to do with perpetuating this state of affairs after we have natural means at command for rendering the situation more humane. Moreover, on the political side we fail to note that so-called laissez-faire individualism, with its extreme separatism and isolation of human beings from one another, is in fact a secularized version of the doctrine of a supernatural soul which has intrinsic connection only with God.

Fear and hate for that which is feared accompany situations of great stress and strain. The philosophic attempt to hold the rise of naturalism accountable for the evils of the present situation, as the ideological incarnation of the enemy democratic peoples are fighting, is greatly accentuated by the emotional perturbations that attend the present crisis. Intense emotion is an all-or-none event. It sees things in terms of only blackest black and purest shining white. Hence, persons of scholastic cultivation can write as if brutality, cruelty, and savage intolerance were unknown until the rise of naturalism. A *diabolus ex machina* is the natural emotionalized dramatic counterpart of the *deus ex machina* of supernaturalism. A naturalistic writer being human may yield to the influence of fear and hate. But in so far he abandons his humanistic naturalism. For it calls for observation of concrete natural causal conditions, and for projection of aims and methods that are consonant with the social conditions disclosed in inquiry. His philosophy commits him to continued use of all the methods of intelligent operation that are available. It commits him to aversion to the escapism and humanistic defeatism inherent in anti-naturalism.

As the war is a global war, so the peace must be a peace that has respect for all the peoples and "races" of the world. I mentioned earlier the provincialism which regards the non-Christians of the world, especially of Asia (and later Africa will come into the scene) as outside the fold, and which philosophical non-supernaturalism admits within the truly human compass only upon conditions its own metaphysics dictates. A philosophic naturalist cannot approve nor go along with those whose beliefs and whose actions, if the latter cohere with their theories, weaken dependence upon the natural agencies, cultural, scientific, economic, political, by which a more humane and friendly world must be built. On the contrary, to him the present tragic scene is a challenge to employ courageously, patiently, persistently and with wholehearted devotion all the *natural* resources that are now potentially at our command.

Valuation Judgments and
Immediate Quality

There is much in Mr. Philip B. Rice's recent article in the *Journal of Philosophy* with which a neo-empiricist is happy to agree.[1] He will agree, on the critical side, with opposition to the metaphysical "realism" that locates the "objectivity" of value in "objects" that are so-called because of lack of any connection whatever with human behavior. He will agree also with the opposition to those views which admit a human factor in values, but which interpret it in such a way that the result is sceptical denial of the possibility of any genuine judgments about them. These agreements are based upon those positive aspects of Mr. Rice's paper which (1) identify the problem of the possibility of genuine judgments of value with the problem of the possibility of reaching conclusions about value that are capable of providing guidance to life-behavior; and (2) which identify the "objectivity" of judgments with verifiability by empirical evidence. The view that value-judgments are "objective" for the same reason that other judgments are accepted as valid,—because, that is, they are verifiable by the hypothetico-inductive method,[2] is that upon which the neo-empiricist stands.

1. "'Objectivity' in Value Judgments," Vol. XL (1943), pp. 5–14 [Appendix 3, this volume].
2. *Op. cit.*, p. 12 [this volume, p. 410]. In view of this emphasis upon verifiability, it seems a matter of regret that no allusion is made to the articles by Dr. Lepley dealing with this point.

[First published in *Journal of Philosophy* 40 (10 June 1943): 309–17. For Philip Blair Rice's article to which this is a reply, see Appendix 3. For Rice's second article, see Appendix 4. For a further reply by Dewey and rejoinder by Rice, see pp. 73–83 and Appendix 5.]

I

The greater one's satisfaction with these points of Mr. Rice's article, the greater, however, will be one's disappointment that Mr. Rice introduces an element of "subjectivity" which is reached by a different method and depends upon a different kind of criterion than that used in defining "objectivity." The method and criterion are so fundamentally different that they cease to be correlative. For *subjective* is defined in terms of a special order of Being, viz., one that is directly open to observation only by one person, and by a special kind of knowing called "introspection," or "*self*-knowledge";—an order of Being which accordingly is "inner" and "private." It is defined, then, by falling back upon an assumption of a certain sort of epistemological-metaphysical "reality," while "objective," on the other hand, is defined on the basis of evidential support depended upon in all scientific inquiry. Not only does Mr. Rice use a method and criterion that are explicitly rejected in the case of "objectivity," but he further complicates matters by holding that this introspective approach to a private and inner material provides a special kind of verifying evidence with respect to valuation judgments, a kind which can and should be *added on* to the evidence supplied by common and public observation, such as is used in arriving at non-valuation propositions;—a view which renders the "subjective" itself "objective" on the basis of the definition given of objectivity!

Before dealing with this latter matter, I shall say something about the definition of "subjectivity" that would be arrived at on the basis of parity of reasoning and criterion with that used in the case of "objectivity." It would run something as follows: Propositions (judgments, beliefs, or whatever) are *subjective* when they are produced by causal conditions which fail to possess genuine evidential capacity and verifying power, but which nevertheless are taken at the time to possess them and hence to provide acceptance and assertion of the propositions in question. The only "assumption" in this definition is the empirically verifiable fact that all beliefs, right and wrong, valid and invalid, have concrete causal conditions which, under the given circumstances, *produce* judgments; but which in some cases are conditions that warrant or justify the proposition that is generated, while in other cases they are found not to be such as to furnish justifying ground. Epistemological philosophers make a great ado about illusions, hallucinations, forms of insanity. But science proceeds on the basis that there are concrete conditions for their occurrence, and that these conditions are capable of being detected and eliminated, or discounted, as far as capacity to produce acceptance of a given proposition and belief is concerned. It was perhaps "natural" in a backward state of science to lump together concrete and specifiable conditions of error and mistake under the general and supposedly unanalyzable assumption of "a subject," as a name for a general peculiar order of Being. But scientific inquiry has progressed by searching for and detecting specific concrete conditions which are subject to exactly the same kind of public observation and test as are the conditions that warrant and justify sound and valid propositions (judgments, beliefs, or whatever). It is the peculiarity of Mr. Rice's view of evaluative judgments that he has completely rejected the epistemological-metaphysical assumption in the case of "objectivity," while retaining it in the case of the "subjective." The consistent empirical view is that viewed as *events,* as occurrences, the *subjective* and *objective* are both of the same nature. They differ (and differ basically) with respect to the capacity of their respective causal conditions to serve as valid *grounds;* in their ability, that is, to stand up in the exercise of the verifying evidential function.

II

Mr. Rice offers no direct evidence or argument for holding to the existence of material that is private and inner and hence (by its very nature) accessible directly only to observation by a "self" which is single, exclusive, and non-public and non-social. He engages, however, in a discussion of another view whose defects are supposed to provide ground for the position he takes. As this other view is attributed to me, consideration of it may have the disadvantage of seeming to be purely an argument *pro domo.* But I hope the discussion will turn out, as it develops, to deal with two points of much more than personal importance. One of them concerns the matter of subjectivity; the other concerns the capacity of a "value-experience," (as described by Mr. Rice), to serve as supplementary or "plus" evidence in verification of value-*judgments*.

Mr. Rice attributed to me, quite correctly, the view that evaluative judgments are conclusions of inquiries into the "conditions and results of experienced objects." He also points out, quite correctly, that this view is equivalent to holding that "objectivity" resides in "the publicly observable conditions and consequences of value-experiences." And he further states that I am moving in the right direction in seeking objectivity in the evidence for value judgments. The trouble is that I do not go far enough with respect to what is evidential and verifying material. My "social behaviorism leads [me] to ignore one very important kind of evidence, namely, that concerning the immediate quality of the experience of value itself."[3] This statement does not of itself expressly assert that this "immediate quality" is private and subjective. In so far, it is possible to discuss the question of the evidential value of an immediately experienced quality apart from the question of its alleged subjective nature.

Mr. Rice's statement that "value-judgments" are "concerning the immediate quality of the experience of value itself," is joined to a statement that since I *admit* "that 'liking' or 'enjoyment' is a constituent of the value experience itself," it is the more strange that I ignore the evidential and verifying force of the experience of liking and enjoyment.[4]

Now I do a good deal more than hold that qualitative "enjoyment," "satisfaction," is a *constituent* of the experienced material which the valuation judgment is about or "is concerning." I hold that it is the *entire* material that judgment is about. But it is an essential part of my view of valuation judgments that the satisfaction, liking, enjoyment they are about is not itself a *value* save in a figurative way,—a way illustrated in the figure of speech in which a man is called a candidate. For it is not asserted that he is inherently and *per se* a *candidate*, but that he is one in connection with an ongoing course of events of which a future election is an indispensable part:—that is, in a prospective reference. And so an enjoyment is called a *value* with reference to being poten-

3. *Op. cit.*, pp. 9–10 [this volume, p. 407].
4. P. 9 [p. 407]. The word "admits" is not italicized in Mr. Rice's text. My reason for italicizing will be readily gathered from what follows.

tially the material for an evaluative judgment, or in connection with events still to occur. This designation is innocent as a figure of speech; it confuses the entire issue when taken literally.

The strange part of Mr. Rice's criticism of my view is that he himself explicitly insists upon the prospective reference of an evaluation judgment as far as its "objectivity" is concerned—and I fail to see how any statement can be regarded as a *judgment* unless it lays claim to objectivity in the sense of evidential support. The following considerations, quoted from Mr. Rice's article, certainly read as if they were in complete harmony with my view that the mere enunciation that something, as matter of fact, is enjoyed or liked is not a *judgment* of the value of what is enjoyed. For in defining "objectivity" (without a claim to which, as I have just said, no form of words can be termed *judgment*) he says expressly that an ethical judgment is *not* a simple descriptive judgment concerning present or past fact, but "is a *predictive* judgment concerning the *potentialities* of human nature as well as its actuality." And he explicitly states that to say an act, *x*, is good refers to it not in isolation but in connection with a whole system or "pattern of interests"; and that it has "objectivity," in which case it will promote the *pattern* of interests "in the long run . . . to a greater extent than any feasible alternative"; and that *x* has objectivity because it refers "to something *beyond my desire or liking at the moment.*"[5] And while he does not go further than say that my emphasis upon "conditions and consequences" is "in the right direction," he does not indicate on what basis alternative possibilities can be compared and investigated with respect to connection with a system of interests, save on the ground of "conditions and consequences."

III

What then is the difference between us? Why does Mr. Rice find my view to be seriously defective, since he agrees with the two main points of my theory as to *judgments* that are evaluations: namely, as to the points (1) that the problem of *objectivity* of such judgments amounts to the problem of whether intelligent guidance of the course of life-conduct is possible, and

5. *Op. cit.,* p. 11 [p. 409], my italics.

(2) that *objectivity* is possible because value-judgments concern a set, system, or pattern of interests, beyond the immediate occurrence of a given liking or satisfaction? As far as I can make out, the difference is two-fold. My critic holds that the occurrence of a liking or satisfaction affords an added or "plus" verifying *evidence;* and he holds that since what is liked is qualitative it is subjective, in the sense of being directly open only to *self*-observation or introspection, or is private and inner. I take up first his view that the immediate quality of a satisfaction is a necessary part of the *evidence* that the satisfaction is a value. This view seems quite incompatible with Mr. Rice's doctrine that the question of value has to do with the connection of a satisfaction with a system of interests, involving the future and a comparison of alternative acts with respect to their integrative function.

Hence, the force of his statement that my "social behaviorism leads [me] to ignore one very important kind of evidence, namely, that concerning the immediate quality of the experience of value itself" seems to rest upon an equivoke. I am so far from "ignoring" it that, according to my view, the entire valuation process is precisely and exclusively about or concerning this quality in its immediate occurrence. And the statement of Mr. Rice himself to the effect that valuation is not a description of what has happened but is *predictive in reference* reads like an explicit endorsement of the same doctrine. The equivoke consists in taking evidence *concerning* an immediately experienced quality to be identical with evidence *supplied* by that very immediate qualitative satisfaction (enjoyment, liking) although its *doubtful* status with respect to its connection with a whole pattern of interests is the occasion and the ground for a valuation-*judgment!* The equivoke is clear in the assumption made in the following passage. He says that since "Dewey admits that 'liking' or 'enjoyment' is a constituent of the value experience itself . . . it would seem to be a grave sin of omission for an empiricist to exclude this phase of the act from study when seeking evidence for valuations" (p. 9 [p. 407]). The clear implication is that the exclusion of an immediately experienced quality from possession of *evidential and verifying function in judgment* is equivalent to excluding it from all recognition or attention whatever—although in fact this phenomenon is precisely that which judgment is about, or "is concerning," in the attempt to determine its standing *qua* value! And when he says, as a criticism of my view, that "in no other field do we rule out attention to the phenomenon under study itself, to concentrate exclusively upon its conditions and results" (p. 9 [p. 407]), it seems to me clear that there is an illicit transfer from the problem of the *evidential* force and function of a given phenomenon over to the fact that a liking has taken place: A transfer that is illicit because it unwittingly substitutes possession of evidential force for the fact of the bare occurrence of that which evokes and demands judgment with respect to its value-status. It is not easy to understand why and how an inquiry, in the case of a given event, into *its* conditions and results is a case of ruling out attention to it. So much for the question of the evidential worth, with respect to determination of value, of the bare occurrence of an event which as an event is undeniably immediately *qualitative*.

IV

I turn now to the other question, the assumption of Mr. Rice that since what is enjoyed is immediately qualitative it is therefore "subjective." For there is no doubt that it is this assumption that leads him to believe that definition in terms of causes and effects, conditions and consequences, is only a partial definition, being confined to factors admittedly "objective" in Mr. Rice's, as well as my own, sense of the word. I point out that in my general doctrine about judgment and verification, *situation* is the key word, and that a situation is held to be *directly and immediately qualitative*. And it is held that a situation evokes inquiry, terminating in *judgment*, when it is *problematic* in its immediate quality, because of confusing, conflicting, relatively disordered qualities. Hence any inquiry which is evoked is successful in the degree in which further observation succeeds in discovering facts by means of which inquiry terminates in an ordered, unified, situation (as immediately qualitative as the original problematic situation). What is discovered in effecting this kind of transformation from one type of quality to another constitutes its *verifying* status with respect to any theory or hypothesis that is involved in the conduct of observations:—the hypothetico-inductive method to which reference was earlier made.

Since the present matter of discussion does not concern the truth of my theory but its nature, I content myself with a single quotation. A transformed qualitative situation is said to be the *end* of inquiry "in the sense in which 'end' means '*end-in-view*' and in the sense in which it means 'close.'"[6]

Now Mr. Rice gives no argument at all in support of his position that the immediate qualitative material of liking (satisfaction, enjoyment) is *subjective*. Apparently he takes it to be self-evident. But Mr. Rice holds that the reason my theory is defective is because I hold that valuation judgments are determined in terms of "conditions and consequences," thus leaving out of account evidence supplied by material which is "subjective." Hence, it is more than pertinent for me to point out that, according to my theory, while the initial problematic situation and the final transformed resolved situation are equally immediately qualitative, no situation is subjective nor involves a subject-object relation. While this fact shows that my theory is at the opposite pole from "ignoring" qualitative immediacy, its pertinence here lies in the fact that if Mr. Rice wishes to engage in relevant criticism of my theory, he should give arguments in support of his view that qualities, at least in the case of phenomena of liking and satisfaction, are open to direct inspection or observation only by an act of introspection or "self-observation" of material which is inherently "inner and private." And he should give reasons for holding that the events which provide the primary datum are (1) not of the nature of *situations,* and/or (2) that there is satisfactory evidence for holding that situations with respect to their qualitative immediacy are "subjective" instead of being prior to, neutral to, and inclusive of any distinction and relation that can be legitimately instituted between subject and object. For *denial* of the primacy and ultimacy of this relation (supposed to be the inherent epistemological-metaphysical basis and background from which philosophical theory must proceed) is the basic feature of my general theory of knowledge, of judgment and verification, my theory of value-judgments being but a special case of this general theory.

And in calling my theory on this matter a special case of my *general* theory I intend to call attention to the fact that I have

6. *Logic: The Theory of Inquiry,* p. 158 [*Later Works* 12:160].

denied that as judgments, or in respect to method of inquiry, test and verification, value judgments have any peculiar or unique features. They differ from other judgments of course in the specific material they have to do with. But in this respect inquiries and judgments about potatoes, cats and molecules differ from one another. The genuinely important difference resides in the fact of the much greater *importance with respect to the conduct of life-behavior* possessed by the special subjectmatter of socalled value-judgments. For in comparison with the deep and broad *human* bearing of their subjectmatter, the subjectmatter of other judgments is relatively narrow and technical.

V

I am grateful to Mr. Rice not only for his agreement, as far as it goes, with some of the main tenets of my theory but for the opportunity his article gives me for making clear my actual position on the secondary and derived nature of the "subject-object" distinction and relation, and the primary character of situations that are completely neutral to this distinction and relation, for the latter, in my view, is intermediate, transitive and instrumental in the transformation of one type of immediately qualitative situation into a situation of another type in respect to ordering and arrangement of qualities, but of the same type with respect to its immediate qualitative nature, which is neither subjective, nor objective, nor a relation of the two.

I am grateful because I have come increasingly to the conclusion that failure to grasp my view on this matter, and its fundamental position in my discussion of special topics, is the chief factor in producing misapprehension of my view of many special topics I have discussed. A recent article in the *Journal of Philosophy* by Mr. Brotherston is in point. Entitled "The Genius of Pragmatic Empiricism"[7] it sets out by saying this theory holds that "the subject-object relation [obtains] in a field of common sense and scientific procedure which at the very beginning of enquiry is given as an on-going concern" (p. 14). Representatives of the theory have made, according to him, an advance in showing that

7. Vol. XL (1943), pp. 14–21 and pp. 29–39.

there is no explicit awareness of this relation until reflective analysis sets in. But they have made the mistake of not expressly pointing out that it is there from the beginning, with primacy attached to the "subject" factor. Now whether or not we *should* have taken this view, it is in fact so different from that we have taken that it may be called "the *evil* genius" of pragmatic empiricism.[8]

I now recur to the matter of the connection of immediate quality with value-judgments. The view that the bare occurrence of *any* kind of satisfaction is evidence of value seems to me to involve a relapse into that pre-scientific method which Peirce called the method of *congeniality*. Nor is it at all clear to me how a quality said to be private and inner can be added on to qualities which are public to form an evidential whole. Such an addition or joining seems to be something like a contradiction *in adjecto*. But these considerations are not at all incompatible with the fact that marked satisfaction, amounting at times to positive excitement, may qualify situations in which terminate judgments of value are *verified by evidential facts*. But the quality of a satisfaction that arises because of attainment of adequate verification is *toto coelo* different from the quality of a satisfaction that happens to occur independent of evidence as to its status *qua* value. One of the main benefits of a genuine education in use of scientific method is that it produces immediate sensitiveness to the difference between these two kinds of satisfaction.

8. Another article by A. F. Bentley, on "Truth, Reality, and Behavioral Fact" states the actual position correctly, and in particular effects a correction of Mr. Brotherston's misconception of James's "neutral entities" (the *Journal of Philosophy*, Vol. XL, 1943, pp. 169–187). I may refer to an earlier article of mine, "How Is Mind to Be Known?" *ibid.*, Vol. XXXIX (1942), pp. 29–35 [this volume, pp. 27–33]. In an earlier article of mine, "The Objectivism-Subjectivism of Modern Philosophy" (*ibid.*, Vol. XXXVIII, 1941, pp. 533–542 [*Later Works* 14:189–200]), I fear I did not make it sufficiently clear that in speaking of organic and environmental factors as conditions of a situation, what is meant is that they are conditions of the *occurrence* of situations, the distinction when made in respect to *production* being the chief factor in aiding us to bring the quality of situations (in which the relation does not obtain) under purposive regulation.

Further as to Valuation as Judgment[1]

I am grateful to Mr. Rice for giving me further opportunity to clear up points in my view which I have failed to make sufficiently clear in the past. I shall in my present attempt confine myself to two leading theses put forth by Mr. Rice. One of them is that there are certain events which are intrinsically of such a nature that they can be observed only "introspectively," or by the single person or self in whom they occur, such events being so "sequestered and idiosyncratic" as to be private and, psychologically, "subjective." The second proposition is that in spite of their subjective intrinsic nature, they are capable of being used as evidence in the case of judgments of value along with facts of a public and "objective" nature, thus being logically "objective" although subjective in existence.[2]

1. The present paper is called out by the article of Professor Rice on "Types of Value Judgments," the *Journal of Philosophy*, Vol. XL (1943), pp. 533–543 [this volume, Appendix 5]. I add here the remark that while I occasionally use the words "valuation judgments," I regard the phrase as pleonastic, *valuation* being judgment. (*Valuing*, as I pointed out long ago, is an ambiguous word standing both for judgment or evaluation and for direct liking, cherishing, relishing, holding dear, etc.) Since Mr. Rice in his present paper attributes to me an identification of what I called *neo*-empiricism—to distinguish it from traditional sensationalist empiricism—and scientific method with "instrumentalism," I also add the remark that the only identification I made was—and is—with the "hypothetico-inductive method."

2. There is a third point in Mr. Rice's paper which, apparently, gives its caption to his article. It is sufficiently independent of the points just mentioned to merit consideration on its own account and, accordingly, is not touched upon in this reply.

[First published in *Journal of Philosophy* 40 (30 September 1943): 543–52. For Philip Blair Rice's article to which this is a reply, see Appendix 5. For earlier articles see pp. 63–72 and Appendixes 3 and 4.]

I

The first of these two propositions concerns a question of fact. The fact involved is of such a fundamental nature that it has no more bearing upon or connection with the logical question of the evidence that validity supports judgments of valuation than it has with a multitude of other philosophic questions. I shall discuss it, then, *as* a question of fact, noting, however, that in Mr. Rice's view the fact, as he interprets it, plays an important part in judgments about "values." Mr. Rice holds that such events as "shapes, colors, overt movements" have qualities which are open to observation on equal terms by a number of observers, and hence are public and "objective" in their mode of existence. In contrast with such events stand events such as "muscular sensations," thoughts not uttered or enacted, feelings having affective tone, etc. The latter can be observed only by a single person, or "introspectively," and hence are private, subjective. It is expressly held that "both the occurrence and the quality of these events can be directly observed only by the individual in whose organism they are occurring." Physiologically, they are said to be conditioned by proprioceptors and interoceptors, while events of a public and "objective" nature are conditioned by exteroceptors.

There is one difficulty in discussing this question of fact. The kind of event whose character is in dispute can not, by definition, be had by any two observers in common, and hence not by Mr. Rice and myself. Mr. Rice accordingly refers me, quite logically, to "my own" (exclusively my own) "joys, pains, and secret thoughts" for evidence of the existence of privately observed events. Now the bald statement that while I recognize the existence of such events as Mr. Rice gives examples of, I do *not* find them to be "private" or inner as observed and known, does not carry discussion far; it seems rather to leave it at a dead end.

The matter at issue may, however, be approached indirectly. Mr. Rice objects to my characterizing his position as "epistemological-metaphysical." I gave no reasons for that characterization. For I did not intend it to apply in any invidious way to Mr. Rice's view. On the contrary, I intended it to apply to a traditional and still generally accepted doctrine which originated and developed in modern epistemological discussions, and which is "metaphysical" in the sense that it has to do with the inherent nature of two kinds or orders of existence. Since Mr. Rice accepts and promulgates the view, if I understand him aright, that there are two such orders, one psychological and "individual," the other not, I used the characterization in question.[3]

In any case, I wish to repeat my expression of gratitude to Mr. Rice for giving me an opportunity to state my position on this matter as explicitly as possible, since, as I remarked in my earlier article, failure to grasp my actual view seems to account for misapprehension of many points in my general philosophical theory. In this restatement of my view, I begin by stating the conclusion I have arrived at. It is as follows: The undeniable *centering* of the events which are the more immediate condition of the occurrence of events in the way of observation and of knowledge generally, within a particular organism, say that of John Smith, has been taken as proof that the resulting *observation* is itself "individual." I believe further that this conversion of a condition of the occurrence of an event into an inherent and intrinsic property of the event itself (that of observation) is not due to anything in the facts, but is derived from the holdover of an earlier doctrine, of pre-scientific and largely theological origin, of an individual soul as the knower—even though the "soul" part has been thinned down into "mind," "consciousness," or even that supposedly scientific *Ersatz*, the brain of a single organism.

I do not deny, in other words, that the immediate or last conditions of the *occurrence* of a pain, say of a toothache, and the immediate and last conditions of the occurrence of an event in the way of knowing a given event *as* a toothache, are *centered* in particular organic bodies. But I do deny that causal conditions of the *occurrence* of an event are *ipso facto* qualities or traits of the event. I hold that they are extrinsic to the event itself although strictly relevant to its occurrence. And I also hold that while the temporally and spatially terminal conditions of an observation

3. This matter is somewhat complicated in Mr. Rice's last paper by the fact that he freely refers to "subjective" and "objective" as *aspects;* aspects it would seem of "experience," which is taken to have two sides or faces, *x*, one private and one public. I should still regard this view as "metaphysical" in the sense of involving generalizations of the highest degree of generality about the nature of what exists. In any case, since I can not suppose that Mr. Rice is hedging in using the word "aspects," the word seems to need explanation. Mr. Rice's discussion of "muscular sensations, secret thoughts, feelings of affective tone," seems to treat them as events on their own account.

are *centered* in a particular organism, they are not *located* under the skin of the organism. For events outside the skin as well as under it are directly involved in the production of either a pain or an observation of it *as* pain.

I begin with the last point. In making a distinction between what I have called the *centering* of an event and its *location,* I have nothing recondite in mind. Every event that takes place has a certain extensive durational and spatial spread, as long and as wide as all the interacting conditions involved. Environmental conditions are surely as much a part of the occurrence of a toothache as are organic conditions; to *know* the event *as* the toothache it actually is depends on knowledge of the former. The sole difference that exists between environmental conditions and organic conditions is that the former occupy a relatively initial place and the latter a relatively terminal position in the series of occurrences forming a single total event. The operative presence of both environing and organic conditions, on equal terms, is found in events Mr. Rice terms "private" as it is in those he calls "public." The notion that language in the cases when it is not heard by others (is not "uttered or enacted") is on that account private in origin, occurrence, and quality is so extreme that it is hard for me to believe that it is held by any except extreme solipsists. Moreover, if the fact that certain occurrences centre in a particular organism justifies the conclusion that the event thus conditioned is private and "subjective," the doctrine that colors and overt movements *as perceived* are also private seems logically to follow. Mr. Rice has corrected my impression that he holds qualities *as such* to be "subjective." But I think the logic of the matter as far as concerns the grounds for holding that *all* qualities are subjective is with those who make no difference between perceived colors and perceived pains.

As far as the logic of the matter is concerned, why not hold that *all events* have an exclusive, sequestered, private, self-centered aspect? A fire, for example, does not occur at large. It takes place in a particular house and may be confined to a single house: that is, according to the logic employed in behalf of the subjectivistic doctrine, it is "individual." All, except confirmed pan-psychists, who hold that this fact does not render the fire subjective while a similar fact causes the perception of a toothache to be private, seem to have a responsibility for indicating the difference in the two cases—pan-psychists not having that responsibility because they use the same logic all the way through.

Finally and most conclusively, the qualified and restricted relative sense in which a pain-event, say, may properly be said to be *centered*, with respect to its occurrence, in a particular organism has nothing to do with *observational knowledge* of it *as* pain and *as* the pain of a toothache. The fact that under ordinary conditions some one else can see "my own" teeth much more readily than I can, will not, I suppose, be taken to prove that after all what is seen by him belongs to him in a "private" way. Nor will the fact that I can not, under ordinary conditions, see the back of my own head be taken to militate against the fact that, after all, it is the back of "my own" head that is involved. Nor will the fact that from where I now sit I can observe certain things not observable by others from the positions they now occupy be taken as evidence that the things in question are private and subjective.

The examples I have chosen will, presumably, call out the retort that the conditions of perception and non-perception in the cases cited are wholly extrinsic, not affecting the nature or quality of the things perceived. Exactly so. My position is that the causes why a toothache is "felt" directly by one and not by another human being are of a similar extrinsic kind, not at all affecting the observed nature of the event as pain and as pain of a toothache. We are brought back to the matter of the distinction between conditions for the occurrence of a given event and the observed qualities of that event.

We have to *learn* to see, hear, and to feel when "feeling" is taken to mean an identification and demarcation of an event as having the qualities that define it as a kind of event—as happens in the case of identifying and distinguishing an event as pain and as toothache. It is to be hoped, though not too confidently asserted, that, in another generation or so, facts ascertained in biology, anthropology, and other sciences will displace the influence now exerted upon theories of observation and knowledge by doctrines that were framed before the sciences attained anything approaching their present estate. As things now stand, much that still passes as sound psychological knowledge is the result of the seeping in of doctrines it was "natural" enough to hold in earlier conditions, but which are now scientifically nullified.

In recurring to the confusion of events which, in a relative and restricted sense, are conditions of the occurrence of an event with the properties of that event as observed, I mentioned that under ordinary circumstances we do not perceive our own teeth or the backs of our own heads. Nevertheless it is easily "done with mirrors." In principle, though not in practical ease, the same thing holds in the case of a toothache. In case a certain grafting of the proprioceptor nerve-tissues of two organisms could be successfully effected (and events as strange as this have actually taken place) there would exist the conditions for observation on equal terms by different observers—the criterion for that which is said to be "public."

And in connection with the other point, that perception and observation are affairs of identifying and distinguishing an event as *such-and-such,* Mr. Rice evinces a sound sense of fact in his admission that a perception based upon knowledge of the public kind—as in the case of observation by a dentist—is more likely to be valid than the observation of one with less technical knowledge, even though the conditions of occurrence of what is observed happen to centre in the organism of the latter. In fact this admission on the part of Mr. Rice comes so close to taking the view I have been presenting that the matter might be left there.

I add, however, that I believe detailed examination of the case represented by "muscular sensations" would prove especially instructive. At what time and under what circumstances was it that the existence of qualities, which, on the physiological side, are mediated by changes of the nervous tissues in muscular structures, was first detected? I believe that the facts of the case would show that instead of their presence being an affair of direct and easy observation on the part of the one in whose organism the immediately conditioning events take place, it was an affair, at the outset, of a conclusion reached by knowledge of other facts—a hypothetical conclusion which was then tested by setting up special conditions (in principle like the use of a mirror in perceiving the back of one's own head) that enabled direct observation to be made.

I add also that examination of the case of language, whether uttered or "secret," would supply, in my judgment, evidence that is all but crucial. That language is something *learned,* and learned under social or public conditions, hardly needs argument. If we eliminate the influence exerted by traditional doctrines owing their present currency to the force of tradition rather than to scientifically ascertained facts, we shall, I believe, have no difficulty in accepting the view that instead of their first being "thoughts" which are private and which become public by being clothed externally in language, it is by language, by communication, that events otherwise dumb become possessed of "meanings" which, when they are studied in a cut-off way, are called "thoughts." I can imagine that this reference to language deciding the meanings "*pain, toothache*" will seem irrelevant to Mr. Rice. The issue is too large to argue at length here. But the question at issue is accessibility to *observation*. To defend the position of irrelevancy it would be necessary to show that observation of an event as *such-and-such* is possible without use of characteristics determined publicly in language, and/or that conditions without which an event can not occur are not relevant to its characterization.[4]

---

4. Mr. Rice was kind enough to send me a copy of his rejoinder, published in the same issue, to this article. Accordingly I append a few brief comments bearing upon the foregoing section. (1) I began the present article by saying that the first thesis of Mr. Rice which I should criticize is the view of the "*intrinsic*," and "*unique*," inaccessibility of certain events to public (i.e., dual or plural) observation. For I understood Mr. Rice to hold to the *intrinsic* character of the inaccessibility of certain events to dual observation. And I do not find in his rejoinder any disavowal of this position. It is retracted, however, if I understand him, in one case, a case usually cited as typical, that of the pain of a toothache. But, if I understand him, there is still not the retraction of the view of *intrinsic* inaccessibility which seems to follow. (2) My point was that cases like this one proved that the number of observers to whom a given event is observable is an *extrinsic* matter, just as with the fact that *under present conditions* I am the only observer to whom events in the room where I am now writing are "accessible." (3) I was so far from attributing to Mr. Rice the view that *he* bases *his* distinction between public and private events upon the causal conditions of their occurrence, that I pointed out that his failure to do so was a case of his regarding inaccessibility under specifiable conditions of time and place as *intrinsic* and absolute—if I understand the words "intrinsic" and "unique" correctly. (4) Hence, instead of taking the position that "external relations can not be used as the 'defining properties' of events" (and of classes of events), my argument is that spatial-temporal *differences* in such "external relations" make the entire difference between the events and classes of events set *intrinsically* apart by Mr. Rice. So that the distinction is as *extrinsic* as is my inability to see, under *usual* space-time conditions, the back of my own head. (5) I am not sure whether Mr. Rice intended to attribute to me the view that I base the distinction between the classes of events in question "on their centering in the organism." But to avoid the possibility of misunderstanding, I add that I do not. On the contrary, my point is that *all* events in the way of observations are *centered* in an organism, while *all* events, those Mr. Rice calls private as well as those he calls public, extend, spatially and temporally, far beyond the skin of the organism in which they come to a head. This consideration adds to the relevancy of reference to language in the matter of observation in which an event is characterized as *such-and-such*.

II

The previous section concerns a matter of fact. While the conclusion reached affects the theory of valuation, it affects it only in the way in which it bears upon discussion of any philosophic topic. Its discussion takes up as much space as is given it in the present paper because the question raised and the criticisms made in previous articles seem to make it necessary. The conclusion I have reached appears at first sight to have left, as far as I am concerned, the question having to do with evidence for valuation in a total *impasse*. For if there are no "subjective" events of the kind indicated, then of course subjective events are not evidential with respect either to valuation or anything else.

The actual question, with respect to valuations, however, is not disposed of in this rather cavalier manner. I do not deny the existence of the kind of *subject-matter* which is called private and inner by Mr. Rice. On the contrary, we agree that this kind of material (whether subjective or objective) is that which valuations are about or concern. The question as to the evidential status for judgment of this material is accordingly still before us. The logical issue as distinct from that of fact needs discussion. Moreover, in his last article Mr. Rice has given illustrations that help define the issue.

Let me begin, then, by repeating as emphatically as possible that the occurrence of events in the way of prizing, cherishing, admiring, relishing, enjoying, is not in question. Nor is their primary importance for human life in any way depreciated; the events are what make life worth having. Nor is it held that they *must* be taken out of their qualitative immediacy and be subjected to judgment. On the contrary, my thesis, as respects valuation, is that only when conditions arise that cause doubt to arise as to their value (not their occurrence) are they judged. There is no single word that covers the entire range of events of the kind mentioned. It is convenient to use a single word to save constant repetition of things admired, enjoyed, liked, held dear, relished, cherished; this list being far from covering their entire range. I shall use the word "the enjoyeds." I use that term rather than "enjoyments" because it emphasizes the fact that actual events are involved; we do not enjoy enjoyments, but persons, scenes, deeds, works of art, friends, conversations with them, and ball games and concertos, to mention Mr. Rice's illustrations.

In his original article, Mr. Rice criticized my view that valuation-judgments proceed by placing the enjoyeds in the context (provided of course by inquiry) of conditions that produce them and consequences that result from them. Mr. Rice did not deny that this operation furnishes evidence, but charged me with neglecting the evidence which is supplied by the very occurrence of the enjoyeds. In fact he even went so far as to imply that I paid no attention to their occurrence in my preoccupation with conditions and consequences. My reply was that so far from neglecting this fact, my theory holds that such are the events the *subject-matter* of valuations; but that since their unsettled or dubious state *qua* value is precisely that which calls out judgment, it is an equivoke to treat them, *in their bare occurrence,* as capable of providing evidence.

In his present reply, Mr. Rice cites the case of a toothache, saying that its immediately dis-enjoyed qualities may, and often do, furnish part of the evidence for the judgment of value: " 'I ought to visit a dentist,' or—though with less initial probability—'I ought to have a cavity filled.' " He continues "The ache is not, as Mr. Dewey seems to hold, merely a 'dubious' element in the situation, but, together with my previous knowledge of similar situations, it constitutes *prima facie* evidence for these value judgments." I do not know just what Mr. Rice has in mind by saying that I seem to hold that the ache is "merely a dubious element in the situation." I do not, however, suppose that he means to impute to me the view that its existence is in doubt. So I repeat that *if* there is a pause for valuation-judgment, it is because there is some doubt, in the total situation, of just what it indicates as to what it is better to do; what *should* or ought to be done. And I insert the *if* because it is by no means necessary that judgment intervene. One having the ache may make it a rule to visit a dentist; the event in question then operates as a direct stimulus—and unfortunately many persons react just by standing an ache until it ceases.

The nub of Mr. Rice's position, however, is found in the sentence containing the phrase "together with," in saying that the qualities of the ache provide, *along with previous knowledge,* evidence. Now there is a meaning of the words "together with" in which the statement made seems just as sensible and evident to me as it does to Mr. Rice. But this meaning is just not that which Mr. Rice gives the words. "Together with" is an ambiguous phrase. Mr. Rice gives it the meaning his own theory requires; that it is itself evidence as far as it goes, evidence which is then *added on* to evidence supplied by previous knowledge of a similar situation. My understanding of the words is that which, I believe, would occur to one independent of any theory. When the event of an enjoyed is judged with respect to estimating its value, its occurrence *qua* value is passed upon by means of taking it out of its isolated occurrence and bringing it into connection with the other facts, primarily those supplied by memory-knowledge of what has happened in the past in similar situations. By being viewed "together with" such facts, judgment is formed as to what the event indicates to be better or as to what should be. From my point of view, then, the meaning Mr. Rice gives the phrase repeats the equivoke with which he was charged in my previous article.

Mr. Rice's sense for facts leads him, even so, to qualify the evidential status of the event; he calls it "*prima facie* evidence," and goes on to speak of the need of "further evidence" being sought for to confirm (or, I suppose, perhaps to refute) evidence that is only *prima facie.* My point is that this further evidence is "together with" the enjoyed in question in precisely the same sense in which the knowledge of previous situations is together with it: the means of determining a valuation of it.

Mr. Rice gives some further examples of the same general type, referring to valuations regarding events to happen in the future. He says in the case of a judgment that it will be enjoyable to go to a Beethoven concerto or a ball game between the Dodgers and the Reds, "it is in part because I remember that similar occasions in the past have been accompanied by enjoyment, and because I discover introspectively that my imaginative rehearsal of the probable experience ahead of me is now accompanied by relish." No one can doubt that evidence supplied by the fact that similar events in the past have proved enjoyable is good evidence of the fact that, under like conditions, the same sort of event will be enjoyed in the future. Instead of proving Mr. Rice's contention that the present relish of the prospect is *added* evidence it goes to show that evidence provided by *other* events is summoned to pass upon the quality *qua* value, of the relish in question. I repeat that I don't hold that valuation-judgment *must* intervene. One may react directly by going to the ball-park or the concert-hall.

Unless perchance Mr. Rice holds that every case of an enjoyed is, *ipso facto*, also a case of occurrence of a valuation-judgment, what are the conditions which according to him, evoke judgment of an enjoyed event in case there is no doubt as to its status *qua* value?

But the reader can analyze for himself the examples cited by Mr. Rice, and decide whether they are in fact instances that what is directly enjoyed are cases of providing additional, even *prima facie*, evidence in *judgments* regarding value, or whether the evidence to which it is said to be *added* is in fact that which decides the *value* of an enjoyed event. And if we were engaged merely in controversy and not in discussion of an issue, I would add that introduction of the phrase *prima facie* is itself a sufficient indication that the latter of the two alternatives describes the facts of the case.

By Nature and by Art

I

Current philosophical theories of knowledge are strangely neglectful of the implications and consequences of the revolution that has taken place in the actual subject-matter and methods of scientific knowledge. In substance, this revolution may be said to be one from knowledge that is such "by nature" to scientific subject-matter which is what it is because it is "by art." The classic scheme, following Aristotle, held that the subject-matter of science, as the highest grade of knowledge, is what it is because of certain inherent forms, essences, or natures. These indwelling and constitutive natures are eternal, immutable, and necessary. It followed that in the Greek-medieval system all *sciences*, from astronomy to biology, were concerned with species or kinds, which are immutably the same and eternally separated from one another by the fixed natures forming their inherent essences or Being.

Other forms of knowledge, such as were called sense-perception and opinion, were also what they were by the nature of their inherent Beings; or, more strictly, by the unchangeable and incorrigible partiality or defect of Being which marked them. For over against fixed and eternal species constituted by inherent essential forms were the things that change; things that are generated and perish. Alteration, modifiability, mutability, are *ipso facto* proof of instability and inconstancy. These in turn are proof of lack of Being in its full sense. It is because of lack, or privation, of self-contained and self-sufficient Being that some things are variable and transient, now one thing and now another. The lack of inherent natures or essences is equivalent to dependence upon circumstances that are external, this dependence upon what is

[First published in *Journal of Philosophy* 41 (25 May 1944): 281–92.]

outside being manifested in their variability. In classic terminology, science is concerned with "formal causes," that is, with inherent natures which "cause" things to be *what* they are. Sense-knowledge and opinion are inferior forms of knowledge concerned with things which by their natures are so mutable that knowledge of them is itself unstable and shifting—as in the case of things touched, heard, seen.

It should not be necessary to dwell upon the fact that according to what is now science what the ancient scheme relegated to an inferior position, namely, efficient and material "causes," constitutes the only legitimate subject-matter of natural science, acceptance of the view that essential forms or natures are its subject-matter accounting for the sterility of science during the period before the scientific revolution occurred. According to the ancient doctrine, the subject-matter of sense-knowledge and opinion on one side, and of science on the other, are forever separated by a gulf that is impassable for the reason that it is cosmological and ontological—that is, due to the very "being" of the subjects involved. In what now constitutes science, the difference is methodological. For it is due to *methods of inquiry*, not to inherent natures. Potentially the subject-matters of sense and opinion are science in the making; they are its raw material. Increased maturity of the procedures and techniques of inquiry will transform their material into scientific knowledge. On the other side, there is no subject-matter of the scientific kind which is eternally the same and not subject to improvement with further development of efficacy in inquiry-procedures.

The scientific revolution, which put science upon the road of steady advance and ever increasing fertility, is connected with substitution of knowledge "by art" for that said to be "by nature." The connection is not remote nor recondite. The arts are concerned with production, with generation, with doing and making. They fall, therefore, within the domain of things which in the classic scheme are mutable, and of which, according to that scheme, scientific knowledge is impossible. According to the present conduct of science and according to its conclusions, science consists of knowledge of *orders of change*. While this fact marks a complete departure from the classic view, it does not suffice of itself to justify calling scientific knowledge an art, though it provides a condition without which that designation is not warranted; for it completely breaks down the grounds upon which a fixed and impassable line was originally drawn between the subject-matters of science and of art. For it connects science with change. The consideration that completes the ground for assimilating science to art is the fact that assignment of scientific status in any given case rests upon facts which are experimentally produced. Science is now the product of operations deliberately undertaken in conformity with a plan or project that has the properties of a working hypothesis. The value or validity of the latter is tested, as in the case of any art, by what happens in consequence of the operations it instigates and directs. Moreover, science is assimilated to the conditions defining an art by the fact that, as in the case of any industrial art, production of relevant and effective consequences depends upon use of artificially designed appliances and apparatus as means of execution of the plan that directs the operations which are undertaken.

II

It is an old and familiar story that "nature" is a word of many senses. One of its senses has been mentioned. According to it, the nature of that which is undergoing investigation, say combustion, electricity, or whatever, is the subject-matter of scientific generalizations. We still use the expression "the nature" of something or other in this sense, though, I imagine, with decreasing frequency. But when we do use it in this sense, its meaning is radically different from that possessed by the same expression in the classic scheme. For it no longer designates a fixed and inherent essence, or Being, that makes facts to *be* what they are. Instead, it signifies an order of connected changes, an order which is found to be fruitfully effective in understanding and dealing with particular changes. The difference is radical.[1]

Another meaning of "nature" is *cosmological*. The word is used to stand for the world, for the universe, for the sum total of facts which actually and potentially are the subject of inquiry and knowledge. With respect to this sense of "nature," ancient

1. It may be remarked in passing that the *old* sense of the "nature" of a thing still prevails in discussion of moral and social subjects; and this fact may explain the continued stagnation and infertility of inquiry in these fields.

philosophy has an important advantage over the general tenor of
modern philosophy. For while modern philosophy is conform-
able to actual scientific practice in eliminating an ontological difference, or a difference in kinds of Being, between the eternal and
the changing, it has, unfortunately, tended to substitute for this
difference one equally fixed between supposed subjective and objective orders of Being.[2] "Unfortunately" is in fact too mild and
neutral a word. For the net effect has been to set up a seat and
agency of knowing over against Nature as that known. Hence
the "knower" becomes in effect extra-natural. Historically, the
facts of the case are easily explainable. For while in the Greek
version mind in both its sensible and its rational operations was a
culminating manifestation or terminal "end," of natural facts, in
the medieval version (out of which modern theory grew without
outgrowing some of its major tenets) soul and mind took on definitely supernatural traits. These traits, in a more or less attenu-
ated form, reappear in the extra-natural knowing "subject" of
modern philosophy as that is set over against the natural world
as "object."

To complete the statement of the terms of the question under
discussion, it is necessary to note explicitly the sense of "nature"
and "natural" in which they contrast with "art" and "artificial."
For in the cosmological sense of nature, the saying of Shakespeare
holds to the effect that nature is made better by no mean but nature makes that mean; in the third sense of natural (that just
mentioned), science is definitely and conclusively a matter of art,
not of nature.

We most readily lay hold of the meaning of this statement by
presenting to ourselves a picture of an astronomical observatory
or a physical laboratory. And we have to include as part of the
picture the role of collections of books and periodicals, which
operate in the most intimate and vital working connection with
the other means by which science is carried on. For the body of
printed matter is what enables the otherwise highly restricted
material of immediate perception to be linked with subject-
matters having an indefinitely wide spatial and temporal range.
For only in fusion with book-material does what is immediately

2. Virtual synonyms are "mental" and "physical" orders, and "personal" and
   "impersonal," taken as separate and opposed with reference to their inherent
   stuffs or subject-matters.

present take on scientific status, and only in fusion with the latter does the former cease to be "theoretical" in the hypothetical sense of that word. For only as culturally transmitted material with its deep and wide scope is anchored, refreshed, and tested continually through *here-and-now* materials provided by direct experimental observations does it become a warranted part of authentic science.

A further qualification has to be added to complete the statement that science with respect to both method and conclusions is an art. For there is a sense in which every form of knowledge is an affair of art. For all knowledge, even the most rudimentary such as is attributable to low-grade organisms, is an expression of skill in selection and arrangement of materials so as to contribute to maintenance of the processes and operations constituting life. It is not a metaphorical expression to say that at the very least all animals know *how,* in virtue of organic structure and physiological processes in connection with trans-cuticular conditions, to do things of this sort. When, then, it is said that science, as distinct from other modes of knowledge, is an art, the word "art" is used with a differential property. The operations of *search* that constitute the art or skill marking other modes of knowledge develop into re-search.

A more concrete qualification of the art which constitutes scientific knowledge is its dependence upon *extra-organic* appliances and instrumentalities, themselves artificially devised. The scientific revolution may be said to have been initiated when investigators borrowed apparatus and processes from the industrial arts and used them as means of obtaining dependable scientific data. The use of the lens was of itself almost enough to revolutionize the science of astronomy. As we look back, we note that the bulk of early knowledge was in fact built up through the pursuit of industrial and mechanical arts. The low social status of artisans (in which class were included sculptors, architects, painters of pictures, musicians, in fact all producers save those working with words) was "rationalized" in the doctrine of the inherently inferior state of all knowledge of this kind. At best, it was "empirical" in the disparaging sense of that word. Fundamentally, the scientific revolution consisted of transformation of "empirical" into *experimental*. The transformation was effected, historically, by adoption, as means of obtaining scientific knowledge, of devices and processes previously employed in industry to obtain "material" ends—in that sense of "material" which identifies "matter" with the menial and servile. After a period in which natural knowledge progressed by *borrowing* from the industrial crafts, science entered upon a period of steady and ever-accelerated growth by means of deliberate invention of such appliances on its own account. In order to mark this differential feature of the art which is science, I shall now use the word "technology." [3]

Because of technologies, a circular relationship between the arts of production and science has been established. I have already spoken of the dependence of science as now conducted upon the use of appliances and processes such as were once confined to the "utilitarian" and "practical" ends to which a subordinate and "base" status was attributed socially and morally. On the other hand, before the application in a return movement of science in the industrial arts, production was a routine affair. It was marked by imitation and by following established models and precedents. Innovation and invention were accidental rather than systematic. Application of scientific conclusions and methods liberated production from this state—a state justifying use of the adjective "empirical" in its disparaging sense. Through incorporation into the arts of production of the methods and conclusions of science, they are capable of becoming "rational" in the honorific sense of that word. The phrase "rationalization of production" states a fact. Indeed, it may be said that the distinction between science and other technologies is not intrinsic. It is dependent upon cultural conditions that are extrinsic to both science and industry. Were it not for the influence exerted by these conditions, the difference between them would be conventional to the point of being verbal. But as long as some technologies are carried on for personal profit at the expense of promotion of the common welfare, the stigma of "materialism" will continue to be attached to industrial technologies, and the honorific adjective

3. While a number of writers have brought forward the facts which are involved in this view, Dr. Clarence Ayres, as far as I am aware, was the first one explicitly to call science a mode of technology. It is probable that I might have avoided a considerable amount of misunderstanding if I had systematically used "technology" instead of "instrumentalism" in connection with the view I put forth regarding the distinctive quality of science as knowledge.

"idealistic" will be monopolized by the technology which yields knowledge—especially if that knowledge is "pure"—that is, in the classic view, uncontaminated by being put to "practical" use.

III

Valuable instruction concerning a number of mooted problems in the theory of knowledge may be derived from the underlying principles of the prior discussion. One of them, perhaps the most obvious on the surface, is the fact that many classifications and distinctions which have been supposed to be inherent or intrinsic to knowing and knowledge are in fact due to socio-cultural conditions of a historical, and therefore temporal and local, sort. There is the fact (upon which I have dwelt at length in previous writings) of the arbitrary and irrelevant nature of the sharp line drawn in the classic philosophical tradition between "theoretical" and "practical" knowledge. The gulf that was supposed to separate them is in fact merely a logical corollary of the view that the proper subject of scientific knowledge is eternal and immutable. The connection of science with change and the connection of the methods of science with experimental production of change have completely vitiated this doctrine. The infertility of natural knowledge before adoption of the experimental method is attributable, in large measure, to the fact that ancient and medieval science took the material of ordinary observation "as is"; that is, in lumps and chunks as given "naturally" in a ready-made state. In consequence, the only treatment to which it could be subjected was dialectical.

What is not so obvious upon the surface is that a theory of knowledge based upon the conduct and conclusions of science does away, once and for all, with the fixed difference supposed to exist between sense-knowledge and rational-knowledge. The sensory aspect of knowledge is strictly an *aspect*. It is distinguishable in intellectual analyses that are undertaken for special purposes. But it is not, as it was long taken to be, a special kind of knowledge nor yet a separate component in knowledge. It is that aspect of the system of knowledge in and by which knowledge extending across an indefinitely extensive spatial and temporal range of facts is anchored and focalized in that which is *here-and-now.* Without demonstrated anchorage of this sort, any system, no matter how well organized with respect to internal consistency, is "theoretical" in the sense of being hypothetical. On the other hand, the "rational" aspect of knowledge is constituted by the corpus of extant knowledge which has been constituted by prior inquiries and which is so organized as to be communicable—and hence applicable to results of further inquiry by which the old system is corrected and extended.

The principle underlying these special matters is that the legitimate subject-matter of a *theory* of knowledge consists of *facts* that are known at a given time, with, of course, the proviso that the procedures by which this body of knowledge has been built up are an integral part of it. This view of the grounds of a competent theory of knowledge stands in open opposition to that which underlies the *epistemological* theory: the postulate, namely, that no subject-matter is entitled to be called knowledge until it has been shown to satisfy conditions that are laid down prior to any case of actual knowledge and independently of any conclusion reached in the course of the inquiries by which knowledge in the concrete is arrived at. The completeness of the opposition between the two postulates may be judged from the following consideration. Upon the ground of the first postulate subject-matter is entitled to the name of knowledge when it is determined by the methods of inquiry, test, verification, and systematic arrangement, or organization, which are factually employed in the sciences. Upon the other basis, the antecedent conditions apply to any and every case, good, bad, and indifferent. Hence they are of an entirely different order from the facts of actual investigation, test, and verification, which warrant use of the name "knowledge" in its honorific sense in actual instances.

It was then inevitable, from the standpoint of logic, that the epistemological approach culminated in the Kantian question: How is knowledge possible anyway (*ueberhaupt*)? If the question were put with reference to the "possibility" of any other subject under investigation, the *existence* of the subject-matter under inquiry would be the starting point. It suffices, for example, to show that cancer exists for the question as to its possibility to be simply the question of the specific conditions of an *actuality.* Only in the case of knowledge is it supposed that the question of its "possibility" is one which puts actuality into total doubt until certain universal antecedent conditions have been laid down and shown to be satisfied.

In the case of cancer, for example, the question of possibility means that our knowledge is still in a doubtful and indeterminate state, so that research is going on to discover the characteristic properties, conditions, and consequences of facts whose actual existence sets the problem. Yet strangely enough (strangely, provided, that is, historical-cultural facts are left out of account) the dogmatic and contradictory assumption that there exists knowledge of the conditions of knowledge prior to and conditioning every specific instance of knowledge arrogated to itself the name of a *critical* theory of knowledge!

IV

I do not propose to discuss further this contradiction, beyond saying that the contradiction will be obvious to anyone who views the matter in terms of the facts of knowledge, instead of in terms supplied by the history of philosophical systems viewed in isolation from other cultural events. I propose rather to set forth some of the historical-cultural conditions which generated in general the epistemological assumption of prior conditions to be satisfied; and which, in particular, led to the "subject-object" formula about these conditions. One of the influential factors consists of the conditions existing when the scientific revolution took place. It is hardly possible to over-emphasize the fact that these conditions were those of revolt not merely against long accepted intellectual doctrines but also against customs and institutions which were the carriers of these doctrines, and which gave them a support extraneous to their own constituents. Because of causes which are psychologically adequate, if not factually so, the word "social" has come to be regarded as applicable to that which is institutionally established and which exerts authority because of this fact. The adjective "individual" is identified on this basis with that which marks a departure from the traditionally and institutionally established, especially if the departure is of a quality involving revolt and a challenge to the rightful authority of tradition and custom.

These conditions were fully and strikingly present at the time of the rise of modern science. Every book on the history of philosophy mentions the fact that the philosophical literature of the fifteenth and subsequent centuries is marked by treatises, essays, tractates, that deal with the methods to be adopted and pursued if scientific knowledge is to be actually obtained. The negative aspect of these new ventures is assault, overt or implicit, upon all that had long been accepted as science. There was in effect, if not openly, an assertion that currently accepted subject-matter was hardly more than a systematized collection of errors and falsities. The necessity of radically new procedures of assault upon existing "science" was uniformly treated as an affair of *method*. It was because of the *methods* habitually used and sanctioned that existing "science" was stagnant, and so far removed from its proper mark—understanding of nature. Other documents upon right methods may not have used the words of Francis Bacon's *Novum Organum*, much less endorsed its precepts. But they were at one with him in proclaiming the necessity of a complete break with traditional methods and in stark opposition to the tenets of the *Organon* of Aristotle.

If the movement of protest, revolt, and innovation that was expressed in these documents and put in practice in the new astronomy and "natural philosophy" had been confined to "science" in its technical and isolated aspect, there would not have been the crisis that actually occurred. The facts constituting what is called "the conflict of science with religion"—or theology—clearly and convincingly prove that the movement of innovation, protest, and revolt was not so confined. The new science was treated as morally heretical and as a dangerous menace to the very foundations of a stable and just social order. Upon the Continent, especially, it was treated as rebellion against divinely established authority. In a more fundamental way than in the ecclesiastic movement named Protestantism, it was a protest against established foundations in morals and religion. Its opponents made this point clear when its proponents failed to do so.

Stated in slightly different terms, the subject-object formulation of the conditions to be satisfied before any subject-matter has a right to the honorable title of "knowledge" has to be viewed in vitally intimate connection with those movements in political and economic institutions which popularly bear the name "individualism." For, as has been already remarked, any departure from traditions and customs that are incorporated in and backed by institutions having firmly established authority is regarded as "individual" in a non-social and *anti*-social sense by the guardians of old forms in church and state. Only at a later time, when it is possible to place events in a long historic perspective instead of in the short-time crowded and broken perspective of what is immediately contemporary, can so-called "individualism" be seen to be as "social" in origin, content, and consequences as are the customs and institutions which are in process of modification.

In this cultural situation, the fact that philosophers as unlike as Descartes and Berkeley both refer to the seat and agent of knowledge as "I" or an "ego," a personal self, has more than casual significance. This reference is especially significant as evidence of the new climate of opinion just because no attempt at justification accompanied it. It was taken to be such an evident matter that no argument in its behalf was called for. References and allusions of this kind are the forerunners of the allegedly "critical" attempt of Kant to frame an account of the conditions of knowledge in terms of a "transcendental ego," after Hume had demonstrated the shaky character of the "empirical" self as the source and agent of authentic knowledge.

If we adopt the customary course of isolating philosophies in their historical appearance which is their actuality from other socio-cultural facts, if we treat the history of philosophy as something capable of being understood in the exclusive terms of documents labeled philosophical, we shall look at the outstanding feature of modern philosophy as one of a conflict between doctrines appealing to "sense-experience" as ultimate authority and theories appealing to intuition and reason, a conflict reaching a supposed solution in the Kantian reconciliation of the *a priori* and the *a posteriori*. When these philosophies are placed in their cultural context, they are seen to be partners in a common movement, both schools being in revolt against traditional science in its methods, premises, and conclusions, while both schools are engaged in search for a new and different seat of intellectual and moral authority. There are indeed significant differences between the two schools. But when these are historically viewed, they appear as differences of emphasis, one school inclining to the "conservative" phase of cultural institutions, and the other school to the "progressive" or radical phase.

While those aspects of the new science which express initiative, invention, enterprise, and independence of custom (on the ground that customs are more likely to be distorting and misleading than helpful in attaining scientific knowledge) are necessary conditions for generation of the subject-object formulation, they are far from being its sufficient condition. Unquestioned persistence of fundamental tradition controlled protest against other customs. Medieval institutions centered in belief in an immaterial soul or spirit. This belief was no separate item. It permeated every aspect of life. The drama of the fall, the redemption, and the eternal destiny for weal or woe, of the soul was all-controlling in the accepted view of the creation and history of the universe and of man. Belief in the soul was so far from being just an intellectual tenet that poignant emotion and the deepest and most vivid images of which man is capable centered about it. The church that administered the concerns of the soul was in effect the dominant educational and political institution of the period.

Secularizing movements gradually undermined the monopoly of authority possessed by the church. Although interests of a natural type did not supersede supernatural interests, they tended to push them out of a central into a peripheral position. But supernatural concerns retained such force in moral and religious matters that the theory of knowledge was routed through the channels they had worn after the *facts* of science were wearing a natural channel. This roundabout channel seemed, because of the force of habit, more "natural" than any indicated by the facts of science. The enormous gap between knowledge-facts and epistemological theory which marks modern philosophy was instituted.

In spite of revolt and innovation, the hold of the belief in the soul as knowing subject upon the attitudes which controlled the formation of the theory of knowledge was so firm that it could not be broken until the institutions, upon which the belief in its concrete validity depended had undergone definite degeneration.

Revolt and innovation were sufficient, however, to bring to explicit and emphatic statement one aspect of the Christian doctrine of the soul, an aspect which was kept covert and hidden in the dominant institutionalism of the Middle Ages. This aspect was the *individual* or singular nature of the subject of sin, redemption, punishment, and reward. Protestantism insisted upon making this aspect of the Christian position overt and central in religious matters. The writers who were concerned with the new science performed a similar task in the theories of knowledge they promulgated. The hold of the old doctrine, even upon those most indifferent to its theological phases, is shown in the persistence of belief in an immaterial mind, consciousness, or whatever, as being the seat and agent of knowledge. The influence of the belief upon the new science, even with its fundamental revolt and innovation, is exhibited in identification of the subject and agent of sound knowledge with "individuals" who had freed themselves from the perverting and deadening effect of custom and tradition. Even today those who deny in words that mind and consciousness are organs of knowledge, replacing them with an organic body or with the nervous system of the organism, attribute to the latter an isolation from the rest of nature (including transmitted and communicated culture) which is much more than reminiscent of the lonely isolation of the medieval soul.

It took more than the undeniable but negative fact of the gradual attenuation and decay of the importance once attached to the soul as seat of knowledge to effect an adequate elimination. The new movement of science had to achieve, on the ground of its own methods and conclusions, a positive conquest of those aspects of natural fact that deal with life and human history before complete elimination could occur. Only during the last hundred years (less than that in fact) have the sciences of biology, cultural anthropology, and history, especially of "origins," reached a stage of development which places man and his works squarely within nature. In so doing they have supplied the concrete and verified positive facts that make possible and imperatively demand formation of a systematic theory of knowledge in which the facts of knowledge are specified or described and organized exactly as are the facts of the sciences which are the relevant subject-matter of a theory of knowledge. Only in this way will the facts of our knowledge-systems and those of the theory of knowledge be brought into harmony with one another, and the present glaring discrepancy between them be done away with.

A Comment on the Foregoing Criticisms

I fully appreciate the attention given *Art as Experience* by the distinguished Italian philosopher Benedetto Croce—as I appreciate his heroic resistance to the wave of Fascism which swept so many Italian thinkers and educators off their feet. That he should have read my book and then have taken the trouble to write about it for publication in another country, commands and receives my hearty thanks. I wish also to express my gratitude to Professor Katharine Gilbert for interesting Croce in writing the article, and for sending me a translated copy of it together with the suggestion that I write a reply.

I regret that what I have to say is largely of the nature of a comment rather than being a reply in any distinctive sense of that word. For a reply, as I understand the word, requires a common ground on which both parties stand and from which deviations and departures can be measured. I do not find such a common ground in this present case. And I can perhaps best introduce my comment by telling why I cannot find it. In substance, it is because Croce assumes that I have written about art with the intention of bringing it within the scope of pragmatic philosophy—although I have not, as he sees the matter, carried out successfully the claim involved in this purpose. The actual fact is that I have consistently treated the pragmatic theory as a theory of *knowing*, and as confined within the limits of the field of specifically cognitive subjectmatter. And in addition I have specifically rejected the idea that esthetic subjectmatter is a form of knowledge, and have held that a prime defect of philosophies of art has been treating subjectmatter as if it were (whether the creators and enjoyers of it were aware of it or not) a kind of knowl-

[First published in *Journal of Aesthetics and Art Criticism* 6 (March 1948): 207–9. For Benedetto Croce's article to which this is a reply, see Appendix 6.]

edge of Reality, presumably of a higher and truer order than anything of which "science" is capable. The consequence of this
approach, I concluded early in my studies, was that the subjectmatter is not looked at nor reported in its own behalf and in
its own terms, but by making it over until it seemed to fit into the
categories of some preferred philosophy. As a result, I did *not*
write *Art as Experience* as an appendix to or application of my
pragmatism (which was forbidden in any case for the reason just
stated), or in subjection to *any* system of philosophy. The net
outcome was bad in the eyes of critics who wish to subordinate
creation of art and esthetic enjoyment to a preconceived system
of philosophy; but, I am happy to add, was reasonably satisfactory to some critics who engage in the practice of a fine art.

Lest the foregoing be understood to be an admission on my
part that my approach to different subjects is too disjointed to
possess even the temper of philosophy, I add that my pragmatic
theory of knowledge is based upon the postulate that knowing is
an activity of human beings as *living* beings; that knowing represents a highly important concern of human life; while *that* postulate is also the one from which *Art as Experience* is treated. And
if it be a legitimate question to ask which one of the two, science
or art, owes the most to the other, I should be inclined to award
the palm to art. For not only is scientific inquiry as it is conducted
a highly skilled technology, but the consummatory fulfillments
that are characteristic of the esthetic phase of life-experience play
a highly important part in attaining the conclusions reached
in science.

I had supposed that the presence of the word "experience" in
my title, especially in its close connection with The Live Animal
of the first chapter would indicate the point of view and method
of approach adopted in discussion of the creation and enjoyment of works of art. But it seems that that supposition was over-
optimistic. The meanings belonging to historic empiricist philosophies have been read into the word in spite of the fact that the
pragmatic theory of knowing has systematically criticized these
empiricisms because of their systematic failure to connect experiences with the processes and operation of human life AS life.

The foregoing remarks indicate the absence of common ground
on which to stand in making a reply. But they should also indicate the point of view from which I may reply to certain remarks

of my critic in pleading Not Guilty to suggestions of slighting ac-
knowledgments to writers to whom I am presumably indebted,
and to a kind of Xenophobia with respect to Italian writers in
particular. For good or for evil, as I have already said, I have
learned little from what has been written in the name of the Philosophy of Art and Esthetics, since it has seemed to me to subordinate art to philosophy, instead of using philosophy as an incidental aid in appreciation of art in its own language. I have
learned much however from the writings of essayists and literary
critics, especially from English writers whose works are themselves a part of the great tradition of English literature, and from
what poets, painters, etc., have said about the arts they have
practiced—a source, in my judgment, that is unduly overlooked
by those who philosophize on art. I do not think that I exaggerate in saying that I owe more to the books on the plastic arts
written by the man to whom my book is dedicated, Albert C.
Barnes, than to all the *official* treatises on art composed by
philosophers.

I fear I shall have to be explicit with reference to the bearing of
these statements upon the eighteen points specifically listed by
Croce, along with a suggestion that they are samples of other
cases which might be mentioned. I would not say that those
which are mentioned are of the order of commonplaces; that
would be going too far. But they are reasonably familiar to con-
noisseurs and to cultivated essayists and critics. I shall be surprised if it can be shown that there are any of these points which
have especial dependence upon any philosophical system. In the
case of many of them, I could, by going back over my readings
of general literature over many years, tell the non-philosophic
source from which, in all probability, I derived them. I content
myself with two cases. My treatment of "expression" is derived
from a combination of criticisms I wrote many years ago about
the idea of "Self-expression" as put forward by some educational
theorists and by an English essayist; and also, I hope, from a
kind of condensed precipitation of reflections evoked by a great
number of conversations and readings that I could not begin to
place in memory, either now or when I wrote them down in a
book. There is one other case on which to be specific—the last
one noted by my critic—"that historical knowledge is indispensable for judgment on art." If the works of Dr. Barnes are acces-

sible in Italy and if Croce cares to consult them, he will find there an insistence on the importance of continuity of tradition in *production* of works of art, as well as of critical appreciation of them. Indeed, the whole theory of judgment expressed in my book is hardly more than an echo of what is to be found in what Dr. Barnes has said about the plastic arts, and which I have found a source of instruction with respect to all the arts. If I felt in need of self-defense I should add, in conclusion, that I had no intention of writing the kind of scholarly treatise in which footnotes breed and multiply on every page as authorities for what is said in the text. My aim was much humbler.

Some Questions about Value

When I analyze the discouragement I have experienced lately in connection with discussion of value, I find that it proceeds from the feeling that little headway is being made in determining the questions or issues fundamentally involved rather than from the fact that the views I personally hold have not received general approval. The clear-cut quality of the recent paper by Dr. Geiger [1] moves me to try to do something by way of clarifying underlying issues, with only that degree of attention to answers and solutions as may serve to make the nature of the questions stand out. I do not suppose that any formulation of questions which I can make will be uninfluenced by the answers I would give them. But if others will state the issues that seem to *them* to be basic, perhaps discussion of solutions will be more fruitful in the way of approach to agreement than has been the case. [2]

I begin with a preliminary rough listing.

I. What connection is there, if any, between an attitude that will be called prizing or holding dear and desiring, liking, interest, enjoying, etc.?

II. Irrespective of which of the above-named attitudes is taken to be primary, is it by itself a *sufficient* condition for the existence of values? Or, while it is a necessary condition, is a further condition, of the nature of *valuation* or *appraisal*, required?

1. "Can We Choose between Values?" the *Journal of Philosophy,* Vol. XLI, pp. 292–298 [this volume, Appendix 7].
2. I should add that no attempt is made to list all the questions upon which division in conclusions rests. The view that gives value a *transcendent* character has been omitted, so what is said will not appeal to those who hold that view.

[First published in *Journal of Philosophy* 41 (17 August 1944): 449–55. For George Raymond Geiger's paper to which this is a reply, see Appendix 7.]

III. Whatever the answer to the second question, is there anything in the nature of appraisal, evaluation, as judgment or/and proposition, that marks them off, with respect to their logical or their scientific status, from other propositions or judgments? Or are such distinctive properties as they possess wholly an affair of their subject-matter—as we might speak of astronomical and geological propositions without implying that there is any difference between them *qua* propositions?

IV. Is the scientific method of inquiry, in its broad sense,[3] applicable in determination of judgments and/or propositions in the way of valuations or appraisals? Or is there something inherent in the nature of values as subject-matter that precludes the application of such method?

I

It can not be assumed that the meaning of the words "prizing" and "desiring" (or of any of the words of the first question) is evident on their face. To attempt to define them all is impossible and unnecessary. The word "prizing" is here used to stand for a *behavioral* transaction. If its force is reduced from overt action to an *attitude,* then the attitude or disposition in question must be understood to be taken toward things or persons, and as having no shadow of meaning if it be isolated from that which it is *towards.* Equivalent names would be nourishing, caring for, looking out after, fostering, making much of, being loyal or faithful to, clinging to, provided these words are taken in an active behavioral sense. If this meaning belongs to "prizing," then the first question concerns the connection (or lack of connection) which holds between the way of behaving that is specified and such states, acts, or processes, as "desiring," "liking," "interest," "enjoying," *no matter how the latter are defined.*

That is to say, *if* the latter words are given a behavioral description, the problem is that of the connections sustained to one

3. The phrase "in its broad sense" is inserted to make it clear that "scientific" is not assumed in advance to signify reduction to physical or biological terms, but, as is the case with scientific investigations of concrete matters generally, leaves the scope of the subject-matter to be determined in the course of inquiry.

another by various attitudes or dispositions which are homogeneous in dimension, since all are behavioral. It might, for example, be held that, since what is called *prizing, holding dear,* is a way of behaving tending to maintain something in factual (space-time) existence, *interest* stands for an enduring, or long-time-span, disposition of this nature, one which holds together in system a variety of acts otherwise having diverse directions. *Desire* might then be the behavioral attitude that arises when prizings are temporarily blocked or frustrated, while *enjoying* would be the name for the consummatory phase of prizing.[4] If, however, *desire, interest,* etc., are given a non-behavioral meaning, then it seems that they must stand for something "internal," "mentalistic," etc. In this case, the issue at stake would be a choice between a view which holds that *valuing* is basically a mode of behavior that serves to keep in being a thing that exists independently of being valued, and the view that some kind of a mental state or process suffices to generate value as an uniquely complete product.

Upon the first-mentioned view, "prizing" (as here understood) has definite biological roots, such as, for example, are manifest in the behavior of a mother-bird in nourishing its young or of a mother-bear in attacking animals that threaten her young. The intensity of the "prizing" involved is then measured by the amount of energy that goes into the nourishing or the protecting behavior. Upon this view there is always an event or thing having existence independently of being prized (or valued) to which the quality or property of "value" is added under specified conditions of space-time. From the view that the desire, liking, interest, or whatever, that generates value is solely "internal" or "mental," it seems to follow that if the value in question is then attached to an event or object (something in space-time), it is because of an external more or less accidental association. For if desire or liking is an "internal" state complete in itself, then the fact that it hits upon or bears upon, say, a diamond, or a young woman, or holding an official position, is assuredly so external as to be relatively a matter of accident.

4. The word "might" is used in the text to indicate that the particular descriptions given are intended to serve as sample illustrations of homogeneous behavioral interpretation, not as finalities.

II

Another issue that seems to be basic in current literature concerns the question of the connection or lack of connection between *valuing* and *valuation* in the sense of *evaluating*. Do values come into existence (no matter how they are understood and accounted for) apart from and prior to anything whatever in the way of an evaluating condition? In case they do so arise, what is the relation of subsequent evaluations to a value having prior existence? *How* does a valuation supervene? And *why* does it supervene—that is to say, what is its function, if any?

The statements in the foregoing paragraph are based upon belief that examination of current discussions will show that some hold that nothing having the properties of value can arise save as some factor of appraisal, of measuring and comparing, enters in, while others hold that values may and do exist apart from any operation of this latter sort so that valuation is always wholly *ex post facto* as far as existence of values is concerned.

It is true, I think, that holding dear and valuing are used interchangeably. As far as usage goes, this fact might seem on its face to point to valuing being complete apart from evaluating. But the fact that valuation and valuing are also often used as synonyms is enough to give pause to such a conclusion. Appraisers in the field of taxation, for example, are said to value real estate, and there are expert appraisers in almost every field having to do with buying and selling property. And it is just as true that they *fix* value as it is that they pass upon it. The underlying issue here is whether "value" is a noun standing for something that is an entity in its own right or whether the word is adjectival, standing for a property or quality that belongs, under specifiable conditions, to a thing or person having existence independently of being valued. If the first view is adopted, then to say that a diamond, or a beloved person, or holding an official position, has or is a value, is to affirm that a connection somehow has been set up between two separate and unlike entities. If the second view is held, then it is held that a thing, in virtue of identifiable and describable events, has acquired a quality or property not previously belonging to it. As a thing previously hard becomes soft when affected by heat, so, on this view, something previously indifferent takes on the quality of value when it is actively cared for in a way that protects or contributes to its continued existence. Upon this view, a value-quality loses the quasi-mystical character often ascribed to it, and is capable of identification and description in terms of conditions of origin and consequence, as are other natural events.[5]

When it was suggested above that *appraising* (*evaluating*) is often used interchangeably with *valuing,* there was no intention of intimating that there is no difference between the direct behavioral operation of holding dear and such operations as valuations of real estate and other commodities. There is a decided difference. The point in calling attention to the fact of common usage is two-fold. It definitely raises the question of the relation of *valuation* and *value* to one another. Does *valuation* affect or modify things previously valued in the sense of being held dear (desired, liked, enjoyed), or does a valuation-proposition merely communicate the fact that a thing or person has in fact been held dear (liked, enjoyed, esteemed)? If the latter, what is the function of deliberation? Is it or is it not true that at times questions arise as to whether things previously highly esteemed (desired, liked, etc.) *should* be so viewed and treated? In the latter case, it would seem that reflective inquiry (deliberation) is engaged in for the sake of determining the value-status of the thing or person in question.

The other point in calling attention to occasional interchangeable use of *valuing* and *valuation* is to raise the question whether the undeniable difference between direct valuing and the indirectness of evaluation is a matter of *separation* or of *emphasis.* If there is in direct valuing an element of recognition of the properties of the thing or person valued as *ground* for prizing, esteeming, desiring, liking, etc., then the difference between it and explicit evaluation is one of emphasis and degree, not of fixed kinds. *Ap-praising* then represents a more or less systematized development of what is already present in *prizing.* If the valuing is *wholly* a-rational, if there is nothing whatever "objective" as its ground, then there is complete separation. In this case the

5. If this line of interpretation were carried out, it would indicate that the appearance of value-quality is genetically and functionally continuous, not only with physiological operations that protect and continue living processes, but with physical-chemical interactions that maintain stability amid change on the part of some compounds.

problem is to determine whether valuation (i) is simply a "realistic" apprehension of something already completely there, or (ii) is simply a verbal communication of an established fact but not in any sense a proposition, or (iii) if it does enter at all into formation of subsequent valuings, how does it manage to do so.

III

The third problem grows quite directly out of the one just considered. It may be stated as follows: Is there anything unique or distinctive about valuation-propositions *as propositions?* (If they merely enunciate to others facts already in existence, this question does not arise, since such communications are, *ipso facto,* not *propositions.*) Outright statements that valuation-propositions *qua* propositions and not just because of their subject-matter are of a distinctive kind are not usual in the literature that discusses the subject of value. But positions are frequently taken and topics introduced that do not seem to have any meaning unless that position has been assumed without explicit statement. I give one typical example.

Articles frequently appear that discuss the relation of *fact* and *value.* If the subject discussed under this caption were the relation of value-facts to *other* facts, there would not be the assumption of uniqueness just mentioned. But anyone reading articles devoted to discussion of this issue will note that it is an issue or problem just because it is held that propositions about values are somehow of a unique sort, being *inherently* marked off from propositions about facts. I can think of nothing more likely to be clarifying in the present confused state of the subject than an explicit statement of the *grounds* upon which it is assumed that propositions about values are *not* propositions about space-time facts, together with explicit discussion of the *consequences* of that position. If a question were raised about the relation of geological propositions to astronomical propositions, or of meteor-propositions to comet-propositions, it would not occur to anyone that the "problem" was other than that of the connection between two sets of facts. It is my conviction that nothing would better clarify the present unsatisfactory state of discussion of value than definite and explicit statement of the reasons why the case is supposed to be otherwise in respect to value.

IV

Of late, there has appeared a school of theorists insisting with vigor that genuine propositions (and/or judgments) about values are impossible, because the latter have properties that render them wholly recalcitrant to cognitive treatment. In brief, this school holds that verbal expressions about values are of the nature of exclamations, expressing only the dominant emotional state of the one from whom the ejaculation issues. The ejaculation may be verbally extended into a sentence expressing a desire or liking or an interest. But, so it is said, the only question of a cognitive or intellectual nature that can be raised is whether the verbal expression in question (whether it be a shorter ejaculation or an expanded sentence) actually expresses the emotional state of the speaker or is meant to mislead others by concealing or distorting his actual state.

The practical import of this position may be inferred from the fact that according to it differences as to value can not be adjudicated or negotiated. They are just ultimate facts. In the frank words of one who has taken this position, serious cases of ultimate difference can be settled, if at all, only by "bashing in of heads." I shall not ask here how far this view carries to its logical conclusion the view that some "internal" or mentalistic state or process suffices to bring value-events into existence. I limit myself to pointing out that at the present time serious differences in valuing are in fact treated as capable of settlement only by recourse to force and in so far the view in question has empirical support. This is the case in recourse to war between nations, and in less obvious and complete ways, in domestic disputes between groups and in conflict of classes. In international relations short of war, the view is practically taken in acceptance of an ultimate difference between "justiciable" and "non-justiciable" disputes.

It can not be denied that this particular question is of immense practical import. Using the word "bias" without prejudice, I think it may be stated as follows: Are value-facts bias-facts of such intensity and exclusiveness as to be unmodifiable by any possible consideration of grounds and consequences? The question at issue is not whether some values are now actually treated as if they were of this kind. It is whether the cause of their being so treated inheres in them as value-facts or is a cultural-social phenomenon. If the latter is the case they are capable of modification by socio-cultural changes. If the former is the case, then differences in valuing which are of serious social importance can not be brought within the scope of investigation so as to be settled in a reasonable way. They may not always lead to open conflict. But if not it will be because it is believed that the latter will not be successful, or will be too costly, or that the time is not ripe, or that some more devious method will accomplish a wished-for triumph more effectively.

This fourth question is evidently connected with those previously discussed. If valuing consists *wholly* and exclusively of something inherently recalcitrant to inquiry and adjudication, then it must be admitted that it can not rise above the brute-animal level—save with respect to the *means* most likely to secure its victory over conflicting valuations and values. But if, in answer to the third question, it is decided that there is some element or aspect of valuation on "objective" grounds in every case of prizing, desiring, etc., etc., then it is possible that this element or aspect may itself become so prized, desired, and enjoyed that it will gain in force at the expense of the brute and non-rational factor.

In this connection it seems worthy of note that those writers who hold to the completely a-rational character of valuing begin by accepting the "internal" mentalistic theory of value, and then proceed to endow this quasi-gaseous stuff with powers of resistance greater than are possessed by triple-plate steel. While the four questions that have been formulated are those which seem to me to be more or less openly expressed in current discussion, the fact I have just stated leads me to raise, on my own account, another question which does not often appear in the literature on value, and which, nevertheless, may be more fundamental than those which do appear. Are values and valuations such that they can be treated on a psychological basis of an allegedly "individual" kind? Or are they so definitely and completely socio-cultural that they can be effectively dealt with only in that context? [6]

6. Since the above text was written, I find this question explicitly raised as basic to economic theory, in the book of Ayres, *The Theory of Economic Progress*, especially pp. 73–85, 90, 97.

Are Naturalists Materialists?

Professor Sheldon's critique[1] of contemporary naturalism as professed in the volume *Naturalism and the Human Spirit* consists of one central "accusation": naturalism is materialism pure and simple. This charge is supported by his further claim that since the scientific method naturalists espouse for acquiring reliable knowledge of nature is incapable of yielding knowledge of the mental or spiritual, "nature" for the naturalists is definitionally limited to "physical nature." He therefore concludes that instead of being a philosophy which can settle age-old conflicts between materialism and idealism, naturalism is no more than a partisan standpoint, and contributes no new philosophical synthesis. Whether or not contemporary naturalists have broken new ground in philosophy is too large a theme for a brief discussion, and is in any case a historical question. But the other issues raised by Mr. Sheldon serve as a challenge to naturalists to make their views clearer on a number of points and to remove some obvious misunderstandings concerning the positions they hold. It is to these tasks that the present discussion is devoted.

I

According to Mr. Sheldon, the "real issue" between materialism and other philosophies is the following: "Can the states

1. W. H. Sheldon, "Critique of Naturalism," *Journal of Philosophy,* Vol. XLII (1945), pp. 253–270 [this volume, Appendix 8]. All page references will be to this article. [Page numbers in brackets refer to this volume.]

[First published in *Journal of Philosophy* 42 (13 September 1945): 515–30, and signed by Dewey, Sidney Hook, and Ernest Nagel. For Wilmon Henry Sheldon's article to which this is a reply, see Appendix 8.]

or processes we call mental or spiritual exercise a control over those we call physical, to some degree independent of any spatio-temporal redistributions; or, if we really understood what is going on when minds seem to control bodies, should we see that the spatio-temporal redistributions are the sole factors?" (pp. 255–256 [456]). The issue so conceived is held to be an intensely practical one. For if one answers the second question in the affirmative "you are going to order your life in a very different way from the way you would order it if they are not. . . . When I accuse the naturalists of materialism, I mean a working materialism, a philosophy that goes beyond pure theory to set up a way of life." As Mr. Sheldon sees the issue, the program and method of the naturalists

> leads to or implies that in the last analysis all processes in the known universe, mental, spiritual, vital, or what not, are wholly at the beck and call of the processes we have agreed to call physical, and therefore the only reliable way of control over nature—and over other men—is secured by knowledge of spatio-temporal distributions. That is the only materialism that counts, that has bearing on human life and the prospects of man's future.
> You may, as a materialist, believe in graded levels—inorganic, animal, man, none of which can be wholly described in terms of the levels below it. . . . On the other hand, you may believe each level can be fully defined in terms of a lower level. In either case you may remain a materialist. The crucial point is whether the *behavior* of the higher (mental) level can be *predicted* and therefore *controlled* surely and accurately from a knowledge of the lower. It is power that counts, it is power that the naturalist hopes by his scientific method to gain: power to ensure the arrival of things on the higher level by proper "redistribution" of things on the lower. The question of logical reducibility is beside the point. . . . (P. 256 [456–57].)

It appears at first blush that the issue thus raised is a genuinely factual one which can be settled by appeal to empirical evidence. For the issue seems to be concerned simply with the most effective way in which things and their qualities can be brought into, maintained in, and ushered out of existence. One is a materialist, on Mr. Sheldon's showing, if one believes that power is acquired by learning how to manipulate embodied things, if one attempts to guide the destinies of men and their affairs by redistributing spatio-temporal objects. Everyone who pursues a vocation in this world whether as engineer or physician, sociologist or educator, statesman or farmer, is perforce a materialist. One is a materialist even when one tries to influence one's fellows by communicating ideas to them, for, as Mr. Sheldon notes, such a method of influencing them employs physical means: verbal and written speech, the arts, and other symbolic structures. Apparently, therefore, only those can call themselves non-materialists who maintain that causal efficacy resides in some disembodied consciousness, unexpressed wishes, silent prayers, angelic or magical powers, and the like. A non-materialist, on this conception, is one who regards minds as substances, capable of existing independently of spatio-temporal things, but logically incapable of being adjectival or adverbial of such things. A materialist, on the other hand, is one who believes there is no evidence for the existence of minds so described, and who in addition finds insuperable difficulties in supposing that a mind so conceived can enter into causal relations with anything else. If this is indeed the difference between a materialist and one who is not, then the naturalists whom Mr. Sheldon accuses of materialism are glad to find themselves in his company—for in his *practical* commitments (the only ones that really count, according to himself) if not his theoretical ones, he is certainly a materialist. In any event, the evidence for materialism so construed is overwhelming; and naturalists will cheerfully admit his accusation of themselves as materialists not as a criticism but as an acknowledgment of their sanity.

Nevertheless, it is unlikely that so innocuous an interpretation of Mr. Sheldon's critique can be faithful to his intent. For though he insists that the issue he is raising is a highly practical one, and though he dismisses as so much irrelevant subtlety various types of materialism which naturalists and others have carefully distinguished, his intent is presumably to tax naturalists with a view in which they themselves "sense bad odor" (p. 257 [458]).

What is this view? Unfortunately, Mr. Sheldon nowhere makes it explicit. He accuses naturalists of excluding from nature everything but the physical, and of adopting a method of inquiry which deprives them of any knowledge of the mental. Indeed, he formulates the issue between materialism and idealism in terms of a sharp contrast between the physical and the mental. But he is not very helpful in making clear what are the marks which set off one of these kinds from the other. He does, to be sure, suggest that the physical is simply that which is capable of spatio-temporal distribution and redistribution; and since the mental is for him an exclusive disjunct to the physical, he also suggests by implication that the mental is that which is not capable of such distribution. However, these suggestions are hardly sufficient for the purpose at hand. Are such properties and processes as temperature, potential energy, solubility, electrical resistance, viscosity, osmosis, digestion, reproduction, physical in Mr. Sheldon's system of categories? Since they are all properties or powers or activities of things having spatio-temporal dimensions, the answer is presumably in the affirmative. Nevertheless, though they characterize things having spatial dimensions, none of the items mentioned has itself a spatial dimension; thus, temperature has no volume, solubility no shape, digestion no area, and so on. And if a property is to be regarded as physical provided that it qualifies something having a spatio-temporal dimension, why are not pains, emotions, feelings, apprehensions of meanings, all subsumable under the physical? For to the best of our knowledge such "mental" states and events occur only as characteristics of spatio-temporal bodies—even though, like potential energy or viscosity, they do not themselves possess a spatial dimension. Accordingly, Mr. Sheldon formulates no clear criterion in terms of which the physical can be sharply demarcated from the mental; and he has therefore not provided sufficient hints as to what the doctrine is which he finds naturalists holding. A distinction between two types of materialist doctrine therefore appears to be in order.

According to one type of materialism, the mental is simply identical with, or is "nothing but," the physical. It is of this type that Mr. Sheldon is thinking when he declares that a genuine materialist "will insist that an idea is but a potential or tentative muscular response" (p. 256 [456]). This view can be stated with some precision in approximately the following manner. Let us call those terms "physical terms" which are commonly employed in the various physical sciences of nature; this class of expressions will then include such words and phrases as "weight," "length," "molecule," "electric charge," "osmotic pressure," and so on. And let us call those terms "psychological terms" of which no use is made in the physical sciences, but which are customarily employed in describing "mental" states; this class of expressions will contain such phrases as "pain," "fear," "feeling of beauty," "sense of guilt," and the like. Materialism of the type now under consideration may then be taken to maintain that every psychological term is *synonymous with*, or has *the same meaning* as, some expression or combination of expressions belonging to the class of physical terms. Proponents of this view, if any, can be imagined to argue somewhat as follows: Modern science has shown that the color *red* appears only when a complicated electro-magnetic process also occurs; accordingly, the word "red" has the same *meaning* as the phrase "electro-magnetic vibration having a wave-length of approximately 7100 Angstroms." (This latter phrase is unduly simple. It requires to be complicated by including into it other terms denoting physical, chemical, and physiological states of organic bodies. But the point of the illustration is not affected by the oversimplification.) And those professing this view must be taken to claim that analogous synonyms can be specified for the distinctive psychological terms such as "pain" and "feeling of beauty."

When the consequences of this view (frequently given the label "reductive materialism") are strictly drawn, statements such as "I am in pain" must be regarded as *logically entailing* statements of the form "My body is in such and such a physico-chemico-physiological state." Whether any competent thinker has ever held such a view in the specific form here outlined is doubtful, though Democritus, Hobbes, and some contemporary behaviorists are often interpreted to assert something not very dissimilar to it. Those who do hold it maintain often that the obvious differences between a color and an electro-magnetic vibration, or between a felt pain and a physiological condition of an organism, are "illusory" and not "real," since only physical processes and events (i.e., those describable exclusively with the help of physical terms) have the dignity of reality. But whatever may be said for reductive materialism—and very little can be said in its favor—it can be categorically asserted that it is *not* a view which is professed, either tacitly or explicitly, by the naturalists whom

Mr. Sheldon is criticizing. If "materialism" means reductive materialism, then those naturalists are not materialists.

But there is a second and different type of materialism, though it is sometimes confused with the preceding one. It maintains that the occurrence of a mental event is contingent upon the occurrence of certain complex physico-chemico-physiological events and structures—so that no pains, no emotions, no experiences of beauty or holiness would exist unless bodies appropriately organized were also present. On the other hand, it does not maintain that the specific quality called "pain," for example, is "nothing but" a concourse of physical particles ordered in specified ways. It does not assert that "an idea is but a potential or tentative muscular response." It does not declare that the word "pain," to use the technique of exposition of the preceding paragraphs, is synonymous with some such phrase as "passage of an electric current in a nerve fiber." It does assert that the relation between the occurrence of pains and the occurrence of physiological processes is a contingent or "causal" one, not an analytical or logical one. Many proponents of this view entertain the hope that it will be possible some day to specify the necessary and sufficient *conditions* for the occurrence of mental states and events in terms of the distributions, behaviors, and relations of a special class of factors currently regarded as fundamental in physical science—for example, in terms of the subatomic particles and structures of contemporary physics. Sharing such a hope is not a *sine qua non* for this type of materialism, and in any case whether the hope is realizable can not be settled dialectically but only by the future development of the sciences. However, whether a materialist of this type entertains such a hope or not, he does not claim but denies that propositions dealing with mental events (i.e., those employing psychological terms) are *logically deducible* from propositions dealing exclusively with physical ones (i.e., those containing only physical terms).

The question of the truth of materialism of this type can be decided only on the basis of empirical evidence alone. Many of the details of the dependence of mental upon physical processes are far from being known. Nevertheless, that there is such a dependence can not reasonably be doubted in the light of the evidence already accumulated. A system of philosophy built on a conception of mind incompatible with this evidence is therefore nothing if not wilful and undisciplined speculation. Accordingly, if "materialism" signifies a view something like the one just outlined, Mr. Sheldon is not mistaken in his accusation of naturalists as materialists. And if the issue between materialists and idealists can be settled only by adopting a notion of mind which denies that minds are adjectival and adverbial of bodies, then he is also right in declaring that naturalists have done nothing to settle it. Nor would they wish to resolve an age-old conflict on those terms.

It is relevant to ask now whether naturalists believe the mental to be "wholly at the beck and call" of the physical, and how they would reply to Mr. Sheldon's query whether "the states or processes we call mental or spiritual exercise a control over those we call physical, to some degree independent of any spatio-temporal redistributions." Two things should be noted. First, there is a certain sting in Mr. Sheldon's metaphors which must be removed in order not to prejudice discussion. To speak of the mental as being "wholly at the beck and call" of the physical suggests a degrading status for the mental, a slavish helplessness, which outrages our sense of fact. Physical processes, on any but a magical view of things, do not beckon or call—only human beings do. If there is a suggestion here that the properties of organized matter on any level *must* be read back into matter organized on any other level, then as already indicated naturalists do not subscribe to such notions of the *physical*. Second, if the point of these questions rests on a conception of minds as substantial but ethereal entities, capable nevertheless of controlling or being controlled by physical substances, naturalists will dismiss the questions as not addressed to themselves: they simply do not subscribe to such notions of the *mental*. On the other hand, if these views of the physical and mental are not assumed by the questions, there remains very little for the naturalists to say in reply—as will immediately appear.

For suppose a chemist were asked whether he believed that the properties of water are at "the beck and call" of hydrogen and oxygen atoms, or whether he thought that water "controlled" the behaviors and properties of its constituents. Would he not reply that the questions are meaningful only on the assumption that the properties of water are not only *distinguishable* from those of its constituents taken singly or in isolation from each other, but are also *substantially distinct* from the properties of hydrogen and oxygen atoms when these are related in the way in which water molecules are organized? On the other hand, the chemist would certainly maintain that the existence of water and its properties is contingent upon the combined presence of certain elements interrelated in definite ways. But he would call attention to the fact that when these elements are so related, a distinctive mode of behavior is exhibited by the structured unity into which they enter. Nevertheless, this structured object is not an *additional* thing which, in manifesting its properties, controls from some external vantage point the behavior of its organized parts. The structured object in behaving the way it does behave under given circumstances is simply manifesting the behavior of its constituents *as* related in that structure under those circumstances. To be sure, the occurrence of those properties we associate with water may be controlled by "redistributing" spatio-temporal things—provided always that the combination of the atomic constituents of water can be effected practically. But in undergoing such redistributions the constituents themselves come to behave in precisely the manner in which their relations to one another within a structured molecule of water requires them to behave: their behavior is not *imposed* upon them from without.

The naturalist proceeds in an essentially no different manner in giving his account of the status of minds. Like the chemist in reference to the properties of water, he maintains that the states and events called mental exist only when certain organizations of physical things also occur. And also like the chemist, he holds that the qualities and behaviors displayed by physical things when they are properly organized—the qualities and behaviors called mental or spiritual—are not exhibited by those things unless they are so organized. But these qualities and behaviors of organized wholes are not additional things which are *substantially* distinct from the properties and behaviors of spatio-temporal objects in their organized unity. Accordingly, naturalists most emphatically acknowledge that men are capable of thought, feeling, and emotion, and that in consequence of these powers (whose existence is contingent upon the organization of human bodies) men can engage in actions that bodies not so organized are unable to perform. In particular, human beings are capable of rational inquiry, and in the light of their findings they are able to "redistribute" spatio-temporal things so as to ensure the arrival and departure of many events both physical and mental. They achieve these things, however, not as disembodied minds, but as distinctively organized bodies. To the naturalist, at any rate, there is no more mystery in the fact that certain kinds of bodies are able to think and act rationally than in the fact that cogs and springs arranged in definite ways can record the passage of time or that hydrogen and oxygen atoms ordered in other ways display the properties of water. "Things are what they are, and their consequences will be what they will be; why then should we desire to be deceived?"

II

Mr. Sheldon claims that in adopting scientific method as the way for securing reliable knowledge, naturalists seriously restrict the class of things concerning which they can acquire knowledge. As naturalism envisages the nature of this method, according to him, the method is applicable only to things which are physical or "public," and not to states and events which are mental or "private." How valid is this claim? Are naturalists precluded by their choice of method from ever discovering anything about things divine or angelic if the universe contains them? And, in particular, must a naturalist if he is serious in his adoption of scientific method rule out of court the "private" data of introspective observation?

A preliminary distinction between two meanings of "scientific method" will help clear the way for the naturalist's reply. For the name is often used interchangeably both for a set of general canons with the help of which evidence is to be gathered and evaluated, and for a set of specialized techniques associated with various instruments each of which is appropriate only for a limited subject-matter. Mr. Sheldon draws part of his support for his conclusions concerning the scope of scientific method from this double sense of the name. He contends that methods are not produced *in vacuo,* and are not independent of subject-matter. "No mere methodology," he declares; "a method envisages, however tentatively, a metaphysic" (p. 258 [459]). And he cites in illustration the telescope, which is an excellent instrument for studying the stars, but is hardly suited for dissecting the seeds of plants. No one, surely, will think of denying the truth of this last observation. However, it does not therefore follow that the logical canons involved in testing the validity of propositions in astronomy are different from the logical canons employed in biology; for the fact that a telescope is the suitable technical means for exploring stars but not seeds is not incompatible with the claim that a common set of principles are adequate for appraising evidence in all the physical domains which encompass these subject-matters. Nor does it follow that because principles of evidence are competent to guide inquiries into physical subject-matter, they are not so competent for inquiries into psychological subject-matter. In any event, however, it is scientific method as the use of a set of general canons of inquiry, not as a class of special techniques, which is professed by naturalists as the reasonable way for securing reliable knowledge. And although Mr. Sheldon complains that naturalists have supplied no standard analysis of scientific method (p. 258 [459]), it surely can be no secret to him that the writings of many naturalists are in fact preoccupied with just such general principles of evidence.

But Mr. Sheldon's chief complaint is addressed to the naturalists' account of the nature of the verificatory process. The naturalists maintain that "reliable knowledge is publicly verifiable." Do they not therefore exclude the very possibility of knowledge concerning matters that are not "public" but are "private"? "Does the mystic verify the Divine being by direct observation?" asks Mr. Sheldon. "Can the introspective psychologist experiment with private minds?" (p. 258 [459]). If, however, what is thus private is excluded from the domain of application of scientific method, is not the naturalist forever compelled to remain in the domain of the physical?

The following remarks may serve to clarify the naturalist's position on this matter.

(a) In maintaining that scientific method is the most reliable method for achieving knowledge, the naturalist means what he says. He recommends that method for acquiring *knowledge*, for achieving *warranted assertions*, but not for acquiring esthetic or emotional experiences. He does not wish to deny that men have mystic experiences of what they call the Divine, that they enjoy pleasures and suffer pains, or that they have visions of beauty. He *does* deny that *having* such experiences constitutes knowledge, though he also affirms that such "mental states" can become *objects* of knowledge. Accordingly, while he insists that the world may be encountered in other ways than through knowledge and admits that scientific method possesses no valid claim to be the sole avenue for such encounters, he also insists that not every encounter with the world is a case of knowledge. Indeed, for many naturalists, the experience of scientific method is instrumental to the enrichment of other modes of experience. This point is elementary but fundamental. It completely destroys the vicious circle in which Mr. Sheldon has attempted to trap the naturalist—the circle according to which nature for the naturalist is what is open to scientific method, while scientific method is simply the method recommended for approaching nature (p. 263 [464]). What is viciously circular in maintaining that if anything is to be *known* (in whatever other manner it may be *experienced*), reliable knowledge of it is acquired through the use of scientific method? For things can be encountered without first having to be known, and scientific method can be described and employed without everything in nature having first to be experienced. It no more follows from this that everything in nature is known or can be experienced only as a mode of knowledge, than it follows that since every assertion about anything whatsoever is *statable*, every thing has already been stated or exists only as a possible statement.

(*b*) Though Mr. Sheldon sometimes appears to suggest that the observable alone is confirmable or verifiable, the naturalist maintains that the meanings of these terms do not coincide. Mr. Sheldon declares:

> Scientific method demands experiment and observation confirmable by fellow men. Mental states or processes, just in so far as they are not physical, not "behavior," are not open to such observation. He says they are "inaccessible." But of course they are accessible to their owner; it is only to fellow men, to the public, that they are inaccessible. Scientific method thus means, to the naturalist, that observation of the non-public has no sense or meaning. Publicity is the test; the private and hidden is ruled out of court. . . . (P. 262 [463].)

The crux of this argument resides in the transition from the statement that mental states are not open to observation by one's fellow men, to the conclusion that therefore the private and the hidden are ruled out of court by the naturalist. But this is a *non sequitur*. For let us grant, at least for the sake of the argument, that *A*'s mental states can not be observed by his fellow men. Let us even accept the much stronger claim that statements like "*B* can not experience *A*'s feelings" are *analytically* true, so that it is *logically impossible* for *B* to experience *A*'s feelings. Does it follow that *B* can not publicly verify that *A* does experience some feeling, of pain, for example? That it does not follow will be evident from applying Mr. Sheldon's argument to the supposition that a subatomic interchange of energies is taking place in accordance with the specifications of modern physical theory. No one will claim that such subatomic events are literally observable, at least by human investigators. Nevertheless, though those events are not observable, propositions about them are certainly confirmable or verifiable—and in fact publicly verifiable by observations on the behaviors of macroscopic objects. Evidently, therefore, there may be states and events which are not observable, even though propositions about them are publicly verifiable.

(*c*) Nevertheless, so Mr. Sheldon urges, if the naturalist is consistent he can not rely on scientific method to yield reliable knowledge of the mental *qua* mental or "private." He can not use this method to assure himself that he has an abdominal pain, for example, unless a surgeon first exhibits and publicly verifies the existence of an inflamed appendix.

But the imputation of such views to the naturalist is a caricature of the latter's position. The latter does maintain, to be sure, that *A*'s feelings of pain have their physical and physiological causes. Since, however, the naturalist is not a reductive materialist, he does not maintain that the painful quality experienced by *A* is "nothing but" the physical and physiological *conditions* upon which its occurrence depends. He will therefore not assert that the dentist who notes a cavity in *A*'s tooth experiences *A*'s pain; on the contrary, he will insist that *A*'s body is uniquely favored with respect to the pains *A* suffers—a circumstance which he attributes to the distinctive physiological events that are transpiring in *A*. Accordingly, the naturalist will recognize that the proposition that *A* is experiencing a pain is verifiable in two ways: directly by *A*, in virtue of the privileged position in which *A*'s body occurs; and indirectly by everyone (including *A*) who is in a position to observe processes causally connected with the felt pain.

However, and this is the essential point, the fact that A can directly verify the proposition that he is in pain, without having to consult a surgeon or dentist, does not make the proposition any the less *publicly verifiable*. For the surgeon or dentist can also verify it, not, to be sure, by sharing A's qualitative experience, but in other ways: by asking A, for example, or by noting the condition of A's body. In brief, therefore, to maintain that propositions about the occurrence of pains and other mental states are publicly verif*iable*, does not mean that they must always be verif*ied* indirectly; and, conversely, to acknowledge that propositions about mental states have not been indirectly verif*ied* is not incompatible with the thesis that they are publicly verif*iable*.

(d) The point involved is important enough to deserve some amplification. It is well known that the temperature of a body can be determined in several alternative ways: for example, with the aid of an ordinary mercury thermometer or of a thermo-couple. In the one case, changes in temperature are registered by variations in the volume of the mercury, in the other by variations in the electric current flowing through a galvanometer. The instruments thus exhibit two quite disparate qualitative alterations: for the thermometer is not equipped to register the effects of thermoelectric forces, while the thermo-couple lacks the necessary structure to record thermal expansions. It is evident, therefore, that the qualities and behaviors displayed by each instrument are a consequence of its specific mode of construction and of the special position it occupies in a system of physical transactions. Nevertheless, in spite of the qualitative differences between them, each instrument can be satisfactorily employed for ascertaining temperature variations—at any rate within specifiable limits of such variations. It is well to note, incidentally, that in recording the temperature of some other body, an instrument is at the same time indicating its own temperature. Moreover, if the instruments are both in working connection with some other body so that they serve to measure the latter's temperature, it is possible to use the behavior of either instrument in order to predict certain aspects of the behavior of the other, and thus to determine the temperature of the other. Were the instruments blessed with the powers of consciousness (let us permit ourselves this fancy), the thermometer would experience a unique quality when it was recording the temperature of some body—a quality or state which would be "private" to the thermometer and incommunicable to the thermo-couple. Nevertheless, even though the thermo-couple would be unable, because of its own distinctive mode of organization and unique physical position, to experience the qualities exhibited by the thermometer, it would not be precluded from recording (and thus "verifying") the temperature both of the third body and of the thermometer itself.

Consider now the bearing of this physical illustration upon the issue raised by Mr. Sheldon. *A* can not *experience* *B*'s mental states, any more than the thermometer can exhibit (or experience) the distinctive qualitative behaviors of the thermo-couple, and for the same reasons. But *A* can *know* that *B* is undergoing some specified experience, just as the thermometer can be employed to measure the temperature of the thermo-couple. The distinction between the public and the private, upon which Mr. Sheldon builds his case against the naturalist, thus consists—so far as questions of *knowledge* are involved—in the differences between the causal relations of two distinct or differently organized bodies.

(*e*) In thus admitting as publicly verifiable all the facts designated by Mr. Sheldon as "mental," naturalists do not, of course, thereby commit themselves to the various propositions for which such data are often cited as evidence. Thus, naturalists do not as a matter of principle, deny that mystics have had ecstatic visions of what they call the Divine, any more than they deny that men experience pains; for they believe that the occurrence of such visions and experiences has been publicly verified. On the other hand, recognizing as warranted the proposition that such *events* do occur does not, by itself, decide what further propositions are confirmed by those occurrences. Indeed, this question can not be decided in general, and requires detailed investigation for each proposition considered. The point is that there is surely a difference between admitting as true the proposition that someone has undergone the experience he calls "experience of the Divine," and admitting as therefore true the proposition which affirms the existence of a Deity—just as there is a difference between acknowledging a pain and attributing it to a heart lesion. In either case, the proposition mentioned last requires the confirmation of independent evidence if it is to be counted as a validly established one. The testimony of a mystic is *testimony*, but is not necessarily *evidence* for the proposition the mystic asserts—though it may be evidence for some *other* proposition—no more than a patient's report about his pains is necessarily evidence for the truth of his belief that he is suffering from a fatal disease. If naturalists disagree with those who assert the existence of gods and angels, they do not do so because they rule out of court the testimony of all witnesses, but because the testimony does not stand up under critical scrutiny. The *horror supernaturae* with which Mr. Sheldon not unjustly charges the naturalists is therefore not a capricious rejection on their part of well-established beliefs: it is a consequence of their refusal to accept propositions, like the belief in ghosts, for which the available evidence is overwhelmingly negative.

(*f*) One final point requires some attention, for it is briefly hinted at by Mr. Sheldon and is often given central prominence in discussions such as the present one. The point concerns the alleged greater certainty of some propositions than others, and in particular the greater certainty of propositions about introspective observations than of propositions about other matters.

Mr. Sheldon raises the issue in connection with a behaviorist attempt to establish the fact that someone is undergoing an experience of the beautiful. He believes that if a naturalist, faithful to scientific method, wishes to be sure that someone is having such an experience, he must apply physical apparatus to the glandular and muscular responses of the person in question. For the naturalist, according to Mr. Sheldon, can not take the person's word for it: "that is a report about something private, outside the realm of verifiable truth" (p. 267 [468]). But it should be clear at this stage of the present discussion that Mr. Sheldon would have a point only if the naturalist were a reductive materialist: that is, if the naturalist were to maintain that a feeling of beauty is "nothing but" a glandular and muscular response. However, since the imputation of such a view to the naturalist is a mistaken one, why should the latter proceed in the fashion suggested by Mr. Sheldon? For a man's glandular and muscular responses are no more identical with his feelings of beauty than are his oral reports that he is having them. An oral report may be more reliable evidence for the occurrence of such feelings than is the reaction of some brass instrument—especially since, as in the present instance, we possess little accurate knowledge concerning the glandular and muscular conditions for the occurrence of such feelings. To be sure, the naturalist will not deny himself the use of physical apparatus if such instruments do provide decisive evidence on disputed matters and if people are suspected of prevarication concerning their feelings—witness, for example, the occasional reliance on "lie detectors." But such instruments do not supply *inherently* more reliable evidence simply because they are physical; whether they do in fact supply such evidence is something that must be settled by detailed inquiry.

But does a naturalist, it is sometimes asked, believe himself justified in accepting a proposition about his "private" experiences, if that proposition is not confirmable by others? Does not a naturalist have to maintain, if he holds reliable knowledge to be publicly verifiable knowledge, that such a proposition as "I now have a bad headache" which he might utter is not made certain simply by the pain he is feeling, but must be confirmed by others before it can be regarded as well-established? In brief, must not a naturalist declare *all* propositions to be unwarranted, unless they are verifiable by other than introspective evidence? In answering these questions in the affirmative, so one criticism runs, the naturalist is adopting a dogmatic and arbitrary criterion for warranted knowledge, a criterion in conflict with common sense as well as with the practice of many competent psychologists.

However, a distinction previously introduced must be repeated here. The naturalist takes seriously his characterization of reliable knowledge as publicly verifi*able* knowledge. Accordingly, the proposition "I now have a bad headache," if it constitutes a piece of knowledge, must be confirm*able* by others as well as by the person making it. But it by no means follows from this that the proposition must actually be confirm*ed* by others if the person making it is to be justified in accepting it as true. Just how much confirmatory evidence must be available for a given proposition before it can be accepted as warranted can not be specified once for all. But undoubtedly there are cases (as in the instance of the proposition about the headache) in which a minimum of evidence (i.e., the felt pain) suffices to warrant its acceptance by the person asserting the proposition—so that any additional evidence will be, for him, supererogatory. But the possibility here considered is not unique to propositions about matters of introspective observation. A chemist who observes that a piece of blue litmus paper turns red when immersed in a liquid, will assert that the paper is indeed red and conclude that the liquid is acid. He will normally regard it a waste of time to search for further evidence to support either of the propositions he is asserting, even though other evidence could be found for them.

On the other hand, the naturalist—like disciplined common sense and the experienced introspective psychologist—is sensitive to the dangers and limitations of "pure" introspection. He knows, for example, that introspection alone can not discover the causes (nor, for that matter, the precise locations) of the pains he feels; for statements asserting the mere *existence* of qualities do not provide theoretical knowledge of the *relations* in which those qualities stand to other things. Even the fact that the felt quality of a pain is "private" is not established by introspective methods alone; this fact, like the fact that certain pains are associated with contemporaneous physico-chemical changes in teeth and nerve fibres and can therefore be controlled by "redistributing" spatio-temporal things, can be ascertained only by overt experiment involving manipulation of "public" things. Theoretical knowledge of pains thus opens up fresh directions for human activity and new types of experience—possibilities which remain unrealized as long as attention is directed simply to the sheer *occurrence* of painful qualities. Assured knowledge of the nature of pains, however, is not the product of mere introspective study. In any event, the annals of physics as well as of medicine and psychology have made clear to the naturalist the serious errors into which men fall when they accept introspective observations without further experimental controls. It is needless to belabor this point—even the text-books are full of illustrations for it. As eminent psychologists have themselves noted, introspective observation is not radically different from any other kind of observation. Whether one employs one's body or some recording instrument for making qualitative discriminations, one must in either case take great care in interpreting its reports and drawing conclusions from them. Moreover, the psychological and social sciences would be denuded of nearly everything of interest if the propositions they asserted were exclusively confined to matters that are capable of direct observation or acquaintance, and if those sciences did not attempt systematically to *relate* the qualities and events immediately apprehended with things and events not so experienced. The dichotomy so insistently and frequently introduced between the "inner" and "outer," between the "private" and "public," therefore seems to many naturalists as little more than a relic from a conception of the mind as a substantial, autonomous agent, operating mysteriously in a body which is not its natural home. Neither this conception nor the dichotomy serve to further the progress of either philosophy or science.

Indeed, this conception of mind has tragic consequences for the human values which Mr. Sheldon wishes to defend against what he believes is the threat of scientific method. For it flies in the face of mountains of evidence concerning the place of man in nature, and leaves human values unanchored to any solid ground in experience. It is not the philosophy of naturalism which imperils human values but Mr. Sheldon's dualism. By ruling out as irrelevant investigation into the natural causes and consequences of the value commitments men make, it deprives human choice of effective status, opens the door wide to irresponsible intuitions, and dehumanizes the control of nature and society which scientific understanding makes possible. In spite of Mr. Sheldon's deprecating remarks about the uncertain conclusions which anthropology, social psychology, psychiatry, and the other social sciences have been able to reach concerning the "mental aspect" of human activities (pp. 257–258 [458]), no one familiar with the history of these disciplines will question the claim that our assured knowledge and our control of these matters has increased as a consequence of introducing into those domains the method of modern science. Is there any competent evidence for believing that the continued use of this method will retard the advance of such knowledge and control rather than promote it? What viable alternative to this method does Mr. Sheldon propose that has not already been tried and discredited? What good reason can he offer for entrusting the maintenance and the realization of human goods to a historically provincial dualism between the mental and the physical—a dualism which the progress of science has made increasingly dubious? It is this doctrine from which Mr. Sheldon's critique of naturalism derives, and not the philosophy attacked by him, which requires a responsible defense.

Ethical Subject-Matter and Language

I

Discussion of the topic indicated by the caption of this article centres about a particular thesis put forward by Professor Stevenson in his recent book.[1] Since my article is definitely critical as to this particular thesis, I feel the more bound to indicate at the outset certain points in which I think his book as a whole should command not only the attention but the support of students of ethical theory. Among points of agreement are the following: (i) There is great need for more attention to the language that characterizes specifically ethical judgments or sentences. (ii) Ethical inquiries should "draw from the *whole* of a man's knowledge," since the materials of such inquiries lend "themselves very poorly to specialization." (iii) Ethical inquiry has suffered from "quest for ultimate principles, definitively established"—a procedure that "not only hides the full complexity of moral issues, but puts static, other-worldly norms in the place of flexible, realistic ones." (iv) Finally since "ethical *issues* differ from scientific ones," there should be careful attention to the *way* in which they differ.[2]

There is such ambiguity in the word "issues" that grasp upon

1. *Ethics and Language* by Charles L. Stevenson, Yale University Press, 1944. I wish to express my indebtedness to a review of the book by Dr. Henry Aiken published in the *Journal of Philosophy*, Vol. XLII (1945), pp. 455–470. Since his discussion of what Stevenson says about the relation of attitudes and beliefs seems to me conclusive I say nothing on that point, and am enabled to adopt a different line of approach.
2. The quoted passages are all from page 336 of *Ethics and Language; "whole"* is italicized in the original text while *"issues"* and *"way"* are not. The reason why I have italicized these words is central in my discussion, as will appear as it proceeds.

[First published in *Journal of Philosophy* 42 (20 December 1945): 701–12.]

its double reference is indispensable. In one sense of the word, that moral and scientific issues differ is not just to be admitted as a concession, but is to be insisted upon as characteristic of ethical subject-matter and ethical sentences *qua* ethical. The sense in which *issues* differ, if not a commonplace, is commonly acknowledged in calling ethics a practical or "normative" subject. But in this sense "issue" is equivalent to office, function, use, force; it concerns the contextual "practical" reference, the *objective* of ethical sentences. As far as accomplishment of this function and use is intended on the part of those who engage in forming, accepting, or rejecting ethical sentences, a differential *interest* marks them off from sentences having what is conventionally called a scientific interest. While difference determines the specific facts *selected* as the distinctive content or subject-matter of ethical sentences, it does not constitute a component part of that subject-matter. It is one thing to say that, because of the differential use or function of ethical sentences, certain facts rather than others are selected and that they are arranged or organized in a given way rather than in some other way. A like proposition applies to differences that mark off the sciences from one another—physics, for example, from physiology. It is quite another thing to convert the difference in function and use into a differential component of the structure and contents of ethical sentences. This conversion marks, in effect, Stevenson's treatment.

I may further anticipate the tenor of the discussion which follows by saying that I do not see how it can be denied that the subject-matter which is selected as appropriate and required for sentences which will fulfill the proper office or function of ethical sentences is charged (and properly so) with facts designated by such names as greed-generosity, love-hate, sympathy-antipathy, reverence-indifference. It is usual to give such facts, taken collectively, the name "emotions," or, slightly more technically, the name "affective-motor." It is one thing to acknowledge (and insist) upon this feature of ethical sentences as one demanded by their function or the use they are put to. It is quite another thing to hold that this subject-matter is not capable of and does not need *description*, and description of the kind belonging to sentences having "scientific" standing. I believe that examination of Stevenson's specific treatment of the "emotional" (or the "emotive" in his terminology) will show that he takes the fact

that factually grounded reasons are employed in genuinely ethical sentences in order to modify affective-motor attitudes which
influence and direct conduct, to be equivalent to the presence of
an extra-cognitive constituent in the sentences in question. In
short, the very fact that factual grounds (which are capable of
description) are the means used in genuine ethical sentences to
affect the springs of conduct and thereby to direct and redirect
conduct, is employed as if it introduced into the specific subject-
matter of ethical sentences a factor completely recalcitrant to intellectual or cognitive consideration.[3] One can agree fully that
ethical sentences (as far as their end and use is concerned) "plead
and advise" and speak "to the conative-affective natures of
men."[4] Their use and intent is practical. But the point at issue
concerns the means by which this result is accomplished. It is,
I repeat, a radical fallacy to convert the end-in-view into an inherent constituent of the means by which, in genuinely moral
sentences, the end is accomplished. To take the cases in which
"emotional" factors *accompany* the giving of reasons as if this
accompaniment factor were an inherent part of the judgment is, I
submit, both a theoretical error and is, when widely adopted in
practice, a source of moral weakness.[5]

II

While the previous paragraphs anticipate to some extent
the conclusion to be reached in the following discussion, they are
chiefly designed to indicate the nature of the problem by telling
what it is *not*. Strangely enough (save perhaps on the ground of
the ambiguity which has been mentioned) it is not easy to quote
isolated sentences in which there is explicit statement that ethical

3. The word "genuine" is used in the text because there can be no doubt that
   sentences *claiming* to be ethical often use an extra-cognitive "emotive" factor
   to influence conduct, thereby cooking the factual evidence adduced. Moreover, some theories, like Kant's, have gone so far as to make a directly and
   exclusively "imperative" factor the very core of all ethical judgments.
4. *Op. cit.*, p. 13.
5. I would not overemphasize the matter, but I get the impression that Stevenson
   is influenced at times in connection with the "meaning" of moral judgments,
   by that ambiguity in which "meaning" has the sense of both design or purpose and that which a sign indicates.

sentences as such contain two independent components, one cognitive, the other non-cognitive. It is easy enough to find sentences like the following: "For the contexts that are most typical of normative ethics, the ethical terms have a function that is *both* emotive and descriptive." [6] But in such passages the word "function" appears. Accordingly, I come directly to discussion of the particular grounds upon which Stevenson bases his conclusion about the non-cognitive constituent of ethical sentences. His statement of this ground or reason appears in connection with a discussion of signs and *meanings*. The evidence brought forward for the existence of signs and meanings which are exclusively "emotive" consists of an account (i) of such non-linguistic events as sighs, groans, smiles, etc., and (ii) of linguistic events such as interjections. Unless the occurrence of emotive meanings in a sense which excludes a descriptive reference (and descriptive meaning) can be independently established, there can, of course, be no question of such an element being found in ethical sentences. Hence further discussion centres on this point.

I quote a key passage *in extenso:*

The emotive meaning of words can best be understood by comparing and contrasting it with the expressiveness of laughs, sighs, groans, and all similar manifestations of the emotions, whether by voice or gesture. It is obvious that these "natural" expressions are direct behavioristic symptoms of the emotions or feelings to which they testify. A laugh gives direct "vent" to the amusement which it accompanies, and does so in such an intimate, inevitable way that if the laugh is checked, some degree of amusement is likely to be checked as well. In much the same way a sigh gives immediate release to sorrow; and a shrug of the shoulders integrally expresses its nonchalant carelessness. One must not, merely on this account, insist that laughs, sighs, and so on, are literally a part of language, or that they have an emotive meaning; but there remains an important point of analogy: Interjections, which *are* a part of language, and which do have an emotive meaning, are *like* sighs, shrieks, groans, and

6. *Op. cit.,* p. 84. We do have, however, such phrases as "the independence of emotive meaning," in the sense of its remaining the same when "descriptive" meaning changes (p. 73).

the rest in that they can be used to "give vent" to the emotions or attitudes in much the same way. . . . Emotive words, then, whatever else must be said of them, are suitable for "venting" the emotions, and to that extent are akin not to words which denote emotions, but rather to the laughs, groans, and sighs that "naturally" manifest them. . . . Why is it that "natural" manifestations of emotions are ascribed meaning only in this broader sense [viz., the sense in which a natural event like "reduced temperature may at times mean convalescence," a sense said to be "wider" than any found in linguistic theory], whereas interjections, so like them in function, may be ascribed meaning in a narrower sense?[7]

Discussion of the answer given by Stevenson to this last question, that as to why the meaning of "natural" signs is different from that of linguistic signs, will be postponed until what is said about interjections, and sighs, groans, and so on, as being alike in that both are merely expressive of emotions and hence have no "referent," has been taken up. On the one hand, the events in question are said to *vent*, to *release*; on the other hand, they are said to be *symptomatic*, and to *manifest*, and to *testify*. In the latter capacity they are assuredly signs in a cognitive sense. When the word "express" is used there seems to be an intermediate and ambiguous term; as far as "express" means *convey* a cognitive sign is undoubtedly involved; as far as to *express* means to "squeeze out" it is akin to *venting*.

Now while I have classified venting and manifestings under two heads, one of which concerns signs while the other one does not, it is characteristic of Stevenson's treatment that he identifies the bald fact of venting or releasing with being a sign. Moreover, he treats a venting as a sign not only of emotion in general but as a sign of specific emotions—a groan of discomfort and a sigh of sorrow, etc. How they can be viewed or treated as such apart from aid and support given by a developed system of known things (which are designated linguistically) I am unable to see. And by this remark I do not mean the trivial or tautological fact that one needs language to give a name to them; I mean that giving them a name as events of a genus, namely, emotion, and as

7. *Op. cit.,* pp. 37–39 *passim.*

events of species of that genus, is not possible without identifications and discriminations which involve connection with events
that are outside the bare occurrence of what is said to be a venting. They are, indeed, so far outside that they can be made and
understood only by adults; that is, by those having a rather wide
acquaintance with things to which "description" is applicable.

The point here made comes out even more forcibly, if possible,
in discussion of interjections as *linguistic* signs. This discussion
occupies a central strategic position. For since they are linguistic
signs, if it can be established that they have meaning and yet a
meaning that is exclusively "emotive," there is in so far a factual
basis for the view that "meanings" of this type are ingredients of
ethical sentences. The evidence offered by Stevenson is indicated
in a passage in which, after saying that there is one sense in
which "the 'meaning' of a sign is that *to which* people refer when
they use the sign," a kind of meaning for which the word "referent" may be substituted and which is *descriptive,* he goes on to
say that there is, however, another sort of meaning possessed by
some linguistic signs. Some words (such as "alas") have no referent, but do have a kind of meaning, namely, "emotive meaning."[8] Here we have at least a negative specification of what it is
to be a linguistic sign that is "emotive." Its distinctive characteristic is lack of a *referent.* It expresses a meaning; like a sigh it
gives vent to a feeling. Thus it shows that there are some signs
which are "akin not to words which denote emotions, but rather
to the laughs, groans, and sighs that 'naturally' manifest them."[9]
And yet this very passage, and the whole discussion of which it is
a part, refers to "something called emotion" in general and to
different emotions in particular (amusement, sorrow, etc.) as that
of which interjections are signs! If this is not to "denote," to designate, or name, I do not know what it is. And the denoting in
question occurs only by virtue of identifications and discriminations without which the sounds called interjections are at best
but events in the way of vocalizations—and, of course, to identify an event even as a "vocalization" is to name it in a way that is
made possible only through a set or system of "referents."

It is convenient to introduce further discussion by reference to

8. *Op. cit.,* p. 42.
9. *Op. cit.,* p. 38.

a cough as a "natural" sign. That "a cough may mean a cold" is an undeniable fact. But when it is said that as a natural sign it lacks "the elaborate conditioning developed for purposes of communication," we are given pause.[10] That, as a *natural* event, a cough may *not* be a sign of a cold is, I should say, an undeniable fact. That a cough can be taken and used as a sign without rather elaborate "conditioning" is, I should say, impossible; at least it seems to be possible only if it is in a class with that cake of Alice in Wonderland which bore on its face the words "Eat me." Consider, for example, the ground upon which a physician breaks up coughs of the common or garden variety into signs of a number of different physiological conditions. It does not follow, of course, that a cough is a linguistic sign in the conventional sense of linguistic. But it does follow that in its capacity or status as *sign*, or with respect to *signness*, it does not differ from a linguistic sign. And that a cough can become a sign of a cold, save in and because of a *context* of linguistic signs which enable it to stand for something beside itself, seems most doubtful. By means of its presence in a total context of which language is another member it acquires an ability to refer beyond its mere occurrence. Without such reference it lacks the properties of a sign. And it is worth noting that a *word* is originally a natural event, a sound or spatial marking before and independently of being a sign.

So far, emphasis has fallen upon the respect in which some natural events, groans, etc., are said to be signs *like* some linguistic signs, namely, interjections. It is worth while to notice the reasons given by Stevenson for holding that they are unlike in one important respect, that which renders an interjection linguistic. In giving answer to the question cited above as to why "natural manifestations" of emotion have meaning in the "broader sense" in which other natural events have meaning we find the following: "The expressiveness of interjections, unlike that of groans or laughs, depends upon conventions that have grown up in the history of their usage. . . . People groan in all languages, so to speak, but say 'ouch' only in English." In the same connection it is said that interjections, being recognized grammatical forms of speech, "are of interest to the etymologist and phoneti-

10. *Op. cit.*, p. 57.

cian, whereas the latter [groans, etc.] are of scientific interest only to the psychologist or physiologist."[11] Yet the words "*only to the physiologist and psychologist*" occur in a passage in which they are discussed as of definite interest to the student of signs, namely, as proof of a certain theory about them! What is to be proved concerns their status as *signs*, with respect to *signness;* what is adduced concerns the particular group that investigates them. The specific kind of "training" or "conditioning" involved in the case of what is meant to the grammarian, etc., and to the physiologist is different. But so is the kind of training that is involved in calling the same thing H_2O and *water*.

Stevenson treats a groan as an inherent manifestation, an expression, and as a sign of something, namely, an emotion. He does so only by assuming that there is given at and from the outset of its occurrence *two* things; one an emotion, the other its venting or release. But there is in the first instance but a single total event of the same order as, say, urination, the turning over of a baby in its crib, its gurgling, its shedding of tears. These are total behavioristic acts, not an emotion and its release. Any one of the events mentioned may come to be taken and used as a sign. But it *becomes* a sign; it is not a sign in its original bare occurrence. The problem of how it becomes a sign, under what conditions it is taken as standing for something beside itself, is not even raised in Mr. Stevenson's treatment. If it were discussed, I think it would be clear that the conditions in question are those of a behavioral transaction in which *other* events (those called "referents" or, more commonly, "objects") are joint partners along with the event which as bare event is *not* a sign.

The conditions under which "alas" and "helas" become, respectively, signs to different social groups are not at all those under which both of them have the character of being signs, and signs of the same event, a sorrowful one. I would not cite a dictionary as final authority. But a dictionary statement has suggestive force. In the *Oxford Dictionary* I find the following: "Alas; an exclamation expressive of unhappiness, grief, pity, or concern." Is it expressive of any of these conditions apart from having a specified position in a complex situation in which occur

11. The passage first quoted is from page 39; the latter passage is found on page 38.

also the things the "emotions" are *at, about,* or *of?* Moreover, the four words are not synonyms. Apart from the co-presence of the "objects" they are of and about, apart from a descriptive context, that is, how can it be told which one of these four "alas" is expressive of? And just as certain intonations, gestures, facial expressions are simulated in order to mislead a spectator or listener, and just as such cases need to be discriminated from genuine cases if the "practical" response is to be appropriate to the facts of the case, so with discriminating actual from a pretended "meaning" of an interjection. The *Oxford Dictionary* follows the passage quoted above with the words: "Occ. with dat. obj., or with for." I submit that the word "occasional" refers only to explicit linguistic usage; that when the dative object is not *linguistically* specified it is because it is such a part of the situation shared by speaker and listener that it is superfluous to speak of it. As to the use of "for," we find among the illustrative quotations the following: "'Las, I could weep for your calamity," and "Alas, both for the deed and its cause." Is there any case in which "alas" has meaning apart from something that is of the nature of a calamity, a loss, a tragic event, or some cause or deed which is mourned? I imagine that when a reader sees the word "emotive," he is likely to think of events like anger, fear, hope, sympathy, and in thinking of them he thinks necessarily of other things— the things with which they are integrally connected. Only in this way can an event, whether a sigh or a word like "alas," have identifiable and recognizable "meaning." And yet this is just what Stevenson's theory excludes!

In connection with his theory that all meaning is a case of a "psychological response," Mr. Stevenson, with his usual care and candor, leaves us no doubt of the kind of psychological response, which is definitely characteristic in his theory of the emotive response. Here are his words: After he has spoken of feeling and emotion as synonyms he says: "The term 'feeling' is to be taken as designating an affective state *that reveals its full nature to immediate introspection,* without use of induction." [12] It certainly must be so taken if there is to be a type of meaning which is exclusively "emotive," because of having no "referent," no *to which.* Only on the ground of the allegation that an emo-

12. *Op. cit.,* p. 60; italics not in original text.

tion self-reveals its full nature in the bare fact of its occurrence, including not only the fact that it *is* an emotion but the fact that it is sorrow, anger, etc., can the fact designated by the words "of, about, to" etc., be ruled out as irrelevant. It is out of the question here to go into the question of "the psychological" in general and of "introspective" self-revelation in particular. I must content myself here with pointing out (i) the central position held by these assumptions in Stevenson's doctrine, and (ii) the fact that they *are* assumptions, made as if they were such a matter of course as to be universally acceptable, and hence not in need of evidence nor argument but only of exposition.[13]

III

Discussion up to this point is preliminary to considera-tion of the main theme of Stevenson's book, ethical language. The latter theory loses its main prop (as far as duality of meaning is ascribed to ethical language) if his account of emotive mani-festations, "natural" and linguistic, is invalid. But it is worth while to discuss the effect of his theory on ethical language. His general point of view is fairly presented in the following passage: "For the contexts that are most typical of normative ethics, the ethical terms have a function that is *both* emotive and descrip-tive."[14] In admitting the "descriptive," Stevenson goes beyond those writers who have denied all descriptive force to moral ex-pressions.[15] In so far, Stevenson's treatment constitutes a decided advance upon them. I begin by stating what the point at issue is not. Stevenson says "Ethical terms cannot be taken as fully com-parable to scientific ones. They have a quasi-imperative *func-tion*."[16] Now (as was said earlier) the point at issue does not con-

13. In the title of Mr. Stevenson's third chapter, the words "psychological" and "pragmatic" are used as synonyms. In treating them as such he relies upon the authority of Morris's extraordinary interpretation of Peirce's theory of signs and meanings. I shall discuss Peirce's theory and Morris's misrepresen-tation in a future article in the *Journal of Philosophy* in which I shall take the opportunity to deal with points here left out of consideration.
14. *Op. cit.*, p. 84. I pass over the use of the word "function" as its ambiguity has already been considered.
15. Footnotes on pp. 256–257 of his work give references to the more important among these writers.
16. *Op. cit.*, p. 36; italics not in original.

cern the last of the two sentences quoted. Nor does it concern the
correctness of the statement that "Both imperative and ethical
sentences are *used* more for encouraging, altering, or redirecting
people's aims and conduct than for simply describing them." [17]
The point at issue is whether the facts of *use* and *function* render
ethical terms and sentences not fully comparable with scientific
ones as respects their subject-matter and content. As far as concerns *use* it would not, I believe, be going too far to say the word
"more" in the above passage is not strong enough. Of ethical
sentences as ordinarily used, it may be said, I believe, that their
entire use and function of ethical sentences is directive or "practical." The point at issue concerns another matter: It concerns
how this end is to be accomplished if sentences are to possess distinctively and genuinely *ethical* properties. The theoretical view
about ethical sentences which is an alternative to that put forward by Stevenson is, that as far as non-cognitive, extra-
cognitive, factors enter into the subject-matter or content of sentences purporting to be legitimately ethical, those sentences are
by just that much deprived of the properties sentences should
have in order to be genuinely *ethical*.

Let us note a somewhat analogous case. The practices, often
resorted to by a skilled lawyer in defending a client charged with
a criminal act, often contain non-cognitive elements and these
may sometimes be more influential, more directive, of what the
jury does than evidence of the matter-of-fact or descriptive sort.
Would one say in this case that these means, such as intonations,
facial expressions, gestures, etc., are a *part* of legal propositions
qua legal? If not in this case, why in the case of ethical propositions? And in this connection it is worth noting that in some
cases at least (possibly in all cases) scientific propositions have a
practical office and function. Such is assuredly the case in which
a scientific theory is in current dispute because opposite views
are entertained. Surely evidence adduced is *used* and is *intended*
to be used so as to confirm, weaken, modify, redirect propositions accepted by others. But I doubt if one would hold that the
heat that sometimes accompanies the putting forth of reasons for
changing old views is a part of the *subject-matter* of the propositions *qua* scientific.

17. *Op. cit.,* p. 21; italics not in original text.

Extra-cognitive devices are without doubt employed to effect a result which in consequence is moral only in the sense in which the word "*im*moral" is included in the scope of "moral." Many propositions which are now taken to be immoral have had positive moral property ascribed to them at former times. There is here a strong indication that extra-rational factors played an undue part in forming the earlier propositions and in getting them accepted. It would be foolish to deny that partisanship, "wishful thinking," etc., plays today a great role in not only getting propositions accepted but in determining the *subject-matter* of *what* is accepted. But I should suppose it to be evident that such facts are "ethical" only in the sense in which that word covers the anti-ethical and the pseudo-ethical. If moral theory has any distinctive province and any important function it is, I would say, to criticize the language of the *mores* prevalent at a given time, or in given groups, so as to eliminate if possible this factor as a component of their subject-matter; to provide in its place sound matter-of-fact or "descriptive" grounds drawn from any relevant part of the *whole* knowledge possessed at the time.

I conclude with a point which, as far as it is personal, is of minor importance, but which may be used to illustrate the position or principle taken in the foregoing discussion. Stevenson takes up my use of "to be" in my discussion of evaluative judgments—of which ethical judgments are one species. He finds in my use of "to be" a definite indication that I am compelled to admit a quasi-imperative "force" in ethical propositions.[18] Since I did not explicitly give them a directive force, it seems to Mr. Stevenson that I must give a predictive force to "to be." So he concludes that what I say about evaluative judgments owes its plausibility in considerable degree to the fact that I permit "hortatory to be's" to be absorbed, as it were, "into an elaborate conjunction of predictive ones."

I begin by saying that whatever I have said about "will be," or of a "predictive sort," is of the same kind as what I have said, in connection with evaluations, about what *has* been and what is *now* going on; that is, it is concerned exclusively with giving reasons or grounds, of the matter-of-fact sort, open to description, for taking a specific ground about some *to-be* in the sense of

18. *Op. cit.,* pp. 255 ff.

what *should* be done. I had supposed that my pretty continued mention of the need of inquiry into "*conditions and consequences,*" drawing upon the whole of *knowledge* of fact that is relevant, made it clear that their office was to determine in a reasonable way cases of *to be's.* Since, apparently, I did not make that point clear, I am glad to state again, in the present context, that *evaluative* statements concern or have reference to what ends are to-be-chosen, what lines of conduct are to-be-followed, what policies are to-be-adopted. But it is morally necessary to state grounds or reasons for the course advised and recommended. These consist of matter-of-fact sentences reporting what has been and now is, as conditions, and of estimates of consequences that will ensue if certain of them are used as means. For in my opinion sentences about what *should* be done, chosen, etc., are sentences, propositions, judgments, *in the logical sense* of those words only as matter-of-fact grounds are presented in *support* of what is advised, urged, recommended to be done— that is, worthy of being done on the basis of the factual evidence available.

It is unfortunately true that many moral *theories,* some of them of considerable prestige in philosophy, have interpreted moral subject-matter in terms of norms, standards, ideals, which, according to the authors of these theories, have no possible factual standing. "Reasons" for adopting and following them then involve a "reason" and "rational" in a sense which is expressly asserted to be transcendent, *a priori,* supernal, "other-worldly." According to theorists of this type, to give reasons of the kind found in inquiries and conclusions in other subjects eliminates what is genuinely moral, reducing it, say, to the "prudential" and the expediently "politic." On this basis, ethics can be "scientific" only in a sense which gives the word "science" a highly esoteric significance—a sense in which some writers hold philosophy to be *the* supreme science, having methods and depending upon faculties that are beyond the possible reach of humbly subordinate "natural" sciences. In view of the vogue of this type of moral theory, it was probably inevitable, historically speaking, that in the course of time writers would arise who would take theorists of this type at their word as far as concerns the negative part of their theories; and hence would announce that *all* moral judgments and theories are wholly extra-scientific. It is the merit of

Stevenson's treatment that he has seen that there is *one* component of ethical sentences that demands and is capable of the same
kind of development and test that are found in inquiry into other
subjects. It is because of this positive contribution that it has
seemed to me desirable to subject to criticism that part of his theory in which he has gone but half-way in this direction.

Peirce's Theory of Linguistic Signs, Thought, and Meaning

In a recent article I pointed out that Stevenson's identification of psychological with pragmatic in his *Language and Ethics* rests upon the interpretation of "pragmatic" which is put forward by C. W. Morris.[1] Morris's point of view regarding the *psychological* differs from that of Stevenson, since the former prefers a behavioristic to an introspective approach (*F.S.*, p. 6). But, however important this difference is from certain points of view, it is irrelevant to the issue here under discussion, namely, the account of meaning as pragmatic advanced by Morris on the alleged authority of Peirce. In the sequel, it will be noted that the theory of Peirce also bears directly on Stevenson's theory of some meanings as "emotive." Consideration of Peirce's actual theory of signs in general and linguistic signs (called *symbols* by him) in particular is pertinent not only because of the present interest in Peirce's writings but because the inverted report of Peirce which is given by Morris has influenced, as consultation of recent literature will show, other writers than Stevenson. Since Morris has professed to be sympathetic with Peirce's theory, it is especially important to rescue Peirce's theory by reference to Peirce's own writings before an *Ersatz* takes the place of what Peirce actually held.

1. My article, "Ethical Subject-Matter and Language," was published in the *Journal of Philosophy*, Vol. XLII (1945), pp. 701–712 [this volume, pp. 127–40]. Morris's view is contained in his *Foundations of the Theory of Signs* (referred to hereafter as *F.S.*) in the *International Encyclopedia of Unified Science*, Vol. I, No. 2, Chicago, 1938.

[First published in *Journal of Philosophy* 43 (14 February 1946): 85–95. For Charles W. Morris's reply, see Appendix 9; for rejoinder by Dewey, see p. 331.]

I

     Morris adopts from Peirce the name *semiosis* for the general theory of signs. In an early passage he distinguishes four factors, components, sometimes called aspects, of signs. There is the (i) sign vehicle, that which acts or functions as a sign; (ii) there is that to which the signs refer, the designatum; (iii) there is "that effect on some interpreter in virtue of which the thing in question is a sign to that interpreter," viz., the interpretant. (iv) "The interpreter may be included as a fourth factor." Or, summarizing, "The takings-account-of are *interpretants;* the agents of the process are *interpreters.*" [2] In a later passage the "process of interpreting" is telescoped into the interpretant, and the consolidation is henceforth called the "*interpretant.*" The three factors of semiosis dealt with in the rest of the monograph are, accordingly, "sign vehicle, designatum, interpreter." [3] Since the deviation from Peirce, amounting as has been said to a reversal, is connected with the gratuitous introduction of an "interpreter," and since this introduction is the source from which there flows the account of the pragmatic and of pragmatism given by Morris, it may seem at first sight as if the point at issue in this article were the nature of "pragmatism." So I wish to make it clear at the outset that this is a secondary matter. The primary matter is the theory of signs in general and linguistic signs (symbols) in particular, and of meaning, put forward by Peirce:—a theory in which "relation to interpreters" not only does not describe "pragmatism" in any way whatever, but falls (and this is the primary point) wholly outside of Peirce's theory of signs and meaning and of anything involved in that theory.

    By parcelling out the triadic relation mentioned above, Morris obtains three dyadic "dimensions." The dyadic "relation of signs to that to which they are applicable" is called the *semantic* dimension; "the relation of signs to one another" is called the *syntactical* dimension; while "the relation of signs to interpreters" is called the *pragmatic* dimension. It is further added that in their semantic dimension, signs designate and/or denote; in their syn-

2. *F.S.*, p. 3 and p. 4. Italics in original.
3. *F.S.*, p. 6, where the three matters last named are called "three correlates of the triadic relation of semiosis."

tactic dimension, they implicate; in their pragmatic dimension, they express.[4]

It is, in my judgment, a too frequent practice to attempt to "solve" problems by a distribution of subject-matters into different compartments—a procedure which also, in my judgment, evades the issues that are serious. Mr. Morris thus awards the semantic dimension to the empirical student of the theory of knowledge; to the logician is awarded the syntactical dimension, as appears from the word "implicates" (implies) in the above statement (the formal being thus successfully cut off from factual scientific subject-matter); to the pragmatic dimension there remains the extra-cognitive, extra-logical domain which includes "all the psychological, biological, and sociological phenomena which occur in the functioning of signs."[5] In this connection, it is said that this three-dimensional division enables us to recognize the *validity* of all three points of view, including the pragmatic, which is "inclined to regard a language as a type [*sic!*] of communicative activity, social in origin and nature."

Whether I am correct or not in my general statement about the tendency to solve problems by parcelling out subject-matter into independent domains or dimensions, one has only to read Peirce to see that Morris's account effectually splits apart the very subject-matters with which Peirce labors in order to provide an integrated solution. And while the point at issue is not the nature of pragmatics, much less its correctness, discussion must begin at this place since Morris's misinterpretation, as far as Peirce is concerned, centres at and proceeds from his extraordinary account of what Peirce means by "pragmatic" in connection with linguistic signs. The actual issue, however, is the theory of Peirce concerning the nature of linguistic signs and of meaning. The misrepresentation in question consists in converting *Interpretant*, as used by Peirce, into a personal user or interpreter. To Peirce, "interpreter," if he used the word, would mean *that which interprets,* thereby giving meaning to a linguistic sign. I do not believe

4. *F.S.*, pp. 6–7.
5. *F.S.*, p. 30, for the last quotation; considering that the subject-matter is *linguistic* signs, which present themselves to the factual student as themselves biological-psychological-societal events, this relegation of the latter to an extra-cognitive, extra-logical compartment should prepare the reader for the disintegration to which it gives rise.

that it is possible to exaggerate the scorn with which Peirce would treat the notion that *what* interprets a given linguistic sign can be left to the whim or caprice of those who happen to use it. But it does not follow from this fact that Peirce holds that the interpretant, that which interprets a linguistic sign, is an "object" in the sense of an existential "thing." On the contrary, the interpretant, in Peirce's usage, is always and necessarily *another* linguistic sign—or, better, set of such signs. The following passage is strictly representative: "On the whole, then, if by the *meaning* of a term, proposition, or argument we understand the entire general intended interpretant, then the meaning of an argument is explicit. It is its *conclusion;* while the meaning of a proposition or term is all that that proposition or term could contribute to the conclusion of a demonstrative argument."[6]

Against such statements as the above may be placed the following statements of Morris, in addition to what has previously been cited from him about the pragmatic dimension and the interpret*er*: The relation of language "to the persons who use it"; "that effect on some interpreter in virtue of which the thing in question is a sign to that interpreter"; "the relation of signs to interpreters . . . the pragmatical dimension"; "expresses its interpreter"; "expresses is a term of pragmatics"; "the permanent significance of pragmatism lies in the fact that it has directed attention more closely to the relation of signs to their users."[7]

The extent to which the view presented in these passages inverts Peirce may be gathered from the fact that Peirce uniformly holds (1) that there is no such thing as a sign in isolation, every sign being a constituent of a sequential set of signs, so that apart from membership in this set, a thing has no meaning—or is *not* a sign; and (2) that in the sequential movement of signs thus ordered, the meaning of the earlier ones in the series is provided by or constituted by the later ones as their interpretants, until a conclusion (*logical* as a matter of course) is reached. Indeed,

6. *Collected Papers*, Vol. V, pp. 110–111; "conclusion" not italicized in original. The reader who consults the *Indices*, especially of Vols. II and V, of the *Collected Papers* will be readily convinced of the representative character of this passage. I add, however, the following: "the conclusion of an argument" is "its *meaning*, . . . its intended interpretant. . . . It seems natural to use the word *meaning* to denote the intended interpretant" (Vol. V, p. 108). In the *Indices*, consult *Meaning* and *Symbol*, in addition to *Interpretant*.
7. *F.S.*, pp. 2, 3, 6, 7, and 29; similar statements occur on pp. 30, 31, and 33.

Peirce adheres so consistently to this view that he says, more than once, that signs, *as such,* form an infinite series, so that no conclusion of reasoning is forever final, being inherently open to having its meaning modified by further signs.

Verbally, this intrinsic "relation of signs to one another" sounds like the *syntactical* dimension of Morris. But in the case of Peirce this moving or sequential relation of signs is formal only in the sense of being the form-of-the-movement-of-an-ordered-series-of-signs-to-a-conclusion. The formal treatment of Peirce is found in his *Logic of Relatives,* which is integrally connected with his whole theory of signs. That to Peirce the movement of signs, while it *has* form, is itself material or factual, *not* formal, appears clearly in the following passage: "To say, therefore, that thought cannot happen in an instant, but requires a time, is but another way of saying every thought must be interpreted in another, or that all thought is in signs."[8]

As Morris's translation of "interpretant" into a personal user as its interpreter turns Peirce's view upside down, so his formulation of *semantic,* or the relation of signs to "things," is so contrary to what Peirce says on the latter subject as to make nonsense of it. The most direct way of showing this inversion is by taking what Morris says about the case of a reference to a thing in what he calls a "thing-sentence," which, according to him, is used "to designate any sentence whose designatum does not include signs."[9] The repeated statement by Peirce that signs as such are connected only with other signs is enough of itself to show that according to him a "designatum" of a sign which is not itself a sign is an absurdity. We seem to have here further evidence of the extent to which the type of logic presented by Morris and others is controlled by the epistemological heritage of a knowing subject, person, self, or what have you, set over against the

8. *Collected Papers,* Vol. V, p. 151. The presence of the word "time" in this passage while speaking of a sign-sequence, is sufficient evidence of the fact that to Peirce "the relation of signs to one another" is not just formal.

9. *F.S.,* p. 15. The fact that Morris adopts this term from those who, like Carnap, think that logic can be a purely or exclusively formal or syntactical affair is a good illustration of the confusion that is bound to result when an attempt is made to link up Peirce's theory with the kind of theory which he constantly opposes. Doubtless Morris's unquestioning acceptance of the kind of formalism expounded by Carnap is the reason why he is forced to give an account of Peirce's *pragmatic* that has nothing in common with the latter.

world, or things, or objects, and capable of reference to the latter either directly in virtue of its own faculty (epistemological realism) or through an idea or thought as intermediary (epistemological idealism). The school whose logical tenets are adopted by Morris substitutes a *word* for a knowing mind or subject, endowing it with the same miraculous power formerly attributed to mind or to an idea as a go-between. I do not see how conversion of Peirce's interpretant, which as later sign supplies meaning to the earlier ones, can be explained save as a diluted relic of the traditional epistemological theory, with word or sign taking the place, as *tertium quid,* of the idea, thought, or mental state of that tradition.[10]

We do not have, however, to depend upon inference from what Peirce says about signs as the objects, or designata, of other signs, to observe the departure from him that is involved in the notion that the designatum of a linguistic sign can be an existential thing. In one passage Morris mentions an *indexical* sign; were it not for the presence, in what he says in that passage, of the word "designata," it approximates the actual theory of Peirce concerning how one kind of sign, but *not* word, sentence, or linguistic sign, refers to things. The passage of Morris reads: "Things may be regarded as the designata of indexical signs."[11] To connect *things* with *indexical* signs is, in Peirce's position, a way of *denying* that they are connected with *linguistic* signs, with words, or anything he calls a *symbol.* For an indexical sign is a case of what Peirce calls *Secondness,* while a linguistic sign is a case of *Thirdness.* It is out of the question here to go into details of what in Peirce's writings is the meaning of these terms, along with his *Firstness.* But a reader who consults almost at random any passage referred to by these words in the *Indices* of his volumes will see that they are used to differentiate, with great care and in a fundamental way, the status, force, and unique function of linguistic signs.

Linguistic signs, constituting *thought* and conferring generality, continuity, law, are cases of *Thirdness.* They have of themselves no reference to "things." Such connection as they can have is, accordingly, dependent upon the intervention of another fac-

10. See Bentley's article, "On a Certain Vagueness in Logic," the *Journal of Philosophy,* Vol. XLII (1945), pp. 6–27 and pp. 39–51.
11. *F.S.,* p. 25.

tor. This factor (called Secondness by Peirce) is of a radically different sort from Thirdness. It is particularity as against generality; brute interruption as against continuity; contingency as against law. As respects the difference between indexical signs as cases of Secondness and linguistic signs as cases of Thirdness, the following passage is both representative and conclusive:

> We are continually bumping against hard fact. . . . There can be no resistance without effort; there can be no effort without resistance. They are only two ways of describing the same experience. It is a double consciousness. . . . As the consciousness *itself* is two-sided, so it has also two varieties; namely, action, where our modification of other things is more prominent than their reaction on us, and perception, where their effect on us is overwhelmingly greater than our effect on them. And this notion, of being such as other things make us, is such a prominent part of our life that we conceive other things also to exist in virtue of their reactions against each other. The idea of other, of *not*, becomes a very pivot of thought. To this element I give the name of Secondness.[12]

The passage is quoted at length. It indicates not only how, according to Peirce, reference of linguistic signs to things is accomplished, namely, through their getting into connection with indexical signs, but in its "two-sidedness" anticipates what James, later, but probably independently, called the doublebarreledness of experience. Implicitly, but not explicitly, it anticipates the principle of "indeterminacy," according to which, when a cat looks at a king, there is a bumping in which the king as well as the cat is moved—though not of course to anything like the same extent. Perception of "internal" and "external" worlds is a matter of one and the same event—the event to which, in recent psychology, the name "sensori-motor" is applied. And while Peirce uses the word "internal" to express the organism's part in this two-sided affair, it is equally true that the organism's side is "external" to that of the part of environing conditions in the common transaction. It all depends, so to say, on whose side we are on.

12. *Ibid.*, Vol. I, p. 162. Physical pointing, and the expressions "this," "that," "I," "You," etc., or all demonstrative and personal pronouns, are reflections of Secondness. Peirce says somewhere that instead of pronouns standing for nouns, the reverse is the case; nouns depend upon pronouns.

This perceptual-manipulative behavioral event determines the indexical sign which brings "us" into connection with "things," something it is impossible, according to Peirce, for symbols, linguistic signs, or, in Morris's words, for a "sentence" to do. What the latter calls "semantic reference" takes place, on Peirce's view, when, and only when, there is a conjunction of the "Secondness" of an indexical sign with the movement of linguistic signs, or "Thirdness," thereby bringing the latter to a close in a way which links it into the former, and thereby also conferring generality, reasonableness, upon what in itself is like a sheer bumping of things into one another.[13]

Along with the statements that a "sign is not a sign"—in the linguistic sense—unless it "translates itself into another sign in which it is more fully developed," and that "the immediate object of a symbol can only be a symbol," may be placed the following: "The Sign can only represent the Object and tell about it. It cannot furnish acquaintance with or recognition of that Object; for that is what is meant in this volume by the Object of a Sign; namely, that with which it *presupposes* an acquaintance in order to convey further information concerning it."[14]

In adult experience, there are few cases of pure or exclusive Secondness or Thirdness; indeed, if there were, Peirce would not have had to take such pains to restate traditional theories of knowledge and of logic by the careful discriminations he institutes, Firstness, Secondness, and Thirdness being the names, perhaps not very happy ones, given to the subjects that are differentiated.

It is not part of the present paper to go into detail about the way in which linguistic signs interlock with indexical signs. It suffices to say that such interception takes place and that by and through it linguistic signs get that reference to and connection with "things" which by themselves they lack. It is also true to say that our scientific knowledge (with the exception of mathematics) and those portions of "common-sense" knowledge which possess generality along with existential reference represent an

---

13. As to lack of reference of linguistic signs, or sentences as such, to things, see *Indices* under *Thirdness, Symbols, Continuity, Generality.*
14. The last quotation is from Vol. II, p. 137; italics not in original; the earlier ones from Vol. V, p. 416, and Vol. II, p. 166, footnote. Cf. the following: "A sign is only a sign *in actu* by virtue of its receiving an interpretation, that is, by virtue of its determining another sign of the same object," Vol. V, p. 397.

interlocking of linguistic with non-linguistic modes of behavior. While he does not use the following mode of speech it is, I believe, faithful to his position to say that in the course of cosmic or natural evolution, linguistic behavior *super*venes on other more immediate and, so to say, physiological modes of behavior, and that in supervening it also *inter*venes in the course of the latter, so that through this mediation regularity, continuity, generality become properties of the course of events, so that they are raised to the plane of reasonableness. For, "the complete object of a symbol, that is to say, its meaning, is of the nature of a law."[15]

II

Peirce uses the word "thought" quite freely. The mentalistic associations of the word, which are due to the epistemological tradition, may give the careless reader the impression that Peirce regards linguistic signs as "expressions" of something that is itself mental. The following passage sums up Peirce's constant attitude on this point: "What I could never admit [is] that logic is primarily conversant with unexpressed thought and only secondarily with language." The following passage should provide the basis for whatever one says who sets out to write about the logical theory of Peirce: "The woof and warp of all thought and all research is symbols; and the life of thought and science is the life inherent in symbols; so that it is wrong to say that a good language is *important* to good thought, merely; for it is of the essence of it."[16]

In one passage Peirce explicitly differentiates three kinds of "interpretants." The "interpretant" of an iconic sign, as a form of Firstness, is *emotional;* that of an indexical sign is, as we have already seen in another connection, *energetic.* Meaning, or *intellectual* and *logical,* interpretants are found, however, exclusively, in connection with *linguistic* signs.[17] These signs in their interconnections *are* "thought."

> If we seek the light of external facts, the only cases of
> thought which we can find are of thought in signs. Plainly, no

15. *Collected Papers,* Vol. II, p. 166.
16. *Collected Papers,* Vol. II, p. 284, footnote, and Vol. II, p. 129.
17. *Collected Papers,* Vol. V, pp. 326–327.

other thought can be evidenced by external facts. But we have seen that only by external facts can thought be known at all. The only thought, then, which can possibly be cognized is thought in signs. But thought which cannot be cognized does not exist. All thought, therefore, must necessarily be in signs.[18]

It is worth while to refer to what is said in connection with the phrase "we have seen." For what is here referred to is denial by Peirce of a faculty or power of introspection as the source of psychological knowledge. And certainly any case of reference of signs to their personal users must be a case of psychological knowledge. Now in Peirce, because of denial of introspective knowledge, all psychological knowledge is a case of what Morris calls *semantic,* or of reference to an existential thing. Only it is a reference which is more highly mediated than is a case of reference of a linguistic sign to things "commonly called external." There are, Peirce says, "logicians who . . . [follow] the method of basing propositions in the science of logic upon results of the science of psychology. . . . Those logicians continually confound *psychical* truths with *psychological* truths, although the distinction between them is of that kind that takes precedence over all others."[19] Again, "there is no reason for supposing a power of introspection, and, consequently, the only way of investigating a psychological question is by inference from external facts." Again, "we have no power of Introspection, but all knowledge of the internal world is derived by hypothetical reasoning from our knowledge of external facts. . . . We can admit no statement concerning what passes within us except as a hypothesis to explain what takes place in what we commonly call the external world." Again, "Introspection is wholly a matter of inference. . . . The *self* is only inferred."[20] Since thought consists of

18. *Collected Papers,* Vol. V, p. 151.
19. *Collected Papers,* Vol. V, pp. 332–333. The "precedence" in question is that while linguistic signs as such refer only to one another, what he here calls *psychical* is a case of sheer Firstness, or an iconic sign whose "interpretant" is *feeling.*
20. *Collected Papers,* Vol. V, pp. 150, 158, and 313. As to what is here meant by the "internal" as distinguished from external, see in addition to the passage already quoted from Vol. I, p. 162, the section on "Struggle," Vol. V, pp. 32–40, Vol. V, pp. 326, 334, and 378. It lies outside the scope of the present paper to go in any detail into what Peirce means by "internal." The

signs, it is neither psychical nor psychological; and, as has been said, any reference of a sign to its "users" is more highly mediated, more complex, and more difficult to accomplish than is reference of it to things "commonly called external." The fact that the occurrence and movement of linguistic signs or symbols is neither, according to Peirce, a psychical nor a psychological affair points directly to the fact that according to him "biological" and "sociological" facts are integral and indispensable factors of such signs—not something to be dismissed to a non-logical and non-cognitive dimension.

For wherever there is generality, continuity, there is habit. And even a casual reader of Peirce should be aware that habit on his view is first a cosmological matter and then is physiological and biotic—in a definitely existential sense. It, habit, operates in and through the human organism, but that very fact is to him convincing evidence that the organism is an integrated part of the world in which habits form and operate. As to the "sociological" factor, it is easy to quote many passages from Peirce in which whatever is entitled to the names "logical" and "cognitive" is brought specifically and explicitly within the societal. So far is he from penning the sociological, along with the biological, within "phenomena that occur in the functioning of signs," that he sticks to the observed fact that language and linguistic signs are modes or forms of *communication*, and thus are intrinsically "social." In so many words he says "Logic is rooted in the social principle." "No mind can take one step without the aid of other minds"—mind as thought being defined, be it recalled, in terms

following passages, however, give the clue to any one interested in following out the matter. "The old expectation, which is what he was familiar with, is his inner world, or *Ego*. The new phenomenon, the stranger, is from the exterior world or *Non-Ego*" (Vol. V, p. 40). And in reference to a case of "bumping" or interference with expectation we find "direct experience of the duality of the inward past and the outward present" (Vol. V, p. 378). And, after the statement that the "self is only inferred:" "There is no time in the Present for any inference at all. . . . Consequently, the present object must be an external object if there be any objective reference in it." It is obvious that interpretation in terms of past, present, and future is radically different from that given by the epistemological-psychological tradition to "inner" and "outer." That introduction of the future is relevant is clear from the following passage, the "subjectivity of the unexpected . . . the objectivity of the unexpected" (Vol. V, p. 379). "The consciousness of the present is then that of a struggle over what shall be" (Vol. V, p. 313).

of linguistic signs. "When we come to study the great principle of continuity and see how all is fluid and every point directly partakes the being of every other, it will appear that individualism and falsity are one and the same. Meantime, we know that man is not whole as long as he is single, that he is essentially a possible member of society. Especially, one man's experience is nothing, if it stands alone. . . . It is not 'my' experience but 'our' experience that has to be thought of; and this 'us' has indefinite possibilities."[21]

III

I believe that in the present state of logical theory Peirce has a great deal to say that is of value. There is potential advance contained in the present concern with language and "symbols." But it can not be carried into effect, it is nullified, as long as the shadow of the old epistemological dichotomy hangs over writings that profess to be logical. Peirce uses at times words that have strong mentalistic associations. It is a reasonable conjecture that the explanation of this usage is to be found in the fact that his *cosmology* was closely affiliated with panpsychism. But, as the foregoing discussion shows, he completely repudiated the notion that language is a *tertium quid* in which something called thought is expressed or clothed. With this repudiation goes denial that the names *Self, Mind, Knowing Subject, Person* as user of signs, apply to anything except a particular sort of natural existence, or "thing," which can be *known* only through and by means of the best knowledge we have of other "things," physical, biological, and socio-cultural. "Users" of Peirce's writings should either stick to his basic pattern or leave him alone.

21. *Collected Papers*, Vol. II, p. 398 and p. 129; Vol. V, p. 259, footnote.

Prefatory Note to *Problems of Men*

The Introduction which immediately follows this Note was written expressly for this volume and has not been published elsewhere. The other essays in this book are reprinted from periodicals in which they originally appeared. Most of them have appeared, as is shown by the dates attached in the Table of Contents, fairly recently. One of them was written, however, half a century ago and has not been previously reprinted.* Naturally, there has been some modification of my position in respect to various philosophical matters as the years have passed. The articles of recent date most nearly represent, of course, my present views. Considering the time which has elapsed, the older essay seemed worth reprinting as an anticipation of the direction in which I have moved during the intervening fifty years.

A few of the essays that are included are so technical that on their face they are not about *The Problems of Men*. But a place has been given them because they present aspects of that work of self-criticism, of purging, which, as I said in the Introduction, philosophy needs to execute if it is to perform under present conditions the role that properly belongs to it.

J. D.

---

* "Logical Conditions of a Scientific Treatment of Morality." See Checklist of Dewey's References.

[First published in *Problems of Men* (New York: Philosophical Library, 1946), p. 1.]

Introduction to *Problems of Men*

The Problems of Men and the Present State of Philosophy

A Report was recently issued by a Committee of an organization whose members are concerned with teaching and writing philosophy, The American Philosophical Association. It was invited to "undertake an examination of the present state of philosophy and the role philosophy might play in the postwar world." The invitation came from and was financed by a non-professional body, The Rockefeller Foundation. This fact is an indication that the theme is considered to be of public, not merely professional concern. This intimation is borne out by a statement regarding the task entrusted to the Committee: It was asked to inquire into "the function of philosophy . . . in the development of a free and reflective life in the community." It was also asked to discuss "the function of philosophy in liberal education." The title of the book is *Philosophy in American Education*.

This title suggests that the Committee confined itself to the narrower of the two tasks confided to it. With a few exceptions the body of the book bears out this impression. After asking, "What are we trying to do? Where do we think we are going?", the introduction to the Report goes on to say "There is not in our contemporary situation an authoritatively accepted body of doctrine called 'philosophy' for which duly accredited spokesmen can pretend to speak. There are philosophies and philosophers, and they *differ philosophically on just the issues with which we are called upon to deal.*" The Committee deserves every credit for the frankness of this admission. But as far as concerns interest outside the circle of philosophers, the words I have italicized are, I believe, more revealing about the present state and role of philosophy than anything else said in the whole volume.

[First published in *Problems of Men* (New York: Philosophical Library, 1946), pp. 3–20.]

This is a strong statement. The reason for making it is that the internal divisions which kept the Committee from dealing with the more important of the two tasks entrusted to it is the reflection in intellectual form of confusions and conflicts by which the public community is divided. Before reproaching philosophers for failure to agree we should recal that in the present state of the world agreement among them would be proof positive that philosophy is so technical as to be wholly out of touch with the problems and issues of actual life.

I propose, then, to discuss the present state of philosophy in its human bearings. Within the circle of professional philosophers and in the teaching of philosophy in institutions of learning, differences in the conclusions that constitute systems and isms have their place. But for the public they are of slight importance compared with the question of what philosophers are trying to do and might do if they tried. The interest of the public centres in such questions as: What is the distinctive purpose and business of philosophy anyway? How is it related to those concerns and issues which today stand out as the problems of men?

I

Discussion may well begin with the fact that there *does* exist at the present time one philosophy which holds that it possesses "an authoritatively accepted body of doctrine" having "duly accredited spokesmen" to declare its contents. The fact that representatives of this type of philosophy do not figure in the Report is itself indicative of a profound cleavage in present life. For that philosophy is that of an institution that claims divine origin and continued divine support and direction. Its doctrines are held to be authoritative because of their source in supernatural revelation. The philosophies represented in the Report formulate a standpoint according to which philosophical doctrines should be formulated on grounds that are independent of supernatural revelation and not requiring any special institution as their organ. The supernatural and theological philosophy took shape in the medieval period. The philosophies represented in the Report took shape in ways away from, largely in protest against, the attitudes and interests which controlled the formulation of the older philosophy.

Roughly speaking this division within philosophy represents a cleavage in life between older and newer factors in present life, between the supernatural and what by contrast may be called the secular. It is an expression of conditions which led Matthew Arnold more than a generation ago to speak of contemporary man as

> Wandering between two worlds, one dead,
> The other powerless to be born.

Nevertheless, an account of the present state of philosophy must note that as far as concerns the *aim and office* of philosophy there is one basic agreement between the philosophy of the theological type and at least some philosophies of the secular type. Rejection of the supernatural origin and foundation makes of course a vast difference. But the philosophical tenets that are presented in the Report cling largely, although not exclusively, to the view that the primary aim of philosophy is knowledge of Being or "Reality" which is more comprehensive, fundamental and ultimate than the knowledge which can be provided by the organs and methods at the disposal of the "special" sciences. For, according to this view, the sciences, with the possible exception of mathematics, deal with things that are temporal, changing, contingent while philosophy aims at knowledge of that which is eternal and inherently necessary, so primary and so final that it alone can give sure support to the claims to truths put forth by the lesser forms of knowing.

It is the fact of a profound cleavage that is here important, not the question of which is right and which is wrong. The cleavage in life that has been brought about by "modern" departures from and revolt against older practices and tenets is so widespread that nothing is left untouched. In politics, it is manifested in the movements which in practically every country have resulted in separation of church and state. Developments in industry and commerce have substituted mobility for the relatively static conditions of rule by custom which once prevailed. They have also introduced interests and enjoyments that compete with those made supreme in the period of medieval ecclesiastic control. With respect to natural and historical knowledge the rise of new methods of inquiry has profoundly shaken the astronomy, physics, biology, anthropology and the historical learning with which the theological philosophy had identified itself. The cleavage that has resulted between theology and positive science, between the mundane and the heavenly, between temporal interests and those called eternal has created the special divisions which in the form of "dualisms" have determined the chief problems of philosophies that are "modern" in the historical sense.

Nevertheless, the most striking fact about these modern philosophies is the extent in which they exhibit the influence of the postmedieval movements in politics, industry and science but without having surrendered the old, the classic, view that the chief business of philosophy is search for a kind of Reality that is more fundamental and more ultimate than are or than can be the facts disclosed by the sciences. The outcome has been the controversies as to the organ of knowing that constitute the philosophical isms of the last few centuries. Because of the view that the aim and business of philosophy is with Reality supposed to be behind and beyond the subject-matter of the various authentic knowings that form the sciences, the "possibility of knowledge," conditions of knowing set up before knowing can take place, became the chief "problem" of philosophy. The more actual knowings flourished, the more philosophies, mutually contradictory among themselves, occupied themselves with furnishing "Foundations for Knowledge," instead of employing what is known to direct it in discovering and performing its own tasks. The work that once gave its name to philosophy, Search for Wisdom, has progressively receded into the background. For wisdom differs from knowledge in being the application of what is known to intelligent conduct of the affairs of human life. The straits of philosophy are due to the fact that the more this available knowledge has increased, the more it has occupied itself with a task that is no longer humanly pertinent.

For practical problems that are so deeply human as to be the moral issues of the present time have increased their range and their intensity. They cover practically every aspect of contemporary life, domestic, industrial, political. But during the very period in which this has occurred, philosophy, for the most part, has relegated them to a place that is subordinate and accessory to an alleged problem of knowledge. At the same time actual knowing and the applications of science in life by inventions and technological arts have been going on at such a rate that the alleged problem of its foundations and possibility of knowledge are of but remote professional concern. The net result of neglect with issues that are urgent and of pre-occupation with issues that are remote from active human concern explains the popular discredit into which philosophy has progressively fallen. This disrepute is in turn a decided factor in determining its role in the world.

For what can philosophies do which, in spite of change of conditions in science and in human affairs of basic import, go on occupying themselves with the problem of the *conditions* of knowledge in neglect of the vital problem of its *consequences,* actual and potential? Inquiry that should devote itself to systematic investigation of the consequences of science; of why they are what they are at present; of the causes of that limitation in which scientific method affects the conditions of life only through the medium of institutions to which scientific inquiry is *not* applied; to what the consequences of science *might* be were they so applied; such inquiry might hope to have some role, to play some part, in development of attitudes in the community that are liberal, well tested, and grounded in fact.

II

Under present conditions scientific methods take effect in determining the concrete economic conditions under which the mass of men live. But they are not employed to determine freely and systematically the moral, the humane, ends served by engrossing practical conditions, the actual state of ends and values. Hence the more important things are left to decision by custom, prejudice, class interests, and traditions embodied in institutions whose results are mostly fixed by the superior power in possession of those who manage them. Under these conditions, a recent movement in philosophy demands especial notice. It retains the notion that philosophy's concern is with superior reality, taking its cue in search for it mainly from mathematics and quasi-mathematical symbolisms, but completely repudiating that aspect of philosophy that has gone by the name of search for wisdom. It converts the practical neglect by modern philosophies of political and moral subjects into systematic theoretical denial of the possibility of intelligent concern with them. It holds that the practical affairs of men which are of highest and deepest significance are matters of values and valuations, and that *therefore* they are by their very nature incapable of intellectual adjudication; of either justification or condemnation on rational grounds. The movement retains in the most emphatic form possible the ancient Greek conception according to which "theory" is intrinsically superior to any and every form of practical concern—the latter consisting of things that change and fluctuate in contrast with the eternity of Being. But the movement in question goes, so to speak, the classic doctrine one better. The latter held that practical affairs were the material of inferior sorts of knowledge. The present movement holds that moral affairs, concerned as they are with "intrinsic" values, or "ends-in-themselves," are wholly outside the reach of any sort of knowledge whatever.

A distinguished member of this school of contemporary thought has recently written that "the actions of men, in innumerable important respects, have depended upon their theories as to the world and human life, as to what is good and evil." But he has also written that what men hold about "what is good and evil" is wholly a matter of sheer likes and dislikes. They, in turn, are so completely private and personal—in the terminology of philosophy so "subjective"—as to be incapable of judgment having "objective" grounds. Likes and dislikes are immune to modification by knowledge since they dwell in inaccessible privacy. Values that are "extrinsic" or "instrumental" may be rationally estimated. For they are only means; are not ends in any genuine sense. As means their efficacy may be determined by methods that will stand scientific inspection. But the "ends" they serve (ends which are truly ends) are just matters of what groups, classes, sects, races, or whatever, happen irrationally to like or dislike.

The actual or concrete condition of men all over the world with respect to their opportunities and their relative disadvantages of position, their happiness and their misery, their kind and degree of participation "in good and evil in innumerable respects" is now decided by things which, on this view, are mere means. In addition they are said to be totally arbitrary and irresponsible with respect to the ends they finally produce although these ends are all that mankind prizes! What is the probable destiny of man on earth if regulation of the concrete conditions under which men live continues to increase at its present rate, while the consequences produced by them are necessarily left at the mercy of likes and dislikes that are, in turn, at the mercy of irrational habits, institutions, and a class and sectarian distribution of power between the stronger and the weaker? However technical the "theoretical" view of this school about ultimate reality may be, the truth or falsity of this part of their doctrine is assuredly of public concern.

Were this philosophy to be generally accepted the movement for a "moratorium on science" would be greatly strengthened. For it is from science that are derived the values which are "means" and only means, according to this brand of philosophy. According to it there is no difference capable of intelligent use and test between use of energy due to splitting of the atom for destruction of mankind and its use in peaceful industry to make life more secure and more abundant. This fact does not prove the doctrine to be false. But it certainly gives ground for serious consideration of the grounds upon which it rests. The problem of values and valuations has been coming to the front of late in any case. The challenge here issued should make it the central issue for some time to come.

Meantime, such popular vogue as may accrue to this doctrine will operate, almost automatically, to promote supernatural theological philosophy. For the latter also holds that ultimate ends are beyond the reach of human discovery and judgment. But it also holds that revelation from on high has provided the all-sufficient remedy. In a time as troubled as the present, a philosophy which denies the existence of any natural and human means of determining judgments as to what is good and evil will work to the benefit of those who hold that they have in their possession super-human and super-natural means for infallible ascertainment of ultimate ends, especially as they also claim to possess the practical agencies for ensuring the attainment of final good by men who accept the truths they declare.

III

Another phase of the present state of philosophy demands notice. It repudiates that which the last named movement affirms and it affirms that which the latter denies. It breaks completely with that part of the philosophical tradition which holds that concern with superior reality determines the work to be done by philosophical inquiry. It affirms that the purpose and business of philosophy is wholly with that part of the historic tradition called search for wisdom:—Namely, search for the ends and values that give direction to our collective human activities. It holds that not grasp of eternal and universal Reality but use of the methods and conclusions of our best knowledge, that called scientific, provides the means for conducting this search. It holds that limitations which now exist in this use are to be removed by means of extension of the ways of tested knowing that define science from physical and physiological matters to social and distinctly human affairs. The movement is called in its various aspects by the names of pragmatism, experimentalism, instrumentalism. Not these names are important but the ideas that are held regarding the distinctive aim and business of philosophic inquiry and of how it should be accomplished.

The accusation brought against it of childlike trust in science omits the fact that it holds that science itself is still in its babyhood. It holds that the scientific method of inquiry has not begun to reach maturity. It holds that it will achieve manhood only when its use is extended to cover all aspects of all matters of human concern. It holds that many of the remediable evils of the present time are due to the unbalanced, one-sided, application of the methods of inquiry and test that constitute everything that has a right to the name "science." It holds that the chief present task of philosophy is with issues and problems that are due to this state of things, including the projection of liberal hypotheses as to ways in which the required social change may be brought about.

This view of the aim and office of philosophy involves a decided shift in the meaning of such words as comprehensiveness and ultimacy in their application to the work of philosophy. They lose the significance that was given to them when philosophy was supposed to be an effort to achieve knowledge of "real-

ity" superior to that with which the special sciences are concerned. There are issues in the conduct of human affairs in their
production of good and evil which, at a given time and place, are
so central, so strategic in position, that their urgency deserves,
with respect to practice, the names ultimate and comprehensive.
These issues demand the most systematic reflective attention that
can be given. It is relatively unimportant whether this attention
be called philosophy or by some other name. It is of immense
human importance that it be given, and that it be given by means
of the best tested resources that inquiry has at command.

Reference to place and time in what has just been said should
make it clear that this view of the office of philosophy has no
commerce with the notion that the problems of philosophy are
"eternal." On the contrary it holds that such a view is obstructive, tending to be of use chiefly in defense of the practice of continually rehashing issues which were timely in their own social
condition but that are no longer urgent—save from the standpoint of historical scholarship. The latter is as important in philosophy as in any other humane field. But when it is permitted to
monopolize philosophical activities it chokes out their life. Eternity that is permitted to become a refuge from the time in which
human life goes on may provide a certain kind of consolation.
But emotion and comfort should not be identified with understanding and insight, nor with the direction the latter may supply.

This movement is charged with promotion of "relativism" in a
sense in which the latter is identified with lack of standards, and
consequently with tendency to promote chaos. It is true that the
movement in question holds since the problems and issues of philosophy are not eternal they should link up with urgencies that
impose themselves at times and in places. The "state of philosophy" if it is to be its present state must have to do with issues that
are themselves actively present. The word "relativity" is used as a
scarecrow to frighten away philosophers from critical assault
upon "absolutisms." Every class-interest in all history has defended itself from examination by putting forth claim to absoluteness. Social fanaticisms, whether of the right or the left, take
refuge in the fortress of principles too absolute to be subject to
doubt and inquiry. The absolute is the isolated; the isolated is
that which cannot be judged on the ground of connections that
can be investigated. The kind of "Relativity" characteristic of the

movement in question is that which marks all scientific inquiry. For the latter also finds its only workable "standards" are provided by the actual connections of things; connections which when they are generalized are given the name of space-time.

Dependence upon space-time connections now marks all the victories won by scientific inquiry. It is silly to suppose they terminate in mere particulars. On the contrary, they constantly move toward the general, provided only the generalizations have to do with wider and wider connections, so as not to swim in wordy vacuity. And so it is with a philosophy that employs the methods and conclusions of authentic inquiry as instruments for examination of values that now operate in regulating human habits, institutions and efforts. No span of connections in space-time is too wide or too long provided they are relevant to judgment of issues that are urgently here-and-now. Not "relativity" but absolutism isolates and confines. The reason, at bottom, that absolutism levels its guns against relativity in a caricature is that search for the connection of events is the sure way of destroying the privileged position of exemption from inquiry which every form of absolutism secures wherever it obtains.

IV

The foregoing remarks need illustration. What special problems and issues does this philosophical movement substitute for those which it takes to be now so irrelevant as to obstruct philosophy from performing the role it might exercise in the present world? Were I to reply that, at the very least, philosophy should clean its own house, I might seem to be retreating from human issues and problems back into the more technical concerns of professional philosophy. This would be the case if the things in philosophical doctrines that need to be got rid of were not also obstructive and deflecting in the human situation. Here is one outstanding illustration. Separation of mind and matter, the elevation of what was called ideal and spiritual to the very summit of Being and the degradation of everything called material and worldly to the lowest position, developed in philosophy as a reflection of economic and political division of classes. Slaves and artisans (who had no more political freedom than did outright slaves) were occupied with the "material," and hence with mere means to the good life in which they had no share. Citizens who were free stood totally above the need of any share in these activities, which were only menial. Division between high knowledge which was rational and theoretical and practical knowledge which was low, servile and a matter of mere routine, and the split between the ideal and the material followed as matter of course.

We have moved away from downright slavery and from feudal serfdom. But the conditions of present life still perpetuate a division between activities which are relatively base and menial and those which are free and ideal. Some educators suppose they are rendering a service by insisting upon an inherent difference between studies they call liberal and others they call mechanical and utilitarian. Economic theories of great influence have developed out of and are used to justify the isolation of economic, commercial, and financial affairs from the political and moral. Philosophy relevant to present conditions has a hard task to perform in purging itself of doctrines which seem to justify this separation and which certainly obstruct the formation of measures and policies by means of which science and technology (the application of science) would perform a more humane and liberal office than they now do.

This example of the kind of issue and problem with which present philosophy might well occupy itself suggests another problem so closely allied as to be, in fact, the same problem in another guise. The distinction, current in present day opinion, inside and outside of professional philosophy, between values that are intrinsic and extrinsic, final and instrumental, is an intellectual formulation of the separations set up between means and ends. This form of philosophic "dualism" is a further projection of pre-scientific, pre-technological, pre-democratic conditions into present philosophy in a way so obstructive as to demand total obliteration. Here again, philosophers have a difficult and exacting work to do if they are to take an active part in enabling the resources potentially at our disposal in present science and technology to exercise a genuinely liberating office in human affairs.

It follows that the whole notion of ends-in-themselves, as distinct from ends that are called mere means, represents a perpetuation of earlier conditions that is now definitely obstructive. In its theoretical aspect it is a striking case of adherence to an absolute after *science* has everywhere substituted connectivities. The hold still exerted by the notion is shown when philosophies that regard themselves as peculiarly modern and emancipated— like the type previously described—retain in full flower the notion that there are actually in existence such things as ends which are not also means. Give up the notion, and there vanish all the grounds that are offered for holding that moral ends are not, in theory, capable of the same kind of "objective" factual determination as are technological ends. Democratic abolition of fixed difference between "higher" and "lower" still has to make its way in philosophy.

Reference to this matter of values serves to introduce another example of the work to be done by a philosophy that desires a role in the present world. One reason that is given for eliminating values as values from any contact with grounded judgment is their alleged *subjective* nature. No student of philosophy needs to be told how largely the dualism of subjective and objective has figured in modern philosophy. At one time, in the earliest days of modern science, this dogma was of some practical use. Science had many foes with which to contend. It adopted the device of setting up the "internal" authority of a knowing mind and ego over against the "external" authority of custom and established institutions. Maintaining the separation when the actual advance of science has shown that man is a part of the world, not something set over against it, is one of the chief obstacles now standing in the way of intelligent discussion of all social matters. Wholehearted acceptance in philosophy of the fact that no grounds now exist for fixed division of events into subjective and objective is pre-requisite if philosophy is to have a role in promoting inquiry in social matters.

The things just discussed are examples of matters in which philosophy has now to do a hard and, for many of us, a disagreeable job. This is the work of getting rid, by means of thinking as exact and critical as possible, of perpetuations of those outworn attitudes which prevent those engaged in philosophic reflection from seizing the opportunities now open. This is the critical or, if one please, the negative aspect of the task to be undertaken in the present state of philosophy. But it is not merely negative. It is one side of the positive and constructive work philosophy can, and therefore should, do. Philosophy cannot of itself resolve the conflicts and dissolve the confusions of the present world.

Only the associated members of the world can do this work in cooperative action—a work of which institution of conditions of peace is a sufficiently striking example. But intellectual instruments are needed to project leading ideas or plans of action. The intellectual instrumentalities for doing this work need sterilizing and sharpening. That work is closely allied with setting better instruments, as fast as they take shape, at work. Active use in dealing with the present problems of men is the only way they can be kept from rusting. Trial and test in and by work done is the means by which they can be kept out of the dark spots in which infection originates. The fact that such plans, measures, policies, as can be projected will be but hypotheses is but another instance of alignment of philosophy with the attitude and spirit of the inquiries which have won the victories of scientific inquiry in other fields.

Only a few centuries ago physical science was in a state that today is only of historical interest—so far away is it in method and subject matter from what we now call "science." Obstacles to creation and use of new methods were not once just theoretical. Old beliefs and old ways of knowing were so connected with traditional habits and institutions that to attack one was taken to be an attack on the other. Nevertheless, a few men had the courage to engage in systematic adverse criticism not only of accepted conclusions but of the standpoint and methods that had obtained for centuries. In addition, they projected new hypotheses to direct the conduct of physical inquiry from that time on. Some of these hypotheses were so broad in scope that today they would rate as "philosophical" rather than as "scientific." Nevertheless, in the end they, as well as the work of purging, played a definite role in leading inquiry into the paths along which dependable tested results have been secured.

Today social subjects, as far as concerns effective treatment in inquiry, are in much the same state as physical subjects three hundred years ago. The need is that there be now the kind of systematic and comprehensive criticism of current methods and habits and the same projection of generous hypotheses as, only a few hundred years ago, set going the revolution in physical knowledge. The opportunity is as great as the need. The obstacles to undertaking the work in social questions are greater than they ever were in dealing, say, with the heavenly bodies. The initial step is to promote general recognition that knowing, including most emphatically scientific knowledge, is not outside social activity, but is itself a form of social behavior, as much so as agriculture or transportation. For it is something that human beings do, as they plow the earth and sail ships. On the critical, or "purging" side, systematic rejection of all doctrines that associate knowing with "mind" and an alleged individual ego, as something separate and self-enclosed, is required. On the positive side, this initial step demands systematic observation of the natural, the biological and societal, conditions by means of which knowing actually goes on.

This work is preparatory. On the whole, it is a case of philosophy cleaning its own house, together with doing a certain amount of refurnishing. The important work is to make evident the social conditions—economic, political, moral, and religious—which have restricted scientific inquiry so largely, first to physical and then to physiological matters; conditions that have kept inquiry penned in so that large fields of utmost human concern are treated as if they were sacrosanct, not to be contaminated by contact with concrete investigations. A deeply entrenched and fortified habit of treating economic affairs, industry, trade and business, as mere means having no intrinsic connection with "ultimate" ends which are moral, illustrates the penning-in theory and perpetuates it in practice.

The result is that what pass for moral ideals in the most important forms of social practices are so "ideal" as to be utopian. They are treated as matters of personal exhortation supplemented with use and threats of use of force in reward and punishment. Separation of the "materialistic" and the "ideal" deprives the latter of leverage and impetus, and prevents the things to which the former name is applied from rendering the humane service of which they are capable. The example of what physiological science and its applications have already accomplished in public health, limited as it is, is an instance of the kind of thing the method and results of competent inquiry might bring about in all aspects of human well being. The pragmatic philosophy, so called, has made a start in helping to break down in the field of education that separation of the "utilitarian" and the "liberal" which restricts alike the former and the latter. The belief that "vocational" education cannot be humane is an illustration that would be humorous were it not so disastrous in effect.

Political theory and practice provide another example. Liberalism once did a work of emancipation. But it was so influenced by a heritage of absolutistic claims that it invented the myth of "The Individual" set over in dualistic separation against that which is called "The Social." It obscured the fact that these words are names for traits and capacities of human beings in the concrete. It transformed that which they actually name into entities by themselves. It thereby obscured, indeed prevented, recognition of the fact that actual realization of these traits and capacities depends upon the specific conditions under which human beings are born and in which they grow up. The words *individuality* and *society* under this influence became names for something readymade and inherent—not differing in substance from that belief in occult essences which the new movement in physical knowledge had to assault and eliminate before it could do its work.

V

In what precedes I have mentioned, by way of illustration, some of the tasks that lie open to systematic generalized inquiry. Any inquiry, whatever name be given it, which undertakes this kind of inquiry, critical and constructive, will not have to worry about its role in the world. In closing I shall say a few words about the atmosphere and climate in which the work will have to be carried on. A passage taken from a writing of a distinguished American thinker, written well over a generation ago, will point a contrast. Josiah Royce wrote "You philosophize when you reflect critically upon what you are doing in your world. And what you are doing is, of course, in the first place living. And living involves passions, faiths, doubts, and courage. The critical inquiry into what these mean and imply is philosophy."

Provided that customs, arrangements, institutions, to which passions, such things as doubts, faiths, and courage, are attached, are brought into this view of the office of philosophy, it is tific inquiry, of speech and publication, of the rights of voluntary association and organization. These rights were not violated because their expression had happened to come into conflict with strong special interests nor yet because of some especial emergency. Suppression on these grounds has been known to occur even in our own country. They were denied and assailed in the totalitarian countries on moral grounds. They were asserted to be manifestations of private and class self-interest which weaken fundamental social ties. They were evidence that selfish and divisive egoism had got the better of devotion to the public good. They were the source of national weakness externally and of disorder and disintegration within.

I have not recited these things because I imagine that our own loyalty to the cause for which our country is fighting needs to be strengthened. I mention them because I believe that the very least the present crisis can do for those who believe in the principles and values of free societies is to make us reflect more seriously than we have been wont to do upon the moral foundation and the moral outlook of the various forms of freedom which centre in freedom of mind and conscience. It is perhaps natural that in times of long continued peace we should come to think of the various forms of freedom that are summed up in the phrase "civil liberties" in a rather routine fashion. We know that they are of such importance that they have found lodgment in our Constitution so that they are politically guaranteed by the highest political authority. But it may be that in coming to think of them as primarily political and legal, as matters for the courts and police, we have lost sight of their fundamental connection with the moral and the religious values which free societies exist to express and promote. But when powerful states deny to their own members the exercise of these liberties and strive to impose by force a similar denial upon other peoples, then indeed it is time that we search out the moral grounds for our faith in freedom of science, freedom of worship, freedom to unite voluntarily to pursue common religious, industrial, and educational aims, freedom of thought, of speech and publication. It is especially important that we do so because these forms of freedom are attacked and denied on grounds that are asserted to be moral; more fundamental in moral value, so it is asserted, than are the superficial and materialistic enjoyments these liberties have

not far different from what I have been saying. But then another note is struck. The passage continued "We feel ourselves in a world of law and significance. Yet why we feel this homelike sense of the reality and worth of the world is a matter of criticism. Such a criticism of life, made elaborate and thoroughgoing, is philosophy." In this further passage it is assumed as a matter of course that the world in which man lives is of such significance and worth that we cannot escape the sense of its homelikeness. The work assigned to philosophy is thereby limited to the office of finding, by systematic and thorough reflection, justification for a fact which philosophy is entitled to take for granted.

Times have altered since these words were written. They probably express an assumption and aim common to most classic systems of the past. But a peculiar hopefulness existing during the period when the words were penned made this assumption of worth, significance and unitary order especially easy. We now live in a situation when the world seems alien rather than homelike; in a period in which the tendency of scientific knowledge modifies the earlier faith in "overruling laws." And in most practical matters there is no more widespread sense than that of insecurity. The type of philosophy which now tries to show that all "appearances" to the contrary the world in which we live is "really," fundamentally, one of fixed order, significance and worth takes on the air of theological apologetics.

Philosophy still has a work to do. It may gain a role for itself for turning to consideration of why it is that man is now so alienated from man. It may turn to the projection of large or generous hypotheses which, if used as plans of action, will give intelligent direction to men in search for ways to make the world more one of worth and significance, more homelike, in fact. There is no phase of life, educational, economic, political, religious, in which inquiry may not aid in bringing to birth that world which Matthew Arnold rightly said was as yet unborn. Present day philosophy cannot desire a better work than to engage in the act of midwifery that was assigned to it by Socrates twenty-five hundred years ago.

January, 1946.

Religion and Morality in a Free Society

In about everything save number of years the nineteenth century already seems a long way off. At least, this is true for those of us who are old enough to have framed our moral and political beliefs during its years. The present state of the world is forcing us to ask whether the faith in which we were brought up and the hopes we learned to cherish are illusory. We were quite aware that the societies in which we lived were not entirely free. We knew that many defects existed and many problems remained to be solved. We knew that freedom brought responsibilities we were not meeting. We became as years passed more and more acutely aware of issues which centred about the relation of economic to political liberty. Some thought political action was encroaching upon personal liberty in industrial and financial matters; others thought that in order to render political liberties secure for all, the state would have to restrict still further economic freedom. A favorite topic of academic discussion was the relation of law to liberty and the point at which liberty passed into license.

But relatively speaking such questions lay on the surface. Most of us took it for granted that the values and purposes of a free society provided the core of the definition of civilization, and the measure of our collective moral advance. Those who thought that inevitable progress was the chief law and lesson of history identified progress with the story of the advance of humanity in political and civil freedom; they looked to the future to continue, with only temporary eddies here and there, that advance. Those who were not so sure about the certainty of progress through the

[First published in *The Centennial Celebration of Hollins College* (Hollins College, Va.: Hollins College, 1949), pp. 79–93, from an address delivered 18 May 1942.]

ages believed the advantages of free societies had been so prov by events that no serious backward movement was conceival

We were aware that the curse of war still existed and that dream of universal establishment of international peace wa the future to realize. We knew that the past had left a herita illwill and suspicion that it would take time to remove. B also thought that increased interdependence of the nations earth, and demonstration that this growth was for the g all, together with the realization that resort to brute fo relic of barbarism, would hasten the day in which nation dwell together on the earth in peace. Peace and civilizati we supposed, too closely bound up together to permit in run any other issue. And in this country we thought institutions would combine with the advantages of graphical location to enable it to be a leader in promo the means by which the reign of international peace forwarded.

We were aware that the question of the relation to of different races and religions was still a thorny on too the past had left an evil heritage. But here too that the kindly offices of time, with growth of mutua sympathetic understanding, would gradually hea that lower stages of civilization had created in the hardly need, however, to continue in this vein. Th did not expect was that nations which had advan proofs of civilization as high scientific attainment and technologies of modern industry would pi upon belief in war as the highest token of social gard brutal persecution of those of other faiths ultimate sign of national virility. We thought physical force was at least under such discou might continue for some time no nation clai would hold that its rank in the scale of civiliz by ability to organize every possible resource and moral, for conquest and subjugation.

When the possibility of international und ligious and racial tolerance is deliberately tacked, there is no cause for surprise at articles of liberal faith. For years before th otalitarian nations suppressed freedom ployed to produce in free societies. In carrying the practical struggle in which we are engaged on to its successful conclusion, we also need to make sure of the grounds of our faith in the ideals and methods of a free society, and we need to make sure that these grounds are moral and religious in quality, not matters of external prudence, policy, material gain, ease and comfort.

I suppose that in any modern war, every people engaged in combat needs to be supported by the belief that its cause is morally right and that the enemy stands for forces that are unjust and unrighteous. But in what I just said I have something quite other in mind than an effort to gird our loins for energy in the existing conflict. It is even likely that our achievement in winning the peace after the war is won will depend in some measure upon the degree in which we have taken thought about the moral values of a free society and have rededicated ourselves to their promotion. In any case the present situation is an opportunity, indeed an urgent challenge, to become more deeply aware of the significance of freedom of mind in a free society than we have been:—aware, that is, of the moral values which legal and political forms and methods exist to support and help bring to fruition.

The need for this new realization is illustrated in the fact that after all there is probably no real cause for great astonishment at the resurrection of the ideals and methods of absolutistic societies. For moral absolutism has marked the greater part, by far the greater part, of human history; in comparison, it is the morality of a free society which is the new thing—one might almost say, is the upstart. I would not assert that the absolutist morality that was embodied for untold generations in social institutions was a slave morality. But it did hold in effect if not always in words that in the great mass of people the mind is too weak and character too corrupt to be trusted with freedom, so that social order depends upon the possession of moral authority by a few who have power to impose obedience to moral principles upon the mass. Changes in science and industry might do away with the particular forms through which the old moral code operated. But why should we be surprised that the habits, attitudes and beliefs that developed in the centuries in which this code had institutional incarnation should attempt to grasp the new forces and to utilize them to assert once more the morality of authority, and of discipline, submission and obedience of the many to the few who wield the authority? The question is a speculative one. But nonetheless asking it may help us realize that the emergence of free societies constitutes a moral revolution as well as a political one, and that the permanence of the democratic political order depends upon the energy and sincerity with which we devote ourselves to maintenance of the moral foundations of a free society.

It is often said that the moral and religious import of the struggle now going on is the necessity of maintaining inviolate the sacred character of human personality. There is without doubt a sense in which the statement is true. But like all generalities it is open to various interpretations. It is possible for persons to uphold it who have radically different ideas about the place of freedom of mind and conscience, and of the rights of free communication in the constitution of human personality. It is possible to hold this view without realizing that the moral change involved in the creation of free societies centres about the belief that personality is something that cannot be achieved and maintained without freedom of thought and freedom of communication. For, to repeat, the long course of history is marked by the belief that the true principle of personality depends upon unquestioning submission to superior moral authority exercised and imposed from without. Otherwise how can we explain the very late appearance of religious toleration, and the abolition of special tests of belief as a condition of citizenship?

The depth of the hold of some form of moral absolutism may be measured by asking the question: To what extent shall we tolerate the right to hold and promulgate views that influential groups within society believe are morally injurious? Do not most of us at bottom believe that certain views have a quality akin to that of infectious disease, and that as it is in the interest of the units composing society to prevent the spread of the latter, so there is a right, nay a duty, to use the coercive force of organized society to stamp out opinions whose spread constitutes a moral epidemic, a social plague? At all events, historic events prove that it is not only possible to take this position and to support it by systematically reasoned moral philosophy, but that it is also possible to hold that only by such methods can true moral personality be protected and conserved.

The second of the freedoms of the socalled Atlantic charter

reads "the freedom of every person to worship God in his own way everywhere in the world." Does this freedom include a right *not* to worship any God in any way? Does it include the right to be an atheist? Or since our own practice gives an affirmative reply in carrying the principle of political tolerance to the point where no restriction as to religious belief is imposed as a condition of full citizenship and professed atheists enjoy all political and legal rights, let us ask the important question: Upon what does our practice rest? Does it rest upon faith in the intrinsic principle of freedom of mind? Or to what extent is it a product of a combination of indifference with belief that historic events have proved that it is too much of a practical nuisance in its direct consequences to try to suppress religious error, even though the suppression is theoretically justifiable?

I do not ask this question in order to discuss the answer that should be given to it. I use it to illustrate the point that belief in freedom of intelligence as the central social value and the source of other social goods is a recent affair, going contrary to the principles by which societies have been regulated during the greater course of history. The founders of existing free societies were inventors and pioneers in a moral sense even more than in a political way. There is nothing new in the statement that freedom of the mind is the fundamental and central freedom in maintenance of a free society. What I have been saying is but a repetition of that statement with emphasis upon two considerations that are involved in it. One of them is that wholehearted and single-minded belief in this proposition commits us to the belief that freedom of intelligence is the central article in the moral creed of a free society. The other is that this belief goes contrary to the principles of the moral code upon which societies have been organized during, by far, the greater part of human history.

This underlying principle of moral absolutism has two roots and two trunks. One of them is that the basic truths by which society ought to be governed are primarily in the possession of a relatively small group, which, in virtue of their possession of it, are morally entitled to be what the Nazis call "leaders" of the mass. The other and counterpart principle is that the great mass of the people cannot be trusted to arrive at possession of these truths and an ability to control their own lives by them save under the guidance of those whose monopolistic possession of ultimate social and moral truths gives them the responsibility as well as the right of leadership. The duty and right of others is disciplined obedient subjection to the moral authority of moral leaders.

It is a convenient simplification to regard the philosophy of Fascist and Nazi enemies as unadulterated worship of sheer force and a denial of the worth of any and all moral principles. The simplification may serve temporarily to stir the sluggish; and far be it from any intelligent person to question the role actually played in totalitarian countries by sheer desire for power and the rewards power brings with it. But the actual case is more dangerous for us than any love of power could be that laid no claim to moral support. What makes Nazi possession of power so extremely perilous for all other interests than their own is just the fact that so many firmly believe that it is used for high social ends, and that its victory will contribute positively to the order and peace of all societies. Force that nakedly presents itself as such has never retained power for a long time. When rule is found to rest merely upon superior force its days are numbered. In order to be able to control the lives of men, a ruling power has to clothe its power with authority, with what is at least a semblance of right.

It is through contrast with the moral philosophy of possession of authority by a given class or group and the consequent right of this group to decide what subjects may or may not believe that the moral philosophy of a free society gains its outstanding significance. Nothing could be a weaker basis for justifying freedom of thought and conscience than the notion that ideas and beliefs exist merely inside us so that there is a gap between them, between mind and action. I do not suppose that anybody would put down in black and white a belief that the reason freedom of mind and thought can be allowed is because they make little difference in what men actually do. Yet the doctrine of pretty complete divorce between beliefs which are intellectual or mental and actions which are practical and overt, between ideas within and the world without, played a part in securing the amount of freedom of mind that obtains at present. It was even argued that freedom of mind could not be hindered anyway, but only freedom of speech, as if conditions of action, including those of communication with one's fellows, do not seriously affect our ability to inquire, reflect and judge. On this point we may at least learn something from Nazi philosophy. For their methods evince profound respect for the power of ideas to sway action, including large scale action involving large numbers.

Thus we are brought again to the crucial question of the moral convictions and ideals of a free society. If we learn from Nazi philosophy and practice that the practical importance of ideas is so immense that nothing else compares with them for power in the long run—as a great American liberal has said—, if we learn only that and nothing else, then we shall be committed to imitating their methods of inculcating one fixed set of ideas: The method of filling the air with certain notions every minute of the day and suppressing the expression of every inquiry, opinion and belief that might in any way compete, concentrating the use of that method upon the young who are ingenuous. In so doing we take over in effect the basic tenets of the totalitarian moral code. We express acceptance of the ideas that the truths which have the authority to direct social action are by right the possession of a small superior elite, and that the mass of human beings cannot be trusted to judge and to believe aright in moral matters; that if they are permitted to exercise freedom of mind their policies and decisions will be so swayed by personal and class interests that the final outcome will be division, conflict and disintegration.

If we take the contrary view and hold that freedom of mind is the root of other freedoms and that political and legal institutions are just and worthy in the degree in which they spring from and manifest freedom of mind, the present situation forces us to face the question of the reasons that justify our faith. How shall we defend ourselves against the charge that since moral truth is one and immutable, we can expect only chaos and confusion to result from entrusting its enunciation and reception to the clamor of many voices? How shall we meet the principle that moral truths require authoritative assertion and obedient acceptance, not debate and discussion?

Although negative reasons do not suffice to justify positive faith, yet some that were mainly negative were influential in bringing men to believe in the advantages of free society. What is more important, they point to something positive and constructive. The bankruptcy of absolutist societies played a large part in turning thought and action toward the ideal of self-government. It demonstrated that irresponsible power is poison; that it infects those who use it even more deeply than those upon whom it is directed. Popular government brought with it distribution and decentralization of power, and putting the matter in its very lowest moral terms, it proved that abuses of power tend to offset one another when power to make and enforce social regulations is widely distributed.

Even if it is supposed that those who have the power and who assume the authority to dictate the beliefs and aims of others are in possession of moral truth, history shows that being human they are moved by egotism and love of power for its own sake. We may indeed safely assert that the more certain a group is that it has a monopoly of ultimate moral truth, the more insensate and ruthless will it be if it possesses the power to regulate the lives and property of others, and that there is no kind of power over others as complete as that conferred by ability to regulate their beliefs. Hence the policy of spreading power by widening the area of free inquiry and free communication appealed to the founders of free society as the only safe policy—just as continual extension of the area of subjugation of peoples, bringing them under the heel of absolutism, is the only safe policy for totalitarian states.

This fact, call it negative if you will, points unerringly to the fact that moral truth which has to be physically enforced, or which does not depend upon moral means for its acceptance, ceases to be true. It is corrupted by the means used to secure its recognition, and the corruption is the more certain to occur in the case of those who wield coercive power than in the case of those who are forced to submit. In the particular case of the absolute states we are combatting I do not suppose the incompatibility between principles and ends that claim moral authority and imposition by physical force needs to be argued. The point is brought up because it proves the identity of ends aimed and the means used to realize them in every case of social morality. It is a lesson hard to learn that the means we use decide the kind of ends, the consequences, that actually come into existence. Impatience has always made men want to take short cuts to attain ends they are persuaded are good. They have not been aware that in using other methods than those which are fundamentally educative they show lack of faith in the intrinsic power of the moral principles they profess to make their own way.

Free societies exhibit many shortcomings. For the most part, however, they are due to failure to live up to their own professed ideals in the methods employed for achieving their ends. Assertion of freedom of mind and of freedom of communication as fundamental principles of social order and progress are assertions of the identity of the cause of moral and religious aims with decisions and choices that are reached by the exercise of a free intelligence which is disciplined and developed by partaking actively with others in a common and cooperative quest. This position marks the most momentous change of all human history. The moral principle involved in it is the most difficult to carry into effect of the ideals and faiths that have marked human life on earth. Totalitarian states would not have had the degree of success they have achieved in revival of moral absolutism, even temporarily, if it were not agreeable to human nature to shift to others the responsibility that goes with freedom. Mussolini made part of the reputation of Fascism in Italy by calling upon the young to "live dangerously." If living dangerously means something more than living recklessly and thoughtlessly, if it means daring to take personal part in reaching decisions and forming policies on matters of utmost social moment, then the very nature of a free society is to demand of its members to live with moral nerves constantly on the alert and moral muscles taut for action. One of our shortcomings has been in persuading ourselves and others that the life of a free society is the easy way of life. If the charge that we have dwelt too much upon rights and too little upon duties has a meaning, that meaning lies just here. In a free society rights and duties are not opposed to each other, but the right to be free is identical with the duty to be unremittingly on edge to learn and to do what we can to make whatever we learn available to others.

As a matter of general social philosophy and of scientific sociological doctrine, there is much to be said for the proposition that the essence and life blood of human society, that which makes our connections with one another genuinely social, not just physical, is the existence of *communication*—the fact that by means of language the net outcome of every experience, the meaning of every discovery, the occurrence of every fresh insight and stimulating outlook can be communicated to others, thereby becoming a common possession. And the entire process of education has for its foundation the fact that mind and character

develop through contact and intercourse. The pains taken in totalitarian states to use schools, press, books, pulpit, public meetings, radio, and even personal conversation, as a means for in-
stilling a single uniform set of ideas is a backhanded tribute to
the identity of freedom of mind with the existence of a free
society.

I have said that the long course of history is marked by twin
beliefs in a closed system of moral principles and a select group
of persons who are the possessors and distributors of these principles. In the abstract, it is possible to make a better defense of
this philosophy than we have been accustomed to believe. Moral
truths have such a direct and urgent connection with the ordering of social relations that there must be, so it is said, a code
which is completely fixed in its essentials and which it is the duty
of some group having authority to make known and enforce.
The Nazis might claim that the change they have introduced concerns only use of all the methods, techniques, and instrumentalities of modern science to ensure common acceptance of a
common body of social principles, leaving behind the clumsy
methods of earlier ages which are still employed by democratic
countries. In a way Carlyle set forth the underlying principles of
moral absolutism when he ridiculed popular government by
comparing it to having a number of men settle the truths of the
multiplication table by discussion and voting, inquiring in effect
whether mathematical or moral truths are more important for
the right ordering of social relations. There should be no dodging
the fact that free societies rest upon the belief that the moral
principles applicable to the concrete problems and issues of human relations are not a tight closed system already in possession
of some authority, but are open to continual inquiry and discovery and retain their freshness and vitality only in consequence of
continued search and continued communication.

This attitude is caricatured by believers in fixed and absolutistic moral authority by representing that it is a denial of the
existence at present of any stable regulative principle. It no more
implies such a conclusion than the necessity for continuous inquiry in the natural sciences implies that without this constant
search we should not know that fire burns and water quenches
thirst. The implication in one case as in the other is that what we
already know may and should be used to learn more, and that in

the case of moral insight it is even more necessary than in the case of physical knowledge that what is known be kept alive in the give-and-take of free communication. Belief in a closed and fixed system of truth grew up in and was appropriate to societies that were bound by more than iron-hoops of custom. Now that social change is the rule and changes occur with accelerated speed, the need is imperative that abstract moral principles be constantly translated into the concrete terms of needs and possibilities which are new. There are but two methods by which to achieve this translation. One is that of dependence upon external authority; the other is that of continual search and continual communication of what search discloses. There was a time when it was supposed that in astronomy and physics the method of free inquiry could result only in intellectual confusion. That exercise of the same method, checked by tests inhering in general diffusion, is as required and as rewarding in matters of social morality and even of vital religious faith is a lesson harder to learn. It will require the unremitting effort of many more persons acting together than was needed in physical science.

The shock given to members of free societies by revival of moral and social absolutism may properly have the effect of making us inquire how far our own failure to live up to the principles and ideals of free society has played a part in producing the revival. I believe one such failure can be pointed out with considerable assurance. Upholders of free institutions have been altogether too ready to assume that competent freedom of mind is a native, an aboriginal possession of every normal human being. In consequence we have not given sufficient attention to the conditions that are required if the potential intelligence of individuals is to become an effective reality. We have too often believed that all that was needed is removal of legal and political restrictions, and that with their abolition, liberty of mind would come into full operation. This negative view of freedom is the root of the defects in our socalled "individualism," defects which are justly criticized. We have tried to justify freedom of speech, conscience, assembly and publication on the ground of a freedom already possessed, rather than on the ground that they are necessary agencies in creation of freedom of mind. A right of free expression that is hardly more than a right to spill over in public whatever an alleged purely "private mind" happens to think does not go far. The freedom of mind that justifies faith that it is the sheet anchor of other freedoms is something to be developed, and the conditions which nurture it require unremitting attentive care.

One instance of our failure to attend sufficiently to the conditions by which freedom of mind is made a reality (which is the same as saying an effective operating force) is found in our neglect of the great role played by industrial conditions. Conditions of work are the conditions under which the great mass of persons form their habitual attitudes; they engage in it every day, and it is the means by which they support their families as well as themselves. The habits formed are intellectual and moral, not simply physical. Free communication is a means of developing free mind as well as being the manifestation of such a mind, and it occurs only when there exists sharing, partaking, in common activities and enjoying their results. Belief that free societies have limited freedom unduly to political, in isolation from economic, affairs, accompanied with the assertion that totalitarian societies will provide a more widespread liberty in this respect than democratic societies have done has played its part in winning approval of their claims.

In some cases, it has even led persons in our own society, as well as in Great Britain, to the approval of suppression of civil liberties in a totalitarian state on the ground that this temporary suppression is a necessary part of the operation of establishing a society that is industrially free. Impatience with the slower processes of communication and education misleads persons animated by generous hopes into neglect of the fundamental principle that a society which is better and freer in any respect whatever, that of economic relations included, can be brought into being only by free means—which means extension, not restriction, of agencies of free communication. There is no delusion more deadly than belief that the ends of a free society can be forwarded by methods that involve suppression of the central freedom of free conscience, free inquiry and free speech. In times of distress and uncertainty there is one standard those who believe in free society can unfailingly use: Does a given society and a given movement depend upon extension or upon restriction of the various agencies in which freedom of mind is expressed and by which it is fed and developed?

Another illustration brings me, fortunately, closer to the cause we are commemorating today. The faith of the American people in education has sometimes been criticized and ridiculed on the ground that education has been made a religion, and, in the mind of its critics, a fetich. I know of no illustration of the fact that the kind of freedom of mind which sustains and justifies a free society is the product of deliberate social nurture carried on by processes of constant communication that include continuous sharing, a continuous give-and-take of ideas, experience, knowledge and beliefs in order to create a common moral attitude and outlook than just the devotion to education, of which we are celebrating today one noble example.

The obviously undeniable thing to be said about religion in a free society is that the right of conscience and belief applies with peculiar force in freedom of worship, and that it is secure only where toleration extends beyond merely enduring something that must be borne lest worse things follow. Genuine toleration does not mean merely putting up with what we dislike, nor does it mean indifference and a conviction that difference of faiths is of no importance because none of them matters. It includes active sympathy with the struggles and trials of those of other faiths than ours and a desire to cooperate with them in the give-and-take process of search for more light. But we can go further than the right of worship and the duty of tolerance. Search for ever more and more wisdom and insight may become intense enough to have religious quality. And this religious quality is strengthened and deepened by realization that discovery of the truth that governs our relations to one another in the shared struggles, sorrows and joys of life is our common task and winning it our common reward. There may be, there will be differences on many points. But we may learn to make these differences a means of learning, understanding that mere identity means cessation of power of growth. Amid all differences of religion, we may, I believe, be one in the belief that the religion of a free society includes faith in the possibility of continued development; search for new truth as a condition of growth, and that mutual respect and regard which constitute charity as the inspiration of peace and good will among men.

The Penning-in of Natural Science

In the pages of the March issue of the British *Literary Guide and Rationalist Review*—a journal which should be better known in this country—I have recently read of a series of talks over the British Broadcasting Radio. On two of them the cause of Scientific Humanism was presented by Julian Huxley and Gilbert Murray; in the third a reply was made by a theologian, Dr. Oldham. It would be interesting to read all three, but as far as I know a report is not accessible in this country. The brief account given in the rationalist monthly contains, however, quotations from the address of the theological contributor. I propose to use two of them as a text for some comments.

One passage reads: "In the scientific approach the individual stands over against the world which he seeks to understand and to shape according to his purpose. This attitude is essentially individualistic." This passage is fairly typical of the anti-scientific campaign now taking place—a campaign that can be interpreted as a promising sign provided it is not over-hopeful for us to find in it evidence that scientific humanism is becoming "dangerous" to the reactionaries. The passage is however most significant as an indication of the misrepresentations (amounting to reversal in this case,) of what scientific method and results stand for. For if there is anything in the world that is not "individualistic" in approach, attitude or consequences it is science. Every scientific worker operates with a capital which is the outcome of the cooperative cumulative work done for countless ages by multitudes of human beings all over the world, each of these workers in his own time and place being also dependent upon the non-individualistic work previously done. And every result obtained by any scientific worker enters at once into an ongoing stream of

[First published in *Humanist* 4 (Summer 1944): 57–59.]

non-self, (and non-selfish), non-personal knowledge—which although a stream is more solid than the granite rock that crumbles, instead of growing, through the ages.

I don't suggest, however, that theologians are those originally responsible for the creation and cultivation of this radically inverted view of science. Frankness demands recognition of the fact that a long line of philosophers in the theories of knowledge they have presented have treated knowledge as if it were a product of socalled "individual minds." Even today one can read most of the psychological books which come from the press without finding any intimation that knowledge is through and through a socio-cultural fact. This otherwise strange fact is to be understood as itself a socio-cultural inheritance from a certain historic period. Most of the movements and achievements that are distinctively "modern," science included, involved revolt against established institutions and against traditions that carried a great emotional load. Revolt treated old institutions and traditions as identical with the "social" revolts as if they were "individualistic," though in fact they were through and through as "social" in origin and purport as were the habits and institutions they were replacing.

Candor and intelligence demand recognition also of the fact that habits which are still prevalent and highly influential (even among scientific workers) tend to keep the socio-cultural foundations and properties of scientific knowledge within the limits of a specialized field, a limitation that tends to render "science" technical in a non-humanistic sense; or, in positive terms, that tends to prevent application or use of the scientific approach in the social affairs which contain the serious moral problems of our own time. The cause of scientific humanism may well learn from this fact. It may—and, if it is to prosper, should—ally itself with every effort to break down the notion that the natural and proper concern of natural science is with an "external" and "physical" world. This view is itself an inheritance from a prescientific age in which man was placed outside and above, instead of within nature; an inheritance which at the present time must be ranked as *anti*-scientific.

Another passage is to the effect that the scientific humanist view ignores "the fact of conflict, which is the inevitable consequence of individuality." Since science is anything but "individualistic" the statement is absurd on its face. But the passage may be used to call attention to the fact that "conflict" in scientific operations is a form of competition that carries forward a common enterprise in which all share and all are concerned to promote. Of the kind of competition that marks science one can say with truth what is often falsely asserted about competition in money-making:—namely, that it promotes helpful cooperation in a common cause. If the word "conflict" is used at all in connection with the advance of knowledge it should be used with recognition of the immense gap that separates it from physical conflict—a gap so intrinsic that it would be well not to use the same word in the two cases.

Here too the humanistic movement needs to ally itself with every movement, from any quarter, which serves to develop widespread recognition of the high morale that is potentially present in the scientific attitude. And to this recognition must be joined the fact that this potentiality is as yet far from actualization. For science is still often and influentially relegated to a field which becomes technical in just the degree to which it is cut off from human affairs and humane values. What needs to be emphasized is that the old belief in the supremacy of the supernatural is at the basis of the common separation of man and his moral concerns from the rest of nature; that this separation is ground for the dividing line still commonly drawn between "natural" and "moral" science; and that this line in turn rests upon identification of natural science with subjects taken to be exclusively physical and material. The idea that natural science has to do with an "external" world comes near to being the height of intellectual perversion and of moral ineptness at a time when about every concrete fact in every phase of human life, along with every serious human problem, is what it is because of applications in human life of the *conclusions* of sciences that are alleged to be merely physical, while the scientific *attitude* and method are notable for their absence in connection with these affairs and problems.

The present organized anti-scientific campaign can be turned to significant use if it becomes a means for bringing into existence a widespread recognition of the limitations which still hem in the application of scientific method. It should result in seeing that the evils now laid at the door of science are in fact due to maintenance of the very split between nature and man, between the material and the "ideal," between the physical and the moral, which are products of the knowledge and lack of knowledge characteristic of the earlier pre-scientific stage of mankind.

The Revolt against Science

It would be a waste of time to argue that at the present time we are in the presence of a widespread revolt against science, for its presence is obvious in almost every field. In education it takes the form of setting the humanities up against the sciences, accompanied with the clamorous assertion that all the ailments and failures of the present school system—numerous and serious beyond a peradventure—are the result of subordination of the "humanities" to the sciences. And if I place quotation marks about the word *humanities* it is because the attack which is made in this field proceeds *from* teachers of literary subjects and proceeds *by* identification of the humane with the linguistic and literary.

Upon the side of theory, of pseudo-philosophy, the attack rests upon calling the sciences "materialistic" while literary subjects are identified with whatever is idealistic and "spiritual" in our traditions and institutions. This position rests back upon belief in the separation of man from nature. Man is taken not only as Lord over Nature but as Lord in its oldest and most discredited sense—that of a despotic monarch supposed to rule by mere fiat. This separation, the most fundamental of all forms of isolationism, completely ignores the daily interests and concerns of the great mass of human beings which are bound up in the most intimate way with the conditions of nature they have to face—conditions which so largely affect their welfare and destiny as human beings. Any one who will allow himself to observe the spectacle offered to view by the great mass of human beings in the matter of making and having a decent living alone, will be aware of the monstrous insolence of identification of the humanities with linguistics and literatures.

[First published in *Humanist* 5 (Autumn 1945): 105–7.]

The fact, however, that the identification is made and that the indictment of the sciences is then made to depend upon it is intensely illuminating. It spotlights the background of the revolt against science; it delineates the genuinely humane values and ends at stake, and points to the only road which leads to a genuine and not a sham, advancement of humanism. With reference to the background, with reference to the source of the revolt, it points straight to those who have "authority" against movements which threaten their supremacy by ushering in a new, wider and more humane order. Fundamentally, the attack proceeds from representatives of those who have enjoyed the power of control and regulation of other human beings because of the existing setup in political, ecclesiastical and economic institutions. Superficially and more vocally, it proceeds from teachers who find that their place and prestige in the educational system is being impaired, and who innocently, that is ignorantly, do the work of campfollowers.

It will be found significant as well as interesting to compare the present revolt against science with the earlier movement that bears the name of "Conflict of Science and Religion." In that earlier warfare, attacks upon science hinged upon certain general conclusions reached by the sciences, first in astronomical and finally in biological science. The attacks centered upon the destructive doctrinal effect of the new conclusions upon beliefs that had been established in a primitive stage of human history, and that, in the course of intervening millennia, had become invested with all kinds of intellectual, institutional and emotional sanctions.

It can hardly be said that the scientific doctrines won a complete victory. "Fundamentalism" is still rife in both Roman Catholic and Protestant denominations. But upon the whole the climate of opinion became adjusted to the new views. Attacks upon them are now of sectarian rather than of general social importance. The present revolt against science goes deeper than the earlier one—and this in spite of victories won by scientific men in the intervening period. We no longer have a battle between a new set of beliefs in special matters and old ones which had endeared themselves to the human heart. The attack upon science is now an attack upon the attitude, the standpoint, the methods, which *are* science, with especial reference to their bearing upon human institutional problems, focussing on the supreme issue of who and what shall have authority to influence and to give direction to life.

I shall not attempt here to criticize the underlying philosophy used to provide justification for the attack upon science whenever anyone ventures to apply scientific methods and results beyond the technical "material" now so charitably allotted to it—provided of course it doesn't dare to trespass upon the moral domain of humane concerns. I want rather to point out some of the factors which confer a show of justification upon the attacks made upon science as "materialistic," and upon its materialism as hostile to the humane values. We are all familiar with the distinction commonly drawn between "pure" and "applied" science. I do not intend to repeat here a point which I have repeatedly made elsewhere—namely, that the sharp division which is made is an intellectual relic from the time when, in Aristotle's phraseology, "theory" had to do with things which were supreme because divine and eternal and "practice" had to do with things that were merely mundane, things at worst menial and at best earth-bound and transient.

I want rather to call attention to the fact that however good may be the grounds a small class of intellectuals have for keeping pure and applied science apart, the great mass of people come in contact with "science" *only* in its applications. Science to them *is* what it means in their life day by day; the consequences it has on their daily occupations, the uses, enjoyments and limitations of use and enjoyment that mark their lives in homes, neighborhoods and factories; on their work and in failures to get work.

"Applied" science means, then, somewhat quite different to them from what it means to the philosopher who is engaged in making distinctions. It means something quite different from what it means to the inventor who is engaged in translating mathematical-physical formulae into machines and other power-devices. For it doesn't mean to him technology in the abstract; it means technology *as it operates under existing political-economic-cultural conditions.* Here and not in science, whether pure or abstract, is where materialism as the enemy of the humane is found; and here, not elsewhere, is where attacks should be directed.

When those who pridefully label themselves humanists, guardians of the moral and ideal interests of mankind, begin to attack the habits and institutions which cause the technological applications of science to work with harshness on such vast portions of the population, limiting alike their education and their other opportunities for a generous human life, transforming the potential instruments of security into devices for producing mass-insecurity, shall we have reason for believing that their concern for humane values is honest instead of a device, deliberate or innocent, for maintaining some form of institutionalized class interest. *Human is as human does.*

Democratic versus Coercive
International Organization
The Realism of Jane Addams

The republication of *Peace and Bread* is peculiarly timely. Jane Addams' book is a record, searching and vivid, of human aspects of the First World War. It gives a picture of the development of American sentiment from 1914 to 1922, the year of its first publication. It is a forceful reminder of things that would be unforgettable, did we not live on the surface of the current of the day's events. Her book takes us through the earliest period when that war seemed remote and unreal, and the American public reacted with incredulity and exasperation; through the phase of gradual hardening into sullen acceptance of war as a fact; to the time when, after a delay of two and a half years, we responded to the declaration of war with enthusiastic participation in which the earlier all but universal pacifism was treated as cowardly retreat or as actively treasonable; and then through the post-war years of disillusionment and reaction.

These facts the older ones among us have largely forgotten and the younger ones never knew. The picture the book gives would be of great present value if it merely communicated the warning and gave the instruction provided by traits common to the First World War and to the present war which now afflicts the world on an even greater scale. But the warning and the instruction are increased rather than diminished, when we include in the reckoning certain matters which make the American attitude and response during the present war very different from that of thirty years ago, and that of the eight or ten years immediately following. A brief statement of some of these differences will, I think, disclose the nature of the increased timeliness.

Conditions at home as well as abroad produced a reaction to

[First published in Jane Addams, *Peace and Bread in Time of War*, anniversary ed., 1915–1945 (New York: King's Crown Press, 1945), pp. ix–xx.]

the outbreak of the European war in 1939 very different from that which greeted the events of 1914. Even only eight years after that date Miss Addams could write, "It is impossible now to reproduce that basic sense of desolation, of suicide, of anachronism, which the first news of war brought to thousands of men and women who had come to consider war as a throwback in the scientific sense." And she could also write, "It is very difficult after five years of war to recall the attitude of most normal people during those first years"—years when the reaction against war "was almost instantaneous throughout the country." What was difficult then is practically impossible now. Instead, we have an accentuation of that later development when, as Miss Addams wrote in 1922, "We have perforce become accustomed to a world of widespread war with its inevitable consequences of divisions and animosities."

It is characteristic of the change that, while some thirty years ago the idea of a war to end wars could be taken seriously, we now indulge only in the modest hope of being able to establish a peace that will last a generation or two. Even more significant is the change in the attitude of those who have opposed our taking part in the two wars. In the case of the first war, it was the sense of the stupidity and immorality of war *as war* that animated the opposition. In the case of the present war, vocal opposition came most conspicuously from the nationalistic isolationism that wanted to keep *us* out of the devastation of war, while those who favored participation were those who, for the most part, took the ground of moral obligation.

There is, I believe, nothing paradoxical in saying that such differences as these, great as they are, increase, instead of lessen, the warning and the instruction, the timeliness, of the book Miss Addams wrote almost a quarter of a century ago. The *warning* is against adoption and use of methods which are so traditional that we are only too likely to adopt them:—methods which are called "Terms of Peace," but which in fact are but terms of a precarious interim between wars. The *instruction* concerns the need for adoption of methods which break with political tradition, which courageously adventure in lines that are new in diplomacy and in the political relations of governments, and which are consonant with the vast social changes going on everywhere else.

The term "pacifist" has unfortunately assumed a more restricted meaning during recent years. It used to apply to all persons who hoped and worked for a world free from the curse of war. It has now come to stand almost exclusively for those who are opposed to war under any and all conditions. On the other hand, the significance of the phrase "Peace Movement" has deepened. It used to stand for something which upon the whole was negative, for an attitude that made it easy to identify pacifism with passivism. A large measure of credit for producing this latter change must go to Jane Addams. In her book *The Newer Ideals of Peace,* published some years before the outbreak of World War One, she set forth aims and methods that are so intimately connected with *Peace and Bread* that the two books form a whole. The aims and methods set forth in both are of a kind that more than justify her in referring to them as "vital and dynamic."

Their nature may be gathered from the vigor with which she repudiated accusations that were freely and ungenerously brought against her and her fellow-workers. Speaking of the state of affairs before the First World War, she writes, "The world was bent on change, for it knew that the real denial and surrender of life is not physical death but acquiescence in hampered conditions and unsolved problems. . . . We pacifists, so far from passively wishing nothing to be done, contended on the contrary that this world crisis should be utilized for the creation of an international government able to make the necessary political and economic changes which were due; . . . it was unspeakably stupid that the nations should fail to create an international government through which each one, without danger to itself, might recognize and even encourage the impulses toward growth in other nations." And again she writes, "We were constantly accused of wishing to isolate the United States and to keep our country out of world politics. We were of course urging a policy exactly the reverse, that this country should lead the nations of the world into a wider life of co-ordinated political activity."

Miss Addams repeatedly called attention to the fact that all social movements *outside* of traditional diplomacy and "international law" had been drawing the peoples of different countries together in ever closer bonds, while war, under modern conditions, was affecting civilian populations as it had never done before. Both of these factors have immensely increased since she wrote. The futility of dependence upon old methods, which is referred to in the passage just quoted, has correspondingly increased. Many persons, among whom the present writer enrolls himself, who are not pacifists in the absolute sense in which Miss Addams was one, believe that she has clearly indicated the directions which all peace efforts must take if they are not to be doomed in advance to futility.

Miss Addams remarks in *Peace and Bread* that "Social advance depends as much upon the process through which it is secured as upon the result itself." When one considers the intimately human quality of her writings it sounds pedantic to say that this sentence conveys a philosophy, one which underlies what she has to say about war and the conditions of enduring peace. But the human quality of her position and proposals in this case *is* a philosophy that gives the key to understanding her. Her dynamic and vital contribution to the Peace Movement is her insistence upon the necessity of international organization. Today the idea has become a commonplace. The Wilsonian League of Nations at least accomplished that much. We are assured from all quarters that the Second World War is being fought in order to achieve an organization of nations that will maintain peace. But when we ask about the *process* that is depended upon, we find the word "organization" covers very different things.

The process that looms largest in current discussions is "political" action, by which we usually mean governmental and legal action, together with coercive economic measures. Miss Addams does employ the *word* "political." But the context invariably shows that she uses it in a wide human sense. And while this usage of hers confers upon the word a moral, and in so far an idealistic, significance, her attitude is in fact much more *realistic* than is the attitude that puts its trust in "organization" of the traditional political type. For one can say, with as much justice as is consonant with brevity, that to trust to traditional political "organization" to create peaceful relations between nations involves reliance upon just that exaggerated nationalistic and power politics that has brought the world to its present pass.

In contrast, the process of organization upon which Miss Addams would have us depend is one which cuts *across* nationalistic lines. Moreover, instead of setting up a super-state, it also cuts *under* those lines. Its nature is indicated in a passage which follows the one already quoted, in which she expressed the desire that the United States take the lead in guiding the world "into a wider life of co-ordinated political activity." What fits the United States, Miss Addams holds, for assuming this leadership is precisely the fact that democratic development in this country has in fact increasingly cut under and cut across barriers of race and class. In nothing is Miss Addams' book more timely than in its sense of the positive values contributed by our immigrant populations. The pattern of American life, composed of multiple and diversified peoples, hostile in the countries from which they came but living in reasonable amity here, can and should be used to provide the pattern of international organization. One of the ironies of the present situation is that a war caused in large measure by deliberate Nazi provocation of racial and class animosity has had the effect in this country of stimulating the growth of racial fear and dislike, instead of leading to intelligent repudiation of Nazi doctrines of hate. The heart of the democratic movement, as Miss Addams saw and felt it, is "to replace coercion by the full consent of the governed, to educate and strengthen the free will of the people through the use of democratic institutions" in which "the cosmopolitan inhabitants of this great nation might at last become united in a vast common endeavor for social ends." Since the United States had demonstrated on a fairly large scale the practicability of this method, Miss Addams put her faith in extension of the democratic process to the still wider world of peoples. Its exact opposite she found in the use of "opposition to a common enemy, which is an old method of welding peoples together," a method "better fitted to military than to social use, adapted to a government resulting from coercion rather than one founded by free men."

There are today many persons not pacifists in the present technical sense who will believe that Miss Addams' book is timely because it points directly to the source of the failure of the hopes so ardently entertained a generation ago. Men then thought they could attain peace through an international organization of the traditional political kind, which relies more upon coercive force than upon constructive meeting of human needs. When I try to formulate what Miss Addams wrote informally yet clearly, I come out with a sense of the difference between two methods

and attitudes. On one hand, we can trust to an international political organization of an over-all type to create the organs it requires. On the other hand, we can rely upon organs that have
been formed to take care of human needs (including the need for
change) to develop in the course of their own use an organization
which can be depended upon, because it has become ingrained in
practice. If history has proved anything, it is, I believe, that only
the latter kind of organization is so "vital and dynamic" as to
endure, while the former kind is likely to yield a mechanical
structure of forces so uncertainly "balanced" as to be sure to collapse when old stresses and strains recur in new shapes. It has
become customary to give the name "realistic" to the kind of organization that is based upon opposition to an enemy and that
relies upon armed force to maintain itself. In contrast, the road
indicated by Miss Addams is, I submit, infinitely more "realistic."

There are chapters in *Peace and Bread,* notably the fourth and
the tenth, which supply material that makes concrete and definite
the difference between processes or organizations of the traditional political-legal type, with their emphasis upon force—already war *in posse*—and the human and socially humane processes to which Miss Addams appealed for help. The formation
of UNRRA, even while this war is being waged, is, as far as it
goes, a recognition of the "Food Challenge" for world organization. The energy with which we use and extend this kind of process as the working model for other endeavors at international
organization will decide the success or failure of efforts to achieve
lasting peace. This is no mere prediction, but is based on the
solid experience of the past.

The significance attached by Miss Addams to the need for
food points to a trait which animates almost every page of *Peace
and Bread,* for the association of the two words in the title is fundamental. The need for bread is a symbol of the importance ac-
corded by Miss Addams to natural impulse and primitive affection. Her faith in them was the source of her interest in "social
settlements"; it was nourished by the experiences that centered
in Hull House. All who knew Miss Addams also know of her insistence that sharing in the activities which issued from Hull
House was not a matter of doing good to others as beneficiaries;
those who took part had more to receive than to give. She had a
deep feeling that the simple, the "humble" peoples of the earth

are those in whom primitive impulses of friendly affection are the least spoiled, the most spontaneous. Her faith in democracy was indissolubly associated with this belief. It permeates what she wrote because it was a part of the life she lived from day to day. Her own life was an active anticipation of what a recent writer has put into words: "Society will develop by living it, not by policing it." Miss Addams did not put her trust in the "Carlyle contention that the peoples must be led into the ways of righteousness by the experience, acumen, and virtues of the great man." Her faith was at the opposite pole. Leaders, whether political or intellectual, were to her trustees for the interests of the common people. Theirs was the duty and the task of giving articulate and effective form to the common impulses she summed up in the word "Fellowship." Were Jane Addams with us today her voice and pen would tell us how the events of the years which have intervened between two World Wars have intensified the evils which will surely follow if leaders betray the trust committed to them—events which have deepened the need for those humane processes and organs which alone can bring hope of enduring peace to a tragically torn and bleeding world.

Key West, Florida
January, 1945

Dualism and the Split Atom
Science and Morals in the Atomic Age

There is an immediate issue and a longtime problem presented by the splitting of the atom and the production of the
atomic bomb. The former naturally engrosses public attention
and public discussion. For it concerns the bearing of the discovery and the invention in question upon the urgent problem of the
security of the peoples of the earth, including most emphatically
our own. The urgency is increased because the bomb appeared
as an agency of destruction toward the close of the greatest scene
of human destruction the world has ever seen. The irony of the
situation is that an instrumentality which was developed as a
means of security during war presents itself in the cold light of
the day after as the greatest threat to security that human imagination can encompass.

The long-term problem concerns the position and the use, actual and potential, of physical science and the technologies of industrial production in present and future human life if it is to be
genuinely humane. The particular development of science and
technology is new. But it is only a consummation of the scientific
and industrial developments of the past. The particular culmination is indeed novel, so novel as to seem sensationally unprecedented. But there is nothing new or unprecedented in the scientific and industrial achievements which have led up to it. And
what is more serious—there is nothing new or unprecedented in
the kind of problem that is presented to mankind: the problem of
systematic use of the resources of physical science and the industry based upon it for human security and well-being, instead of
for insecurity and destruction. The advent of the atomic bomb
dramatizes and highlights issues that have been in active process
for generations. Science and industrial technology are themselves

[First published in *New Leader* 28 (22 November 1945): 1, 4.]

too new to have made their way into the more basic conditions of our civilization. They have been superimposed as external strata upon institutions and habits so old as to be established beyond the reach of easy fundamental transformation.

In short, the splitting of the atom as a scientific discovery and production of the atomic bomb as a technological development bring into central focus events that for a long time have been working in piecemeal and scattered fashion. These events have been going on since the scientific revolution of the seventeenth century and the industrial revolution of the eighteenth and nineteenth. In bringing them to a head, the later development as a summation of what had preceded, forces upon our observation tendencies that we had not previously seen—and to some extent had not wanted to see. No intelligent person can henceforth fail to note that the physical science and the industrial technology of our time are out of gear with the heritage of moral values and aims by which we belatedly profess to live.

It is customary to give the name of "cultural lag" to the discrepancy in question. It is that, of course. But merely calling it a *lag* tends to conceal from view the fateful fact that it brings with it a deep tragic split between what is distinctively human on one side and the science and technology we label merely material on the other side. As long as the split exists, science and technology will too often operate in inhuman ways. Voices that learned their speech in an earlier age are accordingly clamorously putting the entire blame for present evils upon the side of science and technology. They say, these things operate inherently on a material and non-moral plane, and that the uses and enjoyments they have brought to mankind have seduced men from proper care for higher "spiritual" things. The materialistic has thus, they say, been allowed to trespass upon a realm where it has no rights. The remedy is to keep physical science and industrial technology in a strict subjection to what representatives of this group *call* "moral," irrespective of the immense changes that are taking place in all the conditions of human life.

One may, or rather must, agree that something is seriously out of joint. But we may and must radically disagree with the creed as to how integration of life is to be achieved. On one hand, the scientific and industrial revolutions are not the kind of revolutions that go backward. It is idle to suppose that exhortations, addressed chiefly to the emotions, will create subjection to abstract moral principles. The impotency of this method is evident; it has lost the support of the traditions, customs, and institutions which once gave it whatever efficacy it possessed. The loss has come about, moreover, through the practical impact of just the scientific and industrial developments which are deplored. The inefficacy of this method is so obvious that added vigor has been given, on the other hand, to those who urge that our only salvation is in a return to obedient acceptance of externally imposed authority; to one that is said to have a monopoly of the higher moral and "spiritual" truths upon which the ordered life of mankind is dependent; to one that has before our very eyes proved itself ineffective.

The claims of the latter group raise a question of fundamental importance: How far do the confusions and conflicts from which we suffer arise from the perpetuation, under changed conditions, of just the doctrines to which we are urged to return? *For one of the main tenets of the latter was precisely that there is a split in the very nature of things, and hence not to be overcome, between what is "material" and what is moral and ideal—that which is euphemistically and emotionally called "spiritual." And the practical consequences of this division are a large part of just the evils that now need to be overcome.*

If the split in question were merely a matter of something labelled philosophy, it would be too remote and anemic to be of consequence. But theoretical formulation of this division originated as an intellectual expression and attempted justification of established institutional conditions. When the work of the world was done by those who, if not slaves or serfs, were politically disfranchised and who were economically dispossessed and disprivileged, who were morally abject, their menial status was inevitably reflected in the idea that the things and processes with which they were occupied were inherently base. Since the industrial arts were matters of custom, acquired by manual apprenticeship on the part of those who practiced them, "reason" and true science were taken to be the manifestation of faculties possessed only by a superior group.

Industrial arts, or technologies are today the product of inventions made possible only by scientific insight which has been acquired through command of highly intellectualized (or "rational") procedures—a fact dramatically demonstrated in the atomic bomb. But it is still true that the great mass of workers are shut out, because of defective education and economic disadvantage, from sharing in the knowledge on which their work is based. The idea that this subjection would be improved or remedied by still more systematic subjection to external authority is the idea that an evil can be improved by intensifying it. And it is still true that in spite of the abolition of slavery and serfdom by means of political emancipation, the workers of the world have little share in control of the work they perform. Actual institutional conditions are still such as to give color and practical support to the philosophy of separation between matter and mind (even though practical dealings with "matter" are the expression of intelligent understanding), between nature and man, between science and morals. Meantime, the actual conditions that are supposedly justified by this philosophy are the source of the main problems and dangers of our time.

What has all this to do with the atomic bomb? The same conditions that render it a threat to human security and well-being are the kind of thing which, before the bomb was dreamed of, threatened the security of masses of people. The very things that occasion fear that the atomic bomb will add power to the forces of destruction are the kind of things that have created those divisions of classes, groups, races, sects, which in turn create recourse to force as the agency for settling differences and conflicts. The way out is not to return to subjection to the alleged authority of representatives of the dogmas and institutions which embody and perpetuate the divisions from which we suffer. It is to carry forward the application of our best scientific procedures and results so that they will operate within, not just outside of and against, the moral values and concerns of humanity. It is the business of modern man to use every effort to see to it that the immense technological resources now at our command are not limited in use to aims which are degraded in advance as merely material or utilitarian in some low sense, but are systematically employed in behalf of human—that is, common and widespread—security and well-being.

And, underlying and overtopping all, is the fact that if the atomic splitting by science and its technological application in the bomb fail to teach us that we live in a world of change so that our ways of organization of human interrelationships must also change, the case is well-nigh hopeless.

World Anarchy or World Order?

The tragedy of our time is that every person on earth actually belongs to a world unit without being a member of world-society. A society exists only where there is a common rule of law; only where there is the machinery of government which can compose or arbitrate the differences among men. The present machinery for settling disputes is war; not just this or that war, but a system of war which enters into and affects every aspect of the lives of every people on earth. It is accidental because it was carried in on the tide of events. It was not foreseen, nor chosen. Nor was any preparation made to meet the great problems which grew out of the vast new forces which have caught the world without warning.

During the past century the nations of the world have become physically interdependent and tied together in a multitude of ways. This change is by far the greatest in the entire history of man on earth. It has taken place so rapidly that old traditions, customs, institutions, habits of sentiment and belief, deep-seated loyalties, fail to provide a workable machinery for dealing with the transformed scene. But until old traditions and habits are transformed they make us powerless to cope with the problems which are indeed related to those traditions and habits. Our thinking, our moral and emotional conditioning, our entire way of life—all these still belong to that early period in history when the peoples of the earth were truly isolated, having but few points of contact and communication, and these only with nearby neighbors. Wars were correspondingly local.

Contrast that period with our own. The change that has been wrought has its tragic symbol in the fact that twice within a short

[From a typescript in the Rare Book and Manuscript Library, Butler Library, Columbia University, New York, N.Y.]

quarter of a century there have been wars of global dimensions. A world whose parts are intimately tied together, but which has no means of keeping those parts from clashing, is actually anarchy.

This condition of world anarchy is displayed most strikingly in the perpetual threat of global war. But this threat is only one of the symptoms and evidences of a world-chaos due to lack of common rule of law and of the machinery necessary to bring about social adjustments in a peaceful way. Consider the vastly increased destructiveness of war. The atomic bomb alone has the power to destroy the globe. Organized research has utilized all the resources of all the sciences to produce this bomb, the deadliest possible instrument of mass destruction. And yet invention and scientific research are the products of knowledge—knowledge which is available, if we wish it, for constructive action of vast and enduring scope. The perversion and distortion involved in this complete reversal of values is convincing proof of the chaos in which a world finds itself when it has become physically one, but has as yet neither the means nor the machinery to create or maintain a world society.

Just as the conditions and consequences of war today are new, so must there be a new way of thinking, planning, and acting on the part of all the peoples of the earth in order to meet the conditions for survival imposed by an Atomic Age. The unutterable seriousness of the physical, industrial, cultural, moral destructiveness of war must be met and countered by equally serious constructive effort. The extensive range of combat must evoke, if civilization is not to go down in ruin, an even greater manifestation of cooperative goodwill. Oldtime diplomacy, power blocs and power politics, precepts of international law, are themselves among the casualties of modern warfare. They are about as outworn and impotent as the oldtime muzzle-loading gun. We shut our eyes to the realities of the situation at our own peril—and, what is even worse, at the peril of generations to come. If we think and act on the ground that the seriousness of the situation requires only that we put forth greater effort to prepare for victory in the next war, then we shall but increase by that much the disintegration that already exists.

II

The peoples of the earth, not just their governmental officials, must find effective answers to the following questions. Is a world-government possible? How shall it be brought into being? By the unilateral and coercive action of some one nation, or by general cooperative action? What shall be its machinery? What responsibilities shall it possess in order that a common rule of law, expressing the needs of a world-society, may substitute a system of peace and security for the present war system? These questions are urgent; it is imperative to face them at once, directly, and with the utmost seriousness. They are not matters of abstract theory but of utmost practical concern. If we fail to find the positive answers, we succeed in finding the way to a new and final war—final because it will mark the destruction of humanity. Only sheer cynicism and defeatism will deny that it is possible to create a workable world government. There have been times when the moral ancestors of present day defeatists would have scornfully declared that a rule of law over a territory anything like as large as our present United States was impossible. They would have said that outside of family groups and small neighborhoods, the custom of every man's hand against other men could not be uprooted.

In the domestic affairs of a nation it is now established as a matter of course that absence of a rule of law is unthinkable. It is as important that the rule of law be common, applying equally without distinction of privilege and special prerogative, as that it be a rule of law. Perhaps it is even more significant that no great political power doubts the practicability of large-scale planning for war during times of so-called peace, while during the period of actual warfare, planning is applied to almost every detail of life. If peoples, especially their rulers, devoted anything like the energy—physical, intellectual and moral—that now goes into planning for war, to planning for an enduring peace system, they could achieve world government. To surrender to defeatism is for intelligence to abdicate. It is to give up the struggle in a cause in which nothing less than the destiny of civilization is at stake.

It is, however, as necessary to appreciate the immense difficulty of the undertaking as it is to have the will to take unreserved part in it.

How shall we bring about world government? Where shall we take hold? By what means, under what auspices, shall the first steps be taken? Shall the matter be left to some one nation? Or, are world-conditions such that only the cooperative effort of all nations can succeed?

There are memories and traditions which have seemingly served in the past to justify the belief on the part of a powerful state that it alone can establish world peace—that is to say, that by its own will it can order peace. The system here is the system of subjection. These memories come to us from the early temporary success of the wars carried on by Alexander the Great, and from the more enduring Pax Romana of the Caesars. There is also the image of the Holy Roman Empire when the conjoint authority of church and political empire created a kind of moral unity in all of western Europe, that is, all the civilized world as then known.

The defeat of Napoleon's effort to unify Europe by means of force and the recent defeat of the attempt of the Fascist Axis to create a world order indicate that this method of instituting a world order is likely to prove a costly, illusory dream.

Why is it impossible today for a single power, through sheer force, to rule the world? It is impossible because the conditions of the world have been radically transformed. At one time, the peoples of different political units had little contact with one another. Even the contacts of war did not mean much more for the daily lives of people than a change in rulers that made little difference beyond the person to whom tribute had to be paid. Today ties between peoples are so numerous and so close that a coercive unification by the action of some one of them brings about a wrenching and distortion that is intolerable. The attempt to subordinate the lives of different peoples to the pattern of some one State is such a violation of established values as to create a solid block of resistance and antagonism.

Even if outward unification were effected by force, the net result would be far from social unity. It could be maintained only by the further use of force. Instead of providing the kind of peace and security nominally aimed at, it would be a continuation of the anarchy of the war-system. The allegiance yielded by subject peoples would be so reluctant and partial as to be meaningless. Metternich, who was far from averse to use of force in political

matters, once remarked that everything could be done with bay-
onets except to sit upon them.

It is a familiar fact that the Napoleonic wars of conquest gave
an immense momentum to the development of nationalism in
Europe. National states were already taking shape. But resistance to foreign rule was an important factor in transforming a
state of affairs into an idea and an ideal. When this had come
about, nationalism as a conscious principle tended to consoli-
date the formerly disperse political and social forces.

The late nineteenth century and the four decades of the twentieth have seen the same thing take place among the peoples of
Asia. They have changed from loose congeries of local communities, having cultural rather than political unity, into political
organizations with nationalistic aims. The menace of subjection
by foreign powers is bringing about an integration which is tying
together many provinces. Efforts to establish a strong central
government follow. A central government with political, legal,
economic, and military organs did not come before nationalism.
It and nationalism are the products of external pressure. Attachment to these organs grows out of the felt need for protecting
ways of life that have been made familiar and dear through centuries of use and wont.

Ways of living are more deeply rooted than are political affilia-
tions, but they are capable of fusing with the latter. When they
do fuse they form a rock on which the attempt to create a world
order by coercive force is broken into pieces. Nationalism is two-
sided. On one side it consists of those intangible bonds that constitute the distinctive moral and intellectual traditions and outlook of a given social group. As a whole, they bear the name of
culture; a name for the fact that there are ways of living so ingrained by long habituation that they form the very fibre of a
people—a fibre so tough that it will resist, often unto death, attempts made from without to destroy it.

It has now become so plain that only the voluntary cooperation of nations can bring into being a world-society (thereby continuing the process by which small local social units gave up their
isolation) that the remaining question has to do with the means
and methods by which obstacles may be overcome. Among these
obstacles the exclusive and aggressive side of nationalism is conspicuous. On its inclusive side—its side of wider social order and

organization—nationalism constitutes a positive advance. The world-society which alone can succeed in maintaining intact and unchallenged an order of enduring peace and security will have to conserve this advance. It will indeed provide added protection to its values. Otherwise, it will not be able to command the loyal support of the peoples of the earth. It may last for a time in a condition of uneasy balance. But in the end it will go the way in which have gone the attempts to establish a world order by sheer superiority of force. A wider community of interests cannot possibly be attained by the negative process of wiping out the communities of belief, action, and mutual support which have behind them centuries of loyalty. Without a basis in them, a world government would lead a precarious existence. If such a government is to deserve the hearty support of the peoples of the earth, it must actively enlist the energies of the national states as dependable organs for execution of its policies. It can accomplish this result only as those policies give the social values of the National States a more secure opportunity to flourish than they now possess.

In view of the burden now put upon national groups by the war-system, this condition should be relatively easy of fulfillment. Even if at the outset the appeal of a world government for general and popular support is mainly on the ground of the relief it affords from the burdens of the war-system it would make little difference if the world-society has a chance to continue to function. For even the relief provided by a world-society will enable nations to do for themselves the desirable things they are unable to as long as they live under the shadow of the war-system, and the result will be the growth of positive allegiance. The one thing indispensable is to make a beginning.

As has been only too tragically proved by two devastating world-wars the movement toward production of more comprehensive social organization, the very movement that brought national states into being has been violently arrested.

The Crisis in Human History
The Danger of the Retreat to Individualism

No question is more urgent than that raised by the editor of *Commentary*. Answers given in discussion are momentous in practice. For the attitude expressed and developed in public inquiry is inevitably a genuine part of the practical answer that will emerge. It is the initial stage of what appears later as more tangible and seemingly more overt activities. The preliminary phase in which belief-attitudes take shape is too commonly dismissed as if it were merely theoretical and contrasted with something else labelled practical. But nothing is of more practical importance than that the question constituting the issue to be dealt with be rightly put. If we get off on the wrong foot, our behavior in later phases is compromised in advance.

These considerations are pertinent because they are not made in empty air. There is already evidence of danger that the issue is wrongly put—and so may confuse, not direct, action. The danger consists in splitting "individual" and "social" from each other at the very start, and then ending with the discovery that they are in opposition to each other. This overlooks the obvious fact that *the debasement which is going on is of the human being in his entirety,* and not of the person in isolation or of society in abstraction.

At the very best, *individual* and *social* stand for traits of unitary human beings; traits, moreover, which are so integral that they are but two aspects of man in his actual existence. Traits which are differential, singular, or individual, in the constitution of human beings have, undoubtedly, been degraded and violated. But the events forming this debasement are aspects of the degradation and violation of the associative ties that hold human beings together. These "social" ties do not inhere in "individuals";

[First published in *Commentary* 1 (March 1946): 1–9.]

they inhere integrally in human beings in their very humanity. Their connection with the traits that mark one human being off from the other is so pervasive and intimate that what happens to the latter cannot be either understood nor effectively dealt with save as the former are held in full view.

This substitution of "human being" for "individual" is in effect one-half of what I have to say about the question before us. "Individual" is as truly but an adjective as is "social." Each word is a name for what is intrinsic in the constitution and development of human beings. That "social" is an adjectival word is commonly recognized, at least as a grammatical fact. But, "individual" is commonly treated as if it were a noun, standing for an entity complete in itself. If one asks for proof of this statement one has only to note how often the phrase "*the* individual" occurs in current discussion, and then note what would happen if the word "human being" were put in its place. Its substitution would not of itself ensure the right way of putting of the issue. But it would at least permit recognition that traits which are "social," in that they are due to the ways in which human beings are associated, have to be taken into the reckoning.

The difference between stating the issue as one concerning what is happening to human beings in their full human capacity, rather than to "individuals" (or to "the individual") is not verbal. Think of any human being you please. If he is thought of in the concrete not in the abstract, there comes into view a creature born so helpless as to be dependent upon others for his very existence. One is almost ashamed to cite facts which are so obvious that it does not seem possible that they could be systematically neglected. I cite but one. Omit language and other means of inter-communication from the account, and no intellectual development of human beings, even in their differential or individual capacities, is conceivable. Think of any human adult in a concrete way, and at once you must place him in some "social" context and functional relationship—parent, citizen, employer, wage-earner, farmer, merchant, teacher, lawyer, good citizen, criminal—and so on indefinitely. Escape from dealing in empty verbal abstractions (of which Individuality and Society, spelled openly or covertly with capitals, are samples), cease converting them into entities, and it becomes glaringly evident that "social" stands for properties which are intrinsic to every human being.

Extend reflection beyond what is immediately obvious, and it is clear that the variety and scope of the connections for which the word *social* is a shorthand expression, are the determining conditions of the kind of actuality achieved by capacities that are individual or differential.

Nothing that has been said indicates a doubt that there is a serious—an even tragic—crisis of human beings in their status as "individuals." It asserts that there is *equally* a crisis in their status as caught up in a complicated meshwork of associations, and that one crisis cannot be viewed in separation from the other. And I would go further than this generality. The very habit of introducing a separation between them has been a powerful factor in justifying and intensifying the factors of which the present crisis is the overt public manifestation. Put in the language of common use, the movement that goes by the name of *Individualism* is very largely responsible for the chaos now found in human associations—the chaos which is at the root of the present debasement of human beings.

These remarks implicitly contain the other half of what I have to say. Separation and opposition of *individual* and *social* has its roots far back in history. It was initiated when man was linked to "the next world" instead of to his fellows in this world. But it would not have culminated in the crisis of our time had it not been reinforced by newer historical factors. The crisis is the overt manifestation of the conjunction of factors that have been working under cover. It is the cumulative expression of converging forces that had been operating piecemeal for a long time. We can not grasp the significance of the crisis without a long look backward into the abyss of time. We cannot judge how to meet it without a long look ahead. My complementary point, in fine, is that we can understand the crisis only as we take it out of its narrow geographical and temporal setting and view it in long historical perspective.

Otherwise we shall deal only with symptoms. We shall allow what is immediately and urgently before our eyes to block vision of the world-wide and centuries-old scene that gives these only too-present events their significance. I have called the two points made here halves of the same whole. What has been called Individualism and Socialism, and then put in opposition to one another, must also be placed in *their* long historical perspective.

The individualistic movement which preceded the socialistic and which provoked the latter by reaction is itself an illustration of the necessity of paying heed to a long course of events. This statement is true whether we take account of its earlier beneficent liberalizing aspect or its later bankruptcy.

Viewed in this way, individualism in its earlier phase appears as a movement of release. It freed conditions and factors of human life that arose with the insurgence of new forces from control by oppressive institutions—Church and State. The emerging state of human life was not seen, however, as a new system of *social* arrangements in which individual or differential proclivities and interests obtained a release. Old traditions and institutions, which had so largely been oppressive, instead of being supports of organized life, were identified with "social." Freedom was regarded largely as the cutting loose of "the individual" from the "social." This tendency was most marked at first in the development of the new physical science and in the efforts made by agencies of belief-attitudes embodied in old institutions to suppress it by force. Subsequent events in politics and in the industrial and commercial aspects of life continued and intensified the belief that social organization was the enemy of human enlightenment and progress. Something called *the* Individual was made absolute.

For the time being the emancipating release that was taking place in many areas concealed the disintegration that was going on. In particular the executives and administratives of the new movements in production and distribution of goods assumed and effectively taught that they were the chief and indispensable agents of all that was liberating. They were aided and abetted by the restrictive consequences of the perpetuation of feudal customs in industry, politics, and religion. But in noting the historic course of the rise and bankruptcy of the individualistic movement, no mistake is greater than to overlook the substantial *moral* support given to Individualism in its laissez-faire Liberal career by the heritage bequeathed from certain religious traditions. These taught that men as inherently singular or individual souls have *intrinsic* connection only with a supernatural being, while they have connection *with one another* only through the extraneous medium of this supernatural relationship.

There took place a peculiar conjunction of conflict between

the new conditions and the old tradition and an alliance between them. In this conjunction, the moral and religious features of the old tradition were so deployed as to give support to the more in-human of the new conditions, especially in industry. The ambiva-lence of what is called "the individual" cannot be understood without taking into account the underlying alliance as well as the open conflict of old and new. The conflict was exhibited in grad-ual undermining of old institutional arrangements in religion, industry, and politics. But the translation of the antagonisms within a particular kind of "social" organization into inherent separation of "social" and "individual," and the assignment of superiority, authority and prestige in this opposition to "the indi-vidual," could not have taken place unless the latter had ab-sorbed into itself the substance of the moral individualism con-tained in the accepted religious tradition.

II

The upheavals in church and state, which were condi-tions and consequences of the breakdown of long established in-stitutional forms of human association, would not have taken the form they did take apart from the events constituting the In-dustrial Revolution. An incidental, yet significant, illustration of this fact is found in the disruption of old ties that resulted from extensive migrations of peoples from old lands. The immediate occasion was a combination of religious and political factors, to which, later, desire for economic betterment was added. The net effect presented itself as a creative release of personal freedom. But the change, with its breaking off of old institutional ties, could not have taken place without new scientific developments and new technical agencies. In the fusion of scientific, religious, political and industrial motivations and movements, the indus-trial finally gained the upper hand. It gained it, moreover, in a peculiar *economic* form in which the feudal pattern of superior and subordinate reappeared in the disguise of voluntary "indi-vidual" agreements between employer and employed, without the stabilizing features of feudalism. A century ago Carlyle gave this particular aspect of social arrangement the apt name of "cash-nexus." But at the same time his magnification of the hero and his contempt for the masses as literally a mass in the sense in which the mass is an inert lump, is a vivid illustration of union of the old repressive institutionalism with the new "individualism." The ironic upshot was that the merely cash-nexus was to be brought into a state of enduring stability by means of the Captain of Industry in his capacity of conquering hero.

That the new individualism was marked by release of powers of discovery and invention (which are genuine traits of human beings in their severalty or "individuality") is undoubted. But the thing needing explanation is the large part played by them in promoting the conflicts, uncertainties and fears that operated to create a "social" reaction in a totalitarian form. For it cannot be said too often in the present state of opinion that this seemingly sudden *out*break of totalitarian collectivism was in fact the breaking *through* the surface, into overt manifestation, of underlying phases of the previous individualism.

A volume, not a few paragraphs, would be needed to tell in adequate detail how the one-sided "individualistic" passed over into an equally one-sided "socialistic" movement. I have learned more on this matter from Polanyi's *The Great Transformation* than from any other source. It shows in detail how policies that had been justified by the prevailing doctrines of "individualism" created, one by one, evils that demanded special legislative and administrative measures to ensure defense and protection of human interests threatened with destruction. The cumulative effect of these "social" measures was all the greater because they were undertaken piecemeal. Each one was regarded as if it stood alone as a mere specific remedy for some danger or evil also regarded as if it stood alone.

In this connection, it is important for even an elementary understanding of events to observe that not just Russia alone but all fascist countries have professed to be "socialistic," and to be engaged in protecting the great mass of their members from the destructive consequences of those "individualistic" measures, baptized with the names of liberalism and democracy, which had brought the population to a state of miserable insecurity. Placing the socialistic in stark opposition to the individualistic was not the creation of Fascism and Totalitarianism. It was a direct inheritance from the laissez-faire "Liberalism" which arrogated to itself the protection of human "individuals" from oppression by organized society. So-called "free enterprise" in business and finance was taken to be identical with the very essence of freedom. When it became apparent as to such Freedom that its net result was recurrent industrial depressions, each one more severe than its predecessor, in which the mass of human beings were reduced to a state of insecurity and fear, it is hardly surprising that peoples who were already habituated to dependence upon superior political authority preferred "the road to serfdom" which promised them some stability of life. The fact that there were at hand the technical means for the establishment of a decent and secure standard of living immensely brightened the prospect—especially when it was viewed as an alternative.

III

Outwardly, superficially, the change was an abrupt one. It caught the world without preparation. It is this seeming abruptness that makes it the more necessary to pay heed to its deep roots in the past. The generally accepted religion of western Europe played a part as already said, because of its teaching that each human being is "spiritually," and hence fundamentally, an entity whose connections with other human beings exist only in the medium of connection with a supreme over-natural Being, God. It followed that men in themselves are external and physical, rather than morally connected. Indeed, human beings in their "natural" estate were so earthly as to be in themselves standing sources of moral evil. In their natural and secular state they shared in the sinful fall of Mankind. As long as a single ecclesiastical institution dominated the life of western Europe, it could claim to possess and administer the means for filling this moral vacuum. The rise of Protestant dissent contributed to the release of its underlying and basic "individualism."

This isolationism is far from being the only source of the moral phase of the contemporary crisis. A gulf had been established in philosophy in ancient Greece between things that are merely means and things that are exclusively ends; between the "material" and the "spiritual." In early and medieval Christianity, the split ceased to be a matter of philosophy; it was enforced in the habitual attitudes that obtained. The split into mere means and mere ends was most marked in relegation of the economic aspects of human life to that which was base because merely "material." But it affected also the political aspects of life, save as the latter were definitely under domination by the ecclesiastic institution which regarded itself as the sole agency for the higher intrinsic "spiritual" values that were ends in themselves, supreme and ultimate. There is probably no attitude more habitual than the one which regards everything economic as having the status of mere means, because concerned only with "material" things which must then be moralized, if at all, from *without*. The doctrine naturally became effective for harm in just the degree in which industrial, commercial and financial factors have come to hold an ever-increasing importance in actual human life.

The doctrine and its practice were conjoined in a peculiar way that reinforced the beliefs in isolated individualism. Kant taught, for example, that every human individual is an "end-in-himself." The teaching was noble in purpose. It was meant as a protest against despotism in Germany. It was meant as a welcome to and support of the rising republican tendencies initiated in the American and French Revolutions. But as an "ideal" it was presented in the sense in which "ideal" means that which is totally separate from the actual. That it was named "noumenal" and contrasted sharply with what was "phenomenal" and "empirical" is a clear disclosure of its direct descent from the earlier separation of the supernatural and the human. It is one thing to protest against practices that reduce *some* beings to a state in which they are mere tools to serve the profit and power of some other human beings. But the doctrine that men are only ends-in-themselves and never means to serve others is equivalent to repudiation of all the cooperative ties which bind human beings together.[1]

Practices which express, and are justified by, doctrines according to which there is a sharp division between things that are inherently but means and other things that are inherently but ends, and which teach that the former division covers the whole range of the economic aspects of life are an abiding part of the present crisis.

1. Although the Kantian formulation forbids treating man *merely* as a means, the dualism between ends that are super-sensible and means that are natural, which pervades his whole philosophy, leads to a conception of men as constituting a community of isolated ends-in-themselves. On this approach, the nature of their actual empirical, communal ties out of which differential personalities develop, cannot be made intelligible.

The intimate association of economic issues with political concerns is such a conspicuous fact of life-conditions that its presence does not need to be argued. Totalitarian socialism is without paradox a legitimate consequence of and reaction to the laissez-faire Liberalism that proclaimed the subordination of the political to the economic.

That economic activities in production, commerce and finance are carried on by "individuals" in their individual capacity is probably the most successful as well as the most harmful myth of modern life. It owes its capacity for evil largely to its alliance with this view that things which are means are set off from things which are ends—ends-in-themselves as the phrase goes. In fact means are the things and the only things that count in producing consequences. No doctrine could possibly be as effective in shielding the actual human consequences of actual economic conditions from judgment in humane or moral terms as the view that they are *merely* means, *merely* material. The economic aspect of human association decides the conditions under which human beings actually live. The decision includes their effective ability to share in the accumulated values of culture and to contribute to the latter's further development. Separation of "ends-in-themselves" from the conditions that are the only active means of ends actually accomplished renders the former utopian and impotent, and the actual conditions brought about by the means in use inequitable and inhuman.

The resulting state of affairs went far to confer attraction upon any and all measures that promised relief. The separation of means and ends, material and spiritual, economic and moral, which sustain the cultural conditions producing this effect, goes so far back in human history, that any explanation which passes over this fact is sure to err radically in diagnosis of the present crisis. The attempt to moralize industry, commerce and finance (namely the conditions under which human beings actually live) by exhortations addressed to the conscience of "The Individual" is the application of a sentimental poultice. On the other hand, a "socialistic" governmental action which represents a sheer swing of the pendulum from the extreme "individualistic" position is bound to travel the old road of division between ends and means, the material and spiritual, at an accelerated rate.

Some reporters of the present scene have advanced far enough to hold that its ills should be remedied by calling in those who have at command both the "technics" of effective action *and* the "morals" of the spiritual adviser. This is on the par with the notion that those suffering from mental disturbance should be attended by one kind of healers for "bodily" disorders and by another for disorders of "mind" or "soul." What is needed in one case as in the other is a report and treatment from the standpoint which recognizes the unity of human beings. There is some slight advance in the idea that there is need for a kind of social therapy from both sources. But it consists only in an undercurrent that may lead forward to a continuous and cooperative observation of men in their unitary structure and function. Otherwise there is but a perpetuation of the old division that is at the root of the troubles. Adding one isolated factor to another one equally isolated does not heal inner division.

A further but closely allied illustration of the necessity of seeing the present crisis in extensive perspective is furnished by the case of Nationalism. Anyone who has read the literature of a century or so ago—Mazzini for example—will be aware that the words *Nation* and *Nationality* were once charged with fine humane aspiration. They were used to protest against both the narrowness of long established local and provincial units of association, and against the kind of levelling, obliterating unification attempted by a Napoleon. It was in effect a revolt against the footless cosmopolitanism of eighteenth century idealists, as well as against the nascent imperialism which would impose a Roman unity and peace. The words were taken to stand for vital communities of tradition and of aspiration: of all the factors that make up the shared culture that results from free inter-communication. These national communities were to cooperate with one another in behalf of the still wider international community—humanity— each putting its moral resources into a common human pool, diversity thus enriching unity.

Today Nationalism is largely a synonym for collective aggressive egoism. Peoples have measured their own national state by its power to expand, and "Great Powers" have been those which were alone secure as nations. This change from the ideal of measuring national unity by its contribution to the welfare and progress of humanity as an inclusive whole is vast and devastating.

The actual conditions of national life were taken over, captured, one by one by the union of new economic forces with old political and militaristic institutions. The latter acquired an effective power they had never known. The former were largely deflected from the human service they were capable of rendering into agencies of oppression. Periodically they were deflected into agencies of active destruction, each new cycle of war being more devastating than the preceding one. The capture of new forces by old institutions and customs immensely reinforced their power for evil. The ardent expectation that the development of commerce would create a state of interdependence that could and would compel a condition of widespread harmony of interests and of mutual trust was converted, in the course of events, into a condition in which human beings in their capacity of "nationals" lived in a state of chronic fear.

War is one of the oldest of human institutions. Its alliance with the organization of human beings into diverse political units is also old. The inviolability of human beings in their individual capacities has never been secure at any time or place when and where war prevailed. War and militaristic policies are intrinsically totalitarian in tendency.

Recent conditions have but given an overpowering overt demonstration of this fact. But here again it is not new factors in isolation that are accountable. The "social" factors which have captured the new forces and which turn them to production of human debasement and violation are as old as history. The "technics" of invention and manipulative control of natural energies have conferred upon war and upon national energies organized for war an unparalleled power for suppression and destruction of human values. But the factors thus intensified are very old.

Despite what I have said to safeguard against misunderstanding, it is likely that some readers will interpret my criticism of religious, moral, political and economic "individualism," as a plea for a swing over to "collectivistic," governmentally conducted "socialism." The criticism however is directed against the *separation* of individual and associative aspects of the unitary human being. As totalitarian events in Fascist Italy, Bolshevist Russia, and Nazi Germany have demonstrated (to all who are able and willing to see) a swing from one pole to the other is but an effective perpetuation of the old separation with a change in the kind of suppressions it inevitably entails. Nevertheless, there are many signs at present that revolt against the manifest tragic evils of totalitarian "socialism" is producing a swing back to magnification of something called *the individual,* although this time with an aversion to the "economic" individual and devotion to the ideal of making the "spiritual" individual supreme. Something called "personalism" is being advanced as the alternative to totalitarianism, especially among and by frustrated former devotees of a one-sided socialistic creed. The outcome is a view which, in the actual words of one of them, ascribes "independent reality and ultimate value to the individual person alone"! Apparently, an absolutist once, an absolutist always. The clothing has changed but not the monistic cut and pattern.

We shall be in a position to understand and to frame policies intelligently only when we substitute observations which are necessarily pluralistic for pseudo-observations which proceed from wholesale points of view, enshrined in philosophy under the title of various monisms. There are all kinds of "individual" traits—in fact, if we take the word "individual" seriously there are as many as there are "individuals." If we once recognize this fact we shall also recognize the absurdity of talking about "The Individual," economic *or* spiritual. We shall be concerned with the specific and plural conditions of association under which traits that are so differential as to be individual obtain a desirable instead of stunted and perverted development. Meantime assertion that the individual is the ultimate reality and value is, if taken seriously, an invitation to an unrestrained egoism—which is not the more attractive for being labelled "spiritual."

The habit of using "society" and "social" as wholesale monistic terms (whether by way of praise or condemnation) is equally harmful. There are all kinds of associations. The gangster is as highly "social" in one connection as he is anti-social in other connections. Observation and intelligence with respect to human life in its associated phases will not begin to approach the progress made, and still being made, in physical matters until we substitute recognition of *specific* forms and modes of connection of human beings for the conceptual abstractions still largely in control of sociological doctrines in all their aspects. A reading of a telephone directory to note the immense variety of human associations and their vast interrelations might well prove more enlightening than reading most lucubrations on the subject of the "individual" and the "social."

What has been said will be completely misapprehended if it is taken to indicate a belief that a happy issue out of the present Crisis is certain or even highly probable. For its import is restricted to a special point—the disastrous logical, psychological, social and moral consequences of introducing separations where there are no separations. Nothing is implied as to the probable outcome of the present Crisis save under conditions of specific qualification. The purpose is to say that the events constituting the present Crisis will be dealt with in a way to produce a desirable outcome only in the degree in which they are viewed in their own concrete context. This context is one of a long historical spread and wide geographical scope. An artificially one-sided separation of "social" and "individual" is now the chief obstacle to seeing the Crisis in its right perspective. There are ominous signs of continuation of this distortion.

I close by adding that while there is no guarantee for optimism, there are resources within our grasp which, *if used*, will tend toward a favorable outcome. The undecided matter is how soon, if at all, we shall use them. The foregoing discussion has referred to individual, singular, differential aspects of human beings as the source of all inventions and discoveries that are not made by chance. They are the medium of all *deliberate* innovation and variation. But only the inventions and technical advances that spring from the intelligence that takes in a wide range of conditions and consequences determines the *direction* they take, and hence the issue they are likely to have.

Intelligence dealing with physical matters has learned this lesson. Physical discoveries and their application in technological invention depend, as a matter of course, upon accumulation of factual conclusions in comprehensive systematic form. Such procedure is definitely *not* the case in the field of our specifically human and humane activities. Here the policies we initiate, the measures we employ to secure results, are decided by very different sorts of considerations. Stated in a summary manner we have no discoveries, inventions and technologies in human affairs comparable at all to those we command in physical matters. Our humane knowledges are relatively speaking in an infantile state.

One reason for this backward condition of humane knowledge and technics has been indicated. No surer way would have been devised to produce and maintain the present tragically one-sided development of knowledge and practice than division of life into material and spiritual, with the economic assigned to the baser and inherently meaner part. The technics of industry have come to monopolize virtually the entire impact of systematic observation and report. The other portion of life, thus torn asunder, is left under the control of a complex of institutions and traditions that took shape in a static period when changes in life were the work of chance, often of catastrophe. No answer can be given to the question whether "the contemporary crisis is due to technology and large scale planning" that does not place at the centre of consideration the arbitrary limitation thereby created. To attribute to "science," to technology, and to large scale planning the evils due to the one-sided and torn conditions of tragically divided human life is to work for perpetuation, yes towards intensification, of the Crisis.

Our present general attitude is one of impatience and haste. We are not inclined "to stop and think"; to engage, that is, in observation that reaches backward and forward. Emotional reactions restrict vision to what is close at hand in time and space. The emotions are themselves as legitimate as they are inevitable in every rightly constituted human being. But they should be used to promote, not to block, wide observation and a planning that is large-scale: that is, large enough in scale to integrate the economic with the moral and humane, and, by striving to give that which has been debased as material its positive place in promoting secure and widely extended humane values, bring unity into our future life. Would there were prophets who are genuine seers who will warn against reactions to the past and who will show us how to take full advantage of the new resources now at our disposal!

Liberating the Social Scientist

In the last year or so *Commentary* has published a number of articles on recent work in the social sciences, under the heading "The Study of Man." Although these articles deal with a variety of topics, I find it significant that they converge toward a common conclusion. This conclusion emerges both from their criticism of the basic defect they discern and in the constructive suggestions they make for improvement. The common element is a troubled awareness of a narrowness, a restraint, a constriction imposed upon the social sciences by their present "frame of reference," i.e. the axioms, terms, and boundaries under which they function today.

Parenthetically, may I remark that while I shall use the phrase "social inquiry," I would prefer the phrase "study of man" (and/or "inquiry into human relationships," or into the "cultures of associated life"). These are better names; they do not prejudge the subject matter of study as does the name "social" in its present usage, with its weighty suggestion of something set over against "individual."

In his "Government by Manipulation" (*Commentary*, July 1946), Nathan Glazer raised the question whether it was appropriate for social study to intervene in the conduct of affairs merely as a "trouble-shooter" to reduce friction between groups (racial friction between Japanese and "whites" on the West Coast during the War, in the material dealt with), rather than with the broader objective of promoting "formulation and implementation of long-range goals." Mr. Glazer's title, "Government by Manipulation," indicates the criticism of the standpoint and method of most of the studies upon which he reports. His reference to "long-range goals" indicates the nature of his suggestion of a better and more effective "frame of reference."

[First published in *Commentary* 4 (October 1947): 378–85.]

Daniel Bell's article "Adjusting Men to Machines" (*Commentary*, January 1947) contains a detailed account of studies of human relationships in a different field, that of industry as seen in "the sociology of the factory." It opens on a note similar to that of Mr. Glazer. "The resources of the social sciences are called upon more and more frequently to deal with the everyday problems of our society, particularly those arising from conflict and friction between groups"—in this case, that between workers on one side and employers and supervisors on the other side. The net outcome of his careful examination of a large number of such investigations is that those who have conducted the inquiries "operate as technicians, approaching the problem *as it is given to them* and keeping within the framework *set by those who hire them*" (italics mine). Here criticism of current procedures as being restricted within a framework that is fixed prior to and outside of inquiry is clear. The nature of the suggestion as to the need of a wider and freer framework is found in such statements as: "There are under way few studies to see what kind of jobs can best stimulate the spontaneity and freedom of the worker and how we can best alter our industrial methods to assure such jobs."

A second article by Mr. Glazer, "What Is Sociology's Job?" (*Commentary*, February 1947), is also a survey of a specific field. It examines the papers read at the last annual meeting of the American Sociological Society, with the object of finding out the prevailing trends of sociological inquiry. The conclusion offered is that there is paucity of interest in the assumptions and hypotheses that are the "underpinning" of the inquiries carried on, while "practical" topics are the main subjects of research, "practical" meaning "crime, juvenile delinquency, divorce, race relations, absenteeism and restriction of output in industry." Although the inquiry in this case is not restricted by conflicting interests between groups, here too there is nonetheless the definite conclusion that it is limited by extraneous considerations with the result that it is largely given over to "proving" the already obvious.

Finally, there is the highly suggestive article by Karl Polanyi, quite explicit in both criticism and constructive suggestion (*Commentary*, February 1947). Its main title, significantly, is "Our Obsolete Market Mentality," and its subtitle, also significantly, is "Civilization Must Find a New Thought Pattern."

Thus, all of these articles agree in finding the "framework of reference" of the current study of human affairs so restricted as to narrow its potential usefulness to human concerns. All of them, also, indicate the need and the desirability of a wider and freer range in inquiry. The following passage in Mr. Bell's article is reasonably representative of their tenor: "Being scientists, they (that is, those who have conducted the inquiries in question) are concerned with 'what is' and are not inclined to involve themselves in questions of moral values or larger social issues." In quoting this passage, I welcome the quotation marks around "what is." For it is the supreme business of scientific inquiry to ask about and find out about *what is*. In what follows I shall accordingly show that the trouble with the inquiries in question is that they fail to be genuinely scientific precisely because, instead of taking *what is*, the facts of the case in human relationships as the subjects of their investigations, they start with a prejudgment as to what is: one that automatically limits the inquiries carried on. And I shall show that when this *unscientific* limitation is removed, "larger social issues" (and moral values as involved in these issues) are necessarily and inevitably an integral part of the subject matter of inquiry.

That shrewd industrialists engage trained experts to study and report upon the conditions that create friction and lower efficiency and profits, proves only that they are shrewd in conducting their business. That the experts who are engaged employ techniques that have proved efficacious in inquiries that are conducted scientifically without predetermined limitations (particularly those of a monetary kind), is also easily understandable. But that inquiries are scientific which are carried on under conditions of an outlook, standpoint, and aim extraneous to scientific inquiry, is, to state the matter baldly, a delusion. And in the case of "social" inquiry it is a dangerous delusion.

For instead of resulting in liberation from conditions previously fixed (which is the fruit of genuine scientific inquiry) it tends to give scientific warrant, barring minor changes, to the *status quo*—or the established order—a matter especially injurious in the case of economic inquiry. Accordingly, in the governmental and industrial studies reported upon by Glazer and Bell, it is not possible to justify their claim to be "scientific" save on the pertinent ground that they borrow and use some techniques that have proved effective in inquiries carried on free of predetermination in outlook, selection of problems, and methods of procedure.

In genuine scientific inquiry, as may be noted by observation of the more advanced forms, the frame of reference is a *working* matter. It is a product of previous knowings as well as a directive of further inquiries. But in the "social" studies reported upon, the reverse is the case. The frame within which the studies proceed is taken as fixed prior to and outside of inquiry. That fact is exemplified in the seemingly innocent, but actually harmful, use of the adjective "existing" when prefixed to the words "social and/or economic order." The word "existing" is used in a way which excludes from critical examination the very order that is the nominal subject of investigation; for it confines the subject matter investigated within an arbitrarily narrowed local segment and short-time span of "existence."

The case of the *existing* economic order is peculiarly instructive. Were it stated that the subject of study is the *present* industrial, commercial, and financial order, as that is determined by considerations that are largely those of pecuniary success, the scientific limitation would at least be brought out into the open. But the use of "existing," in the cases reported, is conditioned and confined by two assumptions. It is assumed in the first place that "economic" subject matter is so complete on its own account and of itself, inherently, and, as used to be said, "essentially," that it can be scientifically studied in independence of all other social (human) facts. In the second place, it is assumed that what has "existed"—between whatever date is set between the beginning of the present state of industry, business, and finance and the year 1947 as limits—can be treated as a scientific sample or representative of the economic *order* without any reference to its antecedents or its consequences.

The two things mentioned are, however, two faces of one and the same fact. It is only by treating the economic order as complete in isolation, in itself, that a limited local and temporal segment can be treated as complete, as fixed and final, for scientific purposes, in its arbitrarily cut-off "existence," and vice versa.[1]

Summing up what has been said, its import is that much "study

1. Something is said later about the scientific legitimacy of partial or specialized inquiries *provided* they are undertaken in such a way that they can be restored, as need arises, to the total complex of subject matter within which they fall.

of man," as that taking place in sociological science, proceeds upon a fallacious assumption. This assumption is that a study can be scientific apart from a temporal and spatial extension which places given local segments and temporal sectors within that larger stretch of events which includes conditioning anteced- ents and the consequences which are the inevitable outcome of what is locally and immediately at hand. Were inquiry carried on by the "intellect" in terms of pure logic, the monstrosity of this assumption would be apparent. But even when "pure" is taken in the sense of full and *intrinsic* exemption from the influence exerted by institutional traditions, occupations, and interests, there is no such thing as pure economics. Such "purity" as *is* found in the more advanced aspects of scientific inquiry consti- tutes an historic achievement by which such inquiry has itself be- come enough of an institutional tradition and interest on its own account to dictate, to a considerable extent (probably never com- pletely, even in mathematics), the conditions under which it is practiced.[2] Physical inquiry, and to considerable but lesser ex- tent, physiological inquiry are examples of fields that have largely achieved this emancipation and consequent "purity." In this re- spect they hold up a model to be striven for in the backward "so- cial" subjects that are still so largely held in subordination to in- stitutional and other aims and conditions that are alien to the business of inquiry.

In this connection it is worthwhile and, in view of current prejudices, probably necessary to say something about the rela- tion of inquiry to practice and "practical" consequences. In spite of the fact that physical inquiry has, through the medium of tech- nological applications, transformed to an almost revolutionary extent the everyday practices of the larger portion of mankind, the idea still prevails that there is some sort of gulf fixed between science (dignified with the name of "theory" in its classic quasi- godlike sense) and practice. But in the case of the study of man,

2. By one of those curious distortions so over-frequent in philosophical discus- sions, my use of the word "instrumental" in previous writings has been often represented and criticized as if it signified that "knowing" must be limited to some *predetermined specific* end. What I have said, time and again, is precisely to the opposite effect. It is that *scientific* knowing is the only *general* way in our possession of getting free from customary ends and of opening up vistas of new and freer ends.

of "social" studies, it should be obvious that the subject matter studied consists of human practices or activities; that the study of them is itself one variety of human activity or practice, and that its conclusions always intervene in the pre-existing body of human practices in one direction or another. Physical inquiry has now itself attained the status of an institution, and, using the word descriptively, without disparaging connotation, of a vested institutional interest, while the present state of sociological inquiry as reported, shows that it still proceeds in subordination to alien institutional interests, instead of being conducted as an institutional interest in its own behalf.

II

Another statement in the first of Mr. Glazer's two articles. He pointed out that the revolution in the method and results of physical inquiry (beginning, be it recalled, only a short three or four centuries ago) has had momentous human consequences:—nothing less, in fact, than the transformation of the feudal social order into the bourgeois social order. He suggests that development of social inquiry may be followed by an equally extensive transformation of the now and here "existing" order. The remark is pertinent to what has been said about the arbitrary cutting off of the present from its human past and its equally inevitable human future.

But it is equally pertinent in its direct bearing upon the origin or source of the present solid wall that divides physical from human inquiry: a wall that also separates the different aspects of human inquiry from one another, and thereby cuts economics, politics, and morals out from the single and inclusive cultural whole in which their subject matters are indissolubly bound together. The effect on science of the divisions thus instituted is effectively to prevent cross-fertilization of methods and results, so that physical inquiry has a one-sided restricted human application, while human inquiry is kept shut up in the region of opinion, class struggle, and dogmatic "authority."

The story of physical inquiry up to the present time presents two outstanding features. One of them is familiar; it achieved its present measure of emancipation from alien traditional and institutional interests only by means of a severe struggle between church and science, so severe that it commonly bears the name of "warfare." The other feature, though outstanding in its human consequences, is commonly ignored. The victory won was not clear-cut and complete. It was a compromise. In this compromise, the world, including man, even beginning with man, was cut into two separate parts. One of them was awarded to natural inquiry under the name of physical science. The other was kept in possession in fee simple by the "higher" and finally "authoritative" domain—and dominion—of the "moral" and "spiritual." In this compromise, each part was free to go its own way provided it refrained from trespassing upon and interfering with the territory made over to the opposed division.

The course of philosophy from the 16th and 17th centuries can be understood only in terms of efforts to deal with the many "dualisms" mirroring the cleavages this established. But even this is not so important as is the fact that the "victory" won by physical inquiry was one of expediency rather than of principle. The liberation achieved was due in the main to the obvious increase of ease, comfort, and power that followed in the wake of the new science rather than to any grasp of its profound and systematic moral and intellectual import. It is not then a matter of surprise that of late the official representatives of the "spiritual" domain—claiming dominion—have assumed the aggressive. Today they are blaming the serious troubles of the world on physical science, proclaiming that the sole way to salvation is a return to the age when "natural" knowledge was held in strict subjection to the authority (and power) of "spiritual" institutions. Under one condition, this change from suppressed to open conflict is to be welcomed. It is all to the good to have the conflict occur in the light of intelligence rather than in the heat of accusation and counter-accusation.

For once a conflict is adequately brought within the field of intelligent scrutiny, it presents itself as a *problem*: and where there is a problem there are alternative possibilities to be systematically viewed, no longer a mere clash of blind forces. The alternative to subordination of natural inquiry to supernatural authority (more correctly, human authority based on extra-natural grounds) is the development of natural inquiry itself to a point where it is capable of dealing with the troubled difficulties of our social-moral order.[3]

The actual issue is whether inquiry into social-moral issues can be effectively promoted in any other way than by using the methods that have won notable triumphs in the physical field, together with use of the specific conclusions that have been thereby attained. Utilization for the new purpose involves of necessity whatever developments are required in former procedures to render them fruitfully applicable to the new purpose they serve. We need "one world" of intelligence and understanding if we are to obtain one world in other forms of human activity.

It is in this connection that the alternative of subjection of natural inquiry to external "authority" becomes ominously significant. It means either the establishment of a particular institution having the physical power to *enforce* its alleged "spiritual" authority, or it means dumping our actual human problems into the lap of the least developed, the most immature, of all of our modes of knowing: politics and ethics. If we take the former path, we find that its influence, in the form in which it flourishes in academic circles in democratic cultures, is slight, while in the form in which it is potent in actual affairs, it is not a "science" but an ideological reflection and "rationalization" of contentious and contending practical policies.

In this contention, the democratic policy has, from the standpoint of inquiry, at least the advantage that it tolerates and, within limits, encourages free inquiry into specific problems as against suppression of discussion in the totalitarian type. But if we confine ourselves to the side of systematic intellectual formulation, we find that the quasi-official doctrine, *traditional* "liberalism," is based upon acceptance of an economic "individualism" which was humanly significant in the earlier stage of the industrial revolution but that is now non-existent save as a defense of one set of economic institutions. On the totalitarian side, the setting of standards and ends is so predetermined that it is socially treasonable and dangerous to subject them to inquiry.

If we turn to ethics or morals as an intellectual discipline, we find ourselves faced with a sorry spectacle. There is no general

3. The idea that the alternative is reduction of the human order to the terms of the physical order is no alternative at all. It is only a repetition of that assumption of two separate "dominions" which underlies our present confusion.

consensus as to standards of judgment or ends of action. There is also a minimum of agreement as to the methods and "organs" by which standards and aims should be determined. Indeed, for at least the last two hundred years there has been steady deterioration in ethical theory as to these issues. One of the most serious aspects of this situation is that the subject matter of moral inquiry has been increasingly pushed out of the range of the concrete problems of economic and political inquiry. In consequence, there has taken place a reduction by which, in popular attitudes, discussion is "moral" in the degree in which it consists of complaints about what exists and exhortations about what *should*, or "ought" to, exist. In fact, the state of moral inquiry at present is a striking exhibition of the division of social inquiry into a number of independent, water-tight, non-communicating compartments, which embody the net outcome of the cleavages that have their source mainly in the isolation of the physical from the distinctively human.

III

I know of no more effective way of calling attention to the *source* and *nature* of the cleavages that now exist between the "material" on one side and the spiritual and moral on the other, than to quote from a semi-official document and avowed proclamation of the cleavage. The passage in question is the opening sentence of the extensive article on "Economics" in the *Encyclopaedia of the Social Sciences* (Vol. 5, p. 344). It reads:

"Economics deals with the social phenomena centering about provision for the material needs of individuals and groups." Even if the word "material" had been italicized, I doubt if many readers would have been given pause, in spite of its use as the differentiating criterion of one class of "social phenomena" from other classes, presumably those of a moral and "spiritual" kind. For ⁻his division of the facts of human relations into two separate kinds, one low (low in the sense of base and also in that of basic), the other high, authoritative, and moral, is so deeply entrenched in institutional practices and in traditions established through long centuries that its explicit use as *the* standard frame of reference for inquiry into "social" facts occasions no protest. It is so familiarly inbred in our intellectual standpoints as to be "natural."

It goes along with a number of other familiar cleavages: body and soul, flesh and spirit, appetite which is animal and conscience which is superimposed as a warning and restraining factor, sense and reason, and, on a more intellectually refined level, the internal and the external, the subjective and the objective. These are cleavages distilled and precipitated in the distinction between the natural and the supernatural which has long held a central and dominating position in the moral history of the Western world.[4] I doubt whether a more momentous *moral* fact can be found in all human history than just this separation of the moral from other human interests and attitudes, especially from the "economic."

I referred earlier, in another connection, to the assumption that economic phenomena form such an independent and self-enclosed compartment of social facts that they can be *scientifically* treated in complete isolation from their human antecedents and consequences. In view of the determining role exerted by industrial, commercial, and financial factors in all phases—scientific, artistic, political, domestic, and international—of the present world, the practically universal passive acceptance of this position would be *unaccountable* did we not understand its source in the historic institutional background of our culture. There is no need to argue in favor of the thesis that economic facts are so far from being an isolated self-enclosed field that, on one side, they are the offspring of the new physical science, and that, on the other side, they affect, through their consequence, the human values of the whole world with ever-increasing intensity. It is enough to face facts with eyes open.[5]

It would require volumes to present anything like a full exposition of the cultural background of the identification of "economic" with "material" which has so disastrously cut the economic off from wider and larger human values—those called

4. The present revival of the notion of the inherent sinfulness of man as explanation of the troubled state of the world (an explanation which strangely enough is a source of comfort to many persons) is contemporary evidence of how deeply these cleavages are entrenched in our culture. See the article of Dr. Sidney Hook on "Intelligence and Evil in Human History" (*Commentary*, March 1947) for a searching examination of this current revival.

5. Critics of the "materialistic" interpretation of history which is attributed to Marx do not seem to notice that this "materialism" was simply an acceptance of the orthodox view of economics, combined with acute observation of its human consequences. To be effective, the criticisms have to be directed at the basic assumption of the isolation and independence of the "economic."

moral. Two periods of human history, however, are so representative as to have typical significance. One of them dates from ancient Greece, whose economy was a slave economy, and where artisans and laborers, even those not technically slaves, were completely excluded from community membership—which in Athens meant not only political citizenship but participation in all the things that are worthwhile in art, knowledge, and human companionship.

These facts were acutely noted and comprehensively formulated by Aristotle. On their basis as they then and there "existed," he made a sharp separation between some forms of activity as means and means *only,* and other modes of activity that were, by their inherent nature, or essence, ends-in-themselves.[6] Economic activity fell completely into the former division. And this is only the beginning of the story. The science and cosmology of the time, as they also received acute and comprehensive formulation by Aristotle, treated the universe as a hierarchical scheme whose parts were graded on the basis of the place held by what was called "matter," with pure matter at the base (in every sense of the word "base") and with the divine, wholly free from any contact with matter, at the apex. Moreover, on the one side change and mutability were strictly conjoined with "matter," and fixity and immutability with self-sustained Being, on the other side. This view persisted in control of what was accepted as natural science until the scientific revolution gave despised motion a central place and "matter" gained "energy," losing that complete passivity which made it the victim of every external "force."

In consequence, the class that was occupied with production, whether in the field or in the shop, was "by nature"—i.e., universally, eternally, and of necessity—menial, servile, embodying only the animal and fleshly part of man, and cut off from all knowledge that was not concerned with the material and mutable. Since Aristotle lived a long time ago, and since at best his metaphysical cosmology appealed to but a small intellectual elite, these doctrines might have faded into insignificance were it not for another imposing historical event. This latter event, which involved the adoption of the substance of the doctrines of Aris-

6. Unfortunately, the example of Aristotle in taking a local segment and sector of life activities as universal and necessary, because "natural," has been widely adopted in philosophical discourse—even by those who revolt at this special instance.

totle into the reigning religion, left a mark on the culture of the world which, in spite of other immense changes, is as yet almost indelible.

This other event was the spread of Christian faith throughout Europe. The supremacy of the Church in the Middle Ages extended far beyond what today is usually called "religion." It was supreme and authoritative in political, economic, artistic, and educational matters. It officially accepted the cosmology and science of Aristotle as the framework of its own intellectual structure in everything "natural" and in everything amenable to human reason. What might otherwise have been a transitory incident was thereby so firmly embedded in the religious culture of the Western world that even the progressive secularization of both knowledge and the dominant everyday interests of the mass of mankind did not seriously shake its hold with respect to the fixed separation of the material from the spiritual and ideal. The severance of the economic from the moral, making each for the purposes of inquiry an independent self-enclosed field, must be understood as one chapter in this story.

IV

The backwardness of inquiry into human affairs, that is, of the "social" subjects, is an integral part of the record. Social inquiry still clings obstinately to the kind of frame of reference that once controlled physical inquiry, but which was abandoned when systematic scientific advance began. Since the 16th century physical inquiry has shown an ever-growing respect for change; for the *process* of change, to indulge in a pleonasm. Until recently, this respect was limited by the Newtonian framework according to which change took place in changeless space and time, which accordingly were independent of each other. Now physical inquiry has liberated itself (through what, not very happily from the standpoint of popular understanding, is called "relativity") from this limitation.

But the more physical inquiry has developed and fructified through acknowledgment of change and process, the more obstinately orthodox moral inquiry has clung to fixed "first" principles and immutable final or last "ends." The very principle which has transformed physical inquiry from a stagnant condi-

tion to one of steady advance is rejected by professed representatives of moral inquiry as the sure road to disorder and chaos. In
consequence, the progressive practical application of the method
and conclusions of physical inquiry to human affairs has been so
unbalanced as to sustain and widen the very splits and cleavages
that now disturb our life. They reinforce the use of pre-scientific,
pre-technological morals to support, in the name of what is spiritual, the very conditions which are the source of so much of our
moral confusion.

There is another difference in the frame of reference in the two
cases that is allied to that just mentioned. The "natural" world,
the cosmos with which physical scientific inquiry is operationally
concerned, reveals its meanings in the course of that inquiry. It is
not something fixed and permanently behind and beneath that
progressive inquiry, even though it be baptized by such eulogistic
terms as Universe, Reality, etc., and the course taken by inquiry
is not determined by some fixed predetermined standard, whatever high metaphysical names be given it. Inquiry is determined
by the conclusions reached in the previous course of its own developing methods of observation and test. The unanswered questions, the problems, which have emerged in this course provide
its next, immediate directives. The strong points in conclusions
already attained provide the resources with which to attack the
weaknesses, the deficiencies, and conflicts that form weak points
in its present state.

In consequence, inquiry in its most developed and accomplished form has no traffic with absolute generalizations. Its best
theories are working hypotheses to be tested through their use in
application in new fields. The devotion of official moral inquiry
to absolutes, instead of being evidence and source of strength, is
evidence and source of its comparatively stagnant estate. It contributes only to maintain that estate. Its absolutes are formal and
empty. Everybody gives allegiance to them even where in concrete situations their interests and practice are worlds away.
These formal absolutes are largely accountable for the sharp division now existing between economic and moral standpoints.[7]

7. Since the word "moral" is used freely in the above, it may fend off misunderstanding if I say explicitly that, as the word is used, it stands for the human or
"social" in its most inclusive reach, not for any special region or segment. I
venture to add that the word "law" commonly added to the word moral supplies striking illustration of the rigidities due to this frame.

Inquiry—because of its practical disesteem of fixed generalizations (even though they be called "laws")—in its most developed
form can engage freely in a high degree of specification, of "specialization," with the assurance that its results, instead of having
an unfavorable impact upon the total body or system of what is
known, will serve to solidify and extend the latter. While detailed
specialization is carried far beyond anything found in "social"
inquiry, it is exempt from the fixed non-communicating divisions
which are such a prominent feature of the latter.[8]

We are faced, as a net outcome, with the necessity of abandon-
ing that alternative which proposes, in effect if not in so many
words, to subordinate scientific inquiry to predetermined ends.
Instead of that we should adopt, positively and constructively,
the exactly opposite alternative. If we break down the underlying
attitudes, interests, and convictions which maintain the walls of
division that now effectively prevent cross-fertilization and use of
the resources at our command, we shall live in a freer and larger
world. If and when we surrender the intellectual habits that have
come to us as a heritage from the past and use freely the resources that are within our command (because of the development of the frames of reference and the conclusions in physical
and physiological matters), we shall find their use does not im-
prison human inquiry within a fixed physical and "material"
framework, but releases and expands methods and conclusions,
so that they will lift the heavy weight that now depresses and
confines "social" (including moral) subjects.

As the resources that are available are released and expanded,
their application in the intelligent clarification of the existing actual and "practical" confusion will follow surely if slowly. The
dream of a well-ordered transformation of human affairs as extensive as that which followed change in physical inquiry, but
tempered and balanced as that was not, will cease to be a dream.

But we must first get rid of those assumptions, rooted in institutional conditions, from which physical inquiry at its best has
freed itself. To do this we need a clarified view of what physical
inquiry *is*—that is, of what it *does* and how it does it. The mis-

8. This is not to impeach the many valid and valuable inquiries carried on by
   working economists. The criticism is directed against the assumptions regarding the frame of reference that is the theoretical underpinning, which now
   stand in the way, practically, of a broader human use of their conclusions in
   guidance of human affairs.

representation that is still current is well illustrated in the following quotation from a recent publication. The text reads as follows:

"All of the sciences have contributed to the belief that man is the victim of a mechanist world and is anything but the captain of his soul. Physics and chemistry have described the universe as a machine operating by immutable laws of cause and effect. Man is but a cog in this machine. Astronomy has revealed an infinite universe of wheels within wheels held together by the force of gravity. In this great system man is an infinitesimal dot of little consequence, etc., etc." If "science" had *revealed* these things as facts, it is difficult to see why there should be so much emotional heat displayed because they have been found out. But as a matter of fact the passage quoted doesn't attain the level of even the "popular" science of fifty years ago.

The type of sweeping generalization here attributed to physics and astronomy is so unscientific that it now flourishes mainly in what is labeled, unfortunately, *moral* theory. Instead of enslaving man to a fixed and finished structure, the progress of science has been accompanied at every step by an expansion of man's practical freedom, enabling him to use natural energies as agencies, first liberating his aims and then providing him with means for realizing them. It is true that this emancipation is still one-sided. But it is this very unbalanced condition that should give us the strongest possible stimulus for extending the scientific standpoint and procedure to fields which still remain under the control of opinion, prejudice, and physical force, and which are still potent only because pre-scientific attitudes and interests have endowed them with institutional authority in the name of morals and religion.

Henry Wallace and the 1948 Elections

Any one who makes a statement on the above topic in which every sentence does not begin with *"if"* is more daring than I am. First of all the question of whether Wallace will run for President. It is doubtful if even Wallace himself knows the answer to this question. He is undoubtedly in a highly receptive mood, but it is probably qualified with an *if,* depending on the way the political winds are blowing when the time comes for either a public decision or one known to his intimate backers. The amount of voting strength he will have when election day comes, in case he is nominated, is as yet *a* big *if.* And while there is a general assumption that it will be enough to elect the Republican candidate, there are some reasonable grounds on which to question even that. [As we go to press, it is announced that Wallace will announce his candidacy on Monday, Dec. 29.]

While I am not a prophet and haven't even any polls on which to base my outlook, I venture to indulge in a rather positive statement about what will happen *if* he should be a candidate. It seems to me altogether likely that the campaign issue will, as the weeks go by, turn more and more upon issues of foreign policy: to be more explicit—though that is hardly necessary—upon our relations with the USSR, and their lack of relations, apart from the lines of abuse its agents choose to engage in, with us. I do not believe it is wildly fanciful to suppose that at the end of the campaign that will be practically the one issue to receive serious attention.

It is on this ground that I do not, as at present advised, share in the assumption that the candidacy of Wallace assures the success of the Republican candidate. The makers of Democratic campaign policies do not enjoy a very high reputation for eptness.

[First published in *New Leader* 30 (27 December 1947): 1.]

They are now suffering from the loss of their shrewdest and most skillful judge of the direction in which the tides of political sentiment are setting, as well as from the loss of many old-line party men who became disgruntled on account of his policies. Nor have the waverings of President Truman served to repair these losses. But I cannot believe that the Democratic leaders who shape the issues on which the campaign is conducted are hopelessly inept.

And they would be hopelessly stupid if they do not see, first, that their chance of success depends upon weaning away enough Republicans to offset the loss they will undoubtedly undergo on the Democratic side, and, secondly, taking the foremost issue to be one forced upon us by the Bolshevik-Soviet regime offers by far the best chance of gaining the needed vote to offset their prospective loss. It can hardly be expected that the rank-and-file of the Republican Party will be more lenient in their judgment of the expansionist political policies of the Russian political leaders, or less fearful of their economic policies, than the rank-and-file of the Democratic Party. And considering the place of the captains of industry and finance within the Republican Party, it is hardly likely they will be eager to add to the standing of the candidate who has the active support of Communists and fellow-travelers both in and outside of labor organizations. I am not foolish enough to imagine they will on that account lift a finger to aid a Democratic candidate, but it will be highly surprising if they can exert their customary influence—particularly on the members of AFL unions who are numerous although being in a decided minority.

The remarks I have just made do not indicate that the prospect of a campaign conducted largely on the issue just stated fills me with pleasure even if it tends, as I believe it will, to favor the election of a Democrat. The reverse is the case. There is already enough bitterness, enough of lack of mutual respect, in the average presidential campaign. I can think of nothing more likely to exacerbate the bitterness. Nor would it end with just bitterness. It would have a tendency to divide the nation at a time when a moral unity of outlook and aim, below political differences, is most urgently needed. The need is great enough in the most favorable conditions. I see nothing more sure to shake and shiver the prospect of furthering such a moral unification than a political campaign conducted on friction and opposition with respect to a foreign country. The Communist issue already occupies a disproportionate place in our political discussions and life—not that there is not a serious political issue involved but that it is getting out of balance with respect to other issues. One favorite accusation of the PAC supporters of Wallace even now is that the Democratic Party is deserting Roosevelt policies and taking a reactionary stand on domestic issues. This position is theoretically inconsistent with what they themselves are actually doing to divert attention from domestic to foreign issues. But logical inconsistencies do not play a large part in politics. The actual danger is that what they are asserting as a charge in order to affect public opinion will come to be a fact. If that happens the recollection that they themselves bear the primary responsibility for making it so will not yield consolation, much less undo the evils consequent upon a serious split in our national life.

American Youth, Beware of Wallace Bearing Gifts

I was born in 1859, a year which presaged crucial events in the life of our country. It was a year in which the Republican Party, rising out of the disintegration of the Whig Party, was able to become the party of victory and liberator of the enslaved. It was this Republican Party which, combining hitherto disparate elements, was able to withstand the threat of disunion and the dismemberment of our democracy.

Today, 89 years later, I see before us a different kind of new party; this one, the party of illiberalism, the spokesman for the slaveholders of the 20th century. I am addressing myself to the candidacy of Henry A. Wallace, a candidacy which, however it may have attracted the sympathy and the passions of freedom-loving Americans, has its deepest roots in the sub-soil of Soviet totalitarianism.

I write this to the university and college youth of our nation not on behalf of any party or any candidate. For many, many years I sought and actively worked for the creation of a new and liberal party in our political structure. This is a task I have dedicated myself to for so long because I know the need for a party which could nurture the progressive, democratic radicalism indigenous to our country.

Thus I voted for Eugene Debs in 1912 and the elder La Follette in 1924 and since there are no absolutes in politics, I also voted for a Grover Cleveland in 1884 and a Woodrow Wilson in 1916. Yet I never wavered in my belief then, nor do I now, that the overriding need for our land is a truly liberal party.

But with my realization of the urgency for a new liberal party, I have also realized that our greatest weakness as liberals is in organization and that without that organization there is danger

[First published in *Liberal* 2 (October 1948): 3–4.]

that democratic ideals may go by default. Democracy is a fighting faith. When its ideals are reenforced by those of scientific method and experimental intelligence, it is capable of evoking discipline, ardor and organization.

In the Wallace candidacy, however, I see no hope for progressives. The entire history of this putative "new party," as well as a study of its present program and leadership has convinced me of this fact. I say this to those of you who see a hope in the Wallace Party as one who speaks in full sympathy with your aspirations, you, youthful dissidents, whose idealism I cherish because it is the real treasure and substance of our country, because you are seeking to brighten our fear-ridden world and to implement our democratic heritage.

I am not here concerned with the Communists and their less spunky comrades, the fellow-travelers. These have decided, knowingly or not, against human freedom, against Democracy, against civil rights for all. Their support for Wallace is consistent with what they seek—an expansion of Soviet influence and the destruction of the democratic forces in Europe, the debilitation of the Marshall Plan.

There is another force which has proper reason to smile on Wallace and his party. It is the extreme conservatives to whom he offers the hope of a divided progressivism. He offers the conservatives assistance in their efforts to confuse public opinion about the moral status of progressivism. The extreme conservatives are making good use of the Wallace double-standard—one for Negroes in Alabama, another for Socialists in Czechoslovakia; one for our State Department and another for the Soviet Foreign Office. Wallace's use of the language and the idealism that is democracy can only lead to debasement of that language and to cynicism about its ultimate meaning.

The one prerequisite for any man in public life today who decries his opponents as imperialists, as war-mongers, as antidemocratic, is that he stand undeviatingly for those positive ideals in which presumably his opponents are defective.

Yet nowhere have I read anything by Wallace which I could judge to be a decisive contribution to ensuring the peace and prosperity program he speaks for. On the contrary, I do find a consistent emphasis on "understanding" the Soviet government, a recommendation that the world be divided into two spheres of

influence—Soviet and American—and an insistence that whoever objects to this amoral fission is no friend of peace; an acceptance as truth of any Soviet statement and disparagement of
any statement by our own government and a denigration of our
motivations.

Thus, Wallace in his open letter to Stalin and in his subsequent
statements pressed for bilateral conversations with the Soviet
dictatorship and the United States, a step which would exclude
nations overrun by this totalitarianism and shunt aside the very
United Nations which Wallace accuses our government of having
treated so cavalierly. Certainly, I could think of many things for a
public figure who seems to have the ear of the Soviet leader, to
ask Stalin—where are civil liberties in Russia, how much slave
labor is there, what happened to the Russian professors I met in
the Soviet Union in 1928 and why did they disappear, when will
Soviet imperialism and its brutalitarian disregard of rights of
others cease?

But this I know cannot be expected from Wallace or from his
top-bracket supporters, who quite openly declare their Communist affiliation, and who by their own statements take pride in the
fact that it was the Communist Party which aided in the establishment of the Wallace movement.

A new party in the United States must meet three tests:

It must offer a genuinely NEW position in the extension and
enrichment of democracy, acting as the mediator in social transi-
tions, availing itself of what is good and useful in the past to
strengthen the present and the future.

It must offer responsible, competent, thoroughly democratic
leadership, a leadership which would believe it morally repre-
hensible to explain away the excesses of a police state.

It must be rooted in the trade union movement, which for all
its faltering, has carried forward our liberal heritage.

The Wallace movement meets none of these tests. Wallace has
surrounded himself with the very men who opposed his Vice-
Presidential candidacy in 1940, as they did the candidacy of
President Roosevelt. It was then an opposition based not on the
paramount needs of our country and the other democracies
faced with the threat of extinction but an opposition directed by
the interests of the Soviet Union, then leagued in a pact with
Hitler.

Today, these erstwhile appeasers of Hitler are the directors of the Wallace Party seeking the appeasement of Stalin and the extension of his hegemony. Fundamentally, their concern is not half so much with the repeal of the Taft-Hartley Law or the establishment of sound inflation controls. Their concern is with transforming the United States into an isolationist sphere, anesthetized to the appeals for aid from our brother democracies in Europe.

In the European Recovery Program lies the hope of peace. Our foreign policy, however perverted in isolated cases its application has been, is basically the only way of strengthening the few remaining European democracies. To withdraw our support, as Wallace would have us do, from western Europe would most certainly mean the eventual fall of France, Italy and the Lowlands, and the Scandinavian peninsula to Soviet totalitarianism.

I ask you young people to study the record of Henry Wallace. I ask you to seek an answer to the fact that not a single outstanding liberal leader, not a single democratic-minded trade union leader has joined the Wallace camp. Certainly, the trade union movement with its 16,000,000 members has ample reason to be dissatisfied with the Southern Democratic and Republican Parties. The 80th Congress has sorely injured the interests of our people. Its willing surrender of our interests clearly indicates that we are, in a practical sense, nearer a one-party Federal establishment, than a two-party system.

But having said this, it is all the more remarkable that the leaders of the AFL and the CIO uncompromisingly reject the Wallace candidacy. And it is not merely in the case of these trade unionists a rejection by a handful of officers. The conventions of our free trade unions have uniformly and by overwhelming majorities confirmed this rejection.

I am aware that what I have said may seem to be wholly negative, than which nothing could be more repellent to generous, eager youth. A merely "wait and see" policy is a harmful retreat from reality. But in this campaign of ideas, in this campaign for the soul of European man, support of Wallace is not the only alternative, because Wallace can no more be the saviour of world peace than he can be the guarantor of civil rights in Eastern Europe. He is merely the willing colporteur of a dictatorship which has overswept the great part of the European land-mass and which has its legions posted in Western Europe awaiting The Day.

It is not mere negativism to say that a political party which willingly accepts and welcomes support of Communist leaders has no more place in the liberal growth of our country than a political party which welcomes support from Ku Klux Klansmen or from leaders of the Nazi Bund. To be negative is also to be positive because if you are for, you are also against.

For lack of a liberal mass party, the country suffers a lack of immediate answers to our most immediate problems. There is now no national mass party which I can urge you to support. But there are promising groups giving serious attention to building the kind of movement of which I have spoken. There are groups which believe as I do that there can be no compromise, no matter how temporary, with totalitarianism. Compromise with totalitarianism means stamping an imprimatur on the drive for a pax Sovietica. Compromise means denouncing universal military training in America but acceptance of a huge standing army in the Soviet Union. Compromise means speaking fearlessly against the poll-tax in the South but ignoring political persecution in Eastern Europe and enslavement in Siberia.

This makes it all the more reason for not committing yourselves to a group which is taking advantage of a political vacuum to impose upon this country, under the name and outward cloak of liberalism, political action dictated by the most reactionary imperialistic nation existing in the world today. Think twice and, as students, inquire and reflect and in a way that indicates that you have the spirit of inquiry that marks a student.

Such a course does not mean passivity and postponement of decision. By all means become active. There are national organizations in the country and in the universities and colleges for political education. Join one of them. If there are none, communicate with their national headquarters and start a branch.

Before you make your irrevocable choice, examine the record and weigh the facts. Many of you will vote for the first time in November. It is a vote which will help shape our destinies because we are in the midst of one of the most burdensome crises in the history of humankind.

Ask which candidate and which party will invigorate our democratic faith and which will sap that vigor? Ask if the cause of world peace will be served by men who are legionnaires in the cause of dictatorship? Ask if the man who scoffed at the death of the Czechoslovak Republic and Jan Masaryk is the man to resist totalitarianism?

There is much you must ask as I have asked. The answers you will find, if I know the university youth of America, will enable you to find political expression of which you will be proud and which will be an inspiration to democratically loyal friends and peoples in all the world.

How to Anchor Liberalism

Deterioration of the means of communication, carried sometimes to the point of complete corruption, is a striking feature of our day. It applies externally to systematic use of the radio, press and other mechanical agencies of communication; it applies even more seriously to *words*, the specific ways of human communication. The assumption by totalitarian states of the word "democracy" to name a regime that openly flouts every one of the freedoms of speech, of assembly, of conference and discussion, that have given substance to democracy in the past is sufficient on this point. The piddling efforts of self-styled "semanticists" to deal by external verbal manipulations with a trouble that lies close to the roots of our present social and political disturbances is perhaps the most recent case of trying to keep back an oceanic tide with a mop.

Part of the difficulty does not arise from deliberate perversion for the sake of prestige or other specific class or group advantage. It proceeds from the fact that social changes have been going on at a rate that has defied the ability of human intelligence to keep up with them. Words suffer from the confused mixture of old and new from which all other human institutions suffer. With the exception of economic laissez-faire abuse, "Liberalism" probably suffers more from this source than from deliberate efforts of a partisan group to misinform and mislead public opinion.

It may be helpful to illustrate this historic aspect of the matter by reference to another field, that of education. For centuries the words "liberal arts" were used purposely and exclusively to name *literary* arts as distinct from the useful and practical "mechanical arts" which, at the time, included all industrial occupa-

[First published in *Labor and Nation* 4 (November–December 1948): 14–15.]

tions. Thus restricted use of the word is a historical monument to a period when Athenian life was based upon institutional slavery together with exclusion of all artisans and hand-workers from free citizenship. Medieval feudalism fixed for succeeding centuries a sharp distinction between "liberal" and "vocational" education, with of course the palm of inherent superiority conferred upon the former.

I believe this allusion is pertinent in the case of the wide use of the words "liberal" and "liberalism." Traditional habits are tougher than we realize. Quite apart from deliberate attempts to restrict the word "liberalism" to policies which in the Europe of an earlier day were genuinely liberating in their opposition to the mass of inequities and oppressions that held over from feudalism, the rapidity of industrial, political and other cultural changes tends now to deprive the word of any agreed-upon significance.

My only purpose in calling attention to these facts is to reinforce, as far as I may, the plea made in *Labor and Nation* for a cooperative effort towards something approaching a body of principles, unless the word *liberal* is to be entirely abandoned. When I say principles, I mean precisely that: not the planks of a platform or items of a program, but fundamental considerations that will afford specific tests and criteria by which to judge specific measures and policies. It is not that I am opposed to the development of platforms and programs. They are prerequisites of effective organization. But what we as liberals suffer from is absence of principles (which by the very meaning of the word are what come first) by which to judge proposed items of a program and planks of a platform. I may be unduly influenced by my personal professional training and the preferences and inclinations that have grown up out of it. But I believe the necessary condition of any enduring get-together among liberals depends upon first doing a serious *intellectual* job.

Such a job must have at least a tentative principle at its inception. I suggest as a working hypothesis the need of a thorough examination of what freedom demands under present conditions if it is to be a reality and not just a cover for this and that scheme. It is no longer enough even if the special scheme is put forth with the moral good faith which has marked, say, the historic socialist plans. It is at the furthest remove from endorsement of the arguments which claim that organized social intervention and planning is a return to serfdom to say that the problem of working out the specific means and agencies by which organized planning and intervention will result in promotion of freedom is a deeply serious one. We have to forget a lot of slogans of the past to do this work—among them our meaningless, because footless, talk about "the individual"—talk that usually plays directly into the hands of those who would utilize the existing human confusion and chaos to impose (probably under the name of freedom and of "the individual") some kind of external authority as the only means of attaining order and security. What (in my best judgment) is imperatively required is less talk about the individual and much more study of specific social conditions to try to discover what kind of organization among them will bring about a wider, and hence more equitable distribution of the uses and enjoyments that our present technical resources make possible. It is not just that many of the Marxist proposals of a century ago are now as outdated as if they had been proposed three centuries ago. Attention of an organized intellectual sort must now focus on the problem of the kinds of concrete social reorganization which by their own nature will do what theorizing about the individual has been supposed to do. And nothing can be gained by inserting the words "moral" or, worse yet, "spiritual" before *individual*. For what is needed is precisely to find out what these adjectives specifically stand for under the radically changed condition in which we now have to live. And that, I repeat, is primarily an intellectual job.

The Democratic Faith and Education

Not even the most far-seeing of men could have predicted, no longer ago than fifty years, the course events have taken. The expectations that were entertained by men of generous outlook are in fact chiefly notable in that the actual course of events has moved, and with violence, in the opposite direction. The ardent and hopeful social idealist of the last century or so has been proved so wrong that a reaction to the opposite extreme has taken place. A recent writer has even proposed a confraternity of pessimists who should live together in some sort of social oasis. It is a fairly easy matter to list the articles of that old faith which, from the standpoint of today, have been tragically frustrated.

The first article on the list had to do with the prospects of the abolition of war. It was held that the revolution which was taking place in commerce and communication would break down the barriers which had kept the peoples of the earth alien and hostile and would create a state of interdependence which in time would insure lasting peace. Only an extreme pessimist ventured to suggest that interdependence might multiply points of friction and conflict.

Another item of that creed was the belief that a general development of enlightenment and rationality was bound to follow the increase in knowledge and the diffusion which would result from the revolution in science that was taking place. Since it had long been held that rationality and freedom were intimately allied, it was held that the movement toward democratic institutions and popular government which had produced in succession

[First published in *Antioch Review* 4 (June 1944): 274–83, from an address, read by Jerome Nathanson, before the conference on The Scientific Spirit and Democratic Faith, at the Ethical Culture School, New York City, on 27 May 1944.]

the British, American, and French Revolutions was bound to spread until freedom and equality were the foundations of political government in every country of the globe.

A time of general ignorance and popular unenlightenment and a time of despotic and oppressive governmental rule were taken to be practically synonymous. Hence the third article of faith. There was a general belief among social philosophers that governmental activities were necessarily more or less oppressive; that governmental action tended to be an artificial interference with the operation of natural laws. Consequently the spread of enlightenment and democratic institutions would produce a gradual but assured withering away of the powers of the political state. Freedom was supposed to be so deeply rooted in the very nature of men that given the spread of rational enlightenment it would take care of itself with only a minimum of political action confined to insuring external police order.

The other article of faith to be mentioned was the general belief that the vast, the almost incalculable, increase in productivity resulting from the industrial revolution was bound to raise the general standard of living to a point where extreme poverty would be practically eliminated. It was believed that the opportunity to lead a decent, self-respecting, because self-sufficient, economic life would be assured to everyone who was physically and morally normal.

The course of events culminating in the present situation suffices to show without any elaborate argument how grievously these generous expectations have been disappointed. Instead of universal peace, there occurred two wars worldwide in extent and destructive beyond anything known in all history. Instead of uniform and steady growth of democratic freedom and equality, we have seen the rise of powerful totalitarian states with thoroughgoing suppression of liberty of belief and expression, outdoing the most despotic states of previous history. We have an actual growth in importance and range of governmental action in legislation and administration as necessary means of rendering freedom on the part of the many an assured actual fact. Instead of promotion of economic security and movement toward the elimination of poverty, we now have a great increase in the extent and the intensity of industrial crises with great increase of inability of workers to find employment. Social instability has reached a point that may portend revolution if it goes on unchecked.

Externally it looks as if the pessimists had the best of the case. But before we reach a conclusion on that point, we have to inquire concerning the solidity of the premise upon which the idealistic optimists rested their case. This principle was that the more desirable goals in view were to be accomplished by a complex of forces to which in their entirety the name "Nature" was given. In practical effect, acceptance of this principle was equivalent to adoption of a policy of drift as far as human intelligence and effort were concerned. No conclusion is warranted until we have inquired how far failure and frustration are consequences of putting our trust in a policy of drift; a policy of letting "George" in the shape of Nature and Natural Law do the work which only human intelligence and effort could possibly accomplish. No conclusion can be reached until we have considered an alternative: What is likely to happen if we recognize that the responsibility for creating a state of peace internationally, and of freedom and economic security internally, has to be carried by deliberate cooperative human effort? Technically speaking the policy known as *Laissez-faire* is one of limited application. But its limited and technical significance is one instance of a manifestation of widespread trust in the ability of impersonal forces, popularly called Nature, to do a work that has to be done by human insight, foresight, and purposeful planning.

Not all the men of the earlier period were of the idealistic type. The idealistic philosophy was a positive factor in permitting those who prided themselves upon being realistic to turn events so as to produce consequences dictated by their own private and class advantage. The failure of cooperative and collective intelligence and effort to intervene was an invitation to immediate short-term intervention by those who had an eye to their own profit. The consequences were wholesale destruction and waste of natural resources, increase of social instability, and mortgaging of the future to a transitory and brief present of so-called prosperity. If "idealists" were misguided in what they failed to do, "realists" were wrong in what they did. If the former erred in supposing that the drift (called by them progress or evolution) was inevitably toward the better, the latter were more actively harmful because their insistence upon trusting to natural laws was definitely in the interest of personal and class profit.

The omitted premise in the case of both groups is the fact that neither science nor technology is an impersonal cosmic force.

They operate only in the medium of human desire, foresight, aim, and effort. Science and technology are transactions in which man and nature work together and in which the human factor is that directly open to modification and direction. That man takes part along with physical conditions in invention and use of the devices, implements, and machinery of industry and commerce no one would think of denying.

But in practice, if not in so many words, it has been denied that man has any responsibility for the consequences that result from what he invents and employs. This denial is implicit in our widespread refusal to engage in large-scale collective planning. Not a day passes, even in the present crisis, when the whole idea of such planning is not ridiculed as an emanation from the brain of starry-eyed professors or of others equally inept in practical affairs. And all of this in the face of the fact that there is not a successful industrial organization that does not owe its success to persistent planning within a limited field—with an eye to profit— to say nothing of the terribly high price we have paid in the way of insecurity and war for putting our trust in drift.

Refusal to accept responsibility for looking ahead and for planning in matters national and international is based upon re- fusal to employ in social affairs, in the field of human relations, the methods of observation, interpretation, and test that are matters of course in dealing with physical things, and to which we owe the conquest of physical nature. The net result is a state of imbalance, of profoundly disturbed equilibrium between our physical knowledge and our social-moral knowledge. This lack of harmony is a powerful factor in producing the present crisis with all its tragic features. For physical knowledge and physical technology have far outstripped social or humane knowledge and human engineering. Our failure to use in matters of direct human concern the scientific methods which have revolutionized physical knowledge has permitted the latter to dominate the so- cial scene.

The change in the physical aspect of the world has gone on so rapidly that there is probably no ground for surprise in the fact that our psychological and moral knowledge has not kept pace. But there is cause for astonishment in the fact that after the ca- tastrophe of war, insecurity, and the threat to democratic institu- tions have shown the need for moral and intellectual attitudes and habits that will correspond with the changed state of the world, there should be a definite campaign to make the scientific attitude the scapegoat for present evils, while a return to the beliefs and practices of a prescientific and pretechnological age is urged as the road to our salvation.

The organized attack now being made against science and against technology as inherently materialistic and as usurping the place properly held by abstract moral precepts—abstract because divorcing ends from the means by which they must be realized—defines the issue we now have to face. Shall we go backwards or shall we go ahead to discover and put into practice the means by which science and technology shall be made fundamental in the promotion of human welfare? The failure to use scientific methods in creating understanding of human relationships and interests and in planning measures and policies that correspond in human affairs to the technologies in physical use is easily explained in historical terms. The new science began with things at the furthest remove from human affairs, namely with the stars of the heavens. From astronomy the new methods went on to win their victories in physics and chemistry. Still later science was applied in physiological and biological subject-matter. At every stage, the advance met determined resistance from the representatives of established institutions who felt their prestige was bound up with maintenance of old beliefs and found their class-control of others being threatened. In consequence, many workers in science found that the easiest way in which to procure an opportunity to carry on their inquiries was to adopt an attitude of extreme specialization. The effect was equivalent to the position that their methods and conclusions were not and could not be "dangerous," since they had no point of contact with man's serious moral concerns. This position in turn served to perpetuate and confirm the older separation of man as man from the rest of nature and to intensify the split between the "material" and the moral and "ideal."

Thus it has come about that when scientific inquiry began to move from its virtually complete victories in astronomy and physics and its partial victory in the field of living things over into the field of human affairs and concerns, the interests and institutions that offered resistance to its earlier advance are gathering themselves together for a final attack upon that aspect of science which in truth constitutes its supreme and culminating significance. On the principle that offense is the best defense, respect for science and loyalty to its outlook are attacked as the chief source of all our present social ills. One may read, for example, in current literature such a condescending concession as marks the following passage: "Of course, the scientific attitude, though often leading to such a catastrophe, is not to be condemned," the immediate context showing that the particular "catastrophe" in mind consists of "errors leading to war . . . derived from an incorrect theory of truth." Since these errors are produced by belief in the applicability of scientific method to human as well as physical facts, the remedy, according to this writer is to abandon "the erroneous application of the methods and results of natural science to the problems of human life."

In three respects the passage is typical of the organized campaign now in active operation. There is first the assertion that such catastrophes as that of the present war are the result of devotion to scientific method and conclusions. The denunciation of "natural" science as applied to human affairs carries, in the second place, the implication that man is outside of and above nature, and the consequent necessity of returning to the medieval prescientific doctrine of a supernatural foundation and outlook in all social and moral subjects. Then thirdly there is the assumption, directly contrary to fact, that the scientific method has at the present time been seriously and systematically applied to the problems of human life.

I dignify the passage quoted by this reference to it because it serves quite as well as a multitude of other passages from reactionaries to convey a sense of the present issues. It is true that the *results* of natural science have had a large share, for evil as well as for good, in bringing the world to its present pass. But it is equally true that "natural" science has been identified with *physical* science in a sense in which the physical is set over against the human. It is true that the interests and institutions which are now attacking science are just the forces which in behalf of a supernatural centre of gravity are those that strive to maintain this tragic split in human affairs. Now the issue, as is becoming clearer every day, is whether we shall go backward or whether we shall go forward toward recognition in theory and practice of the indissoluble unity of the humanistic and the naturalistic.

What has all this to do with education? The answer to this question may be gathered from the fact that those who are engaged in assault upon science centre their attacks upon the increased attention given by our schools to science and to its application in vocational training. In a world which is largely what it is today because of science and technology they propose that education should turn its back upon even the degree of recognition science and technology have received. They propose we turn our face to the medievalism in which so-called "liberal" arts were identified with literary arts: a course natural to adopt in an age innocent of knowledge of nature, an age in which the literary arts were the readiest means of rising above barbarism through acquaintance with the achievements of Greek-Roman culture. Their proposal is so remote from the facts of the present world, it involves such a bland ignoring of actualities, that there is a temptation to dismiss it as idle vaporing. But it would be a tragic mistake to take the reactionary assaults so lightly. For they are an expression of just the forces that keep science penned up in a compartment labelled "materialistic and anti-human." They strengthen all the habits and institutions which render that which is morally "ideal" impotent in action and which leave the "material" to operate without humane direction.

Let me return for the moment to my initial statement that the basic error of social idealists was the assumption that something called "natural law" could be trusted, with only incidental cooperation by human beings, to bring about the desired ends. The lesson to be learned is that human attitudes and efforts are the strategic centre for promotion of the generous aims of peace among nations; promotion of economic security; the use of political means in order to advance freedom and equality; and the worldwide cause of democratic institutions. Anyone who starts from this premise is bound to see that it carries with it the basic importance of education in creating the habits and the outlook that are able and eager to secure the ends of peace, democracy, and economic stability.

When this is seen, it will also be seen how little has actually been done in our schools to render science and technology active agencies in creating the attitudes and dispositions and in securing the kinds of knowledge that are capable of coping with the problems of men and women today. Externally a great modification has taken place in subjects taught and in methods of teaching them. But when the changes are critically examined it is found that they consist largely in emergency concessions and accommodation to the urgent conditions and issues of the contemporary world. The standards and the controlling methods in education are still mainly those of a prescientific and pretechnological age.

This statement will seem to many persons to be exaggerated. But consider the purposes which as a rule still govern instruction in just those subjects that are taken to be decisively "modern," namely science and vocational preparation. Science is taught upon the whole as a body of readymade information and technical skills. It is not taught as furnishing in its method the pattern for all effective intelligent conduct. It is taught upon the whole not with respect to the way in which it actually enters into human life, and hence as a supremely humanistic subject, but as if it had to do with a world which is "external" to human concerns. It is not presented in connection with the ways in which it actually enters into every aspect and phase of present human life. And it is hardly necessary to add that still less is it taught in connection with what scientific knowledge of human affairs might do in overcoming sheer drift. Scientific method and conclusions will not have gained a fundamentally important place in education until they are seen and treated as supreme agencies in giving direction to collective and cooperative human behavior.

The same sort of thing is to be said about the kind of use now made in education of practical and vocational subjects, so called. The reactionary critics are busy urging that the latter subjects be taught to the masses—who are said to be incapable of rising to the plane of the "intellectual" but who do the useful work which somebody has to do, and who may be taught by vocational education to do it more effectively. This view is of course an open and avowed attempt to return to that dualistic separation of ideas and action, of the "intellectual" and the "practical," of the liberal and servile arts, that marked the feudal age. And this reactionary move in perpetuation of the split from which the world is suffering is offered as a cure, a panacea, not as the social and moral quackery it actually is. As is the case with science, the thing supremely needful is to go forward. And the forward movement in the case of technology as in the case of science is to do away with the chasm which ancient and medieval educational practice and theory set up between the liberal and the vocational, not to treat the void, the hole, constituted by this chasm, as if it were a foundation for the creation of free society.

There is nothing whatever inherent in the occupations that are socially necessary and useful to divide them into those which are "learned" professions and those which are menial, servile, and illiberal. As far as such a separation exists in fact it is an inheritance from the earlier class structure of human relations. It is a denial of democracy. At the very time when an important, perhaps *the* important, problem in education is to fill education having an occupational direction with a genuinely liberal content, we have, believe it or not, a movement, such as is sponsored for example by President Hutchins, to cut vocational training off from any contact with what is liberating by relegating it to special schools devoted to inculcation of technical skills. Inspiring vocational education with a liberal spirit and filling it with a liberal content is not a utopian dream. It is a demonstrated possibility in schools here and there in which subjects usually labelled "practically useful" are taught charged with scientific understanding and with a sense of the social-moral applications they potentially possess.

If little is said in the foregoing remarks specifically upon the topic of democratic faith, it is because their bearing upon a democratic outlook largely appears upon their very face. Conditions in this country when the democratic philosophy of life and democratic institutions were taking shape were such as to encourage a belief that the latter were so natural to man, so appropriate to his very being, that if they were once established they would tend to maintain themselves. I cannot rehearse here the list of events that have given this naive faith a shock. They are contained in every deliberate attack upon democracy and in every expression of cynicism about its past failures and pessimism about its future—attacks and expressions which have to be taken seriously if they are looked at as signs of trying to establish democracy as an end in separation from the concrete means upon which the end depends.

Democracy is not an easy road to take and follow. On the contrary, it is, as far as its realization is concerned in the complex conditions of the contemporary world, a supremely difficult one.

Upon the whole we are entitled to take courage from the fact that it has worked as well as it has done. But to this courage we must add, if our courage is to be intelligent rather than blind, the fact that successful maintenance of democracy demands the utmost in use of the best available methods to procure a social knowledge that is reasonably commensurate with our physical knowledge, and the invention and use of forms of social engineering reasonably commensurate with our technological abilities in physical affairs.

This then is the task indicated. It is, if we employ large terms, to humanize science. This task in the concrete cannot be accomplished save as the fruit of science, which is named technology, is also humanized. And the task can be executed in the concrete only as it is broken up into vital applications of intelligence in a multitude of fields to a vast diversity of problems so that science and technology may be rendered servants of the democratic hope and faith. The cause is capable of inspiring loyalty in thought and deed. But there has to be joined to aspiration and effort the formation of free, wide-ranging, trained attitudes of observation and understanding such as incorporate within themselves, as a matter so habitual as to be unconscious, the vital principles of scientific method. In this achievement science, education, and the democratic cause meet as one. May we be equal to the occasion. For it is our human problem. If a solution is found it will be through the medium of human desire, human understanding, and human endeavor.

Challenge to Liberal Thought

There is probably no better way to realize what philosophy is about when it is living, not antiquarian, than to ask ourselves what criteria and what aims and ideals should control our educational policies and undertakings. Such a question, if it is systematically followed out, will bring to light things that are morally and intellectually fundamental in the direction of human affairs. It will disclose differences and conflicts that are basic in society as it now exists. It will give concrete and definite meaning to problems and principles that are remote and abstract when they are presented in terms of philosophical systems isolated from human needs and human struggles. For this reason the present campaign of assault upon what is modern and new in education is to be welcomed even by those who believe its tendency is thoroughly reactionary. It has to be faced, and facing it will bring to light beliefs that have too long been kept in the dark. For it is true in education as elsewhere that the Great Bad is the mixing together of things that are contrary and opposed. The drawing of lines that is now going on will not only serve to clear up confusion in our educational estate but will tend to breathe life into the dead bones of philosophy.

We are told that scientific subjects have been encroaching upon literary subjects, which alone are truly humanistic. We are told that zeal for the practical and utilitarian has resulted in displacement of a liberal education by one that is merely vocational, one that narrows the whole man down to that fraction of his being concerned with making a living. We are told that the whole tendency is away from the humane to the materialistic, from the permanently rational to the temporarily expedient—and so on.

[First published in *Fortune* 30 (August 1944): 155–57, 180, 182, 184, 186, 188, 190. For Alexander Meiklejohn's reply, see Appendix 10. For rejoinder by Dewey, see pp. 333–36. For further letters, see Appendix 11 and p. 337.]

Now curiously enough it happens that some of us who disagree radically with the reasons given for criticizing our present system and equally radically with the remedy that is urged, agree that the present system (if it may be called a system) is so lacking in unity of aim, material, and method as to be something of a patchwork. We agree that an overloaded and congested curriculum needs simplification. We agree that we are uncertain as to where we are going and where we want to go, and why we are doing what we do.

In many details our criticisms of the present state of education do not differ widely from those of the critics whose fundamental premises and aims are in sharp opposition to ours. The standpoint from which criticisms are made and the direction in which reform is urged are, however, worlds apart. The issue is taking shape. We agree as to absence of unity. We differ profoundly from the belief that the evils and defects of our system spring from excessive attention to what is modern in human civilization—science, technology, contemporary social issues and problems. Rather we rest our own critical estimate of the present educational situation upon a belief that the factors that correspond to what is living in present society, the factors that are shaping modern culture, are either confusedly smothered by excessive attention to the old or are diverted into channels in which they become technical and relatively illiberal in comparison with what they would be if they were given the central position.

I begin then with the fact that we are now being told that a genuinely liberal education would require return to the models, patterns, and standards that were laid down in Greece some twenty-five hundred years ago and renewed and put into practice in the best age of feudal medievalism six and seven centuries ago. It is true that a theory of education using the word "liberal" as applied to an education having nothing to do with the "practical" was formulated in Greece. From Greece we inherit the tradition that puts "liberal" and "mechanical" education in sharp opposition to each other and that—a fact to be noted—identifies as mechanical anything and everything concerned with industry and useful commodities and services.

This philosophy was faithful to the facts of the social life in which it appeared. It translated into intellectual terms the institutions, customs, and moral attitudes that flourished in the life of Athens. As was proper, a liberal or free education was the education of a free man in the Athenian community. But this has to be placed alongside the fact, totally improper from the standpoint of modern democratic communities, that free citizens were few in number, and that their freedom had a large servile class as its substratum. The class that enjoyed the privileges of freedom and a liberal education was based upon precisely those considerations that modern liberation has steadily striven to get rid of. For a status fixed at and by birth, sex, and economic condition is just what democratic societies regard as *illiberal*. To the Greek philosopher, these differences were necessary; they were fixed "by nature." They were so established in social institutions that any other view seemed irrational even to the wisest men of the time.

This fact might well make us look with suspicion upon an educational philosophy that, at the *present* day, defines liberal education in terms that are the opposite of what is genuinely liberal. Vocational and practical education was illiberal in Greece because it was the training of a servile class. Liberal education was liberal in Greece because it was the way of life enjoyed by a small group who were free to devote themselves to higher things. They were free to do so because they lived upon the fruits of the labor of an industrially enslaved class. Moreover, industry was carried on by routine apprenticeship in ways that were handed down from parents to children.

That the models and patterns followed by craftsmen achieved a high degree of aesthetic development should not be permitted to blind us to this fact. For it marks a striking contrast with the conditions of modern industry. Methods of work are now the result of the continuous application of science. Inventions, themselves the result of application of science, are constantly encroaching upon ways of production that carry over routine and precedent. There was justification in existing conditions for the Greek who distinguished between activities that were the manifestation of rational insight or science and those that were the expression of irrational routine. But there is no excuse for such a view at the present time. There is now more natural science involved in the conduct of our industry than there is anything nearly resembling science in the conduct of our political and social affairs.

The problem of going ahead instead of going back is then a

problem of liberalizing our technical and vocational education. The average worker has little or no awareness of the scientific processes embodied in the work he carries on. What he does is often to him routine and mechanical. To this extent the diagnosis the critics make of present vocational education is correct in too many cases. But their reactionary remedy involves fixation of just that which is bad in the present system. Instead of seeking an education that would make all who go to school aware of the scientific basis of industrial processes, they would draw the lines still more sharply between those who receive a vocational training, deliberately kept illiberal, and the much smaller number who enjoy a liberal education—after the Greek literary model. A truly liberal, and liberating, education would refuse today to isolate vocational training on any of its levels from a continuous education in the social, moral, and scientific contexts within which wisely administered callings and professions must function.

Not to base the materials and methods of the education that does this work upon intelligent selection and arrangement of what is growing and vital in the present, with deliberate omission of that which has served its time, is the sure way to perpetuate the confusion and conflicts of the world in which we now live. Exercise of intelligent courage to make education what it might be would result in an access of both confidence and the wisdom that would justify the confidence.

The situation is no better when we turn to the medieval version of the Greek theory of liberal education. The gulf between serf and landlord was too fixed in medieval society even to attract the attention of the most liberal-minded philosophers. It was accepted as a matter of course, or as "natural." In addition, medieval society had no political citizenship and no community life in the *civic* sense that was supreme in the Athenian city-state. Although words borrowed from Greek philosophy about liberal arts and education were profusely employed, their meanings had nothing in common with those of Athenian life. The important institution was the church, not the city-state. Consequently, in medieval thought the difference between the priest and the layman took the place occupied in Greek philosophical writings by the difference between freeman and artisan. The word *cleric* strikes the keynote of medieval culture in very much the same way that the word *citizen* sounds the keynote of Athenian life.

The result, so far as educational philosophy is concerned, explains how it is that the present reactionary movement is closer to the medieval model than to the Greek. The activity of the free Athenian citizen was directly concerned with the affairs and problems of a civic community in which theocratic interests and religious rites were a regular and subordinate part of the life of a secular and temporal community. Aristotle, moreover, taught that even free political life was not completely free from the taint of the practical. The only completely free life was that devoted to pursuit of science and philosophy. And nature, not the supernatural, was at the heart of ancient Greek philosophy.

To the Greek scientist-philosopher firsthand perception of nature, if not through the senses then through the "intellect," was the source of truth. Writings bequeathed by the past were used for the suggestions they contained, as materials to set forth alternative possibilities. They were never taken as final authority. The one thing forbidden was to permit the opinions of others to come between vision and the facts of nature. But in medieval culture that which had already been said, written down and transmitted by linguistic means from generation to generation, became *the* final authority. It is enough to cite the role of what are significantly known as "the Scriptures." I do not mean that there was not a great display of intellectual acuteness and sharpening of wits. But it was directed to the study, interpretation, adaptation, and organization of letters, of what was linguistically transmitted from previous learning. By and large these writings took the place nature itself had held in Greek philosophy and science. *They* constituted the world to be investigated.

Nevertheless, given the conditions of Europe at the time, this dependence upon letters as the medium of communication with past knowledge was practically necessary. To be liberal is all one with being liberating, with effecting a release of human powers. Failure to realize this is the source of one of the great errors of our neo-scholastics who suppose that the subject matter of a liberal education is fixed in itself. Linguistic arts and the written materials of the past exercised a liberating function in the Middle Ages as nothing else could have done. For all northern Europe was only just emerging from a state of barbarism. Historically speaking, it is practically impossible to see what effective tutor and guide the movement could have had save acquaintance with the products of the infinitely higher culture developed centuries before in the Mediterranean basin. Language, letters, was the sole medium of contact with those products. Clerics were the sole class possessing both the mastery of linguistic tools and the moral authority to make them central in education.

Social and cultural conditions since the Middle Ages have undergone a great, a revolutionary, change. In spirit, we are nearer the culture of antiquity than we are to that of the medieval period. Great as is the change from a servile to a free basis in organization of social relations, it can be said with considerable truth that the change is in line with *principles* stated in Athens. The full significance of these principles could not be perceived by their authors because of the practical pressure exerted by social institutions. Historical illiteracy is thus the outstanding trait of those critics who urge return to the ideas of the Greek-medieval period as if the ideas of the two ages were the same because philosophers of the medieval period used some of the verbal formulas set forth by philosophers of the earlier period.

Language is still fundamentally important in education. Communication is the feature that definitely marks off man from other creatures; it is the condition without which culture would not exist. But the notion that language, linguistic skills and studies can be used for the same ends and by the same methods under contemporary conditions as in Greek, Alexandrian, or medieval times is as absurd in principle as it would be injurious in practice were it adopted. The attempt to reestablish linguistic skills and materials as the centre of education, and to do it under the guise of "education for freedom" or a "liberal" education, is directly opposed to all that democratic countries cherish as freedom. The idea that an adequate education of any kind can be obtained by means of a miscellaneous assortment of a hundred books, more or less, is laughable when viewed practically. A five-foot bookshelf for adults, to be read, reread, and digested at leisure throughout a lifetime, is one thing. Crowded into four years and dealt out in fixed doses, it is quite another thing. In theory and basic aim, however, it is not funny. For it marks a departure from what is sound in the Greek view of knowledge as a product of intelligence exercised at first hand. It marks reversion to the medieval view of dependence upon the final authority of what others have found out—or supposed they had found out—and without the historical grounds that gave reason to the scholars of the Middle Ages.

The reactionary movement is dangerous (or would be if it made serious headway) because it ignores and in effect denies the principle of experimental inquiry and firsthand observation that is the lifeblood of the entire advance made in the sciences—an advance so marvelous that the progress in knowledge made in uncounted previous millenniums is almost nothing in comparison. It is natural enough that the chief advocates of the scholastic reaction should be literary men with defective scientific educations, or else theologians who are convinced in advance of the existence of a supernaturally founded and directed Institution, whose official utterances rank as fixed and final truths because they are beyond the scope of human inquiry and criticism.

Mr. Hutchins wrote as follows: [1]

> We know that there is a natural moral law, and we can understand what it is because we know that man has a nature, and we can understand it. The nature of man, which is the same everywhere, is obscured but not obliterated by the differing conventions of different cultures. The specific quality of human nature . . . is that man is a rational and spiritual being . . .

By his inherent and necessary essence, then, man is the same in all ages, climes, and cultures. Nothing that can happen to him, or in the physical, biological, and social world of which man is a part, can make any difference to his nature. The principles that have authority over his conduct and his moral beliefs are therefore fixed and immutable. Moreover, they are perceived by a faculty independent of, and supreme over, the methods by which patient inquiry, with the aid of experimental observation, discovers natural facts of self, society, and the physical world.

There is nothing novel in this view. We are familiar with it from early childhood. It is a conventionally established part of a large portion of our training in family and Sunday school. Nevertheless, it is the expression of a provincial and conventional point of view, of a culture that is pre-scientific in the sense that science bears today. Men of at least equal penetration (Aristotle

1. *Fortune,* June 1943.

himself for example) with those now asserting the absolute uniformity of human nature and morals taught the same thing about natural objects. Astronomical and biological sciences were once as firmly based upon eternal uniformity as moral science and philosophy are now asserted to be. In astronomy, it was held that the higher heavens have always had and always will have, with everything in them, an unswerving circular movement. The teachings of present astronomical science would then have seemed like a proclamation of chaotic turmoil. In biology, the complete fixity and uniformity of species of plants and animals were taken to be the rational and necessary foundational truths for all scientific knowledge.

In short, the view now so confidently put forth about morals once prevailed in natural science. The foundation of both is that the uniform and unchangeable is inherently superior in perfection and truth to anything subject to change. From the standpoint of society, it is easy to understand the rise of this view. It is appropriate to societies ruled by custom—they fear change as the source of instability and disorder. It was also a natural view when observation was restricted by lack of instruments. Without the use of a telescope, variations in the positions of "fixed stars" could not be noticed. Changes of kind or species in plants and animals were observable only when monstrosities appeared. Belief in the eternal uniformity of human nature is thus the surviving remnant of a belief once universally held about the heavens and about all living creatures. Scientific method and conclusions have had little effect upon persons whose education is predominantly literary. Otherwise they would not continue to assert in one field a belief that science has abandoned everywhere else.

The group in question does not, however, oppose the teaching of science. Far from it. Their claim is that the subject matter of natural science is of subordinate importance; and that, when all is said and done, it belongs with the subjects whose value is technical, utilitarian, practical. Thereby they endorse and tend to confirm the split between natural means of authentic knowing, on the one hand, and everything having moral, ideal, and "spiritual" importance, on the other.

It is hard to see how any thoughtful person can view a split of this kind lightly. There was no such separation in Greek and me-

dieval "science." All fundamental truths about the natural world
and natural objects in their science concerned what was as eternal and unchanging as were moral ends and principles. In fact,
Aristotle, the authority in the medieval period in respect to natural and temporal matters, expressly assigned to the subject matter of astronomy and biology a higher position in respect to
complete constancy than to moral knowledge. For he observed
the undoubted fact that moral practices and aims change from
place to place and time to time.

In truth, the present-day alliance between those who appeal to
Greek philosophy and those who appeal to medieval philosophy
is tactical rather than basic. They are allies in a common dislike,
co-dwellers in a Cave of Adullam. They have the same dislikes
without having the same loyalty and goal. Greek science is indeed marked by traits that are supranatural from the standpoint
of the present science of nature. Nevertheless, according to
Greek science the subjects of science were profoundly natural
and inherently reasonable. According to medieval theological
philosophy, the basis of all ultimate moral principles is supernatural—not merely above nature and reason, but so far beyond
the scope of the latter that they must be miraculously revealed
and sustained.

Some of the theological fellow travelers of Mr. Hutchins make
this point clear. For they characteristically introduce a complete
division between political, civic, and social morality and personal morality. The former is *"natural"*; its virtues are directed
toward "the good of civilization." The latter has to take into account "the *supratemporal* destiny" of man. The teaching of
"natural morality" merely is likely to be influenced by "what are
called the virtues of political life and civilization." It tends to neglect or disparage personal morality, which "is the root of *all*
morality"—a morality, be it remembered, that is supernatural in
origin and destination.

The dilemma in which liberal writers of this school find themselves is illustrated in the fact that they make a plea for an "integral humanism," and for avoidance of cleavage. They then set up
a series of complete cleavages on their own account. There is one
between man and the supernatural; one between the temporal
and the eternal; one between humanity and divinity; one between the inner and the outer; and finally one between the civic

and social (or things of this world generally) and the alleged supratemporal destiny of man—needing, of course, a special supernatural and infallible church to bridge the gulf.

From one point of view, these authors simply manifest the division and conflict characteristic of our present civilization. But in addition they recommend its systematic fixation as the cure of the evils that the cleavage occasions. At that, in view of what the two schools have in common, the one represented by our theological philosopher seems to have the advantage over its temporary partner. For they claim to speak for a divinely founded church, which is permanently directed from on high. When, therefore, the utterances of fallible human reason vary and when the merely civic moralities of different peoples conflict with one another, it can authoritatively point out *the* truth.

The issue raised in educational philosophy is thus significant as a manifestation of a cleft that now marks every phase and aspect of philosophy. It presents the difference between an outlook that goes to the past for instruction and for guidance, and one that holds that philosophy, if it is to be of help in the present situation, must pay supreme heed to movements, needs, problems, and resources that are distinctively modern. This latter view is often countered by caricaturing it. It is said to be based upon insensate love of novelty and change, upon devotion to the modern just because it happens to come later in the course of time. The actual state of the case, however, is that there are factors at work in contemporary life that are of transcendent value in promise, if not yet in achievement. They are experimental science and experimental method in the field of knowledge. This field includes a definite morale and ethic as well as definite conclusions about man and the world. The second modern factor is the democratic spirit in human relations. The third is technological control of the energies of nature in behalf of humane ends. All three are closely linked. The revolution in natural science is the parent of inventions of instruments and processes that provide the substantial body of modern industrial technology. This fact is so obvious as to be undeniable—though there are some persons superficial enough to attribute the great advance in industry not to the methods and conclusions of modern science but to love of pecuniary power. What perhaps is not equally obvious is that the marvelous advance in natural science has come about because of the breaking down of the wall existing in ancient and medieval institutions between "higher" things of a purely intellectual and "spiritual" nature and "lower" things of a "practical" and "material" nature.

For it is a historical fact, evident to all who are willing to look, that the change from relative sterility and stagnation to a career of fruitfulness and continued progress in science began when inquirers used the instruments and processes of socially despised industry as agencies by means of which to know nature. Then the change achieved in production of commodities and services was a great factor in breaking down feudal institutions. Substitution of easy communication in place of the isolation of peoples, groups, and classes has been an agency in bringing the democratic movement into existence.

I come back to the fact that we are living in a mixed and divided life. We are pulled in opposite directions. We have not as yet a philosophy that is modern in other than a chronological sense. We do not have as yet an educational or any other social institution that is not a mixture of opposed elements. Division between methods and conclusions in natural science and those prevailing in morals and religion is a serious matter, from whatever angle it be regarded. It means a society that is not unified in its most important concerns.

I do not understand that those who are urging return to the ancient foundation in morals and social institutions wish to return to earlier conditions in natural science; nor yet to abolish all modern inventions and appliances that are the fruit of experimental extension of science. But the logical and practical import of their scheme is simply to fixate the division, the split from which we suffer. The spirit and method of the pre-scientific period is to prevail in the "higher" sphere while science and technology are relegated to an inherently lower and separate compartment of life. Preaching, or else an external institutional authority, is to keep the latter in its place.

The one outstanding issue concerns, then, the direction in which we are to move. Are we compelled to hold that one method obtains in natural science and another, radically different, in moral questions? Scientific method is now finding its way into the psychological field; it is already at home in anthropological study. As the conclusions reached in these studies find their way into general acceptance, is a conflict between science and moral beliefs to replace the old conflict between science and what was taken to be religion? And the question is the more pertinent because the religion in question was also the expression of a prescientific stage of culture.

The issue as it offers itself in the educational field brings home in a vivid and striking manner this problem of the direction to be taken in philosophy. I do not mean that the question in philosophy is as momentous as the direction we are to take in our practical affairs—in education, industry, and politics. But the two are closely connected. The old metaphysical and theological philosophies reflected the social conditions in which *they* were formulated. By their translation into terms of reason, these conditions were given support. The traditional philosophies provided guidance in the direction taken by social movements. They strive to exercise these functions today. They succeed in so doing, however, only to the extent of introducing confusion and conflict.

I hope I have made it clear that I have no sympathy with the philosophy underlying the views I have been considering. But its active appearance on the scene is to be welcomed. Philosophy needed to be taken out of the hands of those who have identified it with barren intellectual gymnastic exercise and purely verbal analyses. Perhaps it took the severe jolt of the present reaction to bring philosophy back to man. At all events, the educational philosophy here discussed raises all the philosophical problems that now demand attention if philosophy is to have anything to say in the present crisis.

The issue of the immutable versus the changing involves the question of whether the method of inquiry and test that has wrought marvels in one field is to be applied so as to extend and advance our knowledge in moral and social matters. Is there an impassable gulf between science and morals? Or are principles and general truths in morals of the same kind as in science— namely, working hypotheses that on one hand condense the results of continued prior experience and inquiry, and on the other hand direct further fruitful inquiry whose conclusions in turn test and develop for further use the working principles used? Suppose it *were* true in the abstract that moral principles are as fixed and eternally uniform as they are said to be. Has any one indicated even in the roughest way how they are then to be applied? At bottom the issue is drawn between dogmas (so rigid that they ultimately must appeal to force) and recourse to intelligent observation guided by the best wisdom already in our possession, which is the heart of scientific method.

Let me give one illustration of the application of scientific thinking to what was formerly regarded as an unchangeable absolute. It is drawn from the man who more than any other single person is the begetter in philosophy of an attitude and outlook distinctively American, Charles Peirce. The illustration is taken from a subject of crucial moral import, the meaning of truth. Over against the traditional view of truth as a fixed structure of eternal and unchanging principles already in our possession to which everything else should be made to conform, Peirce said that truth "is that concordance of an abstract statement with the ideal limit toward which endless investigation would tend to bring scientific belief." This concordance may be possessed even now and here by a scientific belief in case there is "confession of its inaccuracy and one-sidedness," since this "confession is an essential ingredient of truth." We have here, as in a nutshell, a statement of the profound difference that is made in a crucial instance between belief in fixity and in change. There is also the definite implication that change can mean continuous growth, development, liberation, and cooperation, while fixity means the dogmatism that historically has always exhibited itself in intolerance and brutal persecution of the dissenter and the inquirer. Faith in endlessly pursued inquiry and in an undogmatic friendly attitude toward present possessions (which is the spur to continued persistent effort) is treated by those whose education has failed to encompass the scientific spirit as a kind of systematic indifference and carelessness amounting to demoralization.

The very heart of political democracy is adjudication of social differences by discussion and exchange of views. This method provides a rough approximation to the method of effecting change by means of experimental inquiry and test: the scientific method. The very foundation of the democratic procedure is dependence upon experimental production of social change; an experimentation directed by working principles that are tested and developed in the very process of being tried out in action. Its operation is compromised, however, by the persistent influence of the very philosophy we are urged to fall back upon.

It is no mere accident that continental Europe, which is now the most disturbed portion of the world and the source of tragic disturbance everywhere else, is just that part that has stuck most closely to the educational philosophy we are now being urged to go back to. America must be looked upon as either an offshoot of Europe, culturally speaking, or as a New World in other than a geographical sense. To take the latter view is neither brash patriotic nationalism nor yet a brand of isolationism. It is an acknowledgment of work to be done. Europe has, at least till very recently, led the world in scientific achievement, and it will be a long time before America will rival what the Old World has accomplished in the plastic arts and in literature. But continental Europe in general and Germany in particular has been the home of the practices and the philosophy based on strict separation between science as technical and ever changing and morals conceived in terms of fixed, unchanging principles. If the name "New World" applies to the American scene, it is because we have the task of bringing into cooperative union the things that the philosophy and the education to which we are being urged to return have kept divided.

In short, the chief influence in retarding and preventing the conscious realization that will give unity and steadiness to the democratic movement is precisely the philosophy of dogmatic rigidity and uniformity. In consequence, the chief opportunity and chief responsibility of those who call themselves philosophers are to make clear the intrinsic kinship of democracy with the methods of directing change that have revolutionized science. In that way and only in that way can we be rid of the dualism of standards, aims, and methods—that is to say the very division from which we are now suffering. Technological industry is the creation of science. It is also the most widely and deeply influential factor in the practical determination of social conditions. The most immediate human problem of our age is to effect a transformation of the immense resources the new technology has put in our hands into positive instruments of human being. The contribution that the reactionary philosophy makes is to urge that technology and science are intrinsically of an inferior and illiberal nature!

What exists in social philosophy at the present time is largely an abstract disputation between something called "individualism" and something called "socialism." But the problem is a concrete one. How shall this and that definite factory and field operation be made to contribute to the educative release and growth of human capacities, as well as to production of a large and reasonably cheap supply of material goods? The problem is one that, by its own terms, can be dealt with only by the continuous application of the scientific method of experimental observation and test. Those who feel in need of a specific example of the connection between science and morals, between "natural" facts and human values, will find it here.

A philosophy that glorifies the gulf between the "material" and the "spiritual," between immutable principles and social conditions in a state of rapid change, stands in the way of dealing effectively with this dominant issue. The solution of the issue will not, of course, take place in philosophy. But the opportunity of philosophy is to help get rid of intellectual habits that now stand in the way of a solution.

As far as school education is a part of the required practical means, educational theory or philosophy has the task and the opportunity of helping to break down the philosophy of fixation that bolsters external authority in opposition to free cooperation. It must contest the notion that morals are something wholly separate from and above science and scientific method. It must help banish the conception that the daily work and vocation of man are negligible in comparison with literary pursuits, and that human destiny here and now is of slight importance in comparison with some supernatural destiny. It must accept wholeheartedly the scientific way, not merely of technology, but of life in order to achieve the promise of modern democratic ideals.

The Problem of the Liberal Arts College

Nothing is more striking in recent discussions of liberal education than the widespread and seemingly spontaneous use of *liberating* as a synonym for *liberal*. For it marks a break with the traditional idea that a certain group of studies is liberal because of something inhering in them—belonging to them by virtue of an indwelling essence or nature—as opium was once said to put persons to sleep because of its dormitive nature. This latter view of the liberal arts has the merit, for some writers and educators, of rendering it unnecessary to inquire closely into what the subjects actually accomplish for those who study them. If a particular group of studies is "liberal" in and of itself, such an inquiry is irrelevant. Failure to exercise a liberating educative effect in given cases is not the fault of the studies but of external conditions, such, perhaps, as the inherent incapacity of some students to rise to a truly "intellectual" level. To define liberal as that which liberates is to bring the problem of liberal education and of the liberal arts college within the domain of an inquiry in which the issue is settled by search for what is actually accomplished. The test and justification of claims put forth is found in observable consequences, not in an *a priori* dogma.

The concrete significance of the foregoing generalities in locating the present problem of the liberal arts college is found in outstanding historic considerations. The theory that certain subjects are liberal because of something forever fixed in their own nature was formulated prior to the rise of scientific method. It was consonant with the philosophical theory which was once held about every form of knowledge. For according to that doctrine if anything is knowable it is because of its inherent nature, form or essence, so that knowledge consists of an intuitive grasp by pure

[First published in *American Scholar* 13 (October 1944): 391–93.]

"intellect" of this nature. This doctrine is completely repudiated in the practices which constitute the scientific revolution.

In the second place, the traditional doctrine was embodied in educational institutions in a period that was pre-technological as well as pre-scientific. The liberal arts were sharply contrasted with the useful arts. This contrast had its basis in social and cultural conditions. The useful or industrial arts were acquired by means of sheer apprenticeship in fixed routines in which insight into principles played a negligible part. The industrial revolution which marks the last few centuries is the result of the scientific revolution. Only the most backward "useful" arts are now matters of empirical routine. They are now technological, a fact which signifies that they are founded in scientific understanding of underlying principles.

In the third place, and most important of all, social organization has also undergone a revolution. The distinction between "liberal" and "useful" arts is a product of the time when those engaged in industrial production were mechanics and artisans who occupied a servile social status. The meaning attached to the traditional doctrine of liberal arts cannot be understood except in connection with the social fact of division between free men and slaves and serfs, and the fact that only the former received an "intellectual" education, which under the given conditions necessarily meant literary and linguistic training. At the time in which a scientific revolution was radically changing the nature and method of knowledge, understanding and learning, and in which the industrial revolution was breaking down once for all the wall between the hand and the head, the political revolution of the rise of democracy was giving a socially free status to those who had been serfs. It thereby destroyed the very foundation of the traditional separation between the arts suitable for a "gentleman" and the arts suited to those engaged in production of useful services and commodities: that is to say, the separation between "liberal" and "useful" arts.

It is not possible to grasp and state the present dilemma of the liberal arts college, and of the function it should undertake in our society, except as they are placed and seen in this context of irreversible historic movements. Nothing can be sillier than attributing the problems of the contemporary liberal college in this country to the activities of a number of misguided educationalists, instead of to the impact of social forces which have continually gained in force. If there is anything equally silly, it is the assertion (by those who would resolve these problems by a return to an outworn identification of "liberal" with the linguistic, the literary and metaphysical) that their opponents are complacently satisfied with the present situation. For, in fact, the latter anticipated the former by many years in pointing out the confusions, conflicts, and uncertainties that mark present collegiate education.

When the situation is viewed in historic perspective (a kind of view quite foreign to the victims and adherents of an exclusively literary and metaphysical training) it is seen that scientific studies made their way into the college against the resistance of entrenched orthodoxy because of their growing importance in the conduct of social affairs, not because of intrinsic love of scientific knowledge—much less because of widespread devotion to scientific method. When Latin lost its monopoly as the universal language of communication among the learned, living languages were added to the curriculum. Not only were the degrees of S.B. and Ph.B. added to the old A.B. (or else the latter extended to cover the new studies), but the curriculum became congested and its aim wavering and unsure.

The new modes of social pressure did not stop at this point. A large number of new callings and occupations came into existence. They competed vigorously with the three traditional "learned" professions, and the effect of this competition found its way into the colleges. At the same time, two of the learned professions, medicine and law, were undergoing great changes. New discoveries in chemistry and physiology so changed medicine as to render it virtually impossible to crowd preparation into the time previously allotted. Studies which in effect, if not in name, were pre-medical found their way into the college. The great changes that were going on in industry and commerce together with their social effects affected the practice of law. The consequences for college education were less overt than in the case of medicine, but they are genuinely present.

The net result of the alterations produced by the social changes here briefly noted has been to render the name "liberal arts college" reminiscent rather than descriptive when it is applied to many of our collegiate institutions. Under these circumstances it is hardly surprising that representatives of the older literary and metaphysical point of view who have been on the defensive have now taken the offensive. Consistently with their view that certain subjects are inherently liberal, they are proclaiming that other subjects, notably those that are scientific and technological, are inherently illiberal, materialistic, and utilitarianly servile, unless they are kept in strict subjection. Social revolutions rarely if ever go completely backward in spite of reactions that occur. I do not believe that there is great likelihood that the American under-graduate college will, in any large number of cases, return to the literary and metaphysical course of study of the traditional liberal arts institutions. I seem to notice that those who are verbally active in this direction are not discouraging receipt of funds to add still more new scientific and semi-vocational courses to an already swollen curriculum.

The danger, to my mind, lies elsewhere. It is possible to freeze existing illiberal tendencies and to intensify existing undesirable splits and divisions. At a time when technical education is en-croaching in many cases upon intelligent acquaintance with and use of the great humanistic products of the past, we find that reading and study of "classics" are being isolated and placed in sharp opposition to everything else. *The problem of securing to the liberal arts college its due function in democratic society is that of seeing to it that the technical subjects which are now socially necessary acquire a humane direction.* There is nothing in them which is "inherently" exclusive; but they cannot be liberating if they are cut off from their humane sources and inspiration. On the other hand, books which are cut off from vital relations with the needs and issues of contemporary life themselves become ultra-technical.

The outstanding need is interfusion of knowledge, of man and nature, of vocational preparation with a deep sense of the social foundations and social consequences of industry and industrial callings in contemporary society. On the face of this need we have urged upon us a policy of their systematic separation. I lately received from a man distinguished in public life, not a professional educator, a letter in which he writes: "Millions of our soldiers are coming back reactionaries of a kind through their lack of cultural education to appraise their surroundings and the events that are taking place." I would add that there are at home many other millions who are confused and bewildered, at the mercy of drift and of designing "leaders," because of their lack of an education that enables them to appraise their surroundings and the course of events. The present function of the liberal arts college, in my belief, is to use the resources put at our disposal alike by humane literature, by science, by subjects that have a vocational bearing, so as to secure ability to appraise the needs and issues of the world in which we live. Such an education would be liberating not in spite of the fact that it departs widely from the seven liberal arts of the medieval period, but just because it would do for the contemporary world what those arts tried to do for the world in which they took form.

Implications of S. 2499

The "Education Development Act of 1947" or S. 2499, sponsored by Senators Murray, Morse, and Pepper, appears at first glance to be an instrument of enormous value to public education. The "Declaration of Policy" of the bill suggests that "democratic participation in government, the development of science and the arts, productive employment in a fruitful economy, wise use of leisure, world peace and security, and the general welfare" will be realized once and for all through its measures. There is nothing new about these goals; they have long been part of the American dream. But the disconcerting mixture of reactionary and revolutionary proposals in this bill belies the very essence of that familiar dream; and it is imperative that the consequences of these underlying departures be perceived by the American people as a whole and in particular by educators, who in their devotion to their profession, may be lured by fascinating promises of increased aid to public education;—since the need for additional support is known to school people all too well.

For under cover of an offer of vast material aid to the public schools are hidden provisions which, if put into execution, would do violence to some of the basic principles of the democratic state. Among these basic principles are first, that of the separation of Church and State, and second, that of keeping the school closely connected with the individual and the local community, retaining authority for administration within each state. In S. 2499 the "nonprofit, tax-exempt school" is placed alongside the public school as a beneficiary of governmental aid. Even if the statutory provisions of any given State should forbid the appropriation of public money to private schools of any descrip-

[First published in *Nation's Schools* 39 (March 1947): 20–21.]

tion, the appropriation, according to Section 504 of the bill, is to be made anyway.

The significance of the role of the public school as an agency of democracy must be accurately perceived if we are to understand fully the implications of this bill, especially since it implies that our tradition, explicitly making the public school the sole educational agency of the State, has no special significance for democracy. S. 2499 would make any and all kinds of schools the trusted partners of the government by affording them financial aid. Because of the obvious dangers to democracy, it is imperative to review once more the basic meaning of our democratic tradition and to point out once again the essential place of the public school in the process of maintaining and improving the democratic processes.

It may seem incongruous to say that our American democratic tradition needs to be reviewed at this time since we have just waged a war to protect and further that tradition. However, it may at times be simpler to defend an ideal from attack than to labor at the painful and persistent task of analyzing it in actuality by means of rigorous self-examination and creating it by self-discipline. And every time an incident of race discrimination is condoned or an economic injustice is tolerated or the power of any ecclesiastical organization is enhanced by direct or indirect public subsidy, we prove once more that we have not rightly known the meaning of American principles.

One of the fundamental principles of our cultural tradition is that our common humanity with its common interest in the enrichment and fulfillment of the human personality is the basis of democratic life. There is no place in American democracy for authoritarianism of any kind—economic, educational, political, or ecclesiastical. Devotion to this principle has enabled us to assimilate an amazing heterogeneity of racial, cultural and religious backgrounds to a degree that has not been known in the world before. The progressive harmonization of differences among races, cultures, creeds, and economic levels is the very life principle of American democracy, and remains the most significant contribution we have made to Western civilization. The danger always present is that this process of harmonization, so habitually and even unconsciously shared in by all participants in the public school program, may be accepted as a matter of course, so that instead of devoting ourselves to increasing its measure, we will fall into a state of apathy, repeating rituals and clichés that we no longer even comprehend. Or we will drift into a kind of sentimentality that means death to any active appreciation of our basic principles. Such sentimentality is exemplified in the attitude of those senators who have stated that since the G.I. Bill of Rights permits veterans to obtain their education at non-public institutions, it is only consistent that this right be extended to the children, and possibly even the grandchildren, of veterans. These men are actually saying that there is nothing anti-democratic in allowing one segment of the population to attend private schools of their choice at public expense generation after generation. It should be obvious that such a procedure would create divisions among our people and would lead to permanent conflict among self-perpetuating blocs. Fulfilling our obligations to the individual veterans of World War II is far different from establishing by an Act of Congress a permanent policy inimical to our constitutional background and to the practice of one hundred and fifty years, a policy of dividing public funds among the legitimately authorized agency of government, the public school, and other institutions that may or may not be in accord with democratic principles.

Recognition of and respect for the individual are basic to the continuance of a democratic society and underlie the traditional policy of keeping the schools close to the people. One of the objections to the "Education Development Act of 1947" is that it violates the active expression of this policy by failing to acknowledge the nature of public education. A woman told me once that she asked a well-known American statesman what he would do for the people of this country if he were God. He said, "Well, that is quite a question. I should look people over and decide what it was they needed and then try to give it to them." She said, "Well, you know, I expected that to be the answer that you would give. There are people that would *ask* other people what they wanted before they tried to give it to them." That asking other people what they would like, what they need, what their ideas are, is an essential part of the democratic idea. We are so familiar with it as a matter of democratic practice that perhaps we don't always think about it even when we exercise the privilege of giving an answer. That practice is an educational matter because it puts upon us as individual members of a democracy the responsibility of considering what it is that we as individuals want, what our needs and troubles are. Any proposal for the development of education in America should have as its main objective this practice of seeking from the people information about their needs. However, S. 2499 has the appearance of imposition of benefits from above rather than development from the grass roots.

One of the basic ideas which made possible the creation of a homogeneous society out of the welter of heterogeneous peoples in this New World was that the power of the State came to be irrevocably divorced from the power of any Church and that all of the children of all of the people were permitted and encouraged to gain knowledge in an institution that was free from the control of any sect or class or individual or even of the Federal government. The public school, representing the first free system of education for all the people, was the result of rebellion against centuries of systematic stultification of the human mind and human personality. While at the present time public education is still far from the complete realization of its goals, the shortcomings of the people's schools must not blind us to the fact that through the years strong foundations have been laid, and it is to the steady improvement of this already well-established agency that we should devote our material resources and our moral enthusiasm.

Instead of estimating accurately the role so long played by our public school system and committing itself firmly to its furtherance and improvement, there is actually an implication in S. 2499 that a new system of "national schools" might better bring about the realization of our objectives. And more treacherously and boldly than ever before is suggested the idea that schools sponsored by organizations of various sectarian persuasions should be supported by the public treasury. The divisiveness that would result from this is easily seen when one recalls the great number of sectarian persuasions and private interests that might possibly vie for places at the public board. The Roman Catholic hierarchy, for example, has attempted for many years to gain public fiscal aid and its program has been advanced through active lobbying for school lunches, health programs and school transportation facilities for Catholic schools. The provisions of S. 2499 would greatly increase Catholic school support. It is essential that this basic issue be seen for what it is, namely, as the encouragement of a powerful reactionary world organization in the most vital realm of democratic life with the resulting promulgation of principles inimical to democracy.

We cannot deny that public education needs federal aid in order to equalize opportunity between state and state and between individual and individual. But it would be a poor bargain indeed to gain material aid at the expense of losing our greatest intellectual and moral heritage. The continuance and improvement of the public school system are compelling obligations for a growing democracy, but what we must be perfectly clear about is that vast sums of money will in themselves solve no problem if the policies under which the expenditures are made are not wholly sound and in complete accord with the best and wisest democratic principles.

Reviews

Mission to Moscow Reveals No New Evidence on Soviet Trials

Mr. Davies' book[1] falls into two parts. "Falls" means falls, since the account Mr. Davies gives of his mission is split into two parts. They might be designated "Before and After the Miraculous Revelation." The story reminds the reader of the experience, on the road to Damascus, of the doubter who became an apostle of the Church. In the case of Ex-Ambassador Davies, the holder of the Moscow Mission became a missionary. The revelation occurred after Mr. Davies had returned to the United States. In fact, it didn't happen until June of 1941.

Mr. Davies is honest enough—much more honest than his publishers in their blurb—to head his account of it "A Study in Hindsight." His report is so naive as to be disarming. After making a speech in Chicago, three days after Hitler's invasion of Russia, "someone in the audience asked, 'What about Fifth Columnists in Russia?' Off the anvil, I said, 'There aren't any—they shot them.' On the train that day, that thought lingered in my mind." He goes on to tell how he was then impressed by the contrast of conditions in Russia with events which took place in Czecho-Slovakia, Norway, the Sudeten, Belgium, etc. Then comes the revelation "Thinking over these things, there came a flash to my mind." It was, indeed, hot from the anvil.

Three years, practically to a day, after Mr. Davies had left Moscow, he discovered a meaning for what went on there which totally escaped him while he was on the ground and while he had the benefit of conversations not only with high-up members of the Soviet government but with as intelligent and as well-informed group of newspaper men, American and English, as ever gathered in a foreign capital. A flash, the flash, revealed to him that

1. *Mission to Moscow*, by Joseph E. Davies, Simon and Schuster, New York, 1941.
[First published in *New Leader* 25 (17 January 1942): 5.]

the purges, the whole terror (as he frankly called it when he was in the midst of what was going on) was revealed to him. The statesmanlike and farsighted Stalin was protecting his country from the fifth columnists, traitors, saboteurs, those who years afterwards played havoc with defense against the Nazis in all other European countries. The stubborn Russian defense is thus explained.

Although another steadfast apologist for Stalin, Walter Duranty, is sure that Hitler wouldn't have dared attack Russia were it not for the purges and the terror, Mr. Davies, now well removed in space and time, knows that the events which struck him at the time with horror, proving to him the absence of all guarantees for personal liberty and safety, give the full explanation of the otherwise inexplicable military successes of the Russians. In the words of the street, "Can you beat it?"

Do you want proof? Isn't it a well known fact that Hitler's military success in other countries was promoted by inside aggressors? And isn't it true that he hasn't repeated those successes in Russia? Isn't it also true that no fifth columnists have raised their heads or hands in Russia? What more do you want to prove that what at the time seemed an act of despotic terror to get rid of domestic political enemies was in fact dictated by extraordinary foresight of future events and was undertaken as a measure of protection against foreign enemies? If the logic of the argument sounds more like a collection of fallacies than like logic, remember the flash of revelation from on high.

What, then, of Mr. Davies' *actual* "mission in Moscow"— with emphasis upon "*in*"? His term of service was from early November 1936 to early June 1938—a period of one year and a half including frequent absences. His dispatches to Washington are numbered. They run to well over twelve hundred. There are altogether around forty or fifty official dispatches quoted, under four per cent of the total number. I do not suggest that Mr. Davies suppressed reports that gave an even more unfavorable account of affairs in Russia. But the fact that what is published represents a highly partial selection speaks for itself.

As it is, it would be easy to quote from his official statements material in support of every adverse criticism that has been made of the Soviet state as a totalitarian despotism. Upon the whole, Mr. Davies while on the ground showed himself to be a man of great innocence or ignorance regarding the historic and ideological background, but also a man of considerable practical shrewdness about matters falling within his competency. His reports on conversations with Litvinoff show the latter deserves his reputation as an able diplomat. Mr. Davies often refers to the group of foreign correspondents in Moscow as sources of information, and a number of dispatches tell what other diplomats said to him—without mention of names save in the case of the French ambassador, whose view on the particular matter cited was already in print under his own name.

There is no reason to doubt that Mr. Davies had access to good sources of information during the short time he spent in Moscow, nor that he tried, as he claims, to be objective, even to the point of leaning over backwards. What he says about Russia in bearing out the belief of all intelligent informed persons as to the conditions which prevailed there is therefore of especial interest. Not a word of his definitely unfavorable reports on the Soviets appears, naturally, in the reviews which place Stalin on a pedestal for his extraordinary statesmanship, and which, incidentally, credit Mr. Davies with engaging in a general whitewash of Soviet conditions. So it is worth notice that he comments repeatedly on the complete absence of personal liberty as that is understood in non-totalitarian countries; upon the growth of bitter anti-foreignism extending to persons actually resident and to wholesale arrests and deportations; upon the growth of nationalism and abandonment of the internationalism of Marx and Lenin. He comments unfavorably on industrial efficiency, rating it at about 40 per cent of productivity in comparable American plants. He not only gives a depressing picture of industrial disorganization but attributes it directly to political causes. "There is scarcely an industry that has not been shaken to the foundations of its organization." Even when expressing his belief that, judged according to Russian judicial methods, most of the men who were publicly tried deserved their sentences, he makes no attempt to conceal his distrust of the legal methods used: "Their basic vice was the subordination of the rights of the individual to the state." He even goes so far as to suggest that perhaps the guilt of some of the men consisted in the fact that they retained their original communistic zeal after it had been officially departed from. In his own words "The very earnestness and sincerity of their convictions might contribute to guilt, in so far as these political crimes are concerned."

In view of the revelation that came to him three years after he had left the country, it is worth while to quote at some length what he said at the time about purges, "The Terror here is a horrifying fact. There is a fear that reaches down and haunts all sections of the community. No household, however humble, apparently but what lives in constant fear of a nocturnal raid by the secret police. . . . The extent of this Terror is indicated by the fact that, almost daily through the kitchen and servants' quarters there come reports of whispered and fearful confidences of new arrests, new hardships, new apprehensions, and new fears among friends. . . . This *particular purge is undoubtedly political.* . . . It is deliberately projected by the party leaders, who themselves regretted the necessity for it." His highest point of ideological insight is found in his reference to "historic trends," as the standard put forward by Bolshevists as the one moral ground on which to judge the right and wrong of what was done. If Mr. Davies were to read attentively *Darkness at Noon,* he might conceivably receive another flash of revelation.

I have referred to this aspect of Mr. Davies' dispatches because it is uniformly disregarded by those who are using the book to foster the views of Soviet Russia. Mr. Davies is not altogether free from blame. His selection and arrangement of material, his conviction, undoubtedly patriotic, that everything possible should be done to build up a case for Russia as a means of promoting war on Germany, are, to say the least, unfortunate. But his publishers are much more to blame. In their accompanying document issued by way of instruction to reviewers upon whose ignorance they assume they can rely, they say, "Here is an entirely new angle on the famous and puzzling treason trials. On the basis of evidence and impression accumulated by Mr. Davies *at the time and on the spot,* it is now clear that these trials scotched Hitler's fifth column in Russia."

Such a statement is a flagrant and apparently deliberate misrepresentation. There is *no* new "evidence." While there is much "impression," it was not formed "at the time" nor "on the spot." Whether the misrepresentation comes from zeal in behalf of large sales, or from belief that the cause of the allies is thereby furthered, I have no way of knowing. But commendation of Stalin and Russia for scotching internal aggression would, on the ground of Mr. Davies' own account of the terror—which at the time he attributed to the desire of these in power to strengthen themselves against domestic political opponents—justify if it is accepted as sound the most ruthless, oppressive and despotic illegal elimination of all dissident elements in any country. I am not willing to believe for a moment that Mr. Davies would stand for having similar methods used in our own country in order to weed out critics and destroy all potential criticism. But the sole element of verifiable fact in the idea that the purges warded off elements of internal weakness is the fact that if you kill off every element of political opposition, you will, without doubt succeed in killing them off before they can do anything.

Aside from the Communists and fellow travelers in the country who are using all their energies to exploit Mr. Davies' book as a means of rehabilitating their self-discredited cause, there are others who think it is sound patriotic policy to build up Russia in public esteem, since Russia is now fighting a common enemy. There is such a thing, however, as short-sighted expediency, which will have a tremendous ultimate recoil. All power to Russia from a military point of view by all means, as long as Russia continues to fight the Axis powers. But the false idealization of Russia, now so much indulged in, will complicate our future relations to Russia, including the terms of peace, when once the war against Germany is won. Only persons with short memories will fool themselves into supposing that in the future we shall not also have to pay a high price for building up Stalinites and fellow travelers to a point where their nuisance power will be immense. Surrender to emotional hysteria during war time may result in creating a dangerously false picture of those who at the time are on our side as well as create a hysteria of hate for all who are on the other side. The worst thing about the book of Mr. Davies is that it lends itself to creation of dangerous illusions. It is being deliberately employed by interested parties for that very purpose.

Mr. Davies records on an early page a conversation he had with Troyanovsky (still Russian Ambassador at that time) in Washington before he departed on his mission. The person suggested that earlier relations between the Foreign Office at Moscow and the previous American Ambassador, Mr. Bullitt, might cause at first some coolness of attitude toward himself. In his journal, Mr. Davies wrote, "I shall want to discuss this with Bill Bullitt." If he carried out his desire is not known, for the result is unfortunately omitted.

Bullitt's "revelation" about the character of the Soviet regime came while he was still on the ground. However, Bullitt is not now in a position where he can express frankly his opinion of the book written by his successor. In consequence, the world is without what might otherwise be as racy a piece of literature as ornaments the history of diplomacy.

Behind the Iron Bars

Forced Labor in Soviet Russia, by David J.
Dallin and Boris I. Nicolaevsky. New Haven:
Yale University Press, 1947.

It is fortunate for one who undertakes to write a notice
of this book that the readers of the *New Leader* are already acquainted with the comprehensiveness of David Dallin's and Boris
Nicolaevsky's knowledge of Soviet affairs and the meticulous
pains and thoroughness with which they report the facts. For the
present work is so complete and its materials are so carefully
checked that anything like an adequate review is out of the question. The last pages of the book are entitled "Literature on Forced
Labor in Russia." A mere summary of the available literature occupies ten octavo pages. And one who consults these pages will
note at once the pains taken to discriminate between reliable
first-hand reports, and those suspected of having a hostile propaganda character or coming from second-hand sources. It may be
doubted whether any story of human degradation has ever been
more fully or more accurately told in so short a time after its occurrence, and this in spite of the iron curtain. The enslavement of
subject populations, both Russian and foreign, was on too large
a scale to enable its main facts to be suppressed, in spite of the
severe measures taken. One hesitates to refer to anything in the
tragically cruel record as "fortunate." But from the standpoint
of knowledge of that record, its Polish phase is definitely fortunate. During 1940, somewhere between 1,000,000 and 1,500,000
Poles were deported to "labor camps" and to "migrants' settlements" in Russia. But in the middle of 1941, an alliance was
signed with the Poles under General Sikorski, and an amnesty
was declared for Poles in these camps. About one-quarter of the
Polish prisoners were already dead. But hundreds of thousands
of the prisoners finally got outside of Soviet Russia, and were
able to report what went on in these establishments—which in a

[First published in *New Leader* 30 (13 September 1947): 11.]

remarkably short time had become an organized part of the Soviet regime, economic, industrial and political. Since the hundreds of thousands of deportees from the Baltic Republics and Bessarabia received no amnesty, and since malcontents as well as convicted criminals swelled the numbers, it took only a short time for forced labor to become an outstanding feature of both the foreign and domestic policies of the Stalin regime. According to the most accurate estimates that can be made, the numbers run at any given time from 10,000,000 to 14,000,000.

The authors of the book have done what strikes me as a surprisingly successful work in combining an account of the general policies lying back of forced labor with instructive authentic details. In the main, readers must be referred to the book itself to appreciate how successfully the two things have been woven together. On the side of policy, I quote the following:

> The forced labor system of Soviet Russia is not the invention of a diabolic mind; neither is it a temporary anomaly nor a tumor on the body politic. The system is an *organic* element, a normal component, of the social structure. To understand this phenomenon is an imperative for every intelligent man. . . . Only when considered in their evolution, from the small beginnings to the massive culmination, do these phenomena assume perspective and find their proper place in the sequence of historical formations.

The virtual promise contained in this passage is fully borne out in the organization of the subject-matter of the book. The account of the development of forced labor as a system, an inherent part of both the foreign policy of Bolshevik Russia in dealing with its weaker neighbors; of its domestic system in securing a plenitude of cheap labor without regard for human life and suffering; and also in dealing with rightist and leftist doctrinal deviations among Communists who came to doubt the infallibility of the ruling bureaucracy, gives an extraordinary picture of the workings of the whole system.

I read recently a mild apology for Soviet policy based upon the idea that the insecurity of Russian life due to treatment of the country by foreign nations accounted for the intransigeance of its attitude. There can be no doubt of the vast extent of insecurity that obtains in the population of Russia. But it is safe to say that for one part of it which is caused by even the worst features of the policies of other nations, nine parts are the direct product of the policies of the rulers of Bolshevik Russia. One outstanding feature of the forced labor system is its systematic use as a means of intimidation of any and every expression of dissent. No one knows how many thousands of persons who had once been Communist officials have been completely wrecked in health as well as in their political careers by this engrained instrument of Soviet policy.

There is one special feature of the many noteworthy ones brought out in the book which I cannot refrain from mentioning. The organized hypocrisy of Soviet policy parallels its organized cruelty. I believe no fair observer of some of the early features of Soviet policy, in the period before Stalin consolidated his power, failed to be struck by certain idealistic features attending it. Incredible as it now seems, this holds of the beginning of the labor policies of Russian prisons—a fact clearly brought out by the authors. During the early period, the highest principles of penological reform were sometimes carried into effect. But pressure of the total monolithic system, with its combined need for cheap labor, for suppression of every expression of criticism and doubt by merciless intimidation and for maintenance in power of a bureaucratic clique, wrought after 1928, especially after 1934, a complete change.

But the earlier idealistic utterances were maintained in full force; indeed, were multiplied and intensified, particularly for foreign consumption. (Incidentally, the incredible gullibility of much "liberal" opinion abroad is demonstrated by the course of events.) The complete inversion of the labor union policy actually pursued by the Soviet Government has been paralleled by an equally complete inversion of the facts of its general penal and labor policy.

There is one particular incident of the display of hypocrisy that appears to me as worthy of special mention. For it concerns a Russian leader who now figures largely in the conduct of Russian international relations. Hitler found apt disciples when he taught and practiced that the more stupendous a lie, the more effective is it. Minor lies arouse doubt; reversals of truth cause paralysis of belief. The Bolsheviks borrowed much from the Nazis; in the matter of wholesale falsification, they were especially apt.

In 1931 and 1932, forced labor was sufficiently developed for the facts to leak out. Protests started in Britain and this country against importation of its products. The economic situation of Russia at the time made their exportation highly important to her welfare. A man by the name of Molotov was then beginning his career. He admitted the existence of labor camps, but was not content with a mere denial that *their* products were exported. For good measure, he declaimed about the idyllic conditions existing in the camps, saying that many "an unemployed worker in capitalist countries will envy the living and working conditions of prisoners in our northern regions." The poems of praise and gratitude written by some prisoners as means of gaining special favors are almost incredibly nauseating when put by the side of the facts. A rumor got in circulation that an American Committee of Investigation was on its way to investigate these camps. Orders went out to liquidate the camps; the prisoners were hastily distributed, large numbers dying, and every trace of the kind of work done in them was rapidly obliterated.

This is but one of the multitude of incidents related by the authors which enable the reader to understand the policies that are characteristic of Russia—the actions of Molotov in his personally successful career being included. One is unable to decide whether the ruthless disregard of human life and well-being, or the equally systematic conversion of idealism into the greatest exhibition of hypocrisy the world has ever seen, is the more repulsive aspect of that profound moral humiliation of man which is the official regime of Russia in the world today.

It is my conviction that the authors of this monumental work are justified in saying that it is urgent that every intelligent citizen understand what is going on and how it is controlled. If and when less troubled times come, this book will be an invaluable resource for historians and students of psychology as well as of economic and political science. Meantime, it is a part of the needed intellectual armor of every citizen concerned with peace on the basis of freedom and justice.

Forewords and Introductions

Foreword to *S. O. Levinson and the Pact of Paris*

It was a rare privilege to be associated in any way and in any capacity with Salmon Levinson. The association had a specially significant value when it was connected with the cause of peace among nations—the cause to which Levinson gave his best and constant thought and energy. There was stimulus—indeed, there was a kind of inspiration—in coming in contact with his abounding energy, which surpassed that of any single person I have ever known and which might easily have provided a group or organization with power to carry on extensive activities. It was great physically; but more than that it was moral power. Mr. Levinson was a man who would not and could not be discouraged either by the immensity of the task he set himself or by the obstacles he encountered.

Levinson's vigor and power were given to a cause that was worthy of them. His devotion was selfless. It was so intense it could not help stirring others, if only from a sense of shame, out of their lethargy. His faith was so ardent that indifference changed to warmth in his presence. His faith was wedded to works. He was an outstanding example of the complete union of faith and energy. His faith was in the possibility of the triumph of the cause of peace to which he gave himself. But this faith was rooted in faith in his fellow-beings, in the common people of the earth. He refused to believe that in their heart of hearts they really wanted the wars by which in the end they are so tragically victimized. He strove as a social inventor, as other men have worked at physical and industrial inventions. He wanted to find and to help others to find the social implement and instrumentality by which men could make effective their underlying desire

[First published in John E. Stoner, *S. O. Levinson and the Pact of Paris: A Study in the Techniques of Influence* (Chicago: University of Chicago Press, 1942), pp. vii–viii.]

for peaceful relations. His immediate purpose was defeated as the second World War so tragically testifies. But I believe that the conditions in which we live but emphasize our need to recover and strengthen Levinson's faith that the great mass of men and women would welcome an era in which the war system has no standing and his faith in the possibility of social means by which to secure this end.

As I prized association with Levinson as a rare privilege, so I am greatly honored to be asked to contribute a Foreword to this present volume. I respond the more willingly because of the quality of the pages to which these lines are prefixed. Mr. Stoner has done more than accomplish a fine piece of scholarly research. He has seen the dramatic aspect of the work of Levinson in such a way as to communicate it to readers. It is not often that an important example of historic investigation is done in such close connection with the time of the events dealt with and with such full access to all sources of information. Because of the variety and scope of Levinson's contacts, Mr. Stoner in writing about him has also made, it seems to me, a valuable contribution to many aspects of contemporary history. He has done a solid and substantial work which will remain authoritative in the matters with which he deals. Let us hope that it will be a historic document not only with respect to the past but also in stimulating others to renewed faith in the cause to which Levinson was devoted and in the possibility of its triumph.

Introduction to *The Little Red School House*

A few years ago I ventured to write that the time might not be far off when the "progressive education" movement might drop the word "progressive." The saying did not mean that some schools would cease to represent the advance guard in educational growth or that the movement itself would cease to move forward. It meant that it would become clear in time that the real issue is between education which is genuinely educative and that which is in fact *mis*educative; and that the conflict between the old, the routine and mechanized, and the new, the living and moving, represents in fact the struggle to discover and put in practice the materials and methods which, under the conditions of present life, are truly educative.

The lively and vital story of The Little Red School House, which these prefatory words accompany, is evidence that the new movement is indeed coming of age. No one, I believe, can read the account without being impressed with the great role of inspired common sense, backed by scientific insight, in development of the new methods. When one contrasts what is actually done in a school of the kind here reported upon with the criticisms passed upon progressive schools by those who urge return to ancient and outworn patterns, one can only feel that the former is the one which has its feet on the ground, which is realistic, while the latter is the one which is theoretical in the bad sense of the word, since it is far away from the earth on which we now live. The nine objectives mentioned on an early page and the measures, reported throughout the whole book, by which the ends are attained provide the proof. Another outstanding feature is the demonstration, furnished in ample measure by the continued success

[First published in Agnes de Lima and the Staff of The Little Red School House, *The Little Red School House* (New York: Macmillan Co., 1942), pp. ix–x.]

of this school, of the flexibility, the adaptability of the educational methods of the so-called Activity Program. This book renders in this respect an immense practical service. It supplies the much needed proof that nothing stands in the way of adoption of the new purposes and methods by schools and classes operating under the conditions which affect public school work, even in a great city. This trait alone gives the book a deeply serious claim upon the attention of all who are concerned in making our public school system the power for good it is capable of becoming. It is remarked in the course of the book that the question is not now whether we shall adopt the new methods, but how they shall be most effectively put into operation. The detailed and vivid account of actual school experiences contained in the present book gives an answer to that question which no one interested in public education can afford to ignore.

Foreword to "Method"

An increasing number of teachers, writers and students in the field of philosophy subjects are now dissatisfied with the historic and traditional systems whose problems and solutions still occupy most of the pages of philosophic texts. To speak more correctly, they are profoundly dissatisfied with respect to the applicability of these systems to the vital problems and issues of the present day. For it is possible to combine this discontent, along with a struggle to achieve something better, with admiration for the systems as historic documents. In the latter capacity, many of them are genuinely products of genius as are the classics in other forms of literature. Moreover, they supply unrivaled clues to the qualities of the cultural climates in which they appeared. But their admirable character in these respects is one of the things that unfits them for reflecting adequately the characteristic human problems of the present and for giving effective aid in dealing with them.

To take this point of view is not to assume that the present is better than the past. It simply recognizes that past systems were produced in what, relatively speaking, were pre-scientific and pre-technological ages. When we note, for example, the extraordinary change, amounting to a revolution, that natural science has undergone in the sciences of life in the last two or three generations and in physics during the present generation in the doctrines of relativity and wave-mechanics, even the systems of the sixteenth through seventeenth, eighteenth and even the first half of the nineteenth centuries appear, not indeed pre-scientific, but products of what in comparison with the present is the infancy of science:—of science before it had mastered the arts of easy locomotion and effective speech.

[In H. Heath Bawden, "Method," unpublished typescript, 1944.]

The same thing holds in technology. It is not merely that the arts of mass-production, of rapid transportation and still more of rapid communication, are very recent, post-dating most of the great systematic intellectual systems of the past. Again, it is not merely (important as that is) that their effect on human customs, institutions, and relationships has been vastly accelerated and widely extended during the present generation. It is that the industrial revolution has itself taken on a new form—one which has been pointed to, though not adequately described, in saying that the machine-age has passed into a power-age. *Processes* have won the victory over fixities in the industrial side of our social life.

This fact, in connection with the scientific revolution, demands a corresponding change in the intellectual attitudes and habits that are expressed in philosophic systems inherited from the past. But it is accompanied by a failure, a negative aspect; and this negative aspect sets the most vital problem for the philosophy of today. Our thinking in social and moral matters is still governed by the habits which were formed in pre-scientific and pre-technological ages. Only our physical thinking is genuinely modern. Hence a split exists between our belief-attitudes and practices in physical affairs and those employed in matters of moral and social concern. Classic philosophy set up a gulf between the moral and ideal and the physical and material. But a merely philosophical dualism, if there be one which does not reach beyond technical limits, is of importance only to professional philosophers. When, however, one set of interests and principles effectively controls our work-a-day life while we try rather helplessly to practice an opposed set in connection with the standards and ideals which we hold ought to regulate our lives, the conflict is serious enough to set the chief problem of present philosophy. The application of science in our economics and daily life has now rendered the old dualism a threat and a disaster, not just a metaphysical theory.

Many thoughtful laymen are aware today that something new is coming to birth in philosophic thought. They are desirous of knowing what it is all about. The newer movements have had as yet too short a time in which to attain systematic development. They have engaged in controversies with old systems and in a struggle to find a language in which to express themselves. In these struggles they have, inevitably, become more or less involved in the very things against which they are struggling. An exposition is needed which proceeds from the centre to the circumference. Only such an exposition will serve as a guide. The text of Dr. Bawden serves this purpose admirably. His insight has laid hold of the one theme which is central and controlling. The revolution in science and technology is a result of the development of intelligent method; rather, of a method which *is* intelligence at work. Philosophers have always written a great deal about reason and rationality. What they called reason was, however, something remote. It was too high, too sublime, to be applicable to things of this world and to the practices of daily life. Dr. Bawden shows how the steady development of method in natural science and in technology has made of rationality a working fact of life, not a distant etherial goal. But he also shows that its victory is still one-sided. It remains to develop method in our social-moral affairs and it is they which in the end decide the human consequences produced by physical applications. The problems and tragedies of domestic and international life are the consequences of the split.

Dr. Bawden's book is not entitled an Introduction to Philosophy. He does not indulge in formal listing of systems with verbal descriptions of their traits. But I know of no work that better serves to introduce a reader and a student into what is living and moving in the intellectual endeavors and struggles of the present. He has clarified in my own case the point of view I have expressed in the opening paragraphs of this Foreword. I shall be happy if anything I can say serves to bring to the attention of others, whether they be students in colleges or thoughtful laymen, the assistance in understanding the spirit and the aims of philosophy which this genuinely modern book provides. For, I repeat, as it starts from the centre and works out from there secondary things fall into place and a definite pattern is exhibited.

Foreword to *Education in the British West Indies*

As any intelligent reader will see for himself, Dr. Williams' study of *Education in the British West Indies* has a much wider reach than the title suggests. It has a claim upon the attention of those who have no direct concern with the British colonies in the Caribbean. While the primary appeal is to educators, including administrators, it has a claim upon the attention of many who are not engaged in any direct way in the conduct of educational institutions. And while the immediate occasion of the work is a project for the creation of a University for students throughout the West Indian islands that are under the British Government, its scope, from the educational as well as from the human side, is wider. It is not too much to say that, in connection with his special problem, the author of this book has found himself obliged to go into many of the most important problems that occupy this troubled world at the present time. And he does this work with the fairness which is the mark of a genuine student.

I can tell why I feel justified in making these statements by a few quotations from Dr. Williams' Preface. Its closing words are: "Education in the modern world is, more than anything else, education of the people themselves as to the necessity of viewing their own education as a part of their democratic privileges and their democratic responsibilities." As he points out, the problem which is involved "exists all over the world." It is a heritage not only from the enslavement of the African and other peoples, but from the era of Colonialism that followed the industrial revolution. Economic and political issues are so intimately involved that the educational problem cannot be even studied, much less intelligently tackled, without taking the general framework into

[First published in Eric Williams, *Education in the British West Indies* (Port-of-Spain, Trinidad, B.W.I.: Guardian Commercial Printery, 1946), pp. vii–viii.]

consideration. At the same time I should be giving a totally wrong impression of the book if it were inferred that the author indulges in broad generalizations. The study is a factual one; but the facts regarding education are placed in their proper, their own, factual background of historical and social conditions.

The most direct appeal of the book will be and should be to British agencies and the British public. But the American public, including framers of public policy as well as educationalists, can profit greatly from its pages. This is true since, because of the historical heritage of Negro slavery, our own problems are similar to those considered in the book. It is true because the British colonies are so close to us and because we, too, have a direct stake in the Caribbean area. It is true because the United States is now a world-power and we are forced, whether we like it or not, to form and execute policies which extend even into the Pacific—into every country where the traditional Colonialism of the past is now faced with a rising tide of democratic aspirations; aspirations which we ourselves have had some share in arousing, especially because of our policies in the Philippines. This study of conditions in a particular area is, for those who have eyes to see, a case study of a world problem in which this country is now involved.

Foreword to *Education for What Is Real*

In the following pages Professor Kelley has restated at the outset some educational principles and standards that have been urged upon teachers more or less often in the last half century. If he had not gone beyond that, his book would have been welcome in its vigor and clarity. But it goes definitely beyond that. I doubt if many persons who have been active in forwarding the newer movements in public education during the years mentioned would say today that they were satisfied with what has been accomplished in spite of bright points on the horizon. There are many reasons for this situation. But one is particularly pertinent to the present book.

Excellent reasons have been offered for adoption of the principles which underlie the new processes and conditions of the public school. But none of them had the force of out-and-out demonstration. They did not even have the outward parade of the external mechanics put out by some theories but which nevertheless were lacking in grasp of what is so distinctively human in life that no amount of such parade could begin to make up for its absence. In fact, in many cases it was used simply to add to the efficiency of older mechanical life-chilling and hardening operations.

This phase of the situation is now radically changed. Under the inspiration and direction of Dr. Adelbert Ames of the Hanover Institute, there has been developed an experimental demonstration of the principles which govern the development of perceiving, principles which are found, moreover, to operate more deeply in the basic growth of human beings in their distinctively human capacity than any which have been previously laid bare.

[First published in Earl C. Kelley, *Education for What Is Real* (New York: Harper and Brothers, 1947), pp. v–vi.]

I am aware that these are strong words. As Professor Kelley remarks in his book, "It is not the first writing that has been done on this topic, nor, I predict, will it be the last." The inherent convincingness of the work of Dr. Ames and his associates goes, however, too deep to be welcome in some influential quarters. It will probably take a good many years for it to go through that succession of stages until it will be said, "Oh, that theory; why, everybody always knew that was true." I am, accordingly, especially grateful to Dr. Kelley for permitting me to have a part in calling attention to a work whose significance will prove virtually inexhaustible.

Introduction to *The Way beyond "Art"—The Work of Herbert Bayer*

No more far-reaching or penetrating statement could be made, in my judgment, than that which is made in the early pages of the present volume. We are in the moving presence of a great intellectual transformation scene. It is the counterpart of the intellectual transformation that began in Greece and that has so controlled the subsequent development of philosophic and scientific thought that it may be said to have been their classic pattern. It was, to borrow the words of Dr. Dorner, a search for immutabilities below and behind the changing events of nature and life. The frame of reference appropriate to this point of view became itself so immutable that it controlled even those who rebelled against some of the forms it had earlier taken. The particular things taken to be fixed "changed," but whatever new things took their place were supposed to be equally immutable. Newton is a good example from the side of science. His atoms had no likeness to the fixed forms and species that were the subjects of Greek science. But they were equally fixed and equally independent of each other in the space and time which were also equally fixed and disconnected—or "absolute." Darwin dealt the idea of fixed species of plants and animals a mortal blow. But his successors in biological science took up the search for smaller elementary units which remained immutable under the process of change.

The movement now going on is, as Dr. Dorner points out, a counterpart change. But it is reversed in its direction. The movements that are characteristically "modern" are coming to a head in search for mutabilities below and behind what, both on its face, and according to the language that comes habitually to our

[First published in Alexander Dorner, *The Way beyond "Art"—The Work of Herbert Bayer* (New York: Wittenborn, Schultz, 1947), pp. 9–11.]

lips, is fixed, settled beyond peradventure. Laws that once were taken to be fixed are changing—adherents of the older view would say "dissolving"—into statistical probabilities, in the form of generalizations stable enough to permit reasonably dependable predictions. In philosophy, belief in eternals and absolute universals has far from disappeared. But the idea of *process* is making its way into that which is known and the idea of operations into our account of how we know. "Event" is the aspect which comes out of, which proceeds, from a total process, whose other aspect is *"fact,"* that which is done, finished (in a relative sense) while event and fact enter together as inceptions of new events and new things to be done.

There is one phase of this wide field I should like to call particular attention to. In the older view, a person as individual was thought to be a fixed element in a given larger whole; departure from this fixed place was heresy, in matters of belief; disloyalty in matters of overt action. Later what was called "The Individual" was cut loose entirely, and was supposed to be fixed in himself— a synonym at the time for *by* himself, or in isolation. The author effectively calls attention to something fundamentally important, but usually ignored: the assumption of immutability is common to both cases. In the first instance, the artist was "servant of absolute form"; in the second he was taken to be himself absolute and hence "spontaneous creator." Against these fixations, Dr. Dorner points to the personal individual as a partaker in the "general process of life" and as a "special contributor to it." This union of partaker and contributor describes the enduring work of the artist.

In the confusion that marks a period of conflict of an overlaying old with the incoming new, it is extremely difficult for one who is sensitive to both to find a secure lodgment. In production of works of art some tend to lose their balance. The average spectator and appreciator of works of art more often, almost certainly if he turns professional critic, tends to judge by standards derived from the art of an earlier and more fixed period. To him practically everything characteristically new or "modern" is an eccentricity and originality. In consequence, members of the public who are influenced by critics who judge on the basis of standards appropriate to a by-gone age are indeed fortunate when they come in intellectual contact with critics who see that genuine art is a liberating event to and *by* its producer and *for* the one who perceives it with intelligence, not by pre-formed routine. Opportunity for this kind of intelligent growth in power of perception and enjoyment is generously provided in these pages from the pen of Dr. Dorner. If I express my appreciation of the honor he has done me in dedicating the book to me and asking me to write the introductory words, it is because I know that he has done so not on account of any competency in the field in which he is expert, but because we have an underlying community of belief as to things common to artistic creation and appreciation and to all other vitally significant phases of human life. That community I am happy to share.

Were I to take what Dr. Dorner says about non-three-dimensional forms in productions appealing to visual perceptive enjoyment, I should be taking an illustration from a field in which I should have to live much longer than I am going to live to form a judgment. For to some considerable extent we all have to await the outcome of a movement, we have to see what it is in accomplishment, before we can judge it with security. But I may use his treatment as an illustration, albeit a minor one, of the unusual balance of knowledge of the history of art with personal sensitiveness of perception that permeates and unifies all that he says. And what he says runs the whole gamut from the urgency of our present need to give to time "a higher dignity and a deeper meaning than it has in our present philosophy of art history" (and he might have said of the history of every aspect of human activity) through his account of "Tensions in Contemporary Art," "The Genesis of Contemporary Art," his study of a particular figure in the field, and his conclusion in which, among many things, pertinent remarks are made about Museums of Art. I shall be sorry for those readers who fail to get from reading this book that increment of meaning and vitality to perception, to taste and judgment, to enjoyment that these pages have in them to supply.

Foreword to *The Unfolding of Artistic Activity*

The contribution made in this volume to the philosophies of art and of education is notable from the standpoint of
theory. At the same time, I believe that, important as is the contribution to both of these subjects, there is another one that is its
most distinguished trait. It is that upon which emphasis falls in
these introductory remarks. The principles in question are taken
out of and beyond the territory of theoretical philosophy into the
field of demonstrated fact. I shall, of course, have to confine what
I say to the principles. But I should not be faithful to the book
itself if I did not give first and foremost place to their testing and
confirmation in work carried on over many years and with a variety of groups. This demonstration, reported in words and in
pictorial evidence, gives substance and form to the principles
that are set forth.

The first of the principles to which I would call attention is the
emphasis upon individuality as the creative factor in life's experiences. An immense amount has been said and written about the
individual and about individuality. Too much of it, however, is
vitiated by setting up what these words stand for as if it were
something complete in itself in isolation. Here, it is seen and consistently treated as the life factor that varies from the previously
given order, and that in varying transforms in some measure that
from which it departs, even in the very act of receiving and using
it. This creativity is the meaning of artistic activity—which is
manifested not just in what are regarded as the fine arts, but in
all forms of life that are not tied down to what is established by
custom and convention. In re-creating them in its own way it
brings refreshment, growth, and satisfying joy to one who
participates.

[First published in Henry Schaefer-Simmern, *The Unfolding of Artistic Activity*
(Berkeley: University of California Press, 1948), pp. ix–x.]

Accompanying this principle, or rather inseparable from it, is the evidence that artistic activity is an undivided union of factors which, when separated, are called physical, emotional, intellectual, and practical—these last in the sense of doing and making. These last, however, are no more routine and dull than the emotional stir is raw excitement. Intelligence is the informing and formative factor throughout. It is manifested in that keen and lively participation of the sense organs in which they are truly organs of constructive imagination. Intelligence is also manifested in the organizing activity of which aesthetic form is the result. But nothing could be further away from that conformity to fixed rules, disguised as principles and standards, which is too often taken to be the function of "rationality." Escape from the one-sidedness which attends many philosophies of sense, of reason, of bodily or physical action, of emotion, and of doing and making, distinguishes the work reported upon in the following pages. In their place there is constant observation of the wholeness of life and personality in which activity becomes artistic.

Because of this wholeness of artistic activity, because the entire personality comes into play, artistic activity which is art itself is not an indulgence but is refreshing and restorative, as is always the wholeness that is health. There is no inherent difference between fullness of activity and artistic activity; the latter is one with being fully alive. Hence, it is not something possessed by a few persons and setting them apart from the rest of mankind, but is the normal or natural human heritage. Its spontaneity is not a gush, but is the naturalness proper to all organized energies of the live creature. Persons differ greatly in their respective measures. But there is something the matter, something abnormal, when a human being is forbidden by external conditions from engaging in that fullness according to his own measure, and when he finds it diverted by these conditions into unhealthy physical excitement and appetitive indulgence.

Normally and naturally, artistic activity is the way in which one may "gain in the strength and stature, the belief in his own powers, and the self-respect, which make artistic activity constructive in the growth of personality." It is this fact that distinguishes the demonstrations conducted by Professor Schaefer-Simmern. They take place in a particular field of activity as every form of experimental demonstration must do. But through that field, as well as in it, there is convincing thoroughgoing demonstration that activity which is artistic extends beyond all subjects conventionally named "The Fine Arts." For it provides the pattern and model of the full and free growth of personality and of full life activity, wherever it occurs, bringing refreshment and, when needed, restoration.

I am glad accordingly to close as I began—upon the note of effective demonstration of what is sound and alive in theoretical philosophies of art and of education.

Tributes

Tribute to James Hayden Tufts

Professor John Dewey has expressed deep regret over his inability to be present today, but he has sent the following significant tribute.

For a considerable number of years I enjoyed the privilege of intimate association with James Hayden Tufts, first at the University of Michigan at Ann Arbor, and then for ten years here in Chicago. Because of this fact I count it a privilege to be asked to say a few words at this Memorial Meeting. For the association was more than professional. It went deeper than being a faculty colleague, a fellow-teacher, an active collaborator in philosophical research and publication, significant as were these contacts in my own life. I think of our friend as a scholar, a teacher, a writer, and of him as one who gave freely of his time, energy, and thought to civic issues. But in thinking of him in these relationships I think of him as carrying into them and manifesting through them the personal qualities that made him a valued companion and friend. More than is the case with many of us there was no division, no separation and split, in the case of Mr. Tufts between his professional interests and activities and the qualities of his character and personality that were shown in all aspects of his intercourse with others.

Sturdiness, firmness, dependability, unostentatious acceptance of responsibility were deeply engrained in his constitution. They seemed to be revealed in his very physique. One always knew where Mr. Tufts stood in any situation which arose and where he would stand whenever any moral issue came up. I never knew of his doing anything to show off or to attract attention to himself,

[First published in Frederic Woodward, T. V. Smith, and Edward S. Ames, *James Hayden Tufts* (n.p., [1942]), pp. 19–23. Read in Dewey's absence by Ames at the Memorial Service held in Joseph Bond Chapel, the University of Chicago, on 8 October 1942.]

and I don't believe anybody else ever did. Perhaps this trait should be so taken for granted as not to need mention. But it seems to me that unfortunately there are things in our social make-up that put a premium on show-off and that tend to bring public recognition to those who indulge in it. In any case its complete absence from the life of our friend is evidence of that simple and direct sincerity which was an essential part of everything he did and said, because sincerity was such a natural and unconscious part of himself.

Another trait that made companionship with him attractive and rewarding was that the habit of judiciousness which New England has bred in its best children was strong in him. For some reason this quality, in its special New England form, seems to be always accompanied with a certain quality of humor, and this accompaniment was marked in the case of our friend. There was a certain unpartisan delay, an element of slowness, in pronouncing judgment when a matter came up which had two sides, as there was *no* hesitation when the moral face of a situation was clear. He seemed to say to those whose reactions were quicker because more partisan: "Why be in such a hurry? The fate of the world doesn't depend upon your making up your mind right away." I had no direct contact with the work of Mr. Tufts in connection with industrial disputes. But his impartial habit of mind, a habit both native and trained, fitted him by a kind of pre-established harmony for that work.

I shall not speak at any length of the work Mr. Tufts did in his chosen field of philosophy. But it is characteristic of the man that he was drawn by the impulse of his nature to morals as a social enterprise, to consideration of ethics not as abstract theory but, in the title of one of his books, as *The Real Business of Living*. It is also characteristic of the judicious quality of his mind that the subtitle of his book on *America's Social Morality* is "Dilemmas of the Changing Mores"—the words "changing" and "dilemmas" telling much about his typical approach. His series of chapters on "unsolved problems" in the field of social morals where dogmatists have ready-made solutions for everything, is a development of what he had projected in the fourth part of the volume written fifteen years before. For the first chapter in this part is entitled "New Forces and New Tasks." There are chapters in that part, as in his book called *Our Democracy,* dealing with the domestic and international problems of American life in its attempts to realize democratic ideals. Written during the First World War they come alive in this greater crisis in which our democracy became directly involved in the last months of the long and useful, humanly useful, life of James Hayden Tufts.

I am glad to have been one of the large number whose faith in our common human kind and in the possibilities of human life has been rendered more robust and enduring because of his life and work. May we all have the strength and simple sincerity to help carry on the work in which his powers were enlisted and without fuss, fanfare, or expectation of selfish reward. When I renew acquaintance with the pages of his earlier work, I find no words occurring oftener than "fair" and "unfair." The world and our own America were never more in need of the Fairness which was the chief note of Mr. Tufts' life than in the tragic years we are now passing through.

James Hayden Tufts

James Hayden Tufts, an original member of the American Philosophical Association and its President in 1914, died August 5, 1942, at the age of eighty. After receiving the degrees of A.B. and A.M. at Amherst and of B.D. at Yale, he taught philosophy for two years at the University of Michigan and then studied at Freiburg where he received the degree of Ph.D. The immediate fruit of his studies in Germany was his translation of Windelband's *History of Philosophy*. From 1892–1930 he taught philosophy at the University of Chicago, becoming head of the department in 1905, serving also as Dean of the Faculties, Vice-president, and after the death of President Burton as Acting President until the appointment of President Mason. He found time to give liberally of his energies to civic affairs. He served as chairman of a Committee for Social Legislation for Illinois, and became the head of the arbitration work in the Chicago clothing industry. He was for a time the editor of the *International Journal of Ethics*.

His philosophical interest was increasingly directed to the moral issues of social life. His scholarly command of anthropological and historical material and his sense of the value of this background in dealing with current issues is clearly shown in his contributions to the First and Third Parts of Dewey and Tufts' *Ethics*. It is characteristic of the continuing activity of his interest that during the last years of his life he was engaged in rethinking social issues and problems in their connection with the present international situation.

Mr. Tufts' extensive and unusual participation in concrete practical problems stimulated and reinforced his scholarly and theoretical knowledge and insight. The fruit of this union of

[First published in *Philosophical Review* 52 (March 1943): 163–64.]

knowledge and practical experience is seen in his books: *The Real Business of Living, America's Social Morality,* and *Our Democracy.*

Great and enduring as is the influence of his published writings, this influence is but one aspect of the truth he stated when he said: "It is only through *personal relations* that we enter certain great realms of values, that we come to know honor and justice, love and sympathy, cooperation and a common good." Colleagues, students, fellow-workers and friends of James Tufts all learned to know these values better because of contact with him. In a rare degree his philosophy was one with his very being and his teaching and writing an expression of his single minded, rugged, and unostentatious character. As a younger colleague said of him: "He was of all the men I have known in American education the true image of the ageless Magister. Magisterial he was of mien, of gait, and of intent."

Boyd H. Bode: An Appreciation

I wish to begin with congratulations, first, to Dr. Kilpatrick for establishing the series of recognitions of distinguished service in Philosophy of Education; second, to him and all members of the Committee for their judgment in awarding this recognition to Boyd Bode; and, third, to Dr. Bode himself, not so much, however, for being the recipient as for the long record of teaching and writings on account of which he so amply merits this token of acknowledgment.

Since I have myself been primarily engaged for many years in the pursuit of philosophy as student, teacher, and writer, it is perhaps fitting that I speak of the work done by our common friend from the philosophical point of view. Some of you here are doubtless aware that he began his academic career as a professional student of philosophy with the aim, presumably, of being a teacher of that subject. He received his doctorate in that subject. The *Journal of Philosophy* and the *Philosophical Review* for the year 1905 carried critical articles by him which exhibit the vigor and independence that have marked his whole career. At the time they deserved and evoked the serious and somewhat prolonged attention of William James. But Bode increasingly turned from philosophy for its own sake to philosophy for the sake of its application in fields where he felt it would bear a human fruit denied it as long as its main business was to discuss problems confined to itself.

His reason for leaving philosophy as a subject pursued on its own account and the field that he chose in which to apply it are both of them, to my mind, deeply significant of the spirit that has animated all his work. He felt that philosophy as an end in itself

[First published in *Teachers College Record* 49 (January 1948): 266–67.]

was too remote from human life to command his full energy and regard; he felt that education was the focal and strategic field in which the truths in the possession of philosophy could come to life in human affairs. In my best judgment, the fact that Boyd Bode has always seen both philosophy and education as expressions of human life, in terms of their joint opportunity and responsibility for contributing to the advancement of that life is what makes his educational work so outstanding and so upstanding. Bode has often been over-generous in what he said about the influence of some of my philosophic writings in aiding him to unite philosophy and education. However, it makes me proud and happy to feel that I have had even an indirect part in the work he has done. Nevertheless, strong as is my "will to believe," I have also to tell you that whatever came to him from any source somehow came out different after it had passed through his mind with its unfailing instinct for clarity, his sense of humor, and his constant vision of where and how the ideas in question should and could enter the lifestream of human beings.

What seems to me the distinctive factor within his human frame of reference is the sure grasp with which he has kept the personal and the social in firm and true balance. No one has emphasized more than he the importance of freedom. But he has always seen freedom to be a moral matter and morals to be rooted in an intelligence that is informed and aware of its social responsibilities. And while he is aware of the emptiness of education that does not have a social outlook, he has never thought it the work of education to reflect passively the given order. He has seen it as the agency through which the social order could itself become more just, more free, and more responsive to the duties it owes its members. I may express this more simply and directly by saying that he sees democracy as the moral human order which gives the fullest possible opportunity for development of all its members and sees the schools of democracy as agencies for maintaining and strengthening that order. The service he has rendered to this cause is no lip service of indiscriminate laudation. He has been sensitive to deficiencies and internal divisions and contradictions in our democracy and in our schools. He has worked steadily in behalf of an education in which the spirit of a democratic human order would be so pervasive and so unified as to contribute effectively to the advancement of a similar order in all the human relationship of American life.

I wish to close, as I began, with congratulations. This time I wish to congratulate those who are here today in their capacity as representatives of the much larger number not present that we have Boyd Bode upon whom to confer the honor of this Award.

Letters to the Editor

Rejoinder to Charles W. Morris

To the Editors of the *Journal of Philosophy:*

In his letter to you, published in the *Journal of Philosophy,* Vol. XLIII (1946), p. 196, Dr. Morris states that my article on "Peirce's Theory of Linguistic Signs, Thought, and Meaning" (the *Journal of Philosophy,* Vol. XLIII, 1946, pp. 85–95) focussed its "attention upon the historical problem of how far my views do or do not agree with those of Peirce." Since Peirce was the original formulator of the pragmatic position, and gave it its name, the historical question certainly has its rights, not to be lightly waived aside. But the issue, as stated by Dr. Morris in his letter, is much broader than this particular historical aspect. As far as concerns the views of Dr. Morris, the attention of my article focussed upon his radical misconception of the scope, intention, and method of *Pragmatism.* It was open to him to say that Peirce, James, and the present writer had made a serious mistake in taking the pragmatic position to be one which brings together in one system what *he* regards as the three distinct topics of semantics, logic, and pragmatics—in *his* sense of the term—and that he is correcting that mistake by putting Pragmatism in its proper niche. But he has produced no evidence from any one of the supposed exponents of pragmatic doctrine to warrant his statement that it is concerned with "the study of the relation of signs to" scientists and/or to the "users" of signs. It is to be hoped that in his forthcoming book Dr. Morris will take the opportunity to make it clear that he is putting forth on his own account a radically new version of the subject-matter, intent, and method of pragmatic doctrine, or else will bring forward evi-

[First published in *Journal of Philosophy* 43 (9 May 1946): 280. For letter by Charles W. Morris to which this is a rejoinder, see Appendix 9. For earlier article by Dewey, see pp. 141–52.]

dence that others who have written in the name of that position have actually excluded the theory of logic and the problem of the connection of signs with "objects" from the scope of their theory. The present writer, as the author of a volume called *Logic: The Theory of Inquiry,* will be particularly interested in seeing evidence of that sort. The alternative is that stated above: A plain declaration by Dr. Morris that he is engaged in correcting the serious error of those who have previously written in the name of Pragmatism.

JOHN DEWEY

New York City

Dewey vs. Meiklejohn

To the Editors:

In the January *Fortune* Mr. Meiklejohn has an article entitled "A Reply to John Dewey." The article to which Mr. Meiklejohn supposes himself to reply is published in the August, 1944, issue of *Fortune,* and is entitled "Challenge to Liberal Thought." I say "*supposes* himself to reply" because he misconceives my plain meaning so completely that I have no hesitation in declaring that whatever Mr. Meiklejohn's article is a reply to, it is not to views that I hold or have expressed.

I wrote: "We are now being told that a genuinely liberal education would require return to the models, patterns, and standards that were laid down in Greece some twenty-five hundred years ago and renewed and put into practice in the best age of feudal medievalism six and seven centuries ago." This *return to past ideals* of liberal education is the "challenge" with which I was concerned; different aspects of the movement of return were documented in my article. In Mr. Meiklejohn's "reply" my statement appears with a distorting addition as follows: "Mr. Dewey suggests that a study of Greece 'would require return to the models, patterns, and standards that were laid down in Greece.'" And very naturally he asks "why." He then proceeds to criticize me as if I had assumed that a *study* of the past *requires imitation* of it. Under the impression that he is refuting my position he points out at some length what I should have supposed to be a commonplace, viz., that the present cannot be understood without study of the past.

I do not wish to waste space repudiating the position attributed to me. Not only have I never held it, but I should be

[First published in *Fortune* 31 (March 1945): 10, 14. For Dewey's earlier publication, "Challenge to Liberal Thought," see pp. 261–75. For Alexander Meiklejohn's article to which this is a rejoinder, see Appendix 10. For further letters, see Appendix 11 and p. 337.]

ashamed if I thought I was under the necessity of denying that I held such a silly notion. It is pertinent, however, to note that an important element in my criticism of those whose views I regard as a challenge to liberal thought and education was the superficiality of their account of Greek thought. I charged them with distortion both as to Greek thought and in re-editing it so as to make it tributary to the theological metaphysics of the Middle Ages. Because of my reference to what I called "historical illiteracy" I incurred the wrath of one important member of the group. It is also pertinent that in speaking of Greek thought I explicitly wrote: "In spirit, we are nearer the culture of antiquity than we are to that of the medieval period. Great as is the change from a servile to a free basis in organization of social relations, it can be said with considerable truth that the change is in line with *principles* stated in Athens."

I cannot leave this phase of the matter without reference to other respects in which Mr. Meiklejohn's "reply" fails to reply to what I said and believe. He gave what *in effect* and perhaps in intent is a handsome and welcome endorsement of my position that a genuinely liberal education must include an understanding of "the sciences and technologies by which the life of that age is sustained and determined." But then Meiklejohn went on to say "As against this, the plan of building the liberal education of each pupil around his own vocation, while it may appeal to immediate individual interest, is open to many objections.... Worst of all, it cuts away the moral foundations of liberal education by finding its significance not in its own effectiveness but in its connection with the private, vocational interest of the pupil."

Mr. Meiklejohn nowhere unambiguously says that the "plan" in question is put forward or implied in my position. But others besides myself may wonder what is the relevancy of his statement unless the passage is supposed to represent my position, rather than one I have repeatedly and earnestly opposed. Certainly no reader would gather from the passage that I hold the position I actually took: that the most urgent educational problem of the present day is to give humane direction to technical subjects now *socially* necessary. A similar ambiguous illusiveness attaches to passages in which Mr. Meiklejohn writes that "There is no difference, he seems to say, between the spiritual and the material, between the liberal and the vocational, between values and facts."

One cannot wrestle with shadows and the word "seems" is but a shadow. So I can only say, with utmost positiveness, what every serious student of my rather numerous philosophical writings already knows. The vital problems of philosophy today spring from the need for reconsideration and reconstruction of traditional beliefs about material and spiritual, theory and practice, fact and value. While this reconstruction will involve breaking down rigid dualisms set up in the past, it will be as far from *identifying* the two things as it is from traditional doctrines which completely separate them. In my article the traditional separations are dealt with so far as they impede the needed reconstruction, one for which ample materials are at hand but which is so far from accomplishment that it determines *the* outstanding task of philosophy today.

In spite of appearances to the contrary I am confident that Mr. Meiklejohn's misconception is not due to desire to misrepresent my views. Why then did the misconception occur? I venture the following explanation. Mr. Meiklejohn devotes much the greater part of his article to a spirited defense of St. John's College. This fact is understandable only upon the hypothesis that he supposed that St. John's was the main objective of my criticism. It is also noteworthy that he prefaces his defense with reference to his own educational experiment at the University of Wisconsin. The implication is that while I was directly attacking the educational program of St. John's, I was indirectly attacking his educational philosophy. As to the first, I can say that the philosophy I criticized is so current and so much more influential than is the work of St. John's that there are only a few sentences in my article even indirectly referring to St. John's. Rightly or wrongly, I had not supposed that the program and work of St. John's was of such importance as to justify my use of the pages of *Fortune* in extended criticism of it, especially as a number of effective criticisms had already been made.[1] And so far was I at any point from addressing myself to the educational philosophy and experiment of Mr. Meiklejohn that I had supposed that there were pretty fundamental differences between his and that reigning at

1. Cf. such articles as those of Dr. Hook in the *New Leader* of May 27 and June 3 of last year, and the addresses of Professors Irwin Edman and Arthur Murphy to the Second Conference on "The Scientific Spirit and Democratic Faith" in New York, in May, 1944.—J.D.

St. John's. I am, of course, compelled to bow, though with reluctance, to the superior knowledge of Mr. Meiklejohn if he identifies the two. But even so, I cannot avoid recalling that he nowhere touches on the matter of re-editing Greek thought to make it a support of medieval beliefs, nor can I wholly deprive myself of the hope that later reflection may lead him to realize that his position and that of the context I criticized are in important respects not similar but opposed.

I am encouraged in this hope by the fact that Mr. Meiklejohn more than once expresses belief that his and my fundamental desires as to the future of education have much in common—something which cannot be said of my views and those whom I criticized. As a possible aid to cooperation in a common cause I close with a brief restatement of the issue as I see it.

We are agreed that a genuinely liberal education is badly hampered by confusion of aims and procedures. We are agreed that intelligent knowledge and understanding of the past is a prerequisite for understanding the present and for the formation of effective educational philosophies. For my part, I hold that philosophies and beliefs which separate man and nature, the eternal and the temporal, the rigidly fixed and the changing, the intellectual and the practical—philosophies that draw an impassable line between the operation of intelligence as expressed in scientific method, and validation of values—are obstructive. They stand in the way of building up the attitude which in serving the needs of a genuinely liberal education will also serve the needs of our troubled and divided social life. All who share this point of view will, I am confident, welcome contributions, however critical, from Mr. Meiklejohn provided they really touch issues and problems with which *we* are concerned because the problems themselves grow out of and reflect the perplexities of our common life. If philosophy is to have relevancy and significance at the present time it must make some contribution to effective dealing with these perplexities. And, as I began my *Fortune* article by suggesting, education is the field in which such a philosophy has its most direct and vital impact.

JOHN DEWEY

Rejoinder to Meiklejohn

To the Editors:

My reply to Mr. Meiklejohn sought only to set him straight as to my views. He is entitled to admit that he misconceived them. But when he speaks of a "joint failure" I find him overinclusive. His final words seem to constitute confession by avoidance.

JOHN DEWEY

[First published in *Fortune* 31 (March 1945): 14. For earlier articles in the Dewey-Meiklejohn exchange, see pp. 261–75; Dewey letter, pp. 333–36; Appendixes 10 and 11.]

Russia's Position

Mr. Davies's Book Regarded as Incorrect Picture

To the Editor of the *New York Times*:

Since the *New York Times Magazine* on Dec. 14 published excerpts from former Ambassador Joseph E. Davies's book *Mission to Moscow,* and since Ralph Thompson reviews the book most favorably in your issue of Dec. 29, I venture, in the interest of truth and for the sake of the record, to offer a few observations which are none the less pertinent for being unfashionable now.

Mr. Davies shares the official Soviet view that Stalin's terror, of which the three great Moscow trials and the execution of the Red Army High Command were the outstanding events, was a weeding out of Hitler's agents in the Soviet Union. He reported to the Secretary of State that he was "predisposed against the credibility of the testimony" of the accused in the Pyatakov-Radek trial of January, 1937, which he "assiduously attended," but that the record had convinced him. He seems also to have swallowed without overmuch gagging the execution of the generals without public trial. Also the subsequent Bukharin-Rykov trial of January, 1938—in which, he remarks in a casual footnote, "detailed and specific charges were made for the first time against the Red Army, implicating some of its leaders in 'fifth column' activities." Not detailed and specific proof, mind you, but "charges" which in retrospect seem to Mr. Davies to justify the belief that the generals were guilty.

Such willingness to be persuaded makes it hardly surprising that Mr. Davies, after Hitler's invasion of Russia, needed nothing more than a re-examination of the trial records and his own dispatches at the time to convince him that "practically every device of German fifth-columnist activity as we know it was disclosed

[First published in *New York Times,* 11 January 1942, p. 7. For reply by John L. Childs, see Appendix 12. For rejoinder by Dewey, see pp. 342–44.]

and laid bare by the confessions at these trials of self-confessed Quislings."

I do not know whether or not there were fifth columnists in Russia. I do not know whether there were fifth columnists among the accused in the Moscow trials. But I do know, after careful study of the trial records, that it is impossible to seine any credible evidence of fifth-column activity out of all the contradictions, confusion and patent lying on the part of the accused, the self-inculpating witnesses and the prosecutor. I can say this without taking into account such egregious and promptly exposed lies as the famous testimony about the nonexistent "Hotel Bristol," or that about Pyatakov's alleged secret midwinter flight to Oslo. I know also that any disinterested person who will take the trouble really to study the records—which are available in official English translations published by the Soviet Government— must inevitably reach the same conclusion.

Mr. Davies either does not know or chooses to overlook the political implications of these trials, although he did make one significant observation in his report on the execution of the generals: "The Stalin regime, politically and internally, is probably stronger than heretofore. All potential opposition has been killed off."

If one looks at the trials in the light of this observation a very different picture emerges from that which Mr. Davies chooses to see. It is the picture of a totalitarian dictator consolidating his power by killing off "all potential opposition." What more likely foci of opposition could there have been in Russia than the surviving associates of Lenin and heroes of the revolution and the civil war who were the principals in the Moscow trials?

And what more effective means could Stalin have found to discredit these men than to force them to confess that they had conspired with foreign powers? It is as though Aaron Burr had seized power and had then consolidated it by bringing George Washington, Thomas Jefferson, John Adams, Alexander Hamilton and other American Revolutionary heroes to trial on charges of having conspired with foreign powers against the State they had helped create.

Mr. Davies also chooses to overlook the pertinent fact that Stalin himself, at the very time of the trials and the thousands of executions without trial, was trying very hard to reach an agreement with Hitler. Here the testimony of a former Soviet agent like Krivitsky becomes pertinent. Krivitsky, it will be remembered, predicted the Stalin-Hitler pact months before it was announced. And he predicted it on the basis of Stalin's secret attempts to reach such an agreement, of which Krivitsky had been aware in his capacity of chief of the Soviet military intelligence in Western Europe.

Seen in this light, Stalin's liquidation of the Old Bolsheviki appears not as punishment for their alleged dealings with Hitler but as a possible price of success in his dealings with Hitler.

But Mr. Davies appears to take the view that whatever Stalin does is right. He defended the Stalin-Hitler pact, and he even goes so far as to maintain that if Stalin, now fortuitously fighting on the side of the Allies, shall once more desert to the Nazi camp, the fault will be not his but that of the Allied governments. Need I point out that such a view is not only an insult to Mr. Roosevelt and Mr. Churchill but that it is calculated, if it finds acceptance, to undermine the faith of the democratic peoples in their leaders if and when Stalin shall once more decide that his interest will best be served by leaving the democracies in the lurch?

There is no question that this country should give the Soviet Union every possible aid against the Nazi invasion, which the Russian people and armies have so heroically withstood. But there is equally no question that it is not only unnecessary but dangerous for Mr. Davies or any other public man to present the totalitarian despotism of Stalin in any but its true light.

The American people know that Stalin, now in the Allied camp by Hitler's will, not his, unleashed the present war through his pact with Hitler. They remember that until Russia was invaded Stalin's followers in America worked energetically to prevent this country from aiding Britain or arming itself. And they should bear clearly in mind that Stalin's actions—and those of his agents and sympathizers here—will be governed by his own interest as he conceives it, regardless of the efforts of or the consequences to his present democratic allies.

There is an even more important issue. To justify the Soviet blood purge to the American people is to justify government actions diametrically opposed to the judicial processes of democracy, with their careful safeguards of the rights of accused persons. To excuse a government terror on any basis is to condone by implication the abolition of all those civil rights which protect the citizens of our democracy from persecution by those in power. It is the most dangerous kind of argument in these times when democracy is in grave peril, and when Americans are defending it with their treasure and their lives.

It is possible to rejoice in Russian victories over the common enemy without idealizing Stalin's regime of terror. Never before have democratic peoples been asked to idealize despotism because its political interests happened to coincide with theirs. In our Civil War we received aid from autocratic Russia. We were grateful for that aid, but no responsible American eulogized the Czarist regime because of it. In the First World War the Republic of France was admittedly saved through the aid of Czarist Russia in the first critical stages of the war. Yet no one in France or the other western democracies held up the bloody regime of the last Czar as a model of justice and integrity.

In the matter of a correct attitude toward Stalin, the most powerful of all Russian despots, we may very well allow ourselves to be taught by him. He recognizes a common interest with us. He accepts what aid we can give him. But he does not trust us. There are no democratic agents and sympathizers at large in Russia, as there are Bolshevik agents and sympathizers at large in the democracies. For Stalin knows what his apologists here apparently do not know—totalitarianism and democracy will not mix.

Our future would be much more secure than it now appears if we were to emulate his circumspection instead of indulging in the fatuous one-sided love feast now going on in this country, of which Mr. Davies's book is merely one manifestation among many.

JOHN DEWEY

Key West, Fla., Jan. 7, 1942

Dr. Dewey on Our Relations with Russia

Sir: Dr. Childs cannot say too much or say it too emphatically about the importance of Russia in the after-war situation, including relations between that country, Great Britain and ourselves. It is just this importance which makes the present build-up of Stalin and *Stalin's* Russia dangerous. The build-up is no less sinister in its consequences when engaged in by weak-kneed liberals, "hard-headed" men for reasons of short range expediency and under the standard of patriotism, than when it is a campaign of propaganda maintained by those who were sure the war was a strictly imperialist one as long as Stalin was safely out of it and who carried on active defense of the alliance between the two totalitarian powers as long as both dictators found it to their interests to keep it up.

Danger is imminent. Anyone who reads between the lines of the statements that are already appearing in the newspapers is aware that negotiations are going on to which Great Britain is an active party, and to which for all we know the United States is at least a passive party, for the sacrifice of the Baltic states and of Poland. That the resistance Russia has put up makes it possible for Stalin to exact a high price for staying in the war after the time arrives when Hitler is ready for another deal is no less a fact because we are all happy that German power has received a check for the first time since the war began. Do we want what in effect are secret treaties, like those of the World War, to predetermine final terms of peace and to plant, as happened in the case of the last war, the seeds of another war?

[First published in *Frontiers of Democracy* 8 (15 April 1942): 194. For Dewey's earlier article, see pp. 338–41; and for John L. Childs's letter to which this is a rejoinder, see Appendix 12.]

I do not for a moment include Dr. Childs among those engaged even in the most indirect way in carrying on a dangerous
appeasement of a totalitarian power. His record as well as his article in the March 15 *Frontiers of Democracy* shows that he does
not share the illusions of ignorance that have given Mr. Davies'
book its authorship and its vogue. I mention certain facts in order
that we may be sure to put first things first. At this immediate
juncture, for the sake of future helpful relations between Russia
and such democracies as exist, the first thing is to beware of the
present active campaign to idealize Stalin and *his* domestic and
international policies.

For instance, I venture the statement that 90 percent of the
readers of the Davies book—*the* current best-seller—would say
that Stalin's purges of the military are a strong factor in the resistance Russia finally succeeded in putting up. They would be totally ignorant of the fact that it was *his* generals who lost all the
early battles, and that it was the calling back into active service of
surviving representatives of the band Stalin more than decimated
that accounts for recent successes. This fact may not seem relevant to the point I'm making. But I submit that an enlightened
public opinion is the hope for peace terms that will help on the
cause of permanent peace and of democratic development. As far
as Russia is concerned, public opinion is now in process of being
obfuscated instead of enlightened. It is a well established fact that
the emotionalism which unavoidably attends war-conditions is
the best culture medium for growth of obfuscation. To permit
this, for reasons of temporary expediency, to develop is a policy
we may have to pay a high price for later on. There are plenty of
voices, most of them innocent, some viciously partisan, who are
lending themselves to create the conditions of a bad peace. I am
sure that Dr. Childs no more wants to join in that chorus than
I do.

What is now needed is a sane, realistic appraisal by the men in
this country who know the facts about Stalin's Russia of those
conditions of both the war and the peace settlement which will
eliminate the dangers inhering in Stalinist supremacy, and establish the basis for helpful relations after the peace between a Russia freed from totalitarian menace and Great Britain and this
country: relations in which we can learn from whatever of good

Russia has accomplished and that country can be assisted forward on a genuinely democratic path. When Stalin needs our help is the time to start setting up these conditions; when we need him more than he needs us is the worst time. So I repeat, first things first.

JOHN DEWEY

Key West, Florida

Several Faults Are Found in *Mission to Moscow* Film

To the Editor of the *New York Times:*

The film *Mission to Moscow* is the first instance in our country of totalitarian propaganda for mass consumption—a propaganda which falsifies history through distortion, omission or pure invention of facts, and whose effect can only be to confuse the public in its thought and its loyalties.

Even in a fictional film this method would be disturbing. It becomes alarming in a film presented as factual and documentary and introducing living historical personalities. Our former Ambassador to the Soviet Union, Joseph E. Davies, personally introduces this dramatization of his mission as the "truth" about Russia. And the representation of President Roosevelt talking to Mr. Davies of the film seems to suggest that it is at least semi-official.

Mission to Moscow deals essentially with three things: Soviet history since January, 1937; international relations since that time, and American history since 1939. It falsifies all three.

1. The most important event in Soviet history during Mr. Davies's ambassadorship was Stalin's continuous purge. The film deals with only one aspect of it—the famous Moscow trials.

Immediately after Mr. Davies's arrival in Moscow—on Jan. 19, 1937—he is shown meeting, among others at a diplomatic reception in his honor, Karl Radek, Nikolai Bukharin, and G. G. Yagoda.

Here the film borrows the primary technique of the Moscow trials in representing an event which could not have taken place. Karl Radek was arrested in September, 1936, and never released thereafter. The mass trial in which he was a principal began on

[First published in *New York Times,* 9 May 1943, p. 8, and written with Suzanne La Follette. For reply by Arthur Upham Pope, see Appendix 13. For rejoinder by Dewey and La Follette, see pp. 351–53. For second letter by Pope, see Appendix 14 and for final response by Dewey and La Follette, see pp. 354–55.]

Jan. 23, four days after the real Mr. Davies's arrival. Nikolai Bukharin was also under arrest at the time and was incriminated in Radek's "confession." Yagoda was already in disgrace. It is significant that in the book which the film purports to dramatize Mr. Davies mentions none of these three men in listing his personal acquaintances among the accused.

The film telescopes the trial of 1937 and that of 1938. Dramatic license might possibly excuse representing Radek and Sokolnikov, principals in the 1937 trial, as principals with Bukharin, Krestinsky, and Yagoda in that of 1938, since all were allegedly in the same conspiracy and were actually tried. But there is no excuse for including as an accused in this synthetic trial Marshal Tukhachevsky, who was secretly executed in June, 1937, after no trial at all. To show Marshal Tukhachevsky having his day in court may serve the interests of Soviet propaganda. It does not serve the interests of "truth about Russia."

In this synthetic trial the accused confess that their alleged crimes were directed by Trotsky. What is omitted is the testimony in the actual trials to specific alleged meetings with Trotsky abroad—testimony immediately challenged in the world press and conclusively disproved by evidence offered in rebuttal before the international commission of inquiry of which the undersigned were respectively chairman and secretary. It is not irrelevant to mention here that the commission, after painstaking investigation, concluded that the Moscow trials were frame-ups—a conclusion endorsed by intelligent world opinion at the time of its announcement.

The film falsifies not only the trials but Mr. Davies's own reports on them to the State Department and his comments in letters to individuals. On pages 52 and 53 of his book he says in a letter to Senator Byrnes: "The guarantees of the common law to protect the personal liberty of the individual from the possible oppressions of government . . . never impressed me with their beneficence in the public interest as they did in this trial. All of these defendants had been held incommunicado for months."

In the synthetic trial Mr. Davies's enthusiasm for the beneficent guarantees of the common law is not registered. What is registered is his close attention to the "confessions" (obligingly delivered in English, of course, since Mr. Davies knows no Russian) and his instant declaration of his conviction that the accused are guilty. There is no hint of the "reservation" recorded on page 43 of his book, "based upon the facts that both the system of enforcement of penalties for the violation of law and the psychology of these people are so widely different from our own that perhaps the tests which I would apply would not be accurate if applied here."

In his official reports Mr. Davies said: "The Terror here is a horrifying fact. There . . . is a fear that reaches down into and haunts all sections of the community. No household, however humble, apparently but what lives in constant fear of a nocturnal raid by the secret police. . . . Once the person is taken away, nothing of him or her is known for months—and many times never—thereafter" (page 302).

But the make-believe Russia of the film is gay, even festive, and wherever Mr. Davies goes he encounters a happy confidence in the regime.

In his letters and reports Mr. Davies spoke of the terror as a struggle for power—"This particular purge is undoubtedly political" (page 303); "The Stalin regime, politically and internally, is probably stronger than heretofore. All potential opposition has been killed off" (page 202).

The film, on the other hand, gives the impression that Stalin is killing off not potential political opponents but traitors in the service of foreign powers. In other words, it reflects the sudden belated flash of illumination described by Mr. Davies in the section of the book called "A Study in Hindsight," which revealed to him (in Wisconsin, and not until June, 1941) that the terror was really a purge of fifth columnists.

2. The film represents Stalin as having been driven into Hitler's arms by the Franco-British policy of appeasement. There is no reference to the desperate efforts of France and Britain to reach a defensive alliance with Stalin in 1939, no reference to the presence in Moscow of an Allied military mission vainly waiting to confer with the Soviet General Staff at the very time when the Stalin-Hitler pact was announced. Hitler's armies are shown invading Poland, but not Stalin's.

There is no mention of the Soviet Government's demand for a negotiated peace after Stalin and Hitler had divided Poland, or of Stalin's words after the partition, "Our friendship is cemented with blood," or of Molotov's famous remark that "fascism is just a matter of taste," or of Mr. Davies's own reference to "Russia's ally, Germany." (*Mission to Moscow,* page 474.)

Nor is there in the film even the merest hint that in France, England, the United States—wherever the Communist International was functioning—the Communist parties systematically sabotaged the Allied cause. One would never know that the most determined and noisy isolationists in this country before June 22, 1941, were in the Communist-led American Peace Mobilization. One would never know that for months before that date the Communists fomented strikes in our defense industries, calculated to sabotage our rearmament and our aid to Britain. Communist responsibility for these strikes is a matter of record—*vide* the statements at the time of Attorney General Jackson, high-ranking labor leaders and the entire American press.

The film is subtly anti-British. It harps on the appeasement policy of Chamberlain and represents Mr. Churchill only in the period when he was still in the opposition and comparatively powerless. By the device of leaping over Stalin's collaboration with Hitler and Churchill's direction of British affairs, it conveys the impression that Stalin's foreign policy has always been democratic and anti-fascist and Britain's one of appeasement. One would never suspect that it was Stalin who enabled Hitler to attack Poland and Chamberlain who came to Poland's defense.

The whole atmosphere of the film conveys the impression that Soviet Russia is our ally in the same degree as Great Britain. The Japanese Ambassador is snubbed and insulted at the same diplomatic reception where Mr. Davies could not have met Bukharin and Radek. Mr. Davies is shown visiting a hospital where Russian doctors and nurses are tending Chinese victims of Japanese air raids—though how they got to Moscow is not explained. The doctor in charge tells him that "the Chinese are our friends," and points the moral of the dire results of appeasement.

The effect of all this is to create the impression that the Soviet Union is our ally against Japan. In fact Japan and Soviet Russia have a non-aggression pact to this day; and it must be said for Mr. Stalin that he has never sought to mislead the United Nations about his policy of neutrality in the Far Eastern war. Nothing could be more dangerous than to mislead the American people into believing that the Soviet Union will turn against Japan the moment Hitler is defeated.

The film shows Mr. Davies, back in America, making a swing around the circle in spite of ill health, because it is his "duty" to explain Russia to the American people. The drama of this section is achieved through contrasting flashes—a wild anti-conscription meeting followed by a flash of Mr. Davies explaining Russia; meetings of American business men demanding isolation and business with Hitler, followed by flashes of Mr. Davies explaining Russia. And so on.

Now what are the facts? On July 15, 1941, Mr. Davies told Sumner Welles that he wished to be of every possible help to the Soviet Embassy here (*Mission to Moscow*, page 492). His swing around the circle took place in the Winter of 1941 and 1942—mostly in 1942. The Conscription Act was passed by Congress in September, 1940; and one of the dissenting votes was cast by Representative Vito Marcantonio.

Obviously Mr. Davies's swing around the circle had nothing to do with swinging American opinion behind conscription. Neither had it anything to do with dissuading such American business men as may have wanted to do business with Hitler, for Pearl Harbor was bombed on Dec. 7, 1941, and American business men were just as much against Hitler as was Mr. Davies. Mr. Davies's swing around the circle was no battle royal. It was just an unexciting trip to sell the Soviet Government to an American public already 100 per cent for the Russian people in their magnificent defense of their country.

Finally, a sinister totalitarian critique of the parliamentary system is introduced in the film. The traditional isolationism of some American members of Congress before the war is represented as equivalent to pro-nazism. The whole effort is to discredit the American Congress and at the same time to represent the Soviet dictatorship as an advanced democracy. Such gross misrepresentation can only contribute to confusion in our relations with the Soviet Union. If our collaboration is to continue after the war it cannot be on the basis of Soviet propaganda but only on that of genuine understanding of the differences in our political systems.

The film is, to resume, anti-British, anti-Congress, anti-democratic and anti-truth. It deepens that crisis in morals which is the fundamental issue in the modern world. The picture *Mission to Moscow* and similar propaganda have helped to create a certain moral callousness in our public mind which is profoundly un-American. Only recently the American people received with comparative calm the Soviet Government's announcement that it had executed as "Nazi agents" the two Polish Jews, Ehrlich and Alter, internationally known leaders of Socialist labor whom it had arrested when it invaded Poland. A few more uncritically accepted films like *Mission to Moscow*—for where thousands read books, millions see motion pictures—and Americans will be deadened to all moral values.

Mission to Moscow is a major defeat for the democratic cause. In putting out this picture the producers, far from rendering the patriotic service on which Mr. Davies compliments them, have assailed the very foundations of freedom. For truth and freedom are indivisible, as Hitler knew when he expounded his method of confusing public opinion through propaganda. The picture *Mission to Moscow* makes skillful use of the Hitler technique. To quote Matthew Low of the *New Leader:* "This kind of 'truth' is on the march, and God help us if nothing can stop it."

JOHN DEWEY
SUZANNE LA FOLLETTE

New York, May 6, 1943

Moscow Film Again Attacked

Miss La Follette and Dr. Dewey Reply to Mr. Pope's Arguments

To the Editor of the *New York Times:*

In your issue of May 16 Arthur Upham Pope, attacking our criticism of the film *Mission to Moscow* in your issue of May 9, impugns our integrity and that of the Commission of Inquiry of which we were, respectively, chairman and secretary.

This is no new thing. The Communist press has smeared the commission for years with exactly the same arguments. The commission's two volumes (not one, as Mr. Pope states) are easily available and effectively answer Mr. Pope's stereotyped strictures upon its work. Incidentally, his assertion that our report was not documented is disingenuous. The report bristles with references to documents, all of which are available to any serious student at the Widener Library of Harvard University.

Our preliminary commission did say (Vol. 1, p. xvii, not p. viii) that "the bearing of the witness may be taken into account in weighing the value of the testimony." Mr. Pope's quotation of the remark is intended to leave the impression that we now challenge Mr. Davies's right to take into account the bearing of the witnesses in forming his opinion of the Moscow trials. This, of course, is not the case. What is challenged was the film's falsification of Mr. Davies's own book on this point.

In the book Mr. Davies expressed some doubt whether the tests he would apply to the testimony were valid in Russia. In the film he declares immediately after the trial his conviction that the "confessions" are true. Obviously one attitude or the other can represent the truth about Mr. Davies; but not both.

Mr. Pope charges that back of all our criticisms "is the belief

[First published in *New York Times,* 24 May 1943, p. 14, and written with Suzanne La Follette. For Dewey and La Follette's earlier letter, see pp. 345–50. For Arthur Upham Pope's response to which this is a rejoinder, see Appendix 13. For second letter by Pope, see Appendix 14. For a final response by Dewey and La Follette, see pp. 354–55.]

that Trotsky was innocent of plotting against the Soviet regime, that the Moscow trials were farcical."

The Moscow trials were, of course, not farcical; they were horrible and tragic. But what was back of all our criticisms of *Mission to Moscow* was the fact that the film is farcical as history and totalitarian as propaganda. It is a fact which has outraged more critics than ourselves; a fact, indeed, which makes the film threaten to prove a propaganda boomerang for its producers and its sponsor.

Mr. Pope defends the film's distortions of historical fact by pleading the rights of "fictional technique." Without granting the right of fiction to falsify history, we call attention once more to the fact that the film is introduced by ex-Ambassador Davies as "the truth about Russia." If a film is offered as objective truth, then its distortions of truth must be called by their right name. A work cannot honestly be presented as truth and defended as fiction.

It is not objective truth to show Marshal Tukhachevsky on public trial, and to put into his mouth the words of the accused Muralov. If Mr. Pope wants to believe that Tukhachevsky was tried in camera that is his right. But to argue that a secret trial and a presumption of guilt justify parading the marshal's ghost in open court is to get pretty far away not only from historical criteria but from those of fiction. Would any self-respecting novelist dare pretend that Napoleon tried the Duc d'Enghien before putting him to death?

It is not objective truth to represent the Russians as happy and hopeful in a period when the continuous purge which horrified Mr. Davies kept every Russian household in "constant fear." It is not objective truth to cite the opinion of a small Congressional minority and ignore the sentiments of the vast majority—and even to misrepresent the minority through violence to chronology. It is not objective truth to ignore Stalin's part in precipitating the World War, his invasion of Poland, his collaboration with Hitler, which Mr. Davies himself characterized as an alliance.

It is not objective truth to create the impression that Soviet Russia is our ally against Japan. Russia may be China's best friend, as Mr. Pope contends—although Frederick Vanderbilt Field in the *New Masses* of Jan. 26 complained that one million of Chiang Kai-shek's troops are kept busy riding herd on the Chinese Communists. But whether China's friend or not, the Soviet Union has a non-aggression pact with Japan and is neutral in the Far Eastern war.

It is not objective truth to misrepresent British policy as well as Soviet policy through the device of selection and omission. France and Britain did drive Stalin into Hitler's arms, Mr. Pope says; they didn't send their first-string diplomats—as if Stalin would unleash a terrible war for a reason so frivolous. Stalin was playing for time to arm, adds Mr. Pope—thus by analogy justifying Chamberlain and Daladier at Munich—but he neglects to explain why, if Stalin was gaining strength to fight Hitler, the Communist International sabotaged Hitler's enemies until June 22, 1941.

To sum up, it is not objective truth to juggle or invent opinions, characters, events, dates, with no regard for anything except the picture of Russia and Joseph E. Davies which Mr. Davies and the Warner Brothers want the American people to accept as the truth. By "fictionalizing" history for the greater glory of the Soviet dictatorship the film becomes precisely what we called it—"totalitarian propaganda for mass consumption."

Yet Mr. Pope, in defending this propaganda, pleads for "a cool objectivity, a looking beyond feuds and controversies." Who is objective—those who insist on historical veracity in a historical work, or those who defend falsifications of history? And who started this controversy anyway—such critics of *Mission to Moscow* as Anne O'Hare McCormick, Dorothy Thompson, Eugene Lyons, the editors of *Time* and *Life*, ourselves; or Mr. Davies and the Warner Brothers? Not those who protest against misrepresentation create controversy, but those who offer misrepresentation as truth.

Finally, we do not believe that totalitarian propaganda such as *Mission to Moscow* can strengthen our ties with the Soviet Union, either in the war or in the future peace, or that it can help either the Russian people or our own. The "decent and re-created life" for the sake of whose attainment Mr. Pope invites us to keep silent cannot be built on a morass of historical falsification and deliberate confusion of the peoples of this world. And as chairman of the Committee on National Morale it would seem to be Mr. Pope's business to know this.

JOHN DEWEY
SUZANNE LA FOLLETTE

New York, May 18, 1943

More on *Mission to Moscow*

To the Editor of the *New York Times:*

In closing, as far as we are concerned, the discussion started by Arthur Upham Pope over our criticism of the film *Mission to Moscow*, may we comment upon a single point contained in the letter of Mr. Pope in your issue of June 12?

Mr. Pope argues that since "every one's freedom of speech is somewhat curtailed in wartime, and in moments of peril the common will must be protected from divisive conflicts," the leaders of the government of an ally should not be subjected to criticism. That, as he says, "it is unwise and unfair to malign a gallant ally or its chosen leaders" is, or should be, a truism. Unfortunately, Mr. Pope begs the whole question by identifying criticisms of the falsifications found in a commercial film with maligning.

In addition, as we pointed out in our original letter, the film indulged in aspersions upon our gallant ally Great Britain, who bore from June, 1940, to June, 1941, the entire burden of the war against the Axis powers. In his letter of your issue of May 16 Mr. Pope spoke harshly of the same ally—in order to justify a film. It looks as if Mr. Pope intended his reservation to apply only to the government of the Soviet Union.

It is even more important that in order to attack criticisms which are made in the interest of genuine common understanding as well as of historic truth Mr. Pope completely ignores the fact that the film is responsible for gratuitous introduction of matters of division and conflict—matters, moreover, that occurred in a foreign country. Mr. Pope should address his admo-

[First published in *New York Times*, 19 June 1943, p. 12, and written with Suzanne La Follette. For earlier letters by Dewey and La Follette, see pp. 345–50 and pp. 351–53. For Arthur Upham Pope's replies, see Appendixes 13 and 14.]

nition to the producers of the film. He should address it to those political partisans and fellow-travelers in this country who act as if proper relations between the United States and the Soviet Union depend upon our taking sides with one faction in Russian politics, even at the expense of historic truth. Under these circumstances, defense of the film is equivalent to the suggestion that democracy take a vacation for the duration.

JOHN DEWEY
SUZANNE LA FOLLETTE

New York, June 15, 1943

The Case of Odell Waller

Supreme Court to Be Asked Again to Hear Negro's Petition

To the Editor of the *New York Times:*

Once more our colored citizens, already deeply aroused over discrimination against them in the armed forces and defense industries, have been presented with a grievance. The United States Supreme Court, on May 4, declined without opinion to review the case of Odell Waller, colored sharecropper, convicted of first degree murder in the shooting of his white farmer landlord during a quarrel induced by Waller's attempt to get his share of their wheat crop. Colored people regard this unexplained refusal as just one more evidence that when white people speak of fighting to preserve freedom, they mean freedom for their own race.

It is particularly gratifying, therefore, to learn that Waller's counsel, John F. Finerty, is about to petition the court for a rehearing, and that an *amicus curiae* brief will also be filed with the Court on behalf of the National Association for the Advancement of Colored People, the American Civil Liberties Union and other organizations, and such prominent citizens as Dr. Henry Sloane Coffin, President of the Union Theological Seminary. In such a case the Court, it seems to me, should be mindful of the late Mayor Gaynor's great dictum, "We must act not only with justice but with the appearance of justice."

Waller pleaded self-defense. The only eyewitness to the shooting was a colored boy of 18, in the employ of the slain man's family. This witness refused to talk to the defense attorneys after the shooting. At the trial he testified that Waller, after a friendly conversation in which Davis told him he would get his wheat soon, shot Davis in the back as he turned to go to breakfast. Against this testimony we have Odell Waller's story, which fits much more logically into the known pattern of Oscar Davis's repeated mis-

[First published in *New York Times*, 15 May 1942, p. 18.]

treatment of the Waller family. Waller testified that Davis refused to give him the wheat, cursed him, and reached for the pocket in which Waller had known him to carry a gun. In fear of his life he shot Davis; and the defense contends reasonably enough that the first two shots hit Davis in the side of the head and on the arm, their force, coupled with his attempt to flee, whirling him around so that the second two shots hit him in the back.

It is hard to believe that Waller would have shot a man with whom he had just had a friendly conversation. Moreover, reliable Negroes who know the South insist that it is incredible that any colored man in that region would give testimony against a white employer's interest, in a white man's court, after a conference with a white prosecutor.

Not only the credibility of the testimony is in question. The case also involves the Constitutional right of an accused person to be tried by a jury of his peers. The Virginia Constitution makes the payment of a $1.50 poll tax for three consecutive years the test of a citizen's qualification to vote; a provision which the present Senator Carter Glass, at the time of its adoption, frankly stated was intended to disfranchise Negroes. In effect it disfranchises more white people than colored, and is widely resented. The lists of qualified voters are commonly used in making up the lists of qualified jurors. Thus Odell Waller, a colored man disfranchised by poverty, was convicted by a jury of white voters, ten of them farmers employing sharecroppers. On this basis his attorney contends that he was denied his Constitutional right to trial by a jury of his peers.

In the public discussion of this case I have noted the argument that since payment of the poll tax is not *in law* the condition for jury service in Virginia, this contention of the defense is invalid. But if payment is *in fact* the condition of service, as the defense has proved with sworn statements, then this argument is obviously irrelevant and technical.

The Supreme Court, in failing to state why it refused to review this case, left it unclear whether it regards a jury of poll-tax payers as peers of a man disfranchised by poverty; or whether it considers that because Waller's young trial attorney raised the commonly known fact that jurors are selected from the tax lists, without adducing specific proof, the condemned man must die solely because of this error. It is vital to the integrity of our judicial procedure that the Supreme Court either grant the petition for a rehearing or state its reasons for refusing. If it shall develop that the Court refuses to review the case on the basis of any technicality, dodging the issue of trial by one's peers, the effect will certainly be to weaken the faith of the poor—and especially poor Negroes—in the democratic processes.

And now a word about the social and humanitarian aspects of this case. It is clear from the record that both the slayer and the slain were victims of the economic forces which for some decades have exerted terrible pressure on both white and colored farmers. The white man was a debt-ridden renter; the colored man a destitute sharecropper. As Jonathan Daniels has put it, "both the white man and the Negro were caught at the bottom of an American agriculture in the South which gives so little that fighting over it—maybe even murder over it—is not to be taken as an unexpected result."

In dealing with this profoundly tragic issue, we must invoke something better than the law of "an eye for an eye and a tooth for a tooth." It calls for compassion—for mercy. If the Supreme Court shall once more decline to review Waller's case, a plea for commutation of sentence will no doubt be made to Governor Colgate W. Darden of Virginia, who has already shown humanity and a courageous disregard of political considerations in granting two reprieves. Because of this record, one may dare to hope that Governor Darden will decide that both justice and mercy can be better served through commutation of sentence than through forcing Odell Waller to pay the extreme—and irrevocable—penalty.

JOHN DEWEY

New York, May 15, 1942

John Dewey on *The Theory of Economic Progress*

Sir: The comment I have to make upon Mr. Henry Hazlitt's review of Ayres' *The Theory of Economic Progress* is decidedly belated. But the issue involved is likely to be timely for a long time to come and so I venture to make a comment at this relatively late date.

The thesis of my comment is that nowhere in his notice does Mr. Hazlitt (in spite of the express title of the book) state either the issue, Mr. Ayres' position regarding it, or the reasons given by the latter for taking it. Instead he set up what it would be a compliment to call a straw man. Anyone who depends upon Mr. Hazlitt will get a completely perverted idea of the book.

This is a serious charge. In evidence I select one instance as typical. The theory which Ayres presents and defends, briefly put, is that the state of industry at a given time reflects the state of technology of the period, which in turn reflects the state of scientific knowledge. Hence economic progress depends upon technological advances. The traditional, the "classic," theory of economics is that "the existence and progress of industrial society are contingent upon the accumulation of capital (funds) as the condition of the existence and growth of capital (equipment)." In criticizing this theory Ayres has occasion to criticize an *argument,* in the form of an illustration, presented in support of the theory by Boehm-Bawerk, and he refers to its obvious "fatuity."

At the hands of Mr. Hazlitt, "argument" is transformed into "theory of capital and interest," so that Mr. Hazlitt can say that Ayres regards the *theory* as a fatuity and takes only three paragraphs "in refuting it (the theory) to his own satisfaction." In

[First published in *Saturday Review of Literature* 27 (14 October 1944): 29. For Henry Hazlitt's review of C. E. Ayres's book to which this is a reply, see Appendix 15. For Hazlitt's rejoinder to this letter, see Appendix 16.]

fact the entire book is devoted to criticizing the theory of monetary capital or funds as the source of the progress of industrial society, and to presentation of an alternative theory. And instead of regarding the theory as a "fatuity," Ayres expressly says that "it is to the credit of the classical tradition that this is the issue to which in the main it has been addressed," adding that if it can be established as correct the objections currently brought against the capitalist system, as for example on the ground of injustice and cruelty due to inequality, must be dismissed as part of the price paid for development of civilization. The alternative theory advanced by Ayres is that while accumulation is important, what counts is not accumulation of funds due to abstinence from consumption but "is the cumulative process of industrial technology."

That this instance of misrepresentation is typical of the entire review may be further gathered from the following fact: Ayres' doctrine that technological progress, due to scientific advance, is the main source of progress in industrial society and hence in the civilization connected with the latter becomes in Mr. Hazlitt's representation the theory that progress *itself* consists in "making tools to make tools"!

It is not incumbent upon a reviewer to praise the position of Ayres; it is not incumbent upon him to accept it. On the contrary, it is his proper business to criticize it adversely if he judges it needs such criticism. But I should suppose it to be reasonably axiomatic that the theory criticized should be one which is set forth in the book supposedly under review.

JOHN DEWEY

New York City

Comment on Bell and Polanyi

To the Editor of *Commentary:*

Daniel Bell's paper "Adjusting Men to Machines" seems to me virtually epoch-making, and Karl Polanyi's "Our Obsolete Market Mentality" is a worthy successor of his book, which when I read it, I found the most enlightening account of the important historical events in the last century-and-a-half I had ever read.

JOHN DEWEY

Key West, Florida

[First published in *Commentary* 3 (March 1947): 289.]

Commentary and Liberalism

To the Editor of *Commentary:*

I am glad as a non-Jewish reader to express to you the great satisfaction I take in reading the pages of *Commentary*. There is not an issue in which I do not find one and generally at least two articles of the most genuinely stimulating sort.

The word "liberal" means so many things that it may not signify much to say that I find *Commentary* the most rewarding of all the liberal journals I see. What distinguishes it to my mind is its breadth and the kind of balance that comes only from views free from clichés, *partis pris,* and the declamatory writing that organs of all stripes seem to favor today. There is a sanity about most of the articles in *Commentary* that comes only from the intellectual and moral soundness of maturity which makes preaching unnecessary.

JOHN DEWEY

New York City

[First published in *Commentary* 6 (November 1948): 485.]

Miscellany

Letter in Introduction to
Don't Be Afraid!

New York City

Gentlemen:

I have read Dr. Cowles' ms., *Don't Be Afraid!* with great interest. From the philosophical and psychological point of view I am greatly impressed with the way in which the account connects Body-Mind. Dr. Cowles' work appeals to me as a practical demonstration of the truth of their intimate connection, which I have long held on theoretical grounds. I welcome, accordingly, his practical proof, which is all the more convincing because it grew so directly out of concrete experience.

Even speaking from the philosophical standpoint, I should be somewhat ashamed to speak first of this theoretical aspect of the matter, were it not that I believe the idea of the separation of Body-Mind has done great practical harm. The remarkable success of Dr. Cowles' methods is evidence of the good that can be accomplished by a sound theory. I anticipate a great and useful career for his book, *Don't Be Afraid!* I hope it will find its way into general use in educational institutions. It should be part of the required course of all teachers in training. Thanking you for letting me read the ms., I am

Sincerely yours,

(Signed) JOHN DEWEY

[First published in Edward Spencer Cowles, *Don't Be Afraid!* (New York: Wilcox and Follette Co., 1941), p. xiv.]

Statement on Jefferson

We have only recently celebrated the two-hundredth anniversary of the birthday of Thomas Jefferson. Even those persons who are akin to the men who abused and vilified him while he was alive have given lipservice to his memory. In sober fact, only those who are continuing to fight for the freedoms for which he strove so valiantly have a right to appeal to his name.

Since Jefferson held that free inquiry and a free education that would put all in possession of the truths it revealed was the sole ultimate support and guarantor of a free government and a free society, it is fitting, it is necessary, at this particular time to re-affirm his faith, and to re-state the reasons upon which this faith is grounded. For everywhere around us we find evidences of the growth of recourse to authoritarianism. It is not simply in international politics and in the ambition of totalitarian dictators that the foundations of free inquiry and free education are now undergoing assault. They are found in philosophy, education, in morals, in religion, where they take the form of insidious attacks upon scientific method, and assertion of a necessity to return to unquestioning acceptance of "first principles" as they are laid down by authority that can be investigated or criticized, so we are repeatedly told, at the cost of social confusion and interminable moral conflict.

For this fundamental reason, I welcome with all my heart and conscience the Conference that will discuss on a constructive basis the intrinsic and inalienable connection of the Scientific Spirit with Democratic Faith in a Free Society.

[From a typescript in the Jerome Nathanson Papers, Society for Ethical Culture, New York City; prepared for press release for conference on The Scientific Spirit and Democratic Faith, 29–30 May 1943, New York City.]

Why I Selected
"Democracy and America"

It happens that I have been engaged recently in making a study of the outgivings of Adolf Hitler—not only *Mein Kampf* but the many speeches he made before and after coming to power. As I now write a few words in connection with this reprint of what I wrote a few years ago, the net conclusion which stays with me from my reading is closely connected with what is said in what follows. Hitler fatally misunderstood the significance, the moving spirit, and the force of American democracy. He did so because he did not have the slightest insight into its moral aspects and moral foundation.

He thought democracy was necessarily weak because he identified it with the mechanics of voting and the quantitative aspect of majority-rule; with the degenerate and futile parliamentarianism he has witnessed in Vienna; with the most divisive, and therefore the weakest, aspect of finance capitalism.

Because of the necessities of his own campaign for power, he realized that to be strong a people must be united. He never realized the moral principle embodied in what is strong and enduring in American democracy: That this unity is toughest and strongest when it is the work of a continuously recreated voluntary consent, which in turn is the product of continual communication, conference, consultation, contact; of the free give-and-take of free beings. He thought it had to be the product of force and the kind of propaganda that is possible only by suppression of all free speech, free publication, free assembly, and free education. Whether or not he judged his own people correctly in this matter, his views and his practice rest upon the lowest kind of estimate of the capacities of human nature. The moral source of

[First published in Whit Burnett, ed., *This Is My Best* (New York: Dial Press, 1942), pp. 1099–1100.]

his final defeat will be just this total lack of faith. As far as democracy lives up to its faith in the potentialities of human beings, by means of putting into practical operation the democratic moral means by which these capacities may be realized, American democracy will do more than aid in winning the war. It will also play a significant role in an even more severe test and task, that of winning the peace. For the foundation of a pacified and unified Europe is the discovery by European peoples of the true nature of the democratic ideal and of the democratic methods by which alone the ideal can be made effective.

Message to the Chinese People

Your country and my country, China and the United States, are alike in being countries that love peace and have no designs on other nations. We are alike in having been attacked without reason and without warning by a rapacious and treacherous enemy. We are alike, your country and mine, in having a common end in this war we have been forced to enter in order to preserve our independence and freedom. We both want to see a world in which nations can devote themselves to the constructive tasks of industry, education, science and art without fear of molestation by nations that think they can build themselves up by destroying the lives and the work of the men, women and children of other peoples. We are alike, your country and mine in being resolved to see this fight through to the end.

In one important respect we are unlike. You have borne the burden, heat and tragedy of the struggle much longer than we have. We are deeply indebted to you for the enduring and heroic struggle you have put up. Our task is severe but it is much easier than it would have been were it not for what you have done in holding a powerful enemy at bay through these long years of suffering. We are now comrades in a common fight and in defending ourselves, all our energies are pledged to your defense and your triumph.

The United Nations will win the whole war, and the United States and China will win against Japan. Of that there can be no more doubt than that the sun will rise tomorrow. Because we are a peaceful nation, we, like you, were taken at a disadvantage at the outset. I assure you that the early disaster has been a stimulus

[First published in English in Robert W. Clopton and Tsuin-Chen Ou, eds., *John Dewey Lectures in China, 1919–1920* (Honolulu: University Press of Hawaii, 1973), pp. 305–6, from a typescript in the National Archives, Washington, D.C.]

that has evoked the united energies and the unalterable resolve of the people of this country. We are in it with you and with the other peoples near you, and we shall carry on till complete victory is ours, and till you and they are forever relieved of the menace under which you have lived for so many years. For the twenty-one demands Japan made upon you a quarter of a century ago is an enduring memorial of how many years you have lived under a threat from which you shall not suffer in future years, and you are able to return to the peaceable task of building up your own culture in peaceful cooperation with other nations of goodwill.

You have assumed by your heroic struggle a new position in the family of nations. You have won the undying respect and admiration of all nations that care for freedom. As the result of the victorious outcome of the war all inequalities to which you have been subject will be completely swept away. Our gratitude to you, our respect for you, our common struggle and sacrifice in the common cause guarantee to China an equal place in the comity of nations when the light of victory dawns.

Both of our nations, even in the midst of the sufferings we undergo and the sacrifices we make, can be of good cheer as we make a reality out of our vision of a world in which we can live without constant dread, and where we have taken a step forward toward a world of friendship and goodwill. In this new world you are assured the position of spiritual leadership of Eastern Asia to which your enduring tradition of culture as well as your present heroic struggle so richly entitle you. We cannot forget that as Japan got her technical and mechanical resources, industry and war from Western nations, so she got her literature, her art, and all that is best in her religion from you. The coming victory will restore to China her old and proper leadership in all that makes for the development of the human spirit.

Message to the Teachers of Perú

My dear Professor García Cuadrado:[1]

I welcome this opportunity to send through you to the educators of Perú a message of wholehearted support for their dedication to the goals of our common cause.

I want to say to them that, in spite of the tragic and lamentable signs that current world conditions forebode, there is one promising indication. This is the fact that in your country, as in other Latin American countries, there is a greater feeling of community with the United States. Our awareness of the need for mutual cooperation in a common destiny has become more intense. Such a statement, true of countries in general, is especially significant for those charged with educating youth because they, more directly and intimately than any statesman, can promote unity and cooperation in a world that today finds itself so divided.

Therefore I want to express through you my personal support for the efforts of the educators of Perú in this undertaking and to tell them I know we will continue to move ahead together in our zeal to create conditions that will lead to peace, mutual understanding, and good will.

Sincerely yours,

(Signed) JOHN DEWEY

---

1. Augusto García Cuadrado, President of the Conference.

[First published in *Journadas Pedagógicas Regionales* (Apata, Departamento de Junín, Perú), 20 al 27 de marzo, 1944, p. 11. This translation into English by Jo Ann Boydston first published in *Dewey Newsletter* 2 (October 1968): 21–22.]

Comment on Sidney Hook's *Education for Modern Man*

One who wants a sane appraisal of present problems, controversies, movements, philosophies, in the field of education will find the need met in Sidney Hook's *Education for Modern Man*. It is wisely sane because Modern Man along with the deficiencies, the possibilities and issues of his education is placed in the wide perspective of human history. On its critical side, it is an antidote against the prevalent short-span views (often frantically expressed) that proceed from opposite camps. On the constructive side, the proposals put forth are sane, not because they are a half-and-half compromise, but because they issue from a firm grasp of all the factors of the situation. Those who desire serious understanding of present controversies and issues, of present defects equally with present promises of improvement, will find this book without par. We shall be fortunate if it becomes a guide-book for public understanding and public active effort. It clarifies, it illuminates one of the most confused aspects of the confused situation of Modern Man.

[First published in *Partisan Review* 13 (Spring 1946): 257.]

Comment on *I Want to Be Like Stalin*

There is not a citizen of this country who does not have an interest, whether he is aware of it or not, in understanding the difficulties we have in getting along as a nation with the Soviet Union. *I doubt if there is anything in existence that is the equal for this purpose of* I Want to Be Like Stalin. It is not the product of an outsider; much less of one unfavorably disposed to the USSR. It is a direct translation from official Russian documents; and the documents were not prepared in order to present either outsiders or Soviet citizens with a favorable picture of the aims and policies of the Bolshevik rulers of the USSR. On the contrary, the book is made up of the official instructions issued by governmental authority for the training of teachers and the conduct of the schools (the only schools permitted to exist), from nursery school up through the university, in the USSR.

The world has never even dreamed before of such a solid, well organized, comprehensive system for moulding the characters and minds of the citizens of a country into a single unified rigid pattern permitting no deviation—and in the name of complete democracy! The following passage is no literary flourish. For those who have eyes to see it expels the mysteries that otherwise surround the policies of the Soviet Union.

"The entire work of the school must be directed toward the education of the children in communist morality"; "a morally educated individual being one who in his conduct subordinates his own interests to the service of his Motherland and people."

Moreover, the transformation of the internationalism of Marx and Lenin into burning nationalism is extended in the next sen-

[From a copy of a typescript about Boris Petrov Esipov and N. K. Goncharov, *I Want to Be Like Stalin*, trans. George S. Counts and Nucia P. Lodge (New York: John Day Co., 1947).]

tence, to saying that "such service presupposes wrath and hatred toward the enemies of the Motherland."

I repeat that it is my conviction that this book provides the best key in existence to understanding why disagreement with any phase of Bolshevik policy makes the dissenting nation an enemy to be dealt with by measures that are dictated by wrath and hatred. It is superfluous to express a hope that the book will have the widest possible reading. George Counts has rendered a great public service.

George Seldes and "Fact"

I shall be obliged to you if you will print the following statement. Mr. George Seldes is using my name to advertise his socalled *In Fact*. This use of my name is totally unauthorized. Instead of giving support in any way of even the most remote kind, this use of my name is typical of the way in which facts are twisted in the interest of Stalinism in the writings of Mr. Seldes and in the periodical he has the nerve to call *In Fact*. This procedure is also typical of the usual procedures of Stalinists in this as in every other country, beginning of course with the USSR.

I hope this statement will receive wide publicity, as any more complete distortion of my position could not be produced even by the most expert of those who systematically call falsity by the name of Fact.

[First published in *New Leader* 30 (12 July 1947): 12.]

Man and Mathematics

I want to say a few words regarding the subject of mathematics[1] touched upon in the Autumn number of the *Humanist:* only a few words, for the topic is a highly technical one, and recent developments have upset older theories about the nature of mathematics without having as yet produced a general consensus. I wish to point out that the two alternatives mentioned in the *Humanist* comment by no means exhaust the field. As far as there is agreement among those competent to speak, it is, I believe, that mathematical subjectmatter while certainly applicable to physical and other scientific materials *is* "independent of the external world." But it does not follow in the least that it is mental or tells "about the structure of our own minds." An alternative not mentioned is that it is a construction, *based on postulates.* Many years ago I heard a distinguished English mathematician, Cayley, say there was dispute about whether the method of mathematics was inductive or deductive, but that, as he saw it, it was neither, being more like *poetry.* Cayley was not a commentator *from the outside* but himself a creator in the field. Of course mathematics is more strictly controlled than poetry because its postulates are the net outcome of centuries of creative, constructive work. So are the working "rules" that guide (but do *not* rigidly control) their systematic development. They are rules in the sense in which poetry, the drama, any fine art, has direction, but is not tied down. Humanists need less than others to take a narrow view of the congeniality of creative construction and the

---

1. See "In Periodicals and Books," the *Humanist*, Autumn 1947, p. 101.

[First published in *Humanist* 7 (Winter 1947): 121. For comment to which this is a reply, see Appendix 17.]

cultural capacities of human beings—not just human "minds." Mathematics, in short, is a highly developed language; like language, it is fruitfully applicable in our dealings with the world, but no more than any other language is it a part of that world save *as man himself is part of it.*

Appreciation of the Rand School

I am glad to have this opportunity to express my appreciation of the value of the educational work done by the Rand School. My contacts with the school, including lectures given there, have shown me how eagerly and earnestly busy young men and women take advantage of the educational opportunity the School offers and what a high standard is maintained. It is doing work in education of fine quality and one that reaches a special constituency. . . . The school has a vital claim on all those who call themselves liberals and who believe in the spread of intelligence as a means of orderly social progress and in the maintenance of freedom of inquiry and teaching.

[First published in *General Bulletin, Spring Term, 1948,* Rand School of Social Science, New York, N.Y., p. 2.]

Appendixes

Appendix 1
The Attack on Western Morality
Can European Ideals Survive?
By Julien Benda

It would seem to me that what, in their inquiry, the editors of *Commentary* call the crisis of civilization could be called with fair exactness the crisis of Hellenic-Christian morality, and more exactly still the crisis of Socratic-Christian morality: Socratic in the sense that it obligates men to respect certain values transcending their particular interests of time and place—in other words, and stated in absolute terms: justice, truth, law, fidelity to engagements; Christian, in so far as it requires as its base a respect for the human person, whatever his condition, from the moment that he presents the moral characteristics of the human species. Because of its opposition to the instincts of domination, to what the Church calls the "pride of life," one might also call this: intellectual morality (the morality of the intellectual).

I would have you note at once that I speak of the person in so far as he presents the *moral* characteristics of the human species. My position—and here I am in opposition to the Church and to a certain type of democracy, for which any man is sacred by reason solely of the fact that he presents the anatomical characteristics of the species—my position is that the human person has a right to this designation, and in consequence to the respect it implies, only if he has been capable of raising himself to a certain level of morality, one that consists precisely in respecting this personality in others—let us say, if he is able to rise to the conception of the rights of man.

This amounts to saying that, while I do not admit the concept of biological races, I do admit that of *moral* races, that is, of groups of men who have been able to attain to this morality, of

[First published in *Commentary* 4 (November 1947): 416–22. For Dewey's reply, see pp. 19–26.]

which others have shown themselves incapable. The word "race" is perhaps not altogether accurate here, since nothing proves that the low moral level of these latter groups is in any way fated or that it is forever impossible for them to escape from it; although the deep-seatedness of their cult of force, its tenacity, its at times naive unconsciousness often might lead one to believe that.[1] In any case, in awaiting the liberation of these groups, if it ever will take place, the first groups have the duty to deal with the second in no way on a footing of equality and, if not to subject them, at least to compel their respect.

The Socratic-Christian Morality Was the Only One Honored a Few Years Ago

Let us return to Socratic-Christian morality.

This is the moral atmosphere in which men of my generation—and those much younger—were brought up, at home as well as at college (which was probably the case in your country, too). This atmosphere revealed itself, among other ways, in the teaching we received from our masters, in categorical censure of the dismemberments of Poland in the 18th century, in denunciation of the methods of perjury and *fait accompli* practiced by Frederick II, in the refusal to pay honor to success won by no

1. I cannot refrain from citing an incident that seems symbolic to me. At the time of the occupation of the Rhineland following the armistice of 1918, one of my friends, an officer in the unit at Cologne, was talking about the war with the manager of his hotel, and he was touched by the good sense of that man, by his resignation, by his disposition to acknowledge the wrongs committed by Germany and the legitimacy of her expiation. But when they parted, the good hotel-keeper sighed out this conclusion: "And to think, sir, that all this would never have happened if the Belgians had let us have our way!" To me this candor is the opposite of disarming.

   This constancy of the German spirit seems real to one of the historians who has studied it most seriously: "He [Herder] will reveal to us," says Lévy-Bruhl, "the secret continuity that, in the midst of appearances, binds without interruption the Germany of the 19th century, which we call realistic, to that of the 18th, which we contrast to it as idealistic. The antithesis is false: there are not 'two Germanies'; there has been only one evolution, now favored, now impeded by the intervention of neighboring nations, the different phases of which appear to be more closely interlinked the greater the distance and the higher the elevation from which History surveys them" (*L'Allemagne depuis Leibniz*).

matter what means (little respect for Louis XI, none for Machiavelli), in admiration for the Roman consul Regulus—who returned to Carthage, where the worst tortures awaited him, because he had given the Carthaginians his word—or, again, in the way that Fustel de Coulange's *La Cité antique* was praised to us, in so far as the author therein berated the Romans for "their detestable maxim": "*Salus populi, suprema lex esto* (let the safety of the people be the supreme law)," and applauded the infusion of a certain degree of Christianity into political mores.

The acceptance of such a morality seemed to us a thing so self-evidently established, so commonplace, that we did not even think it could be discussed. We knew, of course, that states did on occasion violate it; but we held that they did so with regret, while denying that they were violating it and, more surely still, refusing to derive any glory from it. Respect—at least verbal, perhaps even hypocritical—for Hellenic-Christian morality seemed to us a definitive achievement of humanity, one we had come to believe natural to such a degree that we could not conceive it possible to put forward any other as an avowed and codified teaching.

Deliberate Assaults Against this Morality at the End of the 19th Century—the Preaching of Pragmatic Morals

Now in this we gave proof of a strange blindness, and our first awakening—how brutal!—was anti-Dreyfusism in 1897. At the end of the 19th century—a capital date, from this point of view, for the moral history of humanity—movements of considerable importance formally came out in opposition to the Hellenic-Christian morality as we have just defined it. They professed in substance that they did not know what this *abstract* justice was, this *abstract* truth, valid for all men in all times and all places. They were acquainted only with justices *of circumstance*, truths *relative and determined by the interests of the group to which they related,* truths that *changed along with those interests.* Even more, they professed themselves ignorant of those so-called rights—even as qualified above—inherent in the human person whatever he might be; and also ignorant of that egalitarianism derived from Christianity of which the French Revolution and democracy have been the inheritors. Instead they believed that there existed categories of men destined to command and that the good of the whole, bound up with the supremacy of these men, might very well necessitate their over-riding the convenience of those whose function it is to obey.

This crusade has shown itself in three great collective deeds.

First, German nationalism: Even at the beginning of the 19th century the Arndts, the Schlegels, the Görres rose up in the name of "the chosen people"; and in attacking the French Revolution in particular, and in coming out against the acknowledgment of any universal principle—against, notably, the universally recognized equality of rights—Arndt expressly opposed any recognition of political rights that Germany might accord to the Jews. And hostility to all idea of a morality fixed and superior to circumstances, the basis of Socratic teachings, is clearly formulated by Fichte in the seventh of his *Addresses to the German Nation:* "The essence of inferior peoples [*read "France"*—J. B.] is their belief in something definitive, firm, immutable. Whoever believes in a principle that is immutable, constant, and therefore dead, believes in it only because he is dead himself." (Note the equation, though grossly sophistical, of immutable principle with dead principle. As if an immutable principle—for example, that of justice—had not been made *living* by the manner in which *living* beings could embrace and defend it. Fichte was able to observe, the day the soldiers of the Revolution crushed the army of his nation at Jena, that men could believe in immutable principles and show themselves singularly far from being "dead themselves.")

On the morrow of their victory in 1870, the pan-Germanists made this position even more plain by declaring, for example, that the future of the Germanic world lay in strengthening still more "what it has been able to save from Christian influence" and that the greatness of Germany consisted in being released from "all sympathy for humanity."[2] In 1914, the same learned

2. Texts cited by Andlér, with hundreds more of the same order, in *Le Pangermanisme Continental,* pp. 67 and 123. See also, and above all, *Le Pangermanisme Philosophique,* by the same author.

men declared that the violation of Belgian neutrality was just because it conformed to the interests of Germany in the circumstances then existing, and asserted that they did not know the meaning of this universal notion of justice with which people were attempting to overwhelm them. Cecil Rhodes had already declared at the time of the Boer War: "This war is just, because it is useful to my country." To be sure, he was only a business man; but an intellectual, Kipling, took a similar attitude. Dare I say that it was quite close, almost violently close, to that of William James at the time the island of Cuba was grabbed by his compatriots (see his *Letters,* II, pp. 73–74)?

It is unnecessary to chronicle how the Nazis brought this movement to its perfection—though they did not invent it—by decreeing that they did not know what a universal truth was, but that, for them, the sole criterion of truth—even scientific—was whether it made the German people strong;[3] while at the same time they officially promulgated the unworthiness of Christianity because of its universality. In addition, their formal opposition to Hellenic-Christian ethics appears sharply in their religion of "dynamism," in the proscription of anything that might arouse in their consciences a brake moderating their avidity.[4] We find, certainly, very little in the way of apology for dynamism in the Socratic dialogues or in the Gospels.

A second movement, of more recent origin, plainly directed against the Hellenic-Christian morality, is Marxism—more exactly, Russian Communism.

We know that one of the principal articles of Marxism is the denunciation of the attachment of certain men to the so-called "transcendental" commandments of the conscience, to what Marx calls with pity the "divine" part (Socrates called it that, too) of humanity, and the declaration that the human species will cease to be enslaved only on the day it frees itself from such afflictions. Marxism similarly admits of no stable truth, but rather of a truth essentially variable and determined by the interests of the moment.

When, at the time of the NEP, Lenin found that he had to call

---

3. Speech of Dr. Frick, the Minister of Public Instruction, to the students of Munich in October 1935.
4. Plato would say, their *pleonexia:* the desire always to have more.

error what he had stated the evening before to be truth, one historian—Mark Vishniak—observed that this about-face was greatly eased for him by his sovereign "disdain for all absolute values." Likewise we may read in Stalin's *Speech on the Five-Year Plan* a vibrant apology for the contradictory as a "vital value" and "instrument of combat."[5] I do not need to remind the reader that if, in a controversy with a Marxist, he invites the latter to have some regard for logic, he finds himself immediately characterized as a "frightful bourgeois" who "still believes in absolute principles of the mind."

Besides, the decision to disqualify all fixed principles and admit no other law than that of circumstances is the essence of the "Hegelian dialectic" as deformed by the Marxists; that is to say, it is the essence of an instrument foreign to all disinterested thought but uniquely adapted to action, and therefore the exact contrary of the Socratic teachings.[6] In addition, disdain for disinterested thought is clearly formulated by this dictum of Marx: "Real [*read "Communist"*—J. B.] humanism has no more dangerous enemy than speculative idealism."

As to the notion of abstract justice as identical with itself for all times and all places, Communism teaches that we have here a pure invention of the metaphysicians; that the idea of justice is dictated to us by the economic conditions in which we live, and varies with them. For our part we have the impression that the nations that Nebuchadnezzar dragged about the plains of Chaldea with rings in their noses, the unfortunate man that the lord of the Middle Ages snatched from his wife and children and bound to the millstone, the youth that Colbert nailed to the bench of the galley for his whole existence, were all very strongly of the opinion that an abstract justice was being violated in their

5. Note a similar declaration by Mussolini: "Let us beware of the mortal pitfall of coherence." We must observe that the novelty here lies in the glorification of the fact of contradiction if interest demands it; for, in point of fact, the contradictory has always existed, and among all nations.

6. We here oppose Sovietism, and more generally Russian civilization, to Socratic Greece, which seems to us to have had no influence upon Russia—but we do not oppose it to the Greece which was irrational and impregnated with Asiatic culture, and of which Dionysianism, Orphism, and a certain philosophy of Plato are the notorious manifestations. Even present-day Russia is far from appearing hostile to the latter Greece, which one may call the anti-Socratic one. Thus the Soviet government has erected a statue to Heraclitus, who, with his denial of all fixed principles, is the direct ancestor of dialectical materialism.

cases and considered that their lot was in no way a just one from the viewpoint of economic conditions of their times. What we stress here is that this *purely relative* conception of justice furnishes an apology to all violators of the human person, to the violators of Belgium in 1914 as well as to the assassins of Czechoslovakia in 1939. Nor did they fail to make use of it.

Finally, a third movement loosed itself, some fifty years ago, against Socratic-Christian ethics—this time among the intellectuals; a movement whose great promoters would seem to be: Nietzsche with his "morality of the master" and his thesis that Socrates, by preaching rationalism, began the decline of Greece; Georges Sorel, with his *Reflections on Violence* (a book that was a world-wide success), and his *Le Procès de Socrate,* in which one can read that the condemnation of that philosopher was justified by reason of his universalist teachings; and, finally, the learned men of the *Action Française.* At least when out of pontifical hearing, these last willingly acknowledge their anti-Christian activity (I speak of them in the present, for they still exist, even if their periodical has disappeared). According to them, Christianity—which they oppose to Catholicism[7]—is the inspiration of many a revolutionary dogma, notably of democratic egalitarianism. Their leader, Charles Maurras, said this a hundred times. They admit their anti-Socratic activities less readily, inasmuch as they make a cult of Greco-Roman humanism. It can hardly be denied, however, that their religion of success, which they assert should be sought "by all means," as well as their rejection of current morality for the class of men to which they themselves belong, derive from the theses of Callicles and his peers rather than from his interlocutor. Likewise, their cult of reason, which, according to them, should work principally for the maintenance of a social hierarchy dear to them, and their cult of truth—but they call this cult barbarous if it operates outside all social considerations[8]—and related to a pragmatism that is indeed the antipodes of the disinterested idealism preached by the master of Crito.

7. An anti-Christian campaign, also in the name of Catholicism, was likewise carried on at the end of the 19th century, but in a manner much more patrician, much less suited to reach the masses, by Rémy de Gourmont and his group of the *Mercure de France.*
8. See my *The Treason of the Intellectuals.*

This third movement, even though it is directed at intellectuals, has not failed, on that account, to become a sizeable one. All the more so since many a Boeotian has thought to acquire the title of intellectual by adhering to it.

The first and third of these movements reinforced each other in one direction: anti-Semitism. Which is, in large part, perfectly logical. Since, as his adversaries declare, the Jew is very often "rootless," he finds himself on that account the natural champion of values stated in absolute terms and the born enemy of those who wish them to be only relative and historical. Moreover, because of his atavism of the oppressed, the Jew is organically and fanatically devoted to respect for the human person. One may well agree with the head of the *Action Française* that Christianity, in so far as it is a school of abstract justice and democratic egalitarianism, stems through the Prophets from a Jewish source.[9]

However, these enemies of absolute values describe them as Jewish not so much because this happens to be true as because these values are thereby rendered *ipso facto* odious to a whole world, thanks to the unpopularity attached to the name of Jew— an unpopularity due to reasons quite different from the political reasons flaunted here, and quite anterior to them. We know what increased strength these learned men derive from this sort of maneuver. Thus the Nazis oppose "German" truth to the "Jewish truth of Einstein." They would evidently find a smaller audience if they contrasted it simply with "scientific truth," above all if they added that this scientific truth was that of such non-Jews as Leibniz, Euler, and Weierstrass, to name some of the great mathematicians from the other side of the Rhine. In the same spirit, certain enemies of Socratic values assert that since Pericles the Greeks have been Jews.

The Treason of the Intellectuals

These considerations demonstrate that the editors of *Commentary* are completely correct in regarding the collapse of moral values here under discussion as being other than a by-

9. In like fashion Rosenberg persecuted the Jewish heritage in Christianity. (See Rauschning: *The Revolution of Nihilism*.)

product of the recent war. And also when they observe that the most serious thing is not so much the downfall of these values as the refusal to believe in the importance of maintaining them—or rather, I would say, the desire to perform a scalp dance over their collapse and raise up hymns to the values that announce their negation. In the face of such a spectacle one thinks of the bandit in Tolstoy's story: the hermit who receives his confession declares with stupefaction, "The others, at least, were ashamed of their immorality; but what is to be done with this one who is proud of it?"

The exaltation of this new "morality" is the work, and could only be the work, of intellectuals, who were also endowed with a literary talent that could hold the attention of the crowd and could furnish it with a semblance of arguments and striking formulas (Nietzsche is the crucial example here).

This, exactly, constitutes what I have called the treason of the intellectuals. To be sure, it has not created this human immorality, but it has brought it to a singular peak. Men did not wait for the author of *Zarathustra* or for Rosenberg to practice the "will to power" in despite of all the rights of others, but morality made them ashamed of doing so. Today a new morality provides them justification, and this increases their self-assurance no little.

Moreover, justification of their violence is offered them by the very institution that was to be expected to scold them: the Papacy recognized Victor Emmanuel III as "Emperor of Ethiopia," and many a prince of the Church bowed down before the resounding slaps in the face administered to human dignity by Hitler, Mussolini, and Franco. How can one expect the man on the street not to mock at the rights of the human person when the highest moral magistracy gives such an example?

Two Forms of Pragmatic Ethics Particularly Triumphant at Present

If the collapse of Socratic-Christian morality in favor of pragmatic morality dates from well before the war, this downfall now seems to me, nevertheless, to be taking on forms that are new—if not in nature, at least in the intensity of their affirmation and in the extent of their adoption. I see two principal new forms:

(1) The religion of *order*. One may say that the religion of order, in so far as it is in opposition to rights of the individual, has replaced, at least in France, the religion of the nation as we saw it manifested at the beginning of the century in Barrès and Maurras. It has so completely replaced it that, with the appearance of fascist states that negated the rights of the individual, the greater part of these Frenchmen—with Maurras at their head—supported the cause of these states, in spite of the latter's expressed intention of humbling the French nation. And the day came when we saw these Frenchmen rejoice—the "divine surprise" of Maurras—over the defeat of their country to the profit of one of those states. It is in the name of order that these people continue to attack French democracy today, making an appeal, not without success, to all the "right-thinking" people of Europe, regardless of whether they belong to a nation, like Germany, fundamentally hostile to their own.

Need I demonstrate that the idea of order is based essentially on the restriction and negation of the rights of the individual? Men seem at all times to have understood this instinctively. I find it significant that they have erected statues to Liberty, Justice, Science, Art, Charity, and Peace, but never to Order. The immense present prestige of the idea of order is a powerful indication of the decline of respect for the person.

(2) The particular good fortune enjoyed today by Marxist dogma in so far, as we remarked above, as it tends to recognize no moral values—justice, truth, reason—except as determined by practical considerations—or, more exactly, by economic interest. I must point to the adherence—very noisy, and impressive to the common man—given today to these doctrines by high scientific and philosophic authorities, at least in France (I think it is the same in America). I think particularly of their adoption of what the Marxists call "dialectical materialism," which teaches that, in order to understand history, it is necessary to commune with the "historical process"—more exactly, the economic process—instead of looking at it from outside. This constitutes a position that is purely mystical and, formally, is a negation of reason, since the essence of the latter is to translate reality into rational terms, not to merge with it. It is a doctrine that is essentially practical or attempts to be so. Dialectical materialism, says

Maurice Thorez, a pupil of Lenin, is "a guide for action"—from which standpoint it is very natural that it should be glorified by a political party whose sole aim is to win out in the here-and-now.

But it is a serious matter when this doctrine is exalted by men whose function it used to be to glorify the exercise of disinterested intelligence, and to act as a counterweight to those who are interested only in how to get the better of others. Let us add that these thinkers want to recognize only a collective consciousness—"the individual consciousness can be no more than the reflection of the collective consciousness," says Marx; with the result that a man on a desert island would have no consciousness. All this includes, whether they wish it or not, disdain for the individual consciousness and its essential inviolability.

Socratic-Christian Morality Could Not Be Saved by Pragmatic Christianity—It Seems Definitively Lost Save for a Few

In the face of this crisis of civilization, it is asked whether a return to religion might not be a remedy. If I call religion Christianity, the return to religion appears to me to be the evident remedy, since the evil consists, according to all that I have just said, in the desertion of it by the world, and—a matter much more serious—in the desertion of it by its moral leaders. Yet we must see a return to a Christianity that, being faithful to its essential nature, preaches eternal values transcending practical considerations, and not to a Christianity that proclaims itself a principle of "action," of "dynamism"—a "shock" Christianity that declares itself a principle of "evolution," a principle of solid political establishment. This latter Christianity is more alive than ever, and, far from acting as a check on the "realism" of the modern world, it seems to me to be its strong adjutant.

As to whether this crisis be "a transition toward another society endowed with better values," I confess that I cannot see how the cult of purely material satisfactions—even in favor of all and not for some people only—can lead to values I would consider "better." I see how these might lead to a humanity happier in one sense, but happiness is not for me the criterion of human value. I think that the cause of civilization such as we understand it is—to borrow a phrase from *Commentary*'s inquiry—a lost cause. There will always remain, nevertheless, isolated beings who will serve it. And, in reality, was it not always this way?

Appendix 2

What Does Mr. Dewey Mean by an "Indeterminate Situation"?

By Donald S. Mackay

The question in the title has to do with the natural origin and development of inquiry in what Mr. Dewey calls its "existential matrix." This matrix, according to his logical theory, provides the biological and cultural foundations of inquiry, and these are not only its natural conditions, but they are or they become the constituents in a process leading to knowledge. Thus, logic is said to be "naturalistic," and logical analysis is properly concerned with the instrumentalities and safeguards of inquiry as it is directed towards knowledge, defined as "warranted assertibility."

The difficulties which I find in this naturalistic theory of inquiry are related to Mr. Dewey's conception of an "indeterminate situation," in so far as this is represented as part of the "existential matrix." One difficulty seems to be the result of a vagueness of exposition or lack of explicitness in his account of the problematic nature of the situation—its supposed existential indeterminateness. The other and more serious difficulty is, I suspect, a material fallacy in the argument from his analysis of the problematic or doubtful situation. I shall consider first the difficulty resulting from vagueness of exposition or lack of explicitness before considering the flaw in the analysis, although I believe that the former is, in part at least, a consequence of the latter. But the vagueness is a symptom and provides a clue to the type of fallacy that Mr. Dewey seems to be committing.

The crux of the difficulties is in his definition of inquiry in the *Logic*. It is fair to regard this as crucial because all of the ensuing chapters, amounting to more than four-fifths of the book, are said by the author to be an expansion of the definition. Inquiry is

[First published in *Journal of Philosophy* 39 (12 March 1942): 141–48. For Dewey's reply, see pp. 34–41.]

defined as "*the controlled or directed transformation of an indeterminate situation into one that is so determinate in its constituent distinctions and relations as to convert the elements of the original situation into a unified whole*" (*Logic*, pp. 104–105 [*Later Works* 12:108]). The term "situation" is said to denote a "contextual whole" within which objects and events are to be understood, although it is not itself an object or event, nor a set of objects or events. The situation, before inquiry begins, is there as a whole, but not as a *unified* whole, the latter being in some sense the eventual outcome of a process of transformation. A situation that lacks unity at the outset becomes unified by means of inquiry, and this is apparently what Mr. Dewey means by a determinate in contrast to an indeterminate situation. But although the transformed situation is determinate, this does not mean that it has become a determinate object or event, set of objects or set of events. Its determinateness pertains to the context and not to the content of the knowledge, or warranted assertibility, to which the inquiry leads. A difficulty is felt as an obstacle to be overcome. It is something directly undergone or suffered in experience. But it may also be perceived as a problem to be solved, or rather it is converted into the definite constituents of a problem. Inquiry then ensues as a response to the confused and perplexing tendencies in the problematic situation. But precisely what does Mr. Dewey mean by the "indeterminateness" of a situation *before* there is any sentient being in that situation to experience doubt and engage in inquiry. In earlier writings on the subject, Mr. Dewey had ascribed the indeterminateness of a problematic situation to an initial uncertainty or hesitancy in the interaction between organism and environment. In the more recent account in the *Logic*, however, the problematic situation is said to be indeterminate in its existential character, independent of and prior to the occurrence of any doubt or ensuing inquiry. There are situations that are doubtful *per se,* whether or not anyone happens to have been perplexed by them, although it is obvious that their problematic nature could not have been disclosed unless someone had been moved to inquire into them. But it seems paradoxical to say that a situation can be doubtful without any actual doubting in it. To add to the paradox, Mr. Dewey remarks that "the original indeterminate situation is not only 'open' to inquiry, but it is open in the sense that its constituents do not hang together" (*ibid.*, p. 105 [*Later Works* 12 : 109]). One might well ask how the constituents of a situation can do anything else but "hang together" in their spatial and temporal relations. And if the situation is existentially indeterminate in some way that is neither spatio-temporal nor cognitive, Mr. Dewey has not made clear what it is.

The point has been raised in a recent debate with Mr. Russell. Against all objections, Mr. Dewey reaffirms his previous position: he *does* mean to say that a doubtful situation can exist without a personal doubter.[1] The source and prototype of such a situation, he says, is the imbalance or disequilibration that recurs in the interactivity of organism and environment. This is exemplified by hunger, which is not merely a subjective "feeling," but a form of organic behavior, manifested in bodily restlessness and bodily acts of search for food. Now, Mr. Russell finds it incredible that Mr. Dewey should mean to say what he *seems* to be saying: "for example, that there were doubtful situations in astronomical and geological epochs before there was life." To be sure, Mr. Dewey never said this or anything like it, but apparently Mr. Russell thinks that this consequence is entailed by the proposition that there can be doubtful situations without personal doubters. However, the views of the two men are not perhaps so far apart as might be suggested by the difference between the situation of a hungry organism in search of food and the situation of a planet in astronomical and geological epoch before there was life. There is no reason to suppose that Mr. Dewey and Mr. Russell are talking about entirely different matters when they use the term "doubtful situation." It is evidently about the nature of the doubtfulness in such a situation that they disagree, and the disagreement results from their different theories of the cognitive and non-cognitive elements of the situation.

In Mr. Russell's type of epistemological realism, the situation can be analyzed into (*a*) particular matters of fact, (*b*) propositions about these matters of fact, and (*c*) various subjective or mental states, such as beliefs, desires, emotions, purposes, and doubts. In this analysis, the doubtfulness of a problematic situation is evidently precluded from (*a*) the matters of fact and from (*b*) the propositions, which must be either true or false. Hence, if

1. *Journal of Philosophy*, Vol. XXXVIII (1941), p. 183 [*Later Works* 14:184].

a situation is to be called "indeterminate," it is only with respect to (c). The subjective or mental states of a personal doubter are such that he has *not* any determinate knowledge about the particular matters of fact in that situation. But in order to be "doubtful," the situation must involve a desire for the solution of the problem, and a purpose directed towards knowledge of a true proposition or set of true propositions concerning the given state of affairs. Clearly, the doubt and the purpose do not exist in the situation apart from the personal doubter, although it might be said that a situation is *hypothetically* doubtful without any actual desire, in the sense that it *would* cause doubt in the mind of a normal man, with the relevant training, desire, and purpose. Nevertheless, the conditions of doubtfulness are held to be mental or subjective, though not in the derogatory sense of subjectivity that Mr. Dewey wishes to avoid.

There is unfortunately a good deal of question-begging in this part of Mr. Russell's criticism. For Mr. Dewey's theory of inquiry involves a behavioral analysis of experience which does not admit the kind of distinction that Mr. Russell makes between the mental and the physical, the subjective and the objective. In opposition to that type of realism, with its causal theory of perception and its correspondence theory of truth, I should agree with Mr. Dewey that the problematic nature of a situation does not depend on any *feeling* of doubt or other "mental" attitude towards the situation in question. In the present war, for example, people are uncertain because the issue is still indeterminate; the issue is not indeterminate merely because people now have feelings of doubt and perplexity about the situation. The war has provided, and probably will continue to provide, occasion for inquiry, as well as for mere oratory and propaganda. Out of it has come an untold amount of investigation, reflected in thousands of books, articles, newspaper columns, and perhaps even some of the broadcasts of radio commentators. Although various decisions have been reached at successive stages of this changing situation, it can hardly be maintained that there is as yet any "warranted assertibility" concerning the causes and consequences of the war. In Mr. Dewey's way of speaking, the situation has not been transformed into a unified whole, in which consequences have been operationally instituted so as to resolve the problem or problems evoking the operations. But the war-situation is also "doubtful" in the subjectivistic sense in which Mr. Russell speaks of a doubtful situation. Some of its apparent uncertainty is an expression of fears and anxieties, the grounds of which may be largely imaginary, just as its seeming certainty of outcome among less apprehensive minds may be an expression of groundless confidence. The situation is colored by the more or less articulate emotional preferences that are sometimes called "value-judgments" in contrast to judgments of fact. But this "subjective" kind of doubtfulness would be only pathological were there not the other kind of doubtfulness which is said to belong to the situation existentially.

If Mr. Dewey's account of the indeterminate situation suffers from vagueness here, it is perhaps from too much rather than from too little specification. "A variety of names serves to characterize indeterminate situations," he says. "They are disturbed, troubled, ambiguous, confused, full of conflicting tendencies, obscure, etc. It is the *situation* that has these traits." The word "et cetera" suggests that Mr. Dewey has in mind some single meaning of indeterminateness, of which obvious variations are mentioned here, while others might readily occur to the reader. But it is far from clear to me that a disturbed situation is indeterminate in the same sense that an ambiguous situation is indeterminate; or that a confused and obscure situation is indeterminate in the sense that it is said to be full of conflicting tendencies. Some of these words seem to denote physical and biological conditions, while others seem to denote psychological and logical conditions. It is clear, however, that a situation, whatever specific traits it may possess, is characterized as indeterminate with respect to its future issue. What, then, does the indeterminateness mean in terms of the issue? There are at least four distinct senses in which the future issue of a problematic situation might be said to be "indeterminate": (1) in the sense that the issue, being future, is still unsettled, inconclusive, not as yet an accomplished fact of which there can be determinate knowledge; (2) in the sense that there is insufficient evidence on which to base a positively verifiable prediction concerning the issue; (3) in the sense that the issue is contingent, not a necessary or inevitable outcome of the activities going on in the present situation; (4) in the sense that there are intelligible alternatives, with a genuine option among them, so that a decision *now* may contribute to the character of the eventual issue in the future. Misunderstanding might be avoided if it were clearly recognized that Mr. Russell, for example, is talking about the indeterminateness of a doubtful situation in *cognitive* terms according to senses (1) and (2); whereas Mr. Dewey is mainly concerned with the *practical* import of indeterminateness according to senses (3) and (4).

The other and more serious difficulty seems to be the result of a mistake in Mr. Dewey's analysis. What does it mean to say that *the existential conditions* in a problematic situation are indeterminate? Assuming that the situation is indeterminate, proleptically, with respect to its eventual issue, Mr. Dewey seems to suppose that the antecedent conditions must also be existentially indeterminate on the ground that the issue is itself an existential and not a merely intellectual affair. But the issue, while still pending and in the future, is an ideal or intellectual affair, an affair of meanings, an anticipated possibility. It may be said in reply to this objection that the issue is a possibility, which, *if* it were fulfilled, *would* be an existential condition. In other words, it would be, at that conjectural time in the future, a matter pertaining to something that is going to exist, or may then exist, and so is not merely a matter of significance. But to argue in this fashion is to commit the same type of fallacy which Mr. Dewey has so often criticized in other philosophical arguments. The fallacy consists of "the conversion of eventual functions into antecedent existence" (*Experience and Nature*, p. 29 [*Later Works* 1 : 34]). It is said to be "a substantiation of eventual functions. The fallacy converts consequences of interaction of events into causes of the occurrence of these consequences" (*ibid.*, p. 261 [*Later Works* 1 : 200]). Mr. Dewey appears to be guilty of the same "philosophic fallacy," but in the converse form. The direct form of the fallacy is that of reading the *determinate* character of an eventual function, *after* its fulfilment, back into a causal antecedent reality. The converse fallacy, which Mr. Dewey seems to be committing here, is that of reading the *indeterminate* character of an eventual function, *before* its fulfilment, back into a causal antecedent reality. In short, the analysis of an "indeterminate situation" confuses an experienced quality of indeterminateness with an indeterminateness of experienced quality.[2] The former has to

---

2. Recalling James's statement: "the feeling of an absence is *toto coelo* other than the absence of a feeling."

do with the felt lack of knowledge in a given situation, where the experienced quality of indeterminateness is to be understood in cognitive terms according to senses (1) and (2) as mentioned above. The latter has to do with the absence of certain operationally identified characters of things or events that are to be eventually determined by means of further inquiry. The indeterminateness of experienced quality is then to be understood in its practical import according to senses (3) and (4). There is a gap between the cognitive indeterminateness of the one and the practical, operational indeterminateness of the other, and Mr. Dewey's doctrine of the continuum of inquiry succeeds only in confusing the two kinds of indeterminateness without bridging the gap between them.

This confusion in Mr. Dewey's theory of inquiry reflects a characteristic weakness in the liberalism of the nineteenth century—a weakness which his philosophical reconstruction of that tradition has never entirely overcome. The source of the confusion is an assumed freedom of indifference and the supposition that values are objectively indeterminate apart from individual preference or interest. The weakness of liberalism, as a philosophical doctrine, is its inability to accept the full consequences of this notion of freedom, which is nevertheless implicit in its traditional assumptions. No one has expressed this freedom of indifference more clearly than Mill, and no one has more persistently evaded its implications, whether in his ethical and political doctrines or in his logic and epistemology. "The sole evidence it is possible to produce that anything is desirable," said Mill, "is that people actually do desire it." From this it follows that the desirability or undesirability of any issue, concerning which there is freedom of choice, would be a matter of complete indifference, were it not for the actual desire that someone happens to have experienced in that situation. The logical counterpart of that view is to be found in Mill's theory of induction, with its doctrine that natural laws are nothing apart from the results of experimental inquiry and inductive generalization, and that the very expression, "Laws of Nature," *means* nothing but the uniformities that have been inductively established among observed phenomena.

It is this same notion of a freedom of indifference and an objective indeterminateness of values, whether intellectual or moral and political, that survives in Mr. Dewey's conception of an "indeterminate situation." It survives, however, with qualifications that lead to serious inconsistencies in his theory of inquiry. For there are three assertions that recur in his writings and they are in conflict with the assumption that a problematic situation is existentially indeterminate, apart from doubt and inquiry. One is the assertion that knowing, as an overt existential act, is part of the ongoing processes of nature and does not in any way transcend or have any reality apart from these natural processes (cf. *The Quest for Certainty*, pp. 244–245 [*Later Works* 4:194–96]). The second is the assertion that inquiry, as the process that leads to knowledge, is an interaction of organism and environment, conditioned by physical, biological, and cultural factors. The third is the assertion that the problematic situation, in its specific qualitative nature, not only evokes inquiry, but exercises control over its special procedures. How, then, can it be consistently maintained that the antecedent conditions of inquiry are indeterminate, prior to any experience of doubt and without reference to the dubious issue of the situation? If the problematic situation does exercise control over the subsequent inquiry, I am unable to understand how the qualitative nature of the situation can be at once specific and indeterminate. And if there is an experienced quality of indeterminateness in the interactivity of organism and environment, it must surely be a *determinate* quality of indeterminateness that gives rise to doubt and evokes inquiry. Finally, the assertion that knowing is an overt existential act, and as such a part of the ongoing processes of nature, implies that knowing is in conformity with the natural laws or the structure of those processes. Since it would be absurd to speak of this structure as indeterminate, it is difficult to understand how the antecedent conditions of inquiry can be indeterminate. For it is asserted that the problematic nature of the situation exercises control over the inquiry, as it moves towards a solution. But this control can hardly be indeterminate in its source, if it is in conformity throughout the process with an antecedently determinate structure.[3]

3. Mr. Dewey makes a further qualification in the statement that "no situation which is *completely* indeterminate can possibly be converted into a problem having definite constituents" (*Logic*, p. 108 [*Later Works* 12:112]). But this proviso is of no avail, because the same difficulties arise in connection with the conditions that *are* indeterminate in an incompletely indeterminate situation.

As a result of this confusion between cognitive and practical indeterminateness, Mr. Dewey fails to clarify the way in which the *form* of the problem in a doubtful situation is able to exercise its control over the course of inquiry. He is so eager to avoid the fallacy of converting the eventual functions of inquiry into its antecedent causal conditions that he neglects the regulative and heuristic elements in the pattern of the original situation. In other words, he leaves out of account the "existential" checks and clues of inquiry that are *antecedent* to the doubt evoking it. The alternatives are not between an intellectually determined form of knowledge and an existentially indeterminate situation. There is also the pattern of a problematic situation, which is as determinate in its own way as is the conclusive form of warranted assertibility, or knowledge. The pattern determines the conditions of the possibility of a solution of the problem and the limits within which inquiry can proceed systematically towards a relevant solution. These limiting conditions and the relevance of the eventual solution presuppose universal and objective standards, with reference to which the problematic nature of the situation is to be defined. But these are the subject of a chapter that could hardly find a place in Mr. Dewey's theory of inquiry.

Appendix 3
"Objectivity" in Value Judgments
By Philip Blair Rice

It seems unlikely that most men are incurably committed to the quest for certainty. Where philosophical criticism does not disillusion them, practical failure if often enough repeated may. Yet giving up the quest for certainty does not entail abandonment of the search for a related but more modest thing often called "objectivity." Even many empiricists, long reconciled to the tentativeness and fallibility of all beliefs, wish to discover a foundation for value judgments which will approximate the degree of probability attained by scientific judgments. Or if we must generally be content with a lower degree of probability than is usually obtainable in, say, physics, we still wish to found our value judgments on evidence and on hypothetico-inductive inference from evidence. Unless we can do so, the alternatives are either some form of apriorist absolutism or a subjectivism which makes valuations dependent on the momentary feeling or whim of the individual.

Absolutism is no solution for our time. The supposedly self-evident axioms or intuitions to which it appeals are seen to be even more variable from individual to individual and from culture to culture than are sense-perceptions themselves; and so the rationalist attitude leads to a scepticism which is more devastating than that which results from empiricism at its crudest. Furthermore, the *a priori* methods of rationalism have been thoroughly discredited in other fields of inquiry which deal with the world of existence. And values, whatever their ontological status, at least manifest themselves in, and control, the realm of existence.

There is an equally persistent effort to escape from the extreme

[First published in *Journal of Philosophy* 40 (7 January 1943): 5–14. For Dewey's reply, see pp. 63–72. For Rice's rejoinder, see Appendix 4. For a final exchange between Dewey and Rice, see pp. 73–83 and Appendix 5.]

forms of subjectivism and relativism, such as are currently represented by those logical positivists who hold that values are wholly relative to the opinion or the immediate feeling of the individual, hence that any alleged statements about them are mere "ejaculations of emotion."

It is in reaction to such views that we find contemporary students of value seeking an objective basis for value judgments. The meanings offered for the term "objectivity"—notoriously one of the danger-signals of philosophical terminology—vary with the solutions proposed. I shall deal only with those that are relevant to an empirical approach to value, for empiricism in this field will stand or fall by its ability to solve this problem. Unless it can do so, it can not serve as a guide in living.

Objectivity with respect to values is currently being sought in the following principal directions: (1) in the properties of valued objects themselves; (2) in universal validity of the rules which guide conduct; (3) in the universal concepts with an objective foundation in reality; (4) in agreement, or the social dimension of valuation; (5) in knowledge of the "conditions" of value experience. It is not my intention to show that all these approaches are worthless, for the resulting analyses have clarified many aspects of valuation. The negative thesis of this essay is, rather, that none of these five by itself, nor all of them together, suffice to answer the basic question, which is: How can we avoid the vicious relativism which makes "x is good" mean merely "A given individual, or a given group, thinks—or feels—that x is good (or desirable, or satisfying, etc.)"?

(1) *Value as a character of the valuable object.* The simplest way of attributing objective status to valuations is that of naïve realism, according to which values are properties of things in the same way that squareness, roundness, and (according to this school) blueness and loudness characterize them. The value properties are carried over into perception just as are the other properties. The mind merely selects them. If any one fails to perceive a value when it is really present, this is due to a failure in his capacity of discrimination.[1]

This position is subject to all the difficulties of naïve realism as

1. The classic statement of this position is to be found in G. E. Moore's *Principia Ethica,* and its standard refutations in Santayana's *Winds of Doctrine,* Ch. IV, and R. B. Perry's *General Theory of Value,* Ch. II.

a general epistemological position: e.g., failure to explain hallucination and error, failure to take into account the complexity of the perceptual process including the rôles of the medium and the responding organism, and neglect of the part that interpretation and reflection play in discrimination.

There are also certain difficulties peculiar to value properties. When an object is valuable to a given person at one time, and not valuable to him at a later time, it is implausible to explain this situation in all cases by saying that he fails to discriminate the value at the later time. For he has already shown his capacity to discriminate the value, and he may on the later occasion deliberately search for it. These conditions usually suffice to reveal other properties of the object that have persisted. But suppose that the interests and emotional habits of the person in question can be shown to have changed. Here is a verifiable alteration in the situation, whereas the supposed change in the value properties of the object is merely conjectural.

An allied position which seeks to take the interests of the experiencer of value into account, and at the same time to place the value in the object, is that of objective relativism. Mr. Eliseo Vivas as spokesman for this view acknowledges that "the value of the object arises out of the interaction of the desiring self and the desired object," and that "the value is not in the object for the self when the self does not desire it." Yet he holds that "value is objective for the valuing organism" in the sense that the "value resides in the outside or object-term of a relational complex which is a value situation, the inside term of which is a self." [2] His principal ground for locating the value in the outside term, or object, is that human beings sometimes, and animals presumably always, may value objects without being explicitly aware of the feelings of satisfaction that accompany the perception of the object. Thus it is asserted to be the bouquet of the cigar or the taste of the milk (these also are assumed to be in the object) to which value attaches, not the satisfaction that accompanies these. Mr. Vivas admits that we can desire, and therefore value, the satisfaction or enjoyment, but he tends to dismiss this attitude as a vagary of hedonists. His position could be attacked on such psy-

2. Eliseo Vivas: "Value and Fact," *Philosophy of Science*, Vol. 6 (1939), p. 435.

chological and epistemological grounds as that the affective element—which is admittedly present and essential—is not itself in the object, and that consequently at least one of the principal ingredients of the value is not in the object. An even more important objection is that this position does not afford an escape from relativistic scepticism. For the objectification of the value may be illusory; on the view in question, the value is in the object only for a given organism, or group of organisms, which may be mistaken in locating it there. Even though the value should in the objective relativist's sense be "in the object," this does not ensure that our *judgments* about the object will be objective. So much is tacitly admitted by Mr. Vivas, when he goes on to find the kind of objectivity we are seeking in the social dimension of value experience. But this will be discussed under (4) and (5).

(2) and (3) *Objectivity as residing in universal rules or concepts.* Certain moral rules, such as "Do not kill," and certain concepts such as "beauty" and "security," are observed to have gained the allegiance of many individuals and of widely varying cultures. Consequently it is hoped to state these rules and define these concepts in such a way as to make them absolutely universal in their compulsiveness. Objectivity, so it is assumed, means primarily universality. But when the rules and concepts are clarified, several obstacles are encountered. The rules or values are found to conflict. "Do not kill" may be found to be incompatible in a particular situation with the rule "Act so as to preserve the lives of your children and friends"; or we may have a choice between beauty and security. Casuistry then gets to work and modifies the rule so as to remove the contradiction: e.g., "Do not kill except when necessary to defend your children and friends." But this rule in turn may conflict with others, and it may be too vague about the circumstances in which it is applied to be of use. When the rule takes all the relevant circumstances into account, it is no longer universal, for every moral situation is unique. Consequently upon analysis the most that can be claimed for rules by empiricists is wide generality, not strict universality. A widely general rule is one that furnishes guidance in a large number of similar and frequently recurring situations; a "value" that claims general allegiance is one that corresponds to basic needs and interests which manifest themselves in many individual lives and

cultures. These are rooted in common human biological structure and in the fundamental structural patterns of human association. In so far as we can discover and formulate these, we have
found guide-posts toward objectivity in our judgments. But these
do not afford a complete solution of our problem. We are not
enabled to determine which rule or value is applicable in a given
particular situation, or whether any hitherto discovered will suffice. Nor is it always the common human or social element that
is decisive: the idiosyncratic factors in a man or a culture may
be the source of the value. For man's biological nature has a
large degree of plasticity, and his environment and his social patterns change.

(4) *Agreement or "social objectivity" as the criterion of value.*
When it is perceived that strict universality is not to be found in
rules or value concepts, then universality is sought in agreement:
"*x* is good" means "Persons *A, B, C* . . . will find *x* good" (the
agreement may be restricted to a specified group or extended to
all mankind). Thus Mr. Vivas, in the article quoted: "When I
say that something is good, and I do not mean merely that I like
it . . . I mean not only that it will satisfy an isolated interest, but
that it will not interfere with the other interests which will make
up my system, but will rather aid and foster them. But I also
mean that the other members of the social group with which I
identify myself will concur with this judgment."[3] The value judgment in this case may be a singular one, "This is good," as well
as a universal rule. The universality is one of assent rather than
logical universality.

But here again the constitution and interests of the individuals
concerned may vary, even within a single social group. In any
case, agreement is at most a rough test of value, not the basis of
its objectivity. For the sum of a number of judgments can not be
objective unless there is a basis of objectivity in each; and further, you can fool all the people some of the time. Consequently
the social dimension of value may be appealed to in a different
fashion:

(5) *Objectivity as residing in the "publicly observable" conditions and results of value experiences.* Thus Professor Dewey:

3. *Ibid.*, pp. 437–438.

"Judgments about values are judgments about the conditions and results of experienced objects; judgments about that which should regulate the formation of our desires, affections and enjoyments."[4] The dominant note in Dewey's discussion of value is an emphasis that reflective inquiry into means is important to the choice of ends: we must know which ends are realizable in the actual world, and this knowledge modifies our ends-in-view. Since the material and social conditions which make the achievement of a given set of values possible or impossible are open to public inspection, these supply an "objective" foundation for our values in opposition to the reliance of extreme "subjectivist" theories on private feeling.

This emphasis of Dewey's has been a useful corrective to such theories as artificially separate means and ends, and then treat ends as chosen purely by feeling. But Dewey admits that "liking" or "enjoyment" is a constituent of the value experience itself. Since the individual has direct access to this through self-observation, and others may have some access to it indirectly, it would seem to be a grave sin of omission for an empiricist to exclude this phase of the act from study when seeking evidence for valuations. In no other field do we rule out attention to the phenomenon under study itself, to concentrate exclusively on its conditions and results.

Thus although, as I shall argue later, Dewey is moving in the right direction when he seeks objectivity in the *evidence* for value judgments, his social behaviorism leads him to ignore one very important kind of evidence, namely, that concerning the immediate quality of the experience of value itself.

To oppose, or to supplement, these five inadequate approaches, I wish to suggest the following primary meaning of objectivity:

(6) A value judgment may be said to be objective without qualification when it is *true*.

This answer is so simple that it has been all but overlooked. As baldly stated, it may seem either obvious or question-begging. That it is not obvious, however, will appear from the fact that none of the above five theories explicitly put the answer in this

---

4. *The Quest for Certainty*, p. 265 [*Later Works* 4:212]; see also his *Theory of Valuation* [*Later Works* 13], *passim*.

way, even though they may presuppose it. Does it beg the question? It may be declared to do so on either of the following grounds:

(a) That the theories in question are themselves concerned with the criteria or conditions of truth in value judgments. E.g., it may be asserted that a value judgment can be true only if values are properties of objects, or if universal value concepts have a foundation in reality. But let us remember the problem from which we started, which was, how we could escape from ethical scepticism, how we could find propositions about values sufficiently reliable to serve as guides in living. Surely, then, the answer we have suggested, if it is valid, must be the direct and primary answer to our problem. For if we can guide our conduct by true judgments we have no grounds for scepticism. Our question, then, is primarily an epistemic question. We are seeking *knowledge* with regard to valuations. It may be that ontological questions, such as some of the above, are involved, and I for one should insist that "truth" is a term containing an ontological reference. But the nature of this reference is an auxiliary question.

(b) The proposed solution may be declared question-begging also for the following reason: that, on empiricist principles, we can never *know* that any proposition is true. All we can assert confidently is that there is evidence which gives the proposition a high degree of probability. These statements are correct, but are compatible with the view offered. Even though we can not with certainty know any valuational proposition to be true, it is only in terms of the ideal of truth that we can define the ideal of objectivity.

But this second objection points to a needed application of the view proposed.

A value judgment is objective *without qualification*, it was said, when it is true. It follows that the judgment can be *known* to be objective only in the degree that it can be *known* to be true.

For practical purposes, then, we can escape from scepticism with regard to values to the extent that we can obtain empirical evidence which is relevant to the truth or probability of value judgments. The sceptic is the man who believes that there is *no* evidence that is relevant to the truth or probability of any proposition, that no proposition has more evidential weight than any other. The non-sceptical empiricist, on the other hand, holds that, while no proposition involving existence can be known with certainty to be true, nevertheless some possess much more evidential support than others, hence possess a much higher degree of probability. And the degree of probability may be so high in many cases that the proposition supplies a reliable guide for action.

Do value judgments, then, conform to the canons of empirical logic? In other words, are they verifiable by the hypothetico-inductive method?

Let us consider the species of value judgment which we encounter most often in ethics. The difficulty arises over the term "ought," or some equivalent, which is always found in the ethical judgment. It is often said that the "ought" can never be reduced to an "is," that "value" is irreducible to "fact." For example, "I ought to do x," or "x is good," can not be equated with "x is desired by me," or "I like x."

If the "ought" is analyzed in this oversimple way, then empiricism in ethics is indeed untenable, and the "ought" becomes something very mysterious. But the meaning of an ethical judgment is capable of analysis in a more complicated and, I believe, more adequate fashion. When I say that I ought to do x, I am referring to something beyond my desire or liking of the moment.

Let us consider the matter first at the purely egoistic level of conduct. When I say that x is good for me, I mean that it will fit in with the whole pattern of my interests and my potential satisfactions. I mean that in the long run act x will promote the system of my interests to a greater extent than any feasible alternative, and also that the resulting satisfactions will be qualitatively superior to those resulting from any other interest pattern.

Similarly on the social or altruistic level. When I say that an act is right or good, I mean that it will promote the interest pattern, actual or potential, of the group, and that this pattern will supply the group with richer intrinsic quality of experience than any alternative.

Briefly, on this view "I ought to do x" means "x will promote the maximum of integration plus qualitative satisfaction."

What we have, then, in the ethical judgment is not a simple descriptive proposition concerning present or past fact, but a predictive judgment involving the potentialities of human nature as well as its actuality. In the large sense of fact, the future is also a fact, and the nature of the world includes what it can be as well as what it is so far. The judgment of value is, then, in this very special sense a judgment of fact.

Is the ethical judgment, so conceived, subject to empirical verification?

I believe that it is. We can obtain empirical evidence both as to the tendency of a given act to promote integration of interests, and also as to its fitness to produce a qualitatively rich experience. Our scientific knowledge, such as our medical knowledge, and our practical experience of the way certain types of act fit into a given context of interests, supply us with evidence as to the integrative or disintegrative tendency of an act. Likewise our observation, largely introspective, of the "inner" quality of various types of satisfaction in the past, and our imaginative experiments with comparatively novel types of act, give us some basis on which to forecast the affective quality of experience, both our own and others'.

To the extent that we have relevant evidence of these kinds, the ethical judgment is "objective." It rests on observed fact and inductive inference from such fact. In so far as introspection plays a part in the knowledge of qualitative satisfaction, the evidence is in the psychological sense "subjective," i.e., it is directly accessible to one observer alone. But it is still evidence, and it is to some extent capable of intersubjective confirmation by indirect means. Even without confirmation, the evidence of one witness has some weight.

One peculiarity of value judgments, then, is that the evidence on which they rest, although it is a matter of empirical observation, is partly of this "private" character. But this fact need not lead, as it is sometimes held to lead, to the extreme relativist position that such evidence is of no worth. For propositions about feelings are themselves true or false, though sometimes only one person from the nature of the case can directly determine their truth or falsity with any adequacy.

Another peculiarity of value judgments is that the basic judgment, and theoretically the only type of judgment that can have complete truth or objectivity, is the *singular* judgment. Each art object is ultimately unique, and so is each ethical situation. So I can say that "*This x* is beautiful (or good)," with more evidential weight than "*All x* is beautiful (or good)."

Objectivity in value judgments, then, attaches primarily to singular judgments, judgments about an individual person in an individual situation. This is why the second meaning of objectivity expounded in the early part of this essay is misleading. By a thorough analysis of the situation, I may assert much more confidently that "This wine is good" than that "All wine is good," and that "For Joe Doakes to kill John Smith under these circumstances is wrong" than that "For any person x to kill any other person y under all circumstances is wrong." Singular judgments of value *can* be either true or false without qualification, though it is necessary to repeat that as empiricists we must say that we can never certainly know them to be true or false. Reputedly universal judgments or rules, however, in this field are more or less rough generalizations possessing at most statistical truth, since they can not take into account the complexities of individual situations involving competing values and disvalues.[5] We need such rules, and we need them in the analysis of particular situations themselves. So far as they serve to guide us here, they have a degree of objectivity. But from the nature of the ethical situation, the proposition which directs an ethical choice is singular, and prescribes a particular line of conduct in an individual situation.

On this view there is a kind of relativism involved in value judgments. When we say that this x is good, we mean that it is good for a given individual or group within a specifiable situation, or at most that an object or action of the type in question is roughly adequate in many or most situations that are similar. But

5. I am referring here to those ethical maxims which prescribe a specific value-content, such as those given above, "All wine is good," or "All killing is wrong." Their terms belong to what roughly corresponds to Carnap's "object-language" in science, and in ethics we may call such a language EL_1. But there is also a "metalanguage" in which ethical theory itself is written, which we may call EL_n. This consists of the definitions and theorems which state the meanings of ethical terms, and which formulate the syntax of EL_1. An example of expressions in EL_n would be the definition of good given above: "'x is good' means 'x will promote the maximum of integration plus qualitative satisfaction.'" Although expressions in EL_n are not exclusively syntactical, or completely lacking in content—since they refer to general aspects of the value situation, that is, of men in relation to their world—they do not suffice to direct action in particular situations. They may, however, indirectly influence action, in so far as ethical dialectic affects specific valuations. Universal propositions in EL_n may be true or false without qualification, though of course they can never be known with certainty to be so, and though a completely adequate formulation of them may be a remote, even an impossible, ideal.

it can not be asserted to be good for all individuals in all situations. For value always involves a *relation* between men and their world, and these latter are highly variable terms.

But this kind of relativism is not "vicious," i.e., it does not lead to scepticism. "*x* is good for person *A* in situation *m*" does not mean "*x* is *thought* or *felt* by person *A*, or by some other person, to be good for *A* in situation *m*." This would lead to as many possible truths as there are observers of the situation, and hence would destroy objectivity in any relevant sense. On the contrary, the judgment means "*x* will promote the maximum of integration plus qualitative satisfaction for *A* (and—if we are speaking on the level of social morality—for the others affected) in situation *m*." Now *x* either will or will not do this. If it will, the proposition is true; if it will not, the proposition is false—regardless of what *A* or anyone else thinks or feels. The person who is most likely to be right is the person who has the most evidence and interprets it most ably. Sometimes the individual most immediately concerned is the least qualified to judge, even though he may have better access to certain types of relevant evidence.

This view of objectivity will suffice for those who are willing to examine each important situation on its merits. It will not satisfy those who persist in demanding rules and value concepts that will prescribe the duties of all individuals in all cultures. But I have not been seeking an objectivity which obviates the necessity for reflection on the nuances of life. Such objectivity would be a moral juggernaut.

Nor is the view of objectivity here presented a comforting doctrine. Evidence concerning the qualitative aspect of different types of experience or patterns of life, obtained as it is through ruthless self-observation and through dramatic rehearsal of the probable experience of others, is slippery and difficult knowledge. The critical person will often have to suspend judgment, or to make a choice from evidence that is heart-rendingly scant, or to act on "hunches" cast up by his subconscious perceptions of fitness. But this would seem to be an inescapable predicament of the human tragi-comedy.

Appendix 4
Quality and Value[1]
By Philip Blair Rice

Nowhere in ethics and general theory of value have greater mystery and confusion abounded than with regard to the category of "quality." The category is one that is deeply embedded in common language and practice. We often say that one object or experience or way of life is qualitatively superior to another, and we make our choices accordingly. Yet the category of quality has been recalcitrant not merely to the efforts of philosophers to define it—for definitions of fundamental categories are always hazardous—but to their attempts to clarify it. The result has usually been either that the category has been accepted as ineffable and unanalyzable, so that judgments of quality become mere dogmatic assertions (perhaps alleged to have a transcendental basis), or else that quality has been explained away by being reduced to some other category such as quantity or integration which offers more footholds for analysis.

The difficulty arises partly from the fact that the term "quality"

1. This paper was written, and accepted for publication, before I had the opportunity to read the manuscript of Professor Dewey's "Valuation Judgments and Immediate Quality" (*Journal of Philosophy,* Vol. XL, 1943, pp. 309–317 [this volume, pp. 63–72]). Since Professor Dewey's paper contains very detailed comments on my earlier paper, "'Objectivity' in Value Judgments" (*Journal of Philosophy,* Vol. XL, 1943, pp. 5–14 [this volume, Appendix 3]), I shall have to defer my reply until a later occasion. The discussion of the "perceptual source of value" in this paper, however, should make it clear to Professor Dewey that I do not conceive all "immediate qualities" to be apprehended by introspection. This is one of the main points upon which he criticized my earlier paper, and I can see that my brief discussion of the question there could easily have led him to misinterpret my position. Most of the points at issue between Professor Dewey and myself, however, are logical and methodological, and consequently do not fall directly within the scope of the present paper. In so far as such questions are relevant to the topic of "immediate qualities," I shall have to postpone a reply to Professor Dewey upon this topic as well.

[First published in *Journal of Philosophy* 40 (24 June 1943): 337–48. For earlier article by Rice, see Appendix 3. For Dewey's reply, see pp. 63–72. For further papers by Rice and Dewey, see pp. 73–83 and Appendix 5.]

as applied to values has a multiplicity of meanings. We may say that one piece of cloth is of better quality than another because it is warmer or more durable. On the other hand, we may praise its quality because it gives an exquisite sensation of sight or touch even though it is flimsy. When a southern Negro judges that certain whites are "quality folks" and is not merely being snobbish, he may be referring either to the considerateness and justice with which they treat their servants and each other, or, since the Negro race is a highly esthetic one, to the charm of a certain manner of living. Probably his judgment is most often a blend of both moral and esthetic considerations.

About all that such usages of the term have in common is that they mean by the quality of an object or an act simply the ground for approving it. When one thing is loosely said to be qualitatively superior to another, we mean merely that it is preferable. But just what properties of it constitute the ground of the preference are left mysterious unless we can pursue the analysis further than this. The term, then, might just as well be abandoned if we can not assign to it a more precise and specific meaning.

As the above examples suggest, the term "quality" as commonly used may include characteristics of objects that are purely instrumental in their value. When a cloth is praised for its durability or an act for its "moral" quality, we are obviously referring to uses and consequences and not merely to immediate or intrinsic properties. On the other hand, the term is often applied to the intrinsic values of an object or experience in contrast to the extrinsic values. This usage is analogous to the logical or metaphysical sense in which a quality is distinguished from a relation.

Before we can suggest a more precise meaning for the term, then, we must find the grounds for ascribing to anything an intrinsic value. This is a question upon which the most influential theories of value now current are far from clear.

Empirical and naturalistic thinkers today generally treat value as a function of needs, desires, interests, and satisfactions. Thus the good or valuable in the most generic sense is defined by R. B. Perry as "any object of any interest."[2] People value that in which they are interested, that which they seek to possess or achieve.

2. *General Theory of Value*, ch. V.

So stated, the theory does not make clear the distinction between instrumental and intrinsic value. Nevertheless, such a distinction seems to be presupposed. That which is valued in the object is an instrumental or relational property, its capacity to lead to the satisfaction of an interest or desire. Intrinsic or consummatory value is realized in the satisfaction of the desire, or in the anticipation of this satisfaction. Intrinsic value, then, in the strict sense, is found in an experience, and only derivatively, or by metonymy, in an object regarded as a potential cause of that experience or as one component of it.

What is it, then, about an experience which gives it intrinsic value? Traditional hedonism would have said "pleasure"; current value theory, for reasons some of which are good and some are bad, prefers to speak of "enjoyment" or "liking" or "consummatory quality." Attaching as it does to the satisfaction phase of the interest-satisfaction nexus, intrinsic value involves feeling, or an affective component, and this is essential. If the attainment of the objective is not accompanied by a positive affective element, we say that we were wrong in desiring the object and hence mistaken in regarding it as the source of intrinsic value. But, as we shall see, the attainment of a desired object nearly always brings some enjoyment or consummatory quality with it, and even when it does not do so, the disappointment may be outweighed by the values of the anticipation; hence the plausibility and the partial truth of the interest theory.

We have been speaking so far of interests in isolation from each other, and hence of value in its most primitive or generic sense. When we consider interests in the total context of life, that is, in relation to each other and to the material and social environment, we see that some interests have to be modified or extirpated. For, as they sprout, our desires may conflict among themselves, and they may aim at objects which the environment can not supply. Hence at the level of value in system an interest theory becomes an integration theory. In order that an object or experience may be judged good, it must not merely satisfy an interest, but must be seen upon reflection to possess such properties that it will promote—or at any rate not hinder—the realization of an organized pattern of interests of the individual or of the group. In Spinoza's language, at this level something is good or valuable if it is "a means of attaining that type of human nature which we have set before us." [3] On this basis, any life that is harmonious or well integrated will possess some intrinsic value. Hence a principle of tolerance: there are many individual ways of life and many cultures that possess value, and we must not insist that they all be cast in one mold.

Yet tolerance does not imply indifferentism, and a pluralism or relativism such as is required by an interest theory must face the recurrent necessity for making a choice. When we are forced to choose between two patterns of life which are equally well integrated, we may make our choice on the ground that one is "qualitatively" richer than another. Thus men have chosen to live in Paris rather than in Boston, or in Tahiti rather than in Paris. We may even, if we choose the life of a poet or an adventurer over that of a business man or a professor, deliberately sacrifice a certain amount of "integration" for the sake of "qualitative richness" of experience.

In order to deal with situations of this kind, we need to examine aspects of value which are ignored by the theories we have been considering. I should like to suggest that the inadequacy of the interest theory, with its consequence the principle of integration, springs from the fact that it takes into account only one of the two chief sources of intrinsic value.

If an experience has intrinsic value when it includes an affective element called "enjoyment" or "liking," we can find two sources for this value. It may attach primarily to conation or to perception, and in the two cases we may speak of conative and perceptual value respectively. The two sources or types of value are nearly always closely interwoven, but they are distinguishable by analysis.

The Conative Source of Value

Conative value springs from the pursuit of a goal or a purpose. I desire something; when I get it (or advance toward getting it or foretaste its attainment), the experience has an affective quality which confers intrinsic value upon the object as experienced or "phenomenal object." This is the type of value

3. *Ethics*, Part IV, Preface.

which is the focus of an interest theory, and it was in part to this type of value that Aristotle was referring when he said that "pleasure" accompanies the performance of any unimpeded activity.[4] The physiological reasons for this tendency of enjoyment to inhere in the working out of conation are obscure. One of the most plausible theories is that a purpose or conation involves a tension, or rather, a series of tensions directed upon the successive phases of the attainment of the end. Enjoyment or consummatory quality, and hence intrinsic value, accompanies the release of the tensions.

Conation is a much more inclusive source of value than many of the proponents of an interest theory themselves have made clear. Our interests or conations may be of a great variety of kinds—"practical," moral, intellectual, and esthetic. We call them practical in the narrow sense when they involve manipulation of the environment and eventuate in possession or consumption of a material object. The "governing propensities" which motivate them may be biological or quasi-instinctive in their origin, or they may be implanted by experience. However they originate, when implemented by choice of the means to realize them, they give rise to specific strivings whose working out brings gratification. The moment of attainment may be brief and the gratification fleeting in consequence; hence the contempt of some moralists and esthetes for "worldly" pursuits. But the practical man may reply that what he enjoys is not so much the victory as the game; that is to say, the successive attainment of subordinate goals auxiliary to the terminal goal.

"Moral" value, in so far as it is not merely instrumental, is similar in character. Morality in the restricted sense is directed toward integration of the individual's needs and toward socialization of them with the interests of others. Although moral activity may thus be initially of an instrumental character, the pursuit of a subordinate end, as we have seen, can bring intrinsic or consummatory values with it. To earn money or write a book or relieve the sufferings of others may involve getting up early in the morning, which at first is disagreeable; but later the habit of early rising may cancel at least part of the disagreeableness

---

4. *Nicomachean Ethics*, Books VII, X. I say "in part," because according to Aristotle pleasure attaches also to contemplation, or the activity of *nous*, which does not involve striving.

through the intrinsic gratification which the accomplishment of any purpose brings with it. As Epicurus put the matter, perhaps with some exaggeration:

> Wherefore prudence is a more precious thing even than philosophy; from it spring all the other virtues, for it teaches that we cannot lead a life of pleasure which is not also a life of prudence, honor and justice; nor lead a life of prudence, honor and justice which is not also a life of pleasure. For the virtues have grown into one with a pleasant life, and a pleasant life is inseparable from them.[5]

Intellectual activity has been so often praised either as purely "contemplative" or else as purely instrumental that we do not have an adequate analysis of its attendant values. The intellect, as the Greeks themselves recognized, is the chief agent of integration; they did not give sufficient emphasis to the consequence that the values of intellectual activity are in considerable measure extrinsic. But intellectual activity also has its intrinsic rewards, whether we conceive it, with the instrumentalists, as "problem-solving," or, with Plato and Aristotle, as directed to the possession of knowledge for its own sake. In either case the intrinsic value is largely, though not wholly, conative. Problem-solving is a type of conation, and has its consummatory values accordingly. Mrs. Langer has given us a modern version of the Greek view in arguing that the need to symbolize experience is a primary human need, or, to use the language of the interest theory, a governing propensity; she cites evidence to show that the human being is interested in symbolic transformation as an end in itself.[6] Intellectual activity, then, possesses conative value not only through its capacity to solve practical problems, but also by satisfying the basic human impulse to find symbols for experience.

The values accompanying conation are so important that we may even, as in games, set up quite arbitrary ends in order to obtain the enjoyment that comes from the pursuit of them. What we value is, to paraphrase Kant, not the purpose but the purposiveness.

5. *Letter to Menoeceus.*
6. *Philosophy in a New Key.*

The Perceptual Source of Value

As prevalent as the values springing from conation may be, this is not the only source of intrinsic value. For some values, or some elements of value, come to us unsought, and therefore do not spring from the release of a tension, since no purposive tension is directly involved.

This second type of intrinsic value we may call "perceptual value," since it seems to arise from perception of the immediate qualities of an object or an act, whether these qualities and their accompanying enjoyment have been anticipated and striven for or not. Very likely we never get an example of perceptual value in an unmixed state, yet it is perhaps seen in its greatest degree of purity in esthetic experience.

Esthetic experience—even from the point of view of the spectator of a work of art—is not indeed purely passive or contemplative; it has its conative aspects. Esthetic perception, as Mrs. Langer has argued, is itself a mode of knowing: the primary human need to symbolize experience may find expression in art as well as in scientific or "intellectual" activity. The scientist symbolizes experience chiefly by analyzing out its relational aspects, while the artist presents its qualities in their particularity. The spectator satisfies vicariously the need for symbolization by sharing in the artist's creative achievement.

Esthetic experience, however, arouses also more specific conations. It involves alertness and the search for form. It includes, like Perry's interests, "expectations"—for example, of repetitions, modulations, and resolutions—and it may give us pantomimic satisfaction of such "governing propensities" as our biological and social drives. But in esthetic experience the goal is set by the artist—or induced by Nature or the rush of life—and our primary purpose, when we consent to submit ourselves, is to perceive the structure, texture, and meaning of the esthetic object. When we enter upon the act of submission, we do not know what the artist's goal is. We do not, as in some other kinds of purposive activity, have a preconceived objective for which we seek to find and execute the means. The artist's activity—which, of course, has a large "practical" element—may involve more or less of this, but not even the artist in the act of making has more than a general aim in mind, and I am speaking here of his audience. We are passive in the sense that we are following and not leading to the goal, however much alertness and anticipation may accompany the process of submission. Our primary purpose, in so far as the activity is purposive, is to perceive what the artist put there for us (or for himself) to perceive. And we value the experience primarily not for the success of our communication with the artist, but for the intrinsic characters of the perception itself—of that which is communicated.

Although part of the total satisfaction or value in esthetic experience comes from our sharing in the artist's purpose of symbolizing experience and from our success in grasping his intent, these conative factors are consequently of secondary importance. And so an interest theory has seemed to be adequate only because so little attention has been given by general theory of value to esthetic value. We must remember that an "interest" has been defined by Perry as including not only a "governing propensity," but also an accompanying "expectation."[7] Now it may be possible to find, or to presume, a governing propensity behind every esthetic experience. In a broad sense of "need," we may say that everything that gratifies us, either by way of conation or by way of perception, responds to a need, even though the need may have been latent or merely potential before the stimulus came which evoked it. To say this is tautologous. If our psycho-physical organism were not congenitally disposed, or shaped by experience, in such a way as to respond gratefully to a perception, we should not so respond to it. But in esthetic experience the "expectations" involved, such as were mentioned previously, are far from adequate to the event. The esthetic object is rich beyond our anticipations. It always contains an element of novelty, of surprise, of superfluity relatively to our specific purposes. Poetry gives us detail, such as imagery, beyond what is required to carry the logical structure of the poem, texture beyond the bare semantical reference of the symbols, rhythmic variety and sonority and intricacy of sound beyond the mechanical demands of the metre and often in conflict with them. The painter, even when he is representing nature, tries to give every portion of his canvas a formal and textural value that parts of his model lack. Far from answer-

7. *Op. cit.,* ch. VII.

ing to some definite pre-existing purpose, the esthetic object may set our strivings to rest by seizing us with the unforeseen splendor of the sensuous manifold. The enjoyment of this component of esthetic value, then, springs from the perception of the qualities before us, not from the release of a conative tension.

I am not suggesting that esthetic perception is the work of a disembodied mind, or that the sensuous element in it is divorced from kinesthetic adjustments and from incipient action-tendencies. Our enjoyment of the "material" factor in a work of art, such as the powder blue or ox-blood red of a Chinese jar, comes nearest to the passivity of pure sensation; and the part that this may play in the total experience suffices to warn us against reducing the whole of esthetic value to the by-products of conation. But in perception of form, taken even at its simplest terms in an ornamental shape, tensions are involved. In such cases—let us say our enjoyment of the shape of the Chinese jar or of a piece of pre-Dynastic Egyptian alabaster ware—the ease with which the eye muscles make the transition from one portion of the curve to another, together with other empathic and peripathic elements—so far as any such factors are relevant to the perception of form, which, of course, has often been questioned—may eventuate in conative value. The distinction of perceptual from conative value here, however, is found in the fact that we enjoy not merely the release from the tensions but the tensions themselves—their equilibrium as well as their resolution. Thus the conflict in a tragedy enriches the play not only because it leads to the dénouement, but also because we relish the symmetrical balance of the opposing forces.

The fact that something more than gratified conation is involved in value seems to be given at least partial recognition by Professor Dewey in his esthetic theory, even though it may be insufficiently emphasized in his general treatments of value. In *Theory of Valuation* and elsewhere, Dewey treats value as something that arises in the implementation of a "need" or a "lack," and hence as primarily conative. In *Art as Experience,* however, we find many qualifying statements such as the following: "An environment that was always and everywhere congenial to the straightaway execution of our impulsions would set a term to growth as surely as one always hostile would irritate and destroy. Impulsion forever boosted on its forward way would run its course thoughtless, and dead to emotion." [8] The environment, he urges, must within measure offer resistance if the activity of adjusting ourselves to it is to possess value. Dewey's principal reason for this is that thereby the objects around us acquire significance, by evoking thought and a greater variety of purposive action. But it can also be argued that obstacles to our action make us more aware of the perceptual qualities of the environment and of our responses to it, together with their attendant values. It is a truism that we are usually so intent on our purposes that we notice only those aspects of the world around us to which we are forced to attend. Our purposes may determine which aspects of the environment we select for attention, but the intrinsic perceptual qualities of that to which we are attending may absorb our notice and even divert us from our purposes so that we contemplate the medium itself as a source of intrinsic perceptual value; hence a part of the value derived from contrast, conflict, and even from "disorder" in a work of art. [9]

The effort to distinguish between the two sources of value is complicated by the fact that an object of perceptual value, even though it may be unsought, immediately acquires an element of conative value when it is experienced. If the perception of it is enjoyable, we have an impulse to hold on to it, to sustain it in consciousness, [10] and this striving when gratified itself acquires an aura of successful purposiveness. But it would seem to be an inversion of the true state of affairs to say, as an interest theory must, that the object is valuable only because we experience the impulse to hold on to it. On the contrary, it may more plausibly be said that we hold on to it because the perception is experienced as intrinsically valuable.

Just as perceptual value in esthetic experience is intermingled with conative value, "practical" activity conversely may contain an element of perceptual value. Pursuit of a preconceived end, even of a biological or economic sort, may involve more or less enjoyment of the sensuous and dramatic qualities of the situation. Only our most hounded activities are entirely void of other sources of gratification besides the release from the tensions that

---

8. *Art as Experience*, p. 59 [*Later Works* 10:65].
9. Cf. S. C. Pepper, *Aesthetic Quality*, and Lawrence Leighton, "Disorder," in the *Kenyon Review*, Vol. 1, No. 2, 1939.
10. See Perry on "recurrent interest," *op. cit.*, ch. IX.

drive us upon our goal. And it is a commonplace that when we are exclusively cramped upon the attainment of a purpose— say the winning of the game—we get less intrinsic value than when we maintain sufficient detachment to perceive the qualities of the process.

Thus when Santayana says that the good life consists in a combination of attachment with detachment, of purposive activity with contemplation, we may translate this to read that the good life makes provision for both the conative and the perceptual sources of value. Since we may acquire an "interest" in perception for its own sake, it follows that, in Santayana's language, the fully rational or harmonious life embraces an element of post-rational contemplation.[11]

Is Quality Analyzable?

Now even when a "qualitative" factor has been recognized, as by J. S. Mill, it has commonly been treated as something unanalyzable or ineffable. Thus Mill, following Plato, resorts to an appeal to authority for the decision between the "higher" and "lower" pleasures: the choice, for example, between pushpin and poetry is left to the wise man or the man who has experienced all types of pleasure.[12] The wise man, presumably, can be quite dogmatic about his decisions; he does not give reasons because, on Mill's principles, he can not. As a result of such an attitude toward the problem, alleged judgments of quality have been rejected as mere "ejaculations of emotion" and hence unverifiable.

The belief that qualitative distinctions, in the sense of judgments about perceptual value, are ineffable, unanalyzable, and unverifiable could be defended so long as esthetics and criticism of the arts were backward studies. But in the last generation we have seen these disciplines come, if not exactly to maturity, at any rate to an intellectually vigorous adolescence. In critics of painting like Roger Fry and R. H. Wilenski, in literary critics like T. S. Eliot, I. A. Richards, J. C. Ransom, and their followers, an unprecedentedly strenuous attempt has been made to develop

11. "Apologia Pro Mente Sua," in *The Philosophy of George Santayana,* edited by P. A. Schilpp, pp. 560–573.
12. *Utilitarianism,* ch. II.

categories and techniques which will permit of a more adequate analysis of the "formal" or perceptual values of a work of art. Philosophical counterparts of this tendency are to be found in such writings as S. C. Pepper's *Aesthetic Quality*. To the extent that a precise language and reliable techniques are devised for the analysis of esthetic experience, we shall be able to talk intelligently about the perceptual sources of value both in the arts and outside them. The judgments of a critic are verifiable in so far as, after due preparation, we can discover in the work with which he deals the formal and other properties to which he calls our attention, and can experience or fail to experience ourselves the same kind of value responses that the critic reports.[13] One reason why the traditional hedonists, such as Mill, were so inarticulate about the qualitative factor in value was that they tried to talk directly about the emotion, instead of approaching it indirectly through an analysis of the perceptual elements which give the feeling or pleasure its specific coloring. Just as we saw, in criticism of interest theories, that the perceptual factor is sometimes the ground of the preference or conation, so we must point out, in criticism of "subjectivistic" or hedonistic views, that the perceptual qualities (which need not be exclusively sensory) are the source and differentia of the feeling.

My intention is not to suggest that all so-called qualitative distinctions among values can be reduced to esthetic or perceptual categories. Terminologically, we have the alternative of restricting "quality" to perceptual factors, or else of continuing to use it comprehensively and loosely to denote the grounds of valuational preference of whatever sort these grounds may be. If we adopt the latter alternative, however, we are now in a better position to be clear as to what we mean by the term in a particular instance. When we use quality to refer to the instrumental values possessed by various types of objects, we can specify the end to

13. The foregoing is not meant to imply that the critic reproduces the perceptual value of the work of art itself—for that would put him in rivalry with the artist—or that esthetic value yields wholly to analysis. I am denying that perceptual value is (*a*) ineffable, on the ground that the artist himself articulates it when he presents it, or (*b*) unanalyzable, on the ground that the critic, when he is successful at his job, can trace, at least in part, the specific factors of esthetic value to their sources. The final judgment of esthetic value is post-analytic; we learn what we can from criticism, and then report on our post-analytic experience of the work of art as a *Gestalt*.

which the object is useful and what properties constitute its utility. When we mean by quality the intrinsic characters of conative value, we can describe the factors in the particular conation. And finally, when we apply the term to the esthetic or perceptual source of value, we can, if we are trained, perform a critical dissection of the properties of the object which contribute to the immediate experience. In none of these cases is the value immune to analysis.[14]

Very often we shall find that more than one type of value is involved. When we speak, for example, of the ethical quality of an act, or make qualitative distinctions between different ways of life, we may mean to include all three elements of value, and so we can adequately deal with the situation only by distinguishing them. We may ascribe greater instrumental value to one of two ways of life because it leads to better integration of our desires with one another and with the physical and social world; we may prefer it because it consequently brings a larger measure of intrinsic value through gratification of the conations involved; and also because it affords a greater richness of perceptual or esthetic content. If "morality" in the narrower sense applies to personal and social integration, the full ethical judgment which is the final arbiter in valuation envisages the good life not only as one that is harmonious, but also as one that is rich in perceptual awareness.

14. Laird's "timological" criterion of value (*The Idea of Value*), and Urban's principle of "authentication" (*Language and Reality*) are merely dogmatic substitutes for the techniques of analysis suggested above; they consequently leave the problem of value as mysterious as it was when the analyses were first undertaken.

Appendix 5
Types of Value Judgments
By Philip Blair Rice

I am grateful to Professor Dewey for giving, in his "Valuation Judgments and Immediate Quality,"[1] such detailed attention to an article of mine,[2] and for the clarification which his paper affords of certain very important points in his theory of valuation. It is also gratifying to have Mr. Dewey's confirmation of my opinion that we are in agreement on certain essential points of an empirical approach to values—for which, indeed, my own views are so largely indebted to his. In what follows, I shall confine myself to those points on which there has been misunderstanding or disagreement.

The central issue is whether data or aspects of events that are "subjective," in the sense that they are directly accessible only to self-observation, can serve as evidence for value judgments. And more specifically, whether introspection of that phase of the value situation which is called "enjoyment" or "satisfaction" can supply evidence relevant to decisions about values. Mr. Dewey holds that it can not; my paper criticized him for this view, and advanced the thesis that it can. My position is that an adequate empiricism with regard to values must take account of such evidence; Mr. Dewey holds that such a view is incompatible with empiricism.

Bearing upon this main issue are four related points of dispute, with which I shall deal in turn:

(1) *Two meanings of the antithesis "subjective-objective."* Mr. Dewey points out that in one context I use the term "subjective" in a sense which is not correlative with the principal use of the

1. *Journal of Philosophy,* Vol. XL (1943), pp. 309–17 [this volume, pp. 63–72].
2. "'Objectivity' in Value Judgments," *Journal of Philosophy,* Vol. XL (1943), pp. 5–14 [this volume, Appendix 3].

[First published in *Journal of Philosophy* 40 (30 September 1943): 533–43. For Dewey's reply, see pp. 73–83. For earlier articles by Rice, see Appendixes 3 and 4. For Dewey's earlier reply, see pp. 63–72.]

term "objective," so that what is subjective by one criterion can be objective by another. Such was my explicit intention. My problem is to find out why Mr. Dewey finds this procedure "disappointing" or *prima facie* paradoxical. The assumption of my paper was that of the many senses in which the antithesis "subjective-objective" is used there are two distinct senses, both of which are pertinent to a study of valuation. These two senses I shall call, in this discussion, (*a*) the logical sense, (*b*) the psychological sense.

(*a*) The logical sense. Mr. Dewey is substantially correct in stating that the primary sense of "objectivity" in my paper identifies it with "verifiability by empirical evidence." Actually and strictly, I identified objectivity with truth rather than with verifiability. I take verifiability to be a criterion (though not the sole criterion) of meaning rather than of truth. Truth is more closely related to verification than to verifiability. I identified "*known* to be true" with "verified," and thus equated for practical purposes an objective judgment with a verified judgment. But this qualification is not important for the present issue, since Mr. Dewey's definition is in the same universe of discourse as mine.

The correlative sense of the term "subjective" is "false," or (on the practical level) "unverified." With qualifications similar to those stated above, I should accept Mr. Dewey's definition of the logically subjective: "Propositions (judgments, beliefs, or whatever) are *subjective* when they are produced by causal conditions which fail to possess genuine evidential capacity and verifying power, but which nevertheless are taken at the time to possess them. . . ." His examples are beliefs of those suffering from illusions, hallucinations, and insanity.

(*b*) The psychological sense. My statement to which Mr. Dewey takes exception was: "In so far as introspection plays a part in the knowledge of qualitative satisfaction, the evidence is *in the psychological sense* 'subjective,' i.e., it is directly accessible to one observer alone." The italics were not in the original, but my clear intent was to state that "objective" (sense *a*) and "subjective" (sense *b*) were compatible predicates.[3]

I do not see anything logically or linguistically scandalous in

3. Strictly speaking, the terms in sense *a* apply to propositions, and in sense *b* primarily to data or evidence. Thus it would be accurate to state that data that are subjective in sense *b* may be used to confer objectivity (sense *a*) on propositions.

this procedure. The antithesis "strong-weak" also has at least two senses, but it is not contradictory to assert that the same man is both physically strong and mentally weak. If there has been a confusion, then, it would seem plausible that Mr. Dewey is confused when he holds that anything which is psychologically subjective is also logically subjective.

If "subjective" (sense *b*) means that which can directly be observed only through introspection, and thus is directly accessible to one observer alone, then "objective" in a correlative sense means that which is perceived by non-introspective or "external" observation, and is equally accessible to more than one observer.

Mr. Dewey asserts, without citing evidence from my paper, that I conceive the subjective (sense *b*) to refer to a "special order of Being," which constitutes "a certain sort of epistemological-metaphysical reality." From similar criticisms of introspection elsewhere in Mr. Dewey's writings, I presume that he is imputing to me something like a Cartesian dualism of mental and material substance. My distinction, however, was quite neutral with regard to metaphysical assumptions, and if any epistemological tenets are involved they are not presuppositions of this view but consequences of it together with other premises.

The distinction was intended to be exclusively one of psychological procedure. It refers to the fact that each individual stands in a unique relation to certain aspects of his own experience, a relation which is not shared by other observers with regard to those aspects of that person's experience. "Introspection" was here used in the sense employed by the late Professor Mead when he said that psychology "does make use of introspection, in the sense that it looks within the experience of the individual for phenomena not dealt with in any other sciences—phenomena to which only the individual has experiential access."[4] It is such phenomena, or rather aspects of phenomena, which I call subjective in the psychologial sense. I say aspects of phenomena because I agree with Mead and with Mr. Dewey himself that the ultimate unit of conduct is most usefully conceived as the total act, or process, or event, and I hold that this is adequately treated only in terms of a total situation involving factors that are both subjective and objective in sense *b*.

4. *Mind, Self and Society*, pp. 4–5.

Examples of aspects of events which are subjective in this sense are muscular sensations, thoughts which are not uttered or enacted, and feelings or "affective" tones. Both the occurrence and the quality of these aspects of phenomena can be directly observed only by the individual in whose organism they are occurring, though others may sometimes infer their occurrence from external symptoms, and consequently may infer their quality from associated "subjective" events which occur under similar conditions within their own experience. The sensory nerves directly concerned in perceiving subjective phenomena are the proprioceptors and interoceptors.[5]

The individual has no such unique vantage-point in observing the "objective" aspects of events and acts (whether others' or his own), such as shapes, colors, and overt movements.[6] These are perceived by use of the exteroceptors, such as the optic and auditory nerves. Persons B, C, and D are on an equality with regard to observation of the color of person A's complexion, his dancing, and his spoken words, so far as bare difference of personal identity goes. A is even at a slight disadvantage in observing these aspects of his own behavior, although he can overcome this disadvantage to some extent by such means as the use of mirrors. A does, however, have a kind of access to the subjective aspects of these phenomena which is denied to B, C, and D, although the latter may be more nearly correct than A in their interpretation of the total act or situation. This is because the total situation includes both subjective and objective aspects, and both are relevant to the judgment on it as a totality. Furthermore,

5. Cf. R. B. Perry, *General Theory of Value*, pp. 270–271.
6. The data or sensations involved in the perception of such phenomena are not necessarily objective in a common epistemological sense in which "primary" qualities are declared to be objective in contrast with subjective or "secondary" qualities, i.e., as asserting that primary qualities resemble certain corresponding properties of their objects, whereas secondary qualities are not thus iconic. This is a third distinct meaning of the antithesis, according to which shapes, e.g., are held to be objective and colors subjective. Furthermore, according to all epistemological schools except the naïve or direct realists, the *sensa* or *data* in the case of "objective" phenomena (sense *b*) are accessible only to the person to whose stream of consciousness they belong, and hence are "subjective" in still a fourth sense, which is partly psychological, partly epistemological. I have dealt with the relation between the second sense of the antithesis (sense *b*) and this fourth sense in another paper, "'Public' and 'Private' Factors in Valuation," which has been accepted for publication by *Ethics*. But here I am trying to avoid epistemological issues.

A, B, C, and *D* may erroneously interpret their psychologically objective data: hence objectivity in sense *b* and in sense *a* need not coincide.

Mr. Dewey states that my paper "offers no direct evidence for the existence of material that is private and inner and hence (by its very nature) accessible directly only to observation by a self which is single, exclusive, and non-public and non-social." I did not state nor imply that the self is "non-public and non-social." I do hold that it has its sequestered and idiosyncratic aspects. From the nature of the case, I can not offer to anyone else "direct" evidence for the occurrence of such aspects. For this, I must ask Mr. Dewey to examine his own joys, pains, and secret thoughts. If he should tell me that he does not have any such, nothing that I might say could refute him. However, as I understand his position from his other writings, he does not deny that experience has such aspects, but merely that they can possess evidential weight.

(2) *How immediate qualities are perceived.* From the above discussion it should be clear that I do not hold, as Mr. Dewey took me to be saying, that all qualities are perceived by introspection. "Subjective" qualities (sense *b*), which include affective tones, are apprehended directly by introspection, and "objective" qualities (sense *b*) are perceived by external or behavioristic observation. The two kinds of qualities are closely associated, and a relation of dependence may subsist between them, so that we may with some probability infer the existence of one from the other in particular cases. In the experience of a painting, for example, the affective tone is derived from, and felt as fused with, the design and color. But the two kinds of qualities are distinguishable even though, in most cases, they are not separable. And the two methods of observation collaborate. Since, as Mr. Dewey holds, values are affective-motor phenomena, affective qualities are of special importance to a theory of value. It is for this reason that in my previous paper I emphasized the rôle of introspection in perception of qualities.[7] In Mr. Dewey's writings on value we read much about the motor element in value experience, but little about the affective element.

7. See also my "Quality and Value," *Journal of Philosophy*, Vol. XL (1943), pp. 337–348 [this volume, Appendix 4].

(3) *"Public" and "private" as aspects of the "problematic situation."* The above definitions of "public" and "private" (for the sake of brevity I shall henceforth use these terms for "objective" and "subjective" respectively, in sense *b*), are, so far as I can see, compatible with analysis of valuation in terms of the *positive* features of Mr. Dewey's "problematic situation." (As I shall suggest below, the conception of the "problematic situation" becomes Procrustean when the attempt is made to fit all valuational and cognitive situations into it, to treat them all in terms of a "motor block.") Let us consider the situation "toothache" or "something-wrong-with-tooth." The "difficulty" which initiates the problem may be either publicly or privately detected. Usually in this case it is detected privately: I observe introspectively a "pain," and this suggests to me the hypothesis "I ought to visit a dentist," or—though with less initial probability—"I ought to have a cavity filled." The ache is not, as Mr. Dewey seems to hold, merely a "dubious" element in the situation, but, together with my previous knowledge of similar situations, it constitutes *prima facie* evidence for these value judgments. However, I seek further evidence to confirm them. This further evidence may consist of non-introspective observation to see if a brown speck can be found on my tooth. Such observation can be carried out by a number of other persons, including my dentist, or by myself with a mirror. If there is a conflict between the public and the private evidence, usually I trust the dentist's public evidence, and permit him to act accordingly. (I should assign superior evidential weight to the private evidence only if the dentist told me that there was nothing wrong with me, or that the pain was good in itself.) The difficulty is fully "resolved" only if the external manifestations of dental trouble disappear, and also if after an appropriate time the pain vanishes. I use the introspectively observed disappearance of the pain as an important part of the evidence that the situation has been resolved, and hence that the value judgment was correct. If the pain is still with me, I use it as initial evidence for a new hypothesis, namely, that the trouble was neuralgia and not decay. The two types of evidence, therefore, may reinforce or correct each other. Just why Mr. Dewey holds that the perception of the ache has no evidential weight is not clear to me.

Mr. Dewey's account of the problematic situation *abstracts from* the aspects of the situation which I have been considering;

it ignores the alternative psychological perspectives from which observations can be made. So I do not know how to interpret his statement that the "immediate qualitative nature" of the situation is neither "subjective, nor objective, nor a relation of the two," if the terms in question are used in sense *b*. Nor do I see that a reference to the immediate quality of the situation is relevant if the terms are used in sense *a*. There is, I suppose, a sense in which the situation as a *gestalt* is perceived as having a unitary quality of its own. But our knowledge of the *total* quality, so far as we can achieve it, is not "immediate," but the result of construction and inference. We can, however, get perspectives upon this total quality by either external observation or introspection, or by both together; the idea of its quality as a whole is put together from the various partial perspectives and the immediate qualities which they supply.

In reading Mr. Dewey's account of mind, I have long been puzzled by what seems to me to be his *standpointless* psychology. I can see why he rejects both introspectionism and Watsonian behaviorism as adequate approaches by themselves, and also why he is dissatisfied with a parallelism which tries to put private and public data together mechanically. His emphasis on the total act is a useful one, and for the purpose of stating psychological laws it is often desirable to ignore the partial perspectives used in particular observations, and to speak in terms of "functions" and other behavioral concepts which cut across the distinction between introspection and external observation. But why this should entail that a distinction between these two chief types of perspective is illegitimate for a descriptive analysis of actual psychological procedures is not clear.

(4) *Evidence "about" enjoyment and evidence "supplied by" enjoyment.* Mr. Dewey holds (*a*) that valuational propositions "concern" enjoyment, but denies (*b*) that such propositions may draw upon evidence "supplied by" observation of enjoyment. He interprets a statement of mine in such a way that he understands me to "identify" these two propositions, and he believes that my view rests upon this supposed "equivoke." I did not intend to assert a logical identity or equivalence between propositions (*a*) and (*b*), although I do hold that they are closely related materially.

When I predict that a certain experience will have value, I do not use introspection of *that* experience to obtain evidence. (Such a view would truly involve the "equivoke" in question.) *That* experience, by hypothesis, has not yet occurred, so I can not introspect it. I may, however, found my prediction in part on introspection of my present *anticipation* of the future experience, and on my *remembrance* of the affective qualities of similar experiences in the past. This view is based, not upon any deductive argument, but upon my empirical analysis of what I—and other persons—actually *do* when making decisions in such matters. If I predict that the experience of a Beethoven concerto, or a baseball game between the Dodgers and the Reds, will bring me "satisfaction" or "enjoyment" and hence value, it is in part because I remember that similar occasions in the past have been accompanied by enjoyment, and because I discover introspectively that my imaginative rehearsal of the probable experience ahead of me is now accompanied by relish. Such predictions have shown themselves to be sufficiently reliable that I continue to use this type of evidence, with discrimination and in conjunction with other kinds. Of course memory and anticipation are fallible with respect to affective qualities, and hence the private evidence is not conclusive. But neither, according to empiricism, is any other kind of evidence conclusive.

Mr. Dewey's second argument against the evidential function of introspectively obtained evidence is that this is incompatible with my view that ethical judgments are predictive in character,[8] that they take into account "the connection of a satisfaction with a system of interests, involving the future and a comparison of alternative acts with respect to their integrative function." That there should be such an incompatibility I do not see, and Mr. Dewey offers no reasons for this view. My decision in such a case as the concert or the baseball game takes account of public factors—the state of my bank account, the demands of other interests beside my musical or sporting interests upon my time, and the fitness of a soloist or a star pitcher—as well as private factors; both may be used for the purposes of prediction. If such public evidence excludes private evidence of the kind that has

8. I do not hold that *all* judgments of value are predictive in the sense that they refer to or are "about" a future event; in the earlier paper I took this position only with regard to a certain type of ethical judgment. Nor do I believe that such judgments depend exclusively upon evidence to be obtained in the future.

been mentioned in the preceding paragraph, the burden of proof that this is so rests upon Mr. Dewey. He should show this by analysis of concrete instances of such experiences and not by deduction from general assumptions concerning empirical method. For it is precisely the adequacy of these assumptions that is in question.

If we had at the present time an adequate doctrine of the logical syntax of empirical knowledge, I believe that the above analysis of valuation could be fitted into it, with resulting clarification of the whole field. Much of the controversy over theory of value among empiricists in recent years has sprung from the failure to recognize that there are many different types of value situations, and consequently that there is a great variety of kinds of "value judgments," with extremely various logical structures. The discussion of value theory by Mr. Dewey, R. B. Perry, and the late D. W. Prall, carried on intensively in the *Journal of Philosophy* between 1914 and 1925, and prolonged by more or less desultory firing between Dewey and Perry since then, will illustrate the point. Thus Mr. Dewey in the course of that discussion wrote: ". . . The articles of mine which Mr. Prall criticized were not concerned with the nature of value, either the quality or the things having the quality, but with the nature of valuation as a judgment. . . . It happens that Mr. Prall is interested in his writings in value, while my interest was logical—that is, was in a certain type of judgment."[9] Perhaps it is because he has recognized the oddity of trying to construct a theory of "valuation" without at the same time offering a theory of "value" that Mr. Dewey on several later occasions has made at least casual attempts to define the latter concept. Thus, in his most recent article, he states that he holds that "qualitative 'enjoyment,' 'satisfaction,'" is "the *entire* material" that a valuation judgment is about. But he goes on to say that enjoyment is equated with value here only in a "figurative" sense; that enjoyment is properly called a value only "with reference to being potentially the material for an evaluative judgment, or in connection with events still to occur." Now here, as in his earlier discussion of the subject, Mr. Dewey has been concerned only with those types of judgment which he calls judgments of practice, and which seek to determine a particular fu-

9. *Journal of Philosophy*, Vol. XX (1923), p. 619 [*Middle Works* 15:23].

ture course of action in the presence of a "difficulty" or motor block. Here the judgment or reflection does create or modify the value involved. On the other hand, Prall, Perry, and most other empirical writers on value start from a simpler type of judgment asserting "valuable" as a predicate, and take this as the archetypal value judgment.

Now I should like to suggest that it is linguistically naïve to continue to dispute about *the* meaning of value, or the characteristics of *the* value judgment. If we should attempt to construct a logical syntax of valuation, we should have to take into account a number of different types of judgments that have been called value judgments. Among these is what might be called an elementary judgment of intrinsic value. The scheme for such a judgment is "x is intrinsically valuable to person A at time t (or in situation m)," and this is equivalent to "A enjoys x at time t (etc.)." This is one common meaning of "valuable"; propositions of this type are true or false and therefore significant, and their verification rests on observation. The label "*elementary* judgments of intrinsic value" is not intended to suggest that such judgments are logically atomic, although they are the simplest propositions which make explicit the three terms—an object, an organism, and a situation—to which a value is relative. The evidence upon which such judgments rest is reported by still simpler propositions analogous to Carnap's "protocol sentences" or, better, Russell's "basic propositions."[10] Some of these simpler propositions are usually based upon introspection, others on external observation. A himself takes into account observations formulable as "Enjoyment now," or "This is enjoyed." Other persons use such indirect evidence as "A looks happy" or "A says he likes this." Both A and the others, furthermore, use public evidence of the type involved in time determination or in description of the other objective factors of the situation.

Another fundamental type of value judgement would be "x has instrumental value in situation m," and this when expanded is equivalent to "x in situation m has such properties that it is capable of promoting intrinsic value y for A in situation n." (Or, in many cases, "x will promote the removal or avoidance of disvalue z. . . .") Likewise, there are elementary judgments of com-

10. *An Inquiry into Meaning and Truth,* chapters X, XI.

parative value, either intrinsic or instrumental. Thus "x has more simple intrinsic value than y for A . . ." would mean "x gives A more enjoyment than does y. . . ." (The definition of "more enjoyment" here is not easy.)

Ethical and esthetic judgments each include a number of subspecies, and are always more complex than the judgments hitherto discussed. In one of the commonest types of esthetic judgment, which we may call the critical judgment, "x has esthetic value" means "x would give perceptual enjoyment to anyone sharing cultural tradition k who was trained to discriminate properties a, b, and c of x." In a common type of ethical judgment, "A ought to do act x" means "x will produce more integration of interests, together with resulting satisfaction, for A and the other persons affected than will any feasible alternative." An adequate treatment of the logical structure of such ethical propositions would show that they in turn rest upon elementary propositions both of simple intrinsic and of simple instrumental value, and perhaps also on esthetic judgments of several types. All these types of judgment would go back for their evidential support to protocol sentences or basic propositions recording observations, introspective or external, and hence would be empirical.

In conclusion, I should like to say a word about Mr. Dewey's identification of "neo-empiricist" or "scientific" method with the instrumentalist position. Empiricism, as I understand the term, is the view that all existential propositions derive their probability from observation. It holds that laws and other complex propositions in any field are obtained by observation, hypothesis, deductive prediction, and verification. Exponents of scientific method have at various times made two further assumptions derived from the study of the methods of the physical sciences: (a) that science must be metric, that it can deal only with quantitative aspects of the subject-matter; (b) that only "public" evidence is admissible. Mr. Dewey rejects the first of these assumptions as essential to empirical or scientific method in the broad sense. What I am suggesting is that instrumentalism and neo-positivism should reexamine the second of these assumptions also. If it should prove too restricting to enable us to deal properly with values, then empiricism as a general doctrine of method can be preserved only by rejecting the assumption. But if empiricism continues to be defended in such a way as to exclude the affective evidence that most men take into account in making value judgments, then the result will be to aggravate that "new failure of nerve" of which Mr. Dewey has written elsewhere, and to turn many of those who are especially concerned with values away from the promising but incomplete contemporary versions of empiricism, to find refuge in some form of intuitionism or apriorism or authoritarianism.

Appendix 6
On the Aesthetics of Dewey
By Benedetto Croce[1]

Dewey's aesthetics is scarcely known at all in Italy; and so far as I am aware, has never been subjected to that detailed critical examination which its intrinsic merits certainly warrant. It furnishes us a new and striking document of the singular mental habit of this thinker—certainly one of the most discerning students of the life of the mind, and possessed of a lively sense of its values, as his ideas on politics and education, and now on art, demonstrate; but at the same time a thinker who continues insistently to call himself an empiricist or pragmatist and to reject and repel, one may almost say with horror, the philosophy commonly called "idealistic." Dewey also uses the appreciative term "organic," but with him it has a touch of mockery. Accustomed as we are in Italy to keep always in mind the history of thought, and to take cognizance of what we call the literature of the subject, in order to become aware of the place which our new conceptions come to occupy in that history and thus confirm their right to it, we feel a certain dissatisfaction in the scarcity or vagueness of such references in Dewey's treatise. In the Preface we read: "I am somewhat embarrassed in an effort to acknowledge indebtedness to other writers on the subject. Some aspects of it may be inferred from authors mentioned or quoted in the text. I have read on the subject for many years, however, more or less widely in English literature, somewhat less in French and still less in German, and I have absorbed much from sources which I cannot now directly recall. Moreover, my obligations to a number of writers are much greater than might be gathered from allu-

1. Translated by Katharine Gilbert.

[First published in *Journal of Aesthetics and Art Criticism* 6 (March 1948): 203–7. For Dewey's reply, see pp. 97–100.]

sions to them in the volume itself" (p. vii [7]).[2] But he must also have availed himself of some Italian authors, though these were perhaps included among the English because read in English translations. However, Dewey expressly mentions my studies more than once in the course of his argument, now to make use of their concepts, for example of my criticism of the separation of the arts from each other; but more often to exorcise with horror, as I said above, my somewhat mad "idealistic" (or rather "organic") way of philosophizing.

Even so, an Italian reader is pleasantly surprised to meet on every page observations and theories long since formulated in Italy and familiar to him. For example, that "expression" in the poetical sense is not to be confused with the expression which goes by the same name but is not expression in and for itself, consisting rather in reflective interpretation of a fact on the part of an observer (p. 61 [66–67]); that the feeling or sentiment in a work of art is not something experienced personally, but has a universal character (p. 68 [73]); that the act of expression does not supervene upon an inspiration already complete, but goes along with it (p. 66 [71–72]); that an artist does not conceive his work in mental terms, translating it afterward into artistic form, but, if he is a sculptor, conceives it in clay, marble or bronze, and so on (p. 75 [81]); that an aesthetic emotion is a distinct thing, yet at the same time not divided by an abyss from other natural experiences (p. 78 [84–85]); that we must reject the formalists' theories of art, which make beauty consist in lines, colors, lights and shadows, and such, separating it from its psychological content and meaning (p. 88 [93–94]); that one does well to avoid even the word "association" [in aesthetics] since by it traditional psychology assumed that the associated material and the immediate sound and color remain separated from each other (p. 99 [104]); that the subject (fable) is one thing and the substance of a work of art another (p. 100 [105–6]); that it is not true that visual qualities are as such, or consciously, central, and other qualities only accessory or associated (p. 123 [128–29]); that technique is one thing and art another (p. 142 [146]); that figures

2. *Art as Experience*, by John Dewey. Minton, Balch, New York, 1934. All page references, unless otherwise indicated, are taken from this book. [Page numbers in brackets refer to *Later Works* 10.]

have in art the value of musical or pictorial tones. This Dewey says wittily, using the words of Matisse to a lady who criticized one of his female figures: "Madam, that is not a woman; that is a picture" (p. 113 [118]). Italians are familiar also with the idea that it is a bad sort of naiveté to separate rhythm and symmetry, and to divide the arts into spatial and temporal, when in reality we have movements and directions in painting and distances and volumes in music (p. 183–84 [187–89]); that there are not such things as aesthetic contents or non-aesthetic contents (p. 187 [191]); that all the other arts are in every art (p. 195 [198–99]); that there are not artistic "things," but only an artistic doing, an artistic producing (p. 214 [218]); that the so-called "modifications of the beautiful" such as the sublime, grotesque, tragic, comic, etc., have practical use but surely not conceptual or dialectical meaning; that the aesthetic process is of great importance for the philosopher, because through it he understands the nature of every psychic process; and therefore aesthetics is indispensable to the work of philosophy (p. 274 [278]); that it is impossible in judging art, to forego either of the two elements: the sensitive and the intellectual (p. 290 [295]); that aesthetic judgment is not that of a court pronouncing in the light of laws or rules (p. 299–300 [303]); that historical knowledge is indispensable for judgment on art.

And so on, for here I note rapidly only certain points. Nor am I setting them down to put forward a claim to authorship or priority, but rather to observe that whatever kind and however much stimulus Dewey has received from the thought of others, he thinks over problems for himself, so that his observations come out with freshness and spontaneity and sustain the reader's interest; particularly the interest of one who, having arrived earlier and by other routes at the same conclusions, and discovering his own ideas in a new form, finds in this an added proof of their truth.

But precisely because of this obvious agreement of his doctrines with so-called idealistic aesthetic, a disciple of Dewey's, and his co-religionist in pragmatism, has very recently raised a respectful and resolute protest against the new book. The book, he says, is unfaithful to the principles and method of pragmatism, being dominantly idealistic and organistic in its aesthetics and admitting an absolute judgment of value on works of art.

This excites his surprise, and he even asks why Dewey does not at once declare himself an Hegelian. The disciple reminds his master that "organicism is a theory of harmony culminating in the great cosmic harmony of the absolute. Pragmatism is a theory of conflict, celebrating struggle and vigorous life in which every solution is the beginning of a new problem, in which every social ideal is an hypothesis of action, in which values thrive on conflicts" (p. 386).[3] To this charge, one must admit, Dewey replies weakly, stating that he remains a pragmatist and has not become an idealist because he does not deduce his aesthetic theory, but makes it spring from the examination of the material before him; moreover, that the terms which he uses, even if to be found in idealistic aesthetics, do not carry in his usage the same signification. In this way he tries to pass off a question of ideas as a question of vocabulary.

But we are not concerned to urge his faults or deviations from pragmatism, except to show that the criticisms he brings against idealistic aesthetics are without foundation. For example, he criticizes Kant for making beauty disinterested, and argues that: "not absence of desire and thought but their thorough incorporation into perceptual experience characterizes esthetic experience in its distinction from experiences that are especially 'intellectual' and 'practical,'" and: "the esthetic percipient is free from desire in the presence of a sunset, a cathedral, or a bouquet of flowers in the sense that his desires are fulfilled in the perception itself" (p. 254 [259]). This correction is not a correction because it states what Kant stated when he distinguished pleasure from beauty (separated *Gefallen* from *Vergnügen*). Then follows what is intended as a real and proper objection, that is, that "esthetic experience is marked by a greater inclusiveness of all psychological factors than occurs in ordinary experiences, not by reduction of them to a single response. Such a reduction is an impoverishment" (p. 254 [259]); but this amounts to a refusal to think, because to think is to distinguish, and one cannot make distinctions without assigning to the mental form thus distinguished its special character of principle; in other words, without using a concept.

3. *The Philosophy of John Dewey,* edited by Paul Arthur Schilpp, in *The Library of Living Philosophers,* Volume 1.

Similarly Dewey, as he proceeds to deny the cognitive character of beauty, agrees that "tangled scenes of life are made more intelligible in esthetic experience; not, however, as reflection and science render things more intelligible by reduction to conceptual form, but by presenting their meanings as the matter of a clarified, coherent, and intensified or 'impassioned' experience" (p. 290 [295]). This is precisely what is called, in philosophical aesthetics, aesthetic or intuitive or pre-logical knowledge (*cognitio inferior, clara sed non distincta*). There follows an objection which really can be reduced to the preceding one, *viz.:* to a prohibition of the thinking that distinguishes, criticizes, and defines: "The trouble I find with the representative and cognitive theories of the esthetic is that they, like the play and illusion theories, isolate one strand in the total experience, a strand, moreover, that is what it is because of the entire pattern to which it contributes and in which it is absorbed. They take it to be the whole" (p. 290 [295]).

Dewey's criticism of me is of the same sort: "The term 'intuition' is one of the most ambiguous in the whole history of thought. In the theories just considered [Aristotle, Plotinus, Hegel, up to the moderns, like Bosanquet], it is supposed to have essence as its proper object. Croce has combined the idea of intuition with that of expression. Their identification with each other and of both with art has given readers a good deal of trouble. It can be understood, however, on the basis of his philosophic background, and it affords an excellent instance of what happens when the theorist superimposes philosophic preconceptions upon an arrested esthetic experience [arrested, let it be noted, because Dewey benevolently grants me, as he does Schopenhauer, greater experience and sensibility in artistic matters than he does to most philosophers]. For Croce is a philosopher who believes that the only real existence is mind, that 'the object does not exist unless it is known, that it is not separable from the knowing spirit.' In ordinary perception objects are taken as if they were external to mind. Therefore, awareness of objects of art and of natural beauty is not a case of perception, but of an intuition that knows objects as, themselves, states of mind. 'What we admire in a work of art is the perfect imaginative form in which a state of mind has clothed itself.' 'Intuitions are truly such because they represent feelings.' Hence the state of mind that constitutes a work of art is expression as a manifestation of a state of mind, and is intuition as knowledge of a state of mind. I do not refer to the theory for the purpose of refutation but as indication of the extreme to which philosophy may go in super-imposing a preconceived theory upon esthetic experience, resulting in arbitrary distortion" (p. 294–95 [299–300]).

Now, without doubt, I hold that poetry and the other arts have for their material not external things (nobody knows what and where such things are) but the "sentiments" or human passion, and I hold that nothing can exist separated from knowing. As I hold these propositions to be true, it is natural that I should use them to establish the place of art in the system of mind. Dewey does not undertake to refute these doctrines of mine because he considers that he has already refuted their very foundation: *viz.* philosophical reflection. He says in another book: "Reason, as a Kantian faculty that introduces generality and regularity into experience, strikes us more and more as superfluous—the unnecessary creation of men addicted to traditional formalism and to elaborate terminology. Concrete suggestions arising from *past* experiences, developed and matured in the light of the needs and deficiencies of the present, *employed as aims and methods of specific reconstruction,* and tested by success or failure in accomplishing this task of readjustment, suffice. To such *empirical suggestions* used in constructive fashion for new ends the name intelligence is given" (p. 95–96 [*Middle Works* 12:134]).[4]

It is certainly strange that a mind so keen and a genius so acute as Dewey's should turn in such vicious circles and positivistic tautologies; and I often ask myself how it could have happened. Perhaps his thought is dominated by the traditional Anglo-Saxon empiricism. Perhaps also the fanaticism and emptiness of the orthodoxy of the Kantians and Hegelians who were his first masters in America stirred in him a revolt which has not yet quieted down. Perhaps this feeling of revolt has prevented him from seeing that the Hegelian and related structures have fallen to pieces and that the Absolute which he found so forbidding, no longer exists as such, but has become one with the world, experience, and history; that the new philosophy has rejected the static elements of Hegelianism in order to preserve and develop the dy-

4. *Reconstruction in Philosophy,* by John Dewey. The italics are Croce's. (K. G.)

namic ones. For the new philosophy is a theory of perpetual conflict, of solutions that generate new problems, of a continual enrichment, such as pragmatism claims to be but cannot logically become. However that may be, his philosophical position is such as I have described above.

Appendix 7
Can We Choose between Values?
By George R. Geiger

Value theory can become very esoteric, as it occasionally tends to become in the technical periodicals. But there are also certain elementary, not to say naïve, aspects of human valuation that should not be lost sight of. Above all—and this is not so naïve—an attempt must be made to choose among the values presented by a culture. However risky or impertinent, that effort is necessary. Any aseptic refusal to make moral choices is to do no more than accept uncritically choices that others have already made. Some assumptions underlying such an attempt will be presented here. And a preliminary one will be the way the term "value" itself is being understood: values, at least so far as they particularly concern ethics, are the results of man's long-time preferences—preferences in the central area encompassing his basic attitudes of life, his deep-rooted tastes and interests, his objects of respect and reverence.

The Biological Basis of Value Decision.—There can be little question that the starting place for decision about human values must be found in the biological wants that drive man's energies. These would include the straight physiological demands for food, shelter, sexual expression, health, and growth; the psychical urge for meaning, self-expression, satisfaction of curiosity, and a widened and heightened sensitivity; the social needs that force the individual to stretch out for others: all of them—physiological, psychic, and social—developing into some kind of pattern, symmetrical or crippled, that will provide the background for a personality. Even this kind of catalogue, of course, is atrociously oversimplified. For example, "health" and "growth," not to mention some of the others, are themselves abstract concepts

[First published in *Journal of Philosophy* 41 (25 May 1944): 292–98. For Dewey's reply, see pp. 101–8.]

when, actually, what they are supposed to represent are specific conditions and processes that require detailed physiological itemizing. Health or growth, or even seemingly more specific needs such as that of sexual expression, are names given *ex post facto* to a series of concrete happenings; to regard them as already established in some *a priori* fashion is to interpret human "drives" as antecedent philosophical principles rather than as tissue changes. Such a qualification does not destroy the validity of listing the possibly abstract human wants that must be considered; it does sound a note of warning when they become hypostatized into biological entities.

Another oversimplification is in the otherwise excellent word, "pattern." For a pattern does not emerge automatically or painlessly out of man's basic wants; it is not like a blend counseled in a recipe, a little of this and a little of that. Human needs, and the interests that arise from them, are in conflict throughout. In this conflict, choices, however unconscious, are made and values come forth as they do on other levels; also, as on other levels, if the conflict becomes unendurable one or more of the interests must go. The personality pattern that begins to issue from this elemental competition is a compromise that has been hammered out of a struggle for existence as savage, even if as private, as any in biological history. All this is not meant to complicate the present argument. It is merely to notice that the phrase, "satisfaction of basic physical needs," is not the primer kind.

But it is primer-simple to insist that in any approach to the problem of human values the beginning is to be found among the biological and psychological wants. This is something of a banal observation. But as commonplace as it is, the point has too often been overlooked by the traditional philosophic approach to value. No ethical system, no hierarchy of values, can be established with any pretense to relevance or permanence without a foundation having been laid; the building-blocks of that foundation can be nothing else but the elemental human wants. Unlike the story about the world resting on a tortoise and the tortoise on something else and so on "all the way down," such a foundation needs no other Atlas to support it. It is itself the massive base of all human history—the base, not necessarily the delicate tracery of the topmost stonework.

Which is to say nothing more than this: that unless man has

sufficient and correct food and shelter he will either die or grow into an unhealthy, stunted caricature; that unless he has opportunities for psychical as well as physical satisfaction, i.e., a chance to develop curiosity, to widen his horizons, to exhaust his capacity for meaning, sensitivity, and intellectual growth, he will become a counterfeit man, the "boob" that cynical Menckens and contemptuous Nietzsches have always held up to scorn; that, finally, unless he participate fully in the society of which he is an integral part, being given the opportunity to contribute whatever his talents permit and to share proportionately in the economic, political, educational, and cultural life of that society, he must turn into a part-man, a false replica of the more complete personality that full social participation could help to create. These may be truisms. Certainly they need the specific elaboration that this paper is not attempting. Nevertheless, as a *sine qua non* for the erection of a system of values, this whole cluster of primal demands must first be grappled with. However precious, even esoteric, ethical and esthetic values may become, they can not cut themselves loose from the framework of biological and psychological and social needs in which human beings have to grow. Reiteration of this elementary point should be unnecessary; unfortunately, it is necessary—at least (occasionally) for philosophers.

The Social Basis.—But preliminary observations like these about the foundation of human values afford little help in making choices between different and conflicting sets of values. *Which* personality pattern is to be applauded and *which* wants? To declare that as many human wants as possible are to be satisfied is incontrovertible, but only in an honorific, not to say a constipated, sense; for there is an unholy struggle constantly going on, and that the pattern which emerges will automatically be entire and symmetrical is a little too much to expect. But even if it were smooth and well-rounded, again, what is the criterion of judgment? Is it symmetrical for the lady's man or for the philosopher? Is the standard that of sacrifice or pleasure, and if so, what kind? Is it happiness?—and what is that? Is the path of life to be one of detached contemplation or of sensual abandonment, of action or of classic restraint, of love or of duty—paths of life that Professor Charles Morris has called by names such as Buddhist, Dionysian, Promethean, Apollonian, Christian, and so on?

The easiest way out perhaps would be to by-pass this most ancient and yet most modern and most tremendous of human decisions by saying, a little of one and some of the other. A harmonious synthesis might seem to be indicated. Something of Gandhi and of John Dewey, and even of Nietzsche, might be prescribed. Indeed, Professor Morris does a little of this in his presentation of Maitreyan Man. However, that kind of synthesis is eminently plausible only, again, in an honorific sense. What would be needed to effect such a laudable amalgam would be a super-culture, one in which the historical and technical differentials between cultures would be, by some over-algebra, canceled out. For there is a struggle—not necessarily overt—between cultures just as there is among man's basic drives. In addition, the diverse values that are championed in such a competition are themselves not accounted for by man's biological needs; those needs, it must be repeated, are the foundation for any system of values, but the way the architecture grows is a cultural, not a biological, matter. It is a technological matter. Therefore, it would seem that the momentous process of choosing among the "paths of life" would also be a cultural and technological one. Certain suggestions about that technique of decision will follow, although it must be realized (without any false modesty) that such a presentation can be no more than a tentative outline.[1]

Laying down a series of assumptions may be the easiest way to sketch that outline. One of those assumptions has already been used in the preceding paragraphs. It is to the effect that the choice among human values can not be made on the basis of an abstract and transcendental criterion which, however noble it may be, stands outside the system it is expected to judge. At least, the choice can not be made legitimately and functionally on such a basis. There would be required for that kind of choice either a super-culture—and, glorious as that would be, it has not yet appeared—or some intuition or revelation of the *right* hierarchy of values. The latter has been tried often enough but seldom with the honesty demanded by Jeremy Bentham's savage formula about "that sort of man who speaks out and says, I am of the

---

1. In suggesting certain elements of this "technological" theory of value, the writer is deeply indebted to the work of Professor C. E. Ayres.

number of the elect; now God himself takes care to inform the elect what is right. . . . If, therefore, a man wants to know what is right he has nothing to do but to come to me."

This assumption, however, is only a negative one. More positive would be the insistence that since we can't get out of a cultural process through tugging at our boot-straps and so arrive at some infinite and all-wise extrapolation, the standard for human value must be located intramurally within a going technology, within a set of functional social institutions. Of course, the words "going" and "functional" are question-begging ones, for what makes a system "go" or be "functional"? The following assumptions, all of them closely related, would attempt to give an answer:

(1) A culture must be judged by its efficiency in maintaining itself and by its progress along a definite technological line.

(2) That line of technological progress is determined by the degree in which men understand their surroundings—surroundings or environment being interpreted in the broadest sense as a culture matrix involving physical, biological, and social factors.

(3) Understanding or knowledge is a matter of doing—of control and change—not simply of contemplation.

Perhaps it may sound imprudent to assert that assumptions like these add up to a test for human values, that qualities like "right," "dynamic," "evolutionary," and so on are to be discovered in the direction in which society is moving. But what else can serve as a test?

The Place of Knowledge in Determining Values.—These assumptions, it will be noted, are pyramided, with the apex pointing to the moral significance of human knowledge and understanding. Now, in a philosophic setting, this is an overly familiar, if not a humdrum and pedestrian, point of view. From Plato and Aristotle on down, the good has been equated with truth, reason, thinking, above all with contemplation. The ultimate end of man is to be intelligent, which, for Aristotle and others, is to be happy. He has a "moral obligation to be intelligent." What, then, is different about an instrumentalist or technological approach to the equation of value with understanding? The answer would seem to lie in the emphasis upon the knowing *process*.

This process of knowing, of inquiry, of scientific method, of reflective thinking—all these are being used here as more or less interchangeable terms—is familiar enough to require no exposition. Fundamental to the procedure is the refusal to accept the traditional elevation of knowing over doing, of theory above practice. Methods are always of supreme interest to the experimentalist, and, by their very nature and use, methods must be operational and active. But this interpretation of knowing means much more than the employment of a tricky machinery. In its widest sense it signifies opposition to fixed ends, system-making, and changelessness; it signifies provisionalism and reconstruction, the reliance upon working hypotheses rather than upon immutable principles. Thus, this kind of knowing is in no wise limited to the professional scientist. It represents an attitude that can function in any area of experience (even valuation), an attitude of free and effective intelligence.

And it is such an attitude that must characterize the knowledge and understanding proposed here as the criterion of value. To put it quite bluntly, the test of human decision—on the social or individual level (if the two can with any meaning be separated)—is *the degree in which it manifests and preserves free intelligent inquiry.* The general ethical standard of human culture is that the scientific attitude (keeping in mind always the broadest possible meaning of that phrase) has become an integral part of it. In the procedures of instrumental knowing—the knowing that alone permits cultures to maintain themselves and to understand and control their surroundings—is to be found the validity of human values. These are all different ways of trying to say the same thing.

So, the free working of human intelligence becomes itself a supreme value. But does not this imply an *ultimate* value or end, one that sounds suspiciously like any other respectable *summum bonum* of historical ethics? John Dewey answers that question:

I have carried on a polemic against ultimates and finalities because I found them presented as things that are inherently absolute, like "ends-in-themselves" instead of ends-in-relationships. The reason they have been proffered as absolutes is that they have been taken out of any and all *tem-*

poral context. A thing may be ultimate in the sense of coming last in a given temporal series, so that it is ultimate *for that series*. There are things that come last in reflective valuations and, as terminal, they are ultimate. Now [one] is quite right in saying that for me the method of intelligent action is precisely such an ultimate value. It is the last, the final or closing, thing we come upon in inquiry into inquiry. But the place it occupies in the *temporal* manifestation of inquiry is what makes it such a value, not some property it possesses in and of itself, in the isolation of non-relatedness. It is ultimate in use and function; it does not claim to be ultimate because of an absolute "inherent nature" making it sacrosanct, a transcendent object of worship.[2]

Like knowledge, values are contextual. They are part of a process, of a technology. Outside their structure, they become meaningless or arbitrary. To be sure, techniques can be overplayed: "Americanism" in the bad sense, that in which gadgets become a compensation for refinement and the bourgeois virtues of successful manipulation are elevated above all, is a result. But that worship is precisely the thing that Dewey deplores. It comes from consecrating a methodology, from making it an end-in-itself; whereas an end-in-view, in a context or situation, functions as a plan of operation that helps to overcome a difficulty. There is nothing irretrievable about the "materialism" and crassness that is alleged to follow from the technological emphasis. In fact, the concentration on methods is itself a point of promise, since, although it can be and has been overdone, it constitutes a powerful prophylactic against the obstinate and pathological concern with human values that are unapproachably aloof.

It would appear, therefore, that to decide between values, between man's long-time cultural preferences, requires the premise that such choices are functions of a technology, that they are situational, not remote or disinfected. A further requirement seems to be that ethics, with its peculiar concern for values, must be fitted in with other aspects of a culture, particularly with those social and biological enterprises which trace the develop-

2. Quoted from *The Philosophy of John Dewey* (The Library of Living Philosophers, Vol. I), p. 594 [*Later Works* 14:77].

ment of behavior patterns. Finally, a much more significant assumption is that value decision rests upon honest discrimination, that acceptance of just "any old" culture is a sign of flaccidity rather than of sophistication. The argument here has been to suggest that the technology which incorporates experimentalist knowing and control must set the norm for modern man.

Appendix 8
Critique of Naturalism
By Wilmon Henry Sheldon

Naturalism is not a new name in philosophy. And like some other words, it may have changed its meaning. Does it mean the same for the 1944 school of naturalism as it meant in James Ward's *Naturalism and Agnosticism,* first edition 1899? Or even in Pratt's *Naturalism* of 1939? Probably not. But the important meaning for us today is the one given it by the 1944 group who so dub their world-view. Their use of the term is now the influential one. For they have emerged in force from the welter of revolts against idealism and dualism in the early 1900's and they form a definite school or type in the philosophic arena. They are full of zeal and energy for the gospel they proclaim as the one thing needful to bring philosophy down out of the clouds (or up out of the bogs). As we should expect, their membership is largely of the younger, more progressive thinkers. Fifteen disciples—or leaders—have lately issued a symposium, *Naturalism and the Human Spirit*[1] (the get-together spirit of our time launches reforms in symposia). In virtue, then, of the vigor and influence of this young school, we take them as the proper exponents of naturalism's meaning. What is that meaning?

To judge it fairly, the obvious course is to read out their written words. Now in the case of an old school, which has had centuries to reflect on what its words might imply or suggest, those words will probably commit their users to just about what the school means to stand for, no more and no less. In the case of a younger school, a school which has but recently come to self-consciousness, this is less likely to be so. A young school believes

1. New York, Columbia University Press, 1944. Quotations will be from this book unless otherwise stated [for Dewey's contribution, see this volume, pp. 46–62; bracketed page numbers refer to this volume].

[First published in *Journal of Philosophy* 42 (10 May 1945): 252–70. For a reply by Dewey, Sidney Hook, and Ernest Nagel, see pp. 109–26.]

that it is stressing a new perspective on the world, or perhaps an old perspective whose value it is the first to realize. It sees in this perspective a way out of the age-long deadlocks of philosophy, a way that will ensure established results on which all philosophers will agree. To emphasize the importance of its discovery, it is likely to coin some new term or phrase for that discovery, or at least to use some old one in a new sense. So we find the names "*phenomenology*," "*logical empiricism*"; and so we find the naturalist of today appropriating the old words "nature" and "scientific method" to his novel uses. But of course "nature," being an old word, has had many meanings: which of these, if any, does he keep, or what new meanings does he bring in? And the like of "scientific method," though to a lesser degree, the phrase being more modern. A plant bedded in bad soil we uproot and put in better ground, but we are likely to bring some of the old dirt unnoticed with the roots. Might this be true of these two favorite terms of the naturalist? Perhaps the reformers are so eager to leave the old beds that they don't notice how much of the dirt they have brought along. Not seldom in the history of philosophy have seemingly novel ideas been found to be old ones under a new name. As Costello prudently remarks, "We must take care lest our suppressed illusions come back to plague us in altered guise, like grinning fiends from out the Freudian deep" (p. 296). And Pratt had said of his book *Naturalism:*[2] "My little book I consider a defense of Naturalism against its most dangerous enemies, the majority of whom are usually found in the ranks of the 'naturalists.'" What then do the symposiasts we are to examine *really* stand for? As we all know, they *say* they stand for the study of nature by scientific method. But what do they mean by nature and by scientific method? To what does their usage of these words commit them?

I now give point to the inquiry by a specific accusation. Namely, their usage of said words in the contexts of the book shows them to be materialists. Their naturalism is just materialism over again under a softer name. They claim to have superseded that perennial type of metaphysic; I believe they slip back into the same old rut. True, they are careful to *define* materialism in such a way as not to be accused of it; but to all intents and purposes they stand

2. New Haven, Yale University Press, 1939. Preface, pp. ix–x.

for the same sort of thing that materialists have always stood for. Thus they do not, as they claim to do, settle the old conflict between idealism and materialism (or for that matter, between scholasticism and process-metaphysic); they perpetuate the conflict by taking sides.

The accusation is at least suggested by what Hook, one of the group, had already said of materialism: "Its differences with idealism were . . . over the massive issue . . . of naturalism and supernaturalism."[3] Certainly materialism and naturalism are alike in their *horror supernaturae*. Certainly some of these naturalists have inveighed mightily against both the idealist and the Thomist traditions, defenders of non-material being. But of course this only gives ground for suspicion. And the naturalists have most emphatically denied that they are materialists. Attend then to the way in which they deny it.

The protagonist Dewey says "he [the naturalist] is aware that since 'matter' and 'materialism' acquired their significance in contrast with something called 'spirit' and 'spiritualism,' the fact that naturalism has no place for the latter also deprives the former epithets of all significance in philosophy" (p. 3 [48]). That is, the naturalist considers "matter" to be, shall we say, a real entity *only* in contrast with spirit or mind taken as another and a *separate* entity. And by this token naturalism, discarding such opposed entities, is on a higher plane, above the opposition between materialism and idealism, dualism and monism, etc.

Now let us at once admit that naturalism is not materialism in the sense of believing in matter as a fixed being, a mindless bit of solid stuff, which would be meaningless unless there were, or appeared to be, minds to be contrasted with it. But we are not talking of materialism in that sense. I spoke of materialism "to all intents and purposes"; I was speaking in instrumentalist terms. Surely the naturalists are just the ones who ought to conceive the issue in such terms. What then *should* we mean by materialism? To answer the question, note this: what makes materialism *vs.* idealism a significant issue for us men is the question: are the states and events we call conscious or mental or spiritual *wholly* at the beck and call of the states and processes we call physical? If they are, you are going to order your life in a very different way

3. *Journal of Philosophy,* Vol. XLI (1944), p. 546.

from the way you would order it if they are not. Materialism, the only sort of materialism that *matters,* declares they are. As Donald Williams, a confessed materialist, puts it: "in the entire universe, including the knowing mind itself, there is nothing which could not be destroyed (or repaired) by a spatio-temporal redistribution of its components." [4] And Williams argues for materialism thus: "Even the idealist or the dualist, when he actually wants to understand or control something, makes use of the spatio-temporal schema." [5] For it is understanding and consequent control of goods that we men want; and once more, surely the naturalist of all people should admit this, for his instrumental philosophy seeks above all things the means of controlling nature for the securing of man's highest values. So the real issue is: can the states or processes we call mental or spiritual exercise a control over those we call physical, to some degree independent of any spatio-temporal redistributions; or, if we really understood what is going on when minds seem to control bodies, should we see that the spatio-temporal redistributions are the sole factors? To accept the latter is to be a materialist. Other definitions ignore the issue. A genuine materialism will, of course, admit that as things are now, when we understand so little of the electrical and radiant energies that govern the nervous system, we have to use the rough-and-ready method of influencing our fellows by communicating ideas (through physical means only, be it noted). But he will insist that an idea is but a potential or tentative muscular response, and the only way to be sure it will work out into the proper deed is to know with precise scientific knowledge the physical laws that rule the behavior of the organism. For after all, what matters about matter is what matter does: what it does *to* us and what we can make it do *for* us. James the starter of pragmatism saw this, but it has been forgotten. So, when I accuse the naturalists of materialism, I mean a working materialism, a philosophy that goes beyond pure theory to set up a way of life. And I say that their program and method leads to or implies that in the last analysis all processes in the known universe, mental, spiritual, vital, or what not, are wholly at the beck and call of the processes we have agreed to call physical, and therefore the only

4. *Philosophical Review,* Vol. LIII (1944), p. 418.
5. *Ibid.,* p. 438.

reliable way of control over nature—and over other men—is secured by knowledge of spatio-temporal distributions. That is the
only materialism that counts, that has bearing on human life and
the prospects of man's future.

You may, as a materialist, believe in graded levels—inorganic,
plant, animal, man, none of which can be wholly described in
terms of the levels below it. You may define thought as some
queer synthesis of sensa, which synthesis is not itself a sensum
(so, for instance, R. W. Sellars). On the other hand, you may believe each level can be fully defined in terms of a lower level. In
either case you may remain a materialist. The crucial point is
whether the *behavior* of the higher (mental) level can be *predicted* and therefore *controlled* surely and accurately from a
knowledge of the lower. It is power that counts, it is power that
the naturalist hopes by his scientific method to gain: power to
ensure the arrival of things on the higher level by proper "redistribution" of things on the lower. The question of logical re-
ducibility is beside the point. What does it amount to, whether
the beautiful contrast of red and black is reducible to the natures
of the red and the black or whether the relation is irreducible to
its terms—so long as we can *get* the relation by placing the colors side by side? We find the naturalistic textbook of Randall and
Buchler[6] laying great stress on the fallacy of reductionism, committed as they say by materialism. But the point is irrelevant,
merely verbal. In fact, a nest of verbal conflicts has grown around
the pivotal point at issue—as Williams has shown in the paper
above mentioned (pp. 424 ff.). Is the materialist a nominalist or
realist in metaphysics, a subjectivist or realist or objective relativist in epistemology; can he substitute the term "experience"
for the terms "mind" and "body" alike, etc., etc.? It is surprising
enough that the new naturalists haven't taken their own instrumentalism seriously here. In particular note what Hook says in
his discussion with Sellars about materialism.[7] Hook finds materialism wrong because "the form or shape of matter is not material, the organization of material particles is not another particle,
a relation between events is not an event." Well, on that showing

6. John H. Randall, Jr., and Justus Buchler, *Philosophy: An Introduction.* New
   York, Barnes and Noble, 1942.
7. *Journal of Philosophy,* Vol. XLI (1944), p. 546.

there never lived a materialist. Even Democritus would not have said that the velocity of an atom was an atom. A Frenchman isn't a Frenchman, for his hair is black! So the naturalist escapes the *name* of materialism by identifying materialism with one side of some irrelevant issue and denying that side. They all seem to sense bad odor in the name. But when it comes to the real test, to what should be their own test, the consequences of their program and platform, I say they are materialists. And now to draw the evidence from what they have written.

Dewey, the acknowledged leader, says: "the naturalist is one who has respect for the conclusion[s] of natural science" (p. 2 [48]). This statement, we suppose, is not meant to be a final definition; only an indicator. It raises questions. How much does the term "natural science" include? Does it include introspective psychology? Here the outsider reflects that the natural sciences which have given well established results, genuine conclusions, are those that deal with physical facts only: physics, chemistry, astronomy, biology, geology. Even these have some undecided points, as all know; but so far as there are decisive conclusions, they are conclusions about facts, processes, laws, which *so far as treated in those sciences have only physical traits*. Take the case of anthropology. This science gives unquestionable results when it tells us what Indians, Negritos, etc., actually do in the body: they meet, they bow, they chant, burn sticks, carve bowls, and so on. When it comes to the question, what their ceremonies mean to us or to them, indecision comes in. The like with sociology, political science, history, and introspective psychology. These sciences haven't got sure conclusions in what we call the mental aspect, that aspect which makes them interesting and valuable to mankind. Like the philosophies, they differ among themselves. Ergo, physical sciences, any sciences so far as they are physical, are the only ones whose conclusions the naturalist should respect. Physical nature is the only nature accessible to sure, or reasonably sure, knowledge about the world. Whatever is to be explained, then, must be explained in physical terms; no other kind of explanation is properly verifiable. True, the naturalists don't want to be dogmatic; they wouldn't say "no other kind could ever possibly be justified." But ought they not to say "from all the evidence we have so far had in regard to the sciences, the physical sciences seem to be the sole purveyors of established truth"? I submit, this is the obvious suggestion from the words of Dewey, even if it is not strictly what he meant.

But doubtless he meant something more. We know well that for him and for the other naturalists it is not so much the conclusions of science that they stress, as the method. That is for them all-important, the *sine qua non*, the one thing needful. Randall, summing up at the end of the book, says that naturalism is "an attitude and temper: it is essentially a philosophic method and a program" (p. 374). And how often has Dewey urged that we apply scientific *method*—experiment, verification—to our social and moral problems: "application of scientific methods of inquiry in the field of human social subject matter" (p. 3 [48]). So let us now turn about from conclusion to method, treating naturalism as a method rather than a body of results. What then does the naturalist's adoration of scientific method commit him to affirm about the world?

For surely one's method indicates his view of the thing investigated. Men don't shoot forth methods *in vacuo;* method is not independent of subject-matter. We don't use the same method to persuade a child as a man; we use a telescope to see stars, not to dissect the seeds of a plant. If a certain method is advocated, the advocate divulges his view of the probable nature of the facts to be studied. No mere methodology: a method envisages, however tentatively, a metaphysic.

Now, I don't know of any standard analysis of scientific method in the naturalist camp. We take for granted experiment and verification by observation; but that leaves us rather in the air. Does the mystic verify the Divine being by direct observation? Can the introspective psychologist experiment with private minds? To find the answer to such specific questions, all we can do is to pick out statements from the present volume, hoping not to misrepresent the writers' meaning. Most of those that I have found are pretty general and vague, while the more definite point decidedly towards materialism. Thus Lamprecht says "in this essay 'naturalism' means a philosophical position, empirical in method, that regards everything that exists or occurs to be conditioned in its existence or occurrence by causal factors within one all-encompassing system of nature" (p. 18). This throws little light on the meaning of the method; "empirical" is claimed by introspective and behaviorist psychologists alike, and explaining by causal factors is common property—except so far as physics now employs chance. Nor can we learn anything about the method from the phrase "all-encompassing system of nature"; does it include only the physical world? Or does it include whatever one might think he has good reason for believing real—e.g., Deity, angels, etc.? More on that question later, when we ask what "nature" means; just now the method only. Hook also mentions method: he defines naturalism as "the wholehearted acceptance of scientific method as the only reliable way of reaching truths about the world of nature, society, and man" (p. 45). Elsewhere Hook says, "There have been many varieties of thought that have gone by the name of materialism and naturalism in the history of philosophy. . . . What is common to them is not a theory of stuff or the constitution of matter or a theory of knowledge or a system of ontology, but the belief that valid knowledge is knowledge warranted by scientific method and the confidence that the application of scientific method (not necessarily the methods and techniques of physics as a special discipline) to all fields of experience, will enlarge our understanding or increase our control."[8] This sounds as if there may be good scientific method in such fields as sociology, politics, or ethics. But alas! it doesn't tell us what that method is. Come to another statement. Edel says: "Reliance on scientific method, together with an appreciation of the primacy of matter and the pervasiveness of change, I take to be the central points of naturalism as a philosophical outlook" (p. 65). "Primacy of matter" sounds materialistic but the context leaves one in doubt whether "matter" may mean only "subject-matter." Anyway, we are not told what scientific method is. Dewey makes a less indefinite pronouncement when he speaks of "scientific method, which after all is but systematic, extensive, and carefully controlled use of alert and unprejudiced observation and experimentation in collecting, arranging, and testing evidence" (p. 12 [57]). But we want to know, for instance, whether or not introspection is good evidence and how evidence is tested. Miss Lavine in fact seems to regard scientific method as a variable affair. She says "surely the growth of the fields of history of science, social anthropology, [etc.] . . . have already cast the gravest suspicion upon the notion of an unconditioned scientific method" (p. 207). To this writer, if I understand her, scientific method is a type of response to the social needs of the day, and as those needs vary from one generation to another, so scientific method may be expected to vary. If that is so, we can hardly look for a cut-and-dried definition of it as the one perennial deliverer of mankind from philosophic bungling—even though the naturalists all feel it to be such. Let us then look only for what the school takes it to mean for the present. After all, that is enough for our purpose. Nagel makes a more definite statement: "perhaps the sole bond uniting all varieties of naturalists is that temper of mind which seeks to understand the flux of events in terms of the behaviors of identifiable bodies" (p. 211). And, of course, this is meat to the materialist, for we presume that Nagel is talking about scientific method. From even so thorough an analyst as Dennes, on the other hand, we get no certain note. He says: "There is for naturalism no knowledge except that of the type ordinarily called scientific. But such knowledge cannot be said to be restricted by its method to any limited field . . . to the exclusion, let us say, of the processes called history, and the fine arts. For whether the question is about forces 'within the atom' or . . . Beethoven's Second Rasumowski Quartette . . . there is no serious way to approach controlled hypotheses . . . except by inspection of the relevant evidence and by inductive inference from it" (quoted with approval by Randall, p. 359). If he would only tell us of what sort is the relevant evidence—whether, for instance, we can trust introspective reports or must use behaviorist methods! It is most unfortunate that these naturalist writings have many passages like this one. Dennes says also, speaking of naturalism's respect for scientific method and rejection of the supernatural, "Its spirit is in these respects very close to the spirit of traditional and more specifically materialistic naturalism. . . . But contemporary naturalism recognizes much more clearly than did the tradition from which it stems that its distinction from other philosophical positions lies in the postulates and procedures which it criticizes and rejects rather than in any positive tenets of its own about the cosmos" (quoted by Randall, p. 359). Yes, we know how it rejects the supernatural. But what positively does it do with the natural? We see plainly that it doesn't want to be called materialist. We see also that when it says something specific and positive about its method, it *actually* looks toward the kind of procedure found in the *purely physical* sciences. Take this statement by Dewey in regard to observation: "the nature of observation . . . is rarely discussed in its own terms—the terms, that is, of the procedures employed by inquirers in astronomical observatories; in chemical, physical, and biological laboratories; in the examinations conducted by physicians; and in what is done in field excursions of botanists and zoölogists" (p. 4 [49]). Note that the sciences mentioned are concerned *only* with physical subject-matter. And so we are not surprised when Larrabee says of naturalism in America, "Far more important than any theory has been the practical materialism of Thomas Jefferson's conviction that 'the business of life is with matter'" (p. 320).

But probably the best test of what scientific method means will be found in the naturalist's treatment of mind and consciousness: a specific problem and at the same time a central one. Turn then to what Krikorian says in his contribution, "A Naturalistic View of Mind." Here we find very definite commitments. Many passages might be quoted; we select a few that show a frank behaviorism. "The naturalistic approach to mind is the experimental approach. This means that mind must be analyzed as behavior, since behavior is the only aspect of mind which is open to experimental examination" (p. 252). "Mind may be defined as control of behavior by anticipation" (p. 252). "The futuristic reference of mind, however, need not be interpreted primarily in introspective terms" (p. 254). "Anticipatory response may have its introspective aspect, yet *introspection itself, as will be shown, may be behavioristically described*" (p. 254, italics mine). Of thought he says: "McDougall demands a psychic entity . . . to perform the activity of reasoning. But why postulate an unverifiable psychic entity for this activity? As Lloyd Morgan puts it, 'May not the relating activity, so called, be just as reasonably assigned to the physiological process in the cortex and the organization as a whole?'" (pp. 257–258). Again, referring to McDougall: "But for a naturalist the analysis of conation does not demand 'purely psychical facts.' Conation . . . has a bodily basis. Conative action as behavior is open to investigation" (p. 259). Again: "Desires are not unobservable entities in some inaccessible realm; they are a certain type of observable behavior. . . . The degree of one's hunger may be verified by the amount of food one eats; the degree of weariness may be determined by the number of hours one sleeps; and the degree of one's pain may be determined by the amount of anodyne one takes" (p. 268). Of mind as an individual personal unit: "Structurally the unity is the biological organism; behaviorally the unity is the integrated action" (p. 269).

Mind is one big bone of contention between idealist and materialist. The naturalist claims to have risen above the quarrel, to a plane where idealism and materialism alike disappear. Has he? His maxim is scientific method. Scientific method demands experiment and observation confirmable by fellow men. Mental states or processes, just in so far as they are not physical, not "behavior," are not open to such observation. He says they are "inaccessible." But of course they are accessible to their owner; it is only to fellow men, to the public, that they are inaccessible. Scientific method thus means, to the naturalist, that observation of the non-public has no sense nor meaning. Publicity is the test; the private and hidden is ruled out of court. And the only publicly observable things are the physical things. Thus the naturalist, when he investigates what men call *mental* affairs, has to *treat* them as bodily or physical affairs. And that is what materialism really amounts to; a working, not a merely verbal, materialism. When, then, it comes to a specific issue, to the issue fought over through the ages between idealist or spiritualist or dualist and materialist, he definitely takes sides with the materialist. That is the commitment to which "scientific method" forces him. So much for the naturalist's usage of that term.

Turn now to the other word, so central to his creed, the word "nature." What does he mean by it? We may best take up the question in two aspects: what nature as he understands it is not, what it definitely excludes, and what it is, what it includes. We begin with the negative aspect: what nature is not.

Well, to be sure, nature is not the supernatural. What then is meant by supernatural? What are typical instances of the supernatural? Says Hook, "The existence of God, immortality, disembodied spirits, cosmic purpose and design, as these have been customarily interpreted by the great institutional religions, are denied by naturalists for the same generic reasons that they deny the existence of fairies, elves, and leprechauns" (p. 45). As the next paragraph begins, "I do not see that anything is gained by blinking the fact that the naturalist denies the existence of supernatural powers" (p. 45), we may fairly presume that "supernatural" would be applied by him to the terms "God," etc., above mentioned. Randall in his summary says, "There is no room for any Supernatural in naturalism—no supernatural or transcendental God and no personal survival after death" (p. 358). So far the objects of Christianity or other religion; but the list is longer. It includes also certain alleged moral principles. Dewey speaks of "the professedly nonsupernatural philosopher who is antinaturalist" and "never ceases to dwell upon . . . the morally seductive character of natural impulse and desire"; also "the doctrine that the truly moral factors in human relations are superimposed from a spiritual non-natural source and authority" (p. 2 [47]). These instances probably illustrate the supernatural, since Dewey calls the thinkers "professedly" non-supernatural, as if they were *really* supernaturalists. He goes on: "in addition to frank supernaturalism there are philosophers who claim to rest their extra- (if not super-) naturalism upon a higher faculty of Reason or Intuition, not upon a special divine revelation. While I am personally convinced that their philosophy can be understood only as a historical heritage from frank supernaturalism . . ." (p. 2 [47]; we need quote no further). If I mistake not, Kant, Fichte, and Hegel would illustrate the last set. So we must add to the religious group the moral intuitionists and the rationalist idealists. Dewey seems to regard all three as enemies of naturalism; probably so would Hook. What then characterizes these enemies, making them so hostile? "Antinaturalism," says Dewey, "has operated to prevent the application of scientific methods of inquiry in the field of human social subject matter" (p. 3 [48]). There lies its poison: the exclusion of scientific method. It would seem to be precisely that exclusion which characterizes supernaturalism or antinaturalism. I find in the present volume no more positive identification than this. Result so far: naturalism stands for scientific method; whatever rules out scientific method—that is the supernatural. We are back where we were. "Nature" means that which is open to scientific method. Scientific method is all we have got.

So far only the negative aspect of "nature." But surely the term must have some positive distinctive trait. Surely naturalism is more than the vicious-circle imperative—"investigate by scientific method that which can be investigated by scientific method." Do the right because it is right to do the right! What *is* right?

How can we identify the things that make up nature, that we may investigate them and consign the rest to oblivion?

Randall says, "There is no 'realm' to which the methods for dealing with Nature cannot be extended. This insistence on the universal and unrestricted application of 'scientific method' is a theme pervading every one of these essays" (p. 358). And he had already said, "naturalism, in the sense in which it is maintained in this volume, can be defined negatively as the refusal to take 'nature' or 'the natural' as a term of distinction. . . . For present-day naturalists 'Nature' serves rather as the all-inclusive category, corresponding to the role played by 'Being' in Greek thought, or by 'Reality' for the idealists. In this sense, as Mr. Dennes recognizes, naturalism, in becoming all-inclusive, ceases to be a distinctive 'ism.' It regards as 'natural' whatever man encounters in whatever way—Nature, as Mr. Costello puts it, is a collective name for 'quite a mess of miscellaneous stuff'" (pp. 357–358). But now consider: "whatever man encounters in *whatever* way" would include "fairies, elves, and leprechauns," immortal souls, Thomistic hierarchies of angels, the Perfect First Cause of the universe, just as much as the social trends of the present age or the law of inverse squares in electrical forces. Does naturalism make any choice between these? Randall is well aware of the danger of being too inclusive, and goes on to say: "But while naturalism . . . holds that everything encountered by men has some natural status in Nature, this does not mean that naturalism can absorb all the philosophic theories of what man encounters and in that sense cease to be a distinctive position" (p. 358). "Naturalism thus merges in the generic activity of philosophy as critical interpretation—the examination of the status of all these varieties of 'stuff' in Nature. . . . Positively, naturalism can be defined as the continuity of analysis—as the application of what all the contributors call 'scientific methods' to the critical interpretation and analysis of every field" (p. 358). Shall we put it this way then: Nature means everything; apply scientific method to everything and you will find out what is sham and what is reality, what is genuine value and what is shoddy. Supernature in the sense of that to which we can't apply scientific method, simply is not. That, I think, is Randall's meaning when he says that naturalism does not absorb all the *philosophical theories* of what man encounters. Some of those theories, the supernaturalist ones, are decidedly wrong, and must be thrown out. There *is* nothing supernatural. To requote: "There is no room for any Supernatural in naturalism—no supernatural or transcendental God and no personal survival after death" (p. 358). And, I take it, the reason why he says this is that as naturalist he believes those two concepts named *have been* investigated and scientific method has found no way of testing, no opening for itself. Thus once more the term "nature" gets whatever definite meaning it has from its working partner, scientific method. The situation is ironically close to the Thomist's matter-form couple: nature the passive matter for investigation gets its specific character by the operation of the active principle or form, the said method. Ironical but not irenical alas! For the naturalist takes the Thomist to be his worst enemy.

Just scientific method then—that is all we can put our hands on. The method itself determines what is fit to be investigated, what is hopeless of investigation. The creed has no longer two articles: nature and method. It has only one: method. Nature, like the scholastic primary matter, is mere potentiality, something that may be subjected to scientific method. And this interpretation is confirmed by a statement made in Randall and Buchler's decidedly naturalistic textbook: "Naturalism excludes what is not scientifically investigable, and calls the domain of possible investigation 'nature'" (p. 183).

Can this one-point interpretation be right? I submit additional evidence. A reader, following the book from the start, soon begins to wonder why the above terms are not carefully defined, especially by *this* young group, usually so insistent on scientific precision. He continues puzzled till he reaches page 121, Schneider's article, a deliberate attempt to define the term "nature." What then does the reader find? Schneider, after dismissing two possible definitions which do not here concern us, proposes a third which he is minded to adopt: nature in the sense of the essence of a thing, in contrast with what is accidental to it. Thus we say—my example only—the nature of man is to think, but whether he thinks about the moon or the table is more or less accidental. This sounds like the Aristotelian-Thomist view, and in fact Schneider says, "I am consciously reverting to this ancient ontology, because I think I see the blunders of its corrupted, medieval guise and the folly of its modern repudiation" (p. 125) (extremes again meet). But for us now the important point is: he takes a thing's nature to mean what it normally is, what it ought to be. A man is what he ought to be when he is true to the human nature he embodies. Nature, says Schneider, "is normative. The real is the genuine. Similarly, 'to be true to one's nature' is not a foolish phrase, though it is redundant. To be one's natural self is to be true, healthy, sound, reliable" (p. 124). "Nature is a norm, but neither a statistical norm nor an ideal" (p. 125). "Natural love is not average love but normal, healthy love" (*ibid.*). "'Natural' means more than probable" (*ibid.*). ". . . it is possible to identify a normal or healthy organism without calculating averages. A normal automobile is a working machine" (pp. 125–126). "That is natural which works" (p. 126). And finally, though he admits that the view is liable to caricature, he says, "I prefer it to the idealist's identification of the real with the ideal, to the orthodox naturalist's belief that all things are equally natural, and to the orthodox empiricist's belief that the probable is natural" (*ibid.*). Thus, unlike the others of this group, he has proposed a specific meaning for "nature" akin to an old "supernaturalist" meaning and in his own words to be preferred "to the orthodox naturalist's belief that all things are equally natural" (*ibid.*). Is this a serious break with the view of "nature" which we got from Randall's words? Randall says of Schneider's view: "Mr. Schneider's suggestive proposal to revive the traditional normative usage of 'nature' and 'the natural' . . . has much to recommend it. . . . Whether Mr. Schneider would go so far as to advocate 'Nature (loud cheers!)' is left unanswered. But as he admits, this normative usage is hardly established in present-day naturalistic thinking, and aside from his paper none of the essays in this volume even suggests it. Some, like Mr. Costello's, seem definitely hostile to the idea" (p. 357, footnote). I think we should heed these words. They throw a definite light on the indefinite meaning of "nature." When one of the group proposes a positive distinctive concept, it is found in Randall's eminently judicious summary to be somewhat at outs with the general understanding of the term. What then is left for us but to see "nature" as just and only any material awaiting approval or condemnation at the hands of scientific method? In sum then, scientific method is the be-all and end-all (or begin-all) of present-day naturalism, the one thing needful, the solver of the great deadlocks of past philosophy, the guarantee of fertile discoveries in the future. As Randall affirms, naturalism "now possesses in great detail a knowledge of the structures or ways of behaving of things, and the elaborate set of techniques and standards of inquiry and verification that constitute the scientific enterprise, the most potent instrument the wit of man has yet devised for analysis and control" (p. 374). The sentence is an apotheosis of science; for the "great detail" of our "knowledge of the structures," etc., has been contributed by the natural sciences, not by philosophy. Let us then stress the second part: "the elaborate set of techniques . . . the scientific enterprise, the most potent instrument," and so on.

True enough, this seems to have been denied elsewhere, by Randall or by the co-author Buchler of the textbook mentioned above. Defining the naturalist's attitude toward scientific method, that book says "nor does it elevate scientific method to the status of a universal panacea. The reason is, first, that it accepts noncognitive experience as well as cognitive—art and religion besides science—as contributing to a world-perspective" (p. 227). But I find this assertion merely verbal. When it comes to the point of testing some alleged religious or artistic insight—for, of course, these would not be accepted uncritically—the test will follow behavioristic methods. Is that picture over there really beautiful? You say yes. I happen to doubt that you really feel it so. I apply suitable physical apparatus to your glandular and muscular responses and find that they are not the responses characteristic of a man's appreciation of beauty. You have deceived yourself. Your supposed artistic insight or experience isn't there. In fact the scientific, the behaviorist method gives the only possible way of being sure that a person *has* an artistic or religious experience. We can't take his word for it: that is a report about something merely private, outside the realm of verifiable truth. If only Randall and Buchler had named some particular artistic or religious contribution to a world-perspective, which they would credit as true beyond a reasonable doubt, needing no scientific confirmation! I have grave doubt that they could. At any rate the writers of *our* symposium have definitely and decidedly elevated scientific method "to the status of a universal panacea." They must; there isn't anything else in their kit-bag.

So let us rest with this account of naturalism's creed. And now return to the charge: the creed drives one into materialism. The reason—to repeat—is this. Whatever else scientific method means, it means that verification involves public confirmation, publicity, the witness of other men. The merely private is the un-verifiable. Now, frankly, the only group of phenomena that is open to the witness of many is the physical group. The behaviorists in psychology have seen this: as C. L. Hull remarks, they don't argue and try to persuade as philosophers do, but simply record facts, physical facts wherein there is no disagreement. And Krikorian the naturalist has seen it, as we have quoted above. Not all the naturalists do see it; but I can find no escape from it in their creed. Even if, as perhaps a last resort, they admit the need of social witness but insist that there is a non-physical or inner aspect in the events we call mental—if they admit that all reality must be embodied but declare that the embodiment isn't the whole of it—even then they can't prove their claim by scientific method unless they can get this inner aspect socially confirmed—which means publicly exhibited, as a physical fact. The well-known societarian emphasis of our naturalists is right in line with their veneration for scientific method. Both drive straight into materialism, the doctrine that all verified truth is of physical events and properties alone.

If they have demonstrated beyond reasonable doubt that the scientific is the only permissible method, they have to the same degree demonstrated that materialism is the only true metaphysic. If they have only assumed the validity of the method as the most promising yet found, then they have only assumed the truth of materialism as the most probable metaphysic. In either case, so far as they are philosophers at all, they are materialists in the working sense of the term. And since there do persist today other types of philosophy which deny the all-sufficiency of scientific method—to wit, Thomism, idealism, mind-body dualism, mysticism, and so on—the naturalists are once more back on the partisan level. Whether right or wrong, they actually renounce the synthetic attitude which Dewey's words seemed to imply.

Now for a personal "Concluding Unscientific Postscript."

If you naturalists believe you have done something positive other than a gesture of welcome to a materialist metaphysic, I address you as follows. And please note that I raise no objection to the instrumentalism that guides you, or to your doctrine of the ubiquity of process. On the contrary, your instrumentalism and your process-perspective seem to me indispensable contributions to philosophy. And what I say is said from the instrumental point of view.

For, on that platform, the merit of a method is to be tested by its results. You have given no new results in philosophy; you point only to the results gotten by the physical sciences. If you think philosophy is anything besides these sciences, you should, on your own showing, if you want us to believe your method is right, experiment with it to see if it gives knowledge *in addition* to what they give: something more than physics, to wit, metaphysics. Not one of you has even tried for this. You have, of course, an implicit metaphysic; every methodist has. But you are apparently afraid to bring it into the open and defend it. That being so, all you can do, as far as we outsiders are concerned, is to ask us to suspend judgment. Your own creed tells you not to believe anything till it is experimentally confirmed. How can you expect us to believe you have the right method for *philosophy* until you show us that it succeeds in giving us objective truth comparable with that of the sciences, truth on which the philosophic experts agree? Will you then be content if the rest of us say: yes, you may have a promising method for philosophy, but we can't make any decision about it till you have used it to give new and specific information about reality? I fear you will not— I fear that you claim to have proved the rightness of your method in philosophy beforehand; an *a priori* claim you should be the last to make.

You may reply: but scientific method *has* been tested, it *has* given proved results, and no other known method has; so by all that's likely we ought to use it in philosophy. What a circle! Scientific method has succeeded with physical things. Granted. So, you say, try it on non-physical things—values, thoughts, angels, immortal souls, and so on. You find it won't apply to them—so they aren't real. As if to say: here is something we are going to apply to all reality, so what it doesn't apply to we shall simply call unreality. Or do you fall back on agreement? The physical sciences are the only ones that give universally accepted results? Of course, if agreement is our only aim, we had better stick to the easier problems of the material world. But are you sure there isn't any reality, any black cat in that dark room of the supernatural? *You* may feel sure, but as far as agreement goes, the majority of philosophers, even in our scientific age, are against you. That doesn't lessen your conviction, does it? Apparently agreement doesn't matter so much. And, after all, as the majority *are* against you—not the majority of an uneducated rabble either— doesn't that suggest that you search out some other way of getting agreement than the scientific way? For of course we all want agreement, but we don't want it at too heavy a cost—at the cost of many views that seem to have shown a survival value for man. By all that's likely, if you are going to appeal to that, your exclusive emphasis on scientific method will only prolong dissension in philosophy. Certainly you can't claim to have proved its rightness for a survey of "whatever man encounters in whatever way."

On the other hand you may deny to philosophy any objective truth peculiar to itself, comparable to the scientific results. You may decide that philosophy is nothing but methodology of science. If so, there will be very little for you as philosophers to do in writing and teaching; the scientists know their own methods better than you do and you should become a physicist or biologist or other particular scientist in order to have weight as a methodologist. If I understand Dewey, he would have philosophers go into sociology or social ethics, in the naturalistic way—that way would be the greatest hope for the future of humankind. But as to teaching philosophy in our universities, in a separate Department, you might continue for a few years until you have got the fundamentals of scientific method pretty well cleared up—but after that what? You might give courses in the history of philosophy to show how false most of the systems are—not a very inspiring educational program. About all you could be is a watchdog of science, barking away any supernaturalist suggestions, or as Sellars has put it "a hanger-on of the various sciences with the courtier-like office of clapping hands."[9] But surely your students, if they heed your teaching, will not themselves go into philosophy; they will apply scientific method in some science or other. For what mind of sizable proportions would wish to devote his life to denouncing the unscientific?

But whatever you do, the fact remains—one more of the ironies of poor human nature—that you instrumental naturalists,

9. *Journal of Philosophy*, Vol. XLI (1944), p. 693.

insisting that all truth must be experimentally tested, have performed no experiments of your own, unless perhaps Dewey's experiments in education. And as to the results of these, opinion is today as divided as it is between idealism and materialism, between Thomism and pragmatism, or any other of philosophy's fighting couples.

The naturalist reform of philosophy rightly urges us to accept only what is established by rigid scientific method, *in the domain of things to which that method is applicable.* But there may be truth available to other methods; through the centuries the majority of philosophers have thought so, and still think so. Such truth may pertain to the hidden private mind of man, to the supernatural, even to certain irrational factors in the world. In ruling it out by an exclusive emphasis on scientific method, naturalism has left us just where we were before, in the arena of partisan conflict. It has contributed nothing new to the cause of philosophic unity or of established truth.

Appendix 9
Reply to Dewey

To the Editors of the *Journal of Philosophy:*

Professor Dewey's discussion in the *Journal of Philosophy* ("Peirce's Theory of Linguistic Signs, Thought, and Meaning," Volume XLIII, 1946, pp. 85–95) of the relation of my monograph, *Foundations of the Theory of Signs,* to Peirce's semiotic may have given to some of your readers the impression that my analysis claimed to be a presentation of Peirce's views. This was not the case. The result may be that the central problem which bothered Dewey (the problem of the relation of a behaviorally oriented semiotic to the work of such "formal logicians" as Carnap) will be missed by his focusing of attention on the historical problem of how far my views do or do not agree with those of Peirce. My monograph certainly did not deal adequately with the place of "logical analyses" in a behavioral theory of signs. I have tried to do more justice to this problem in my book, *Signs, Language, and Behavior,* which is to appear in the next few weeks.

CHARLES W. MORRIS

University of Chicago

[First published in *Journal of Philosophy* 43 (28 March 1946): 196. For Dewey's article to which this is a reply, see pp. 141–52. For Dewey's rejoinder, see pp. 331–32.]

Appendix 10
A Reply to John Dewey
By Alexander Meiklejohn

In the August issue of *Fortune* John Dewey discusses the present state of American educational theory. He is stirred to protest by what he calls "the present campaign of assault upon what is modern and new in education." So deeply and so richly has Mr. Dewey's influence gone into "the modern and the new" of our teaching that any assault so defined must be regarded by him as an attack upon the great achievements of his own career. And yet, with characteristic fearlessness and generosity, Mr. Dewey welcomes the assault. He suggests that it may be "thoroughly reactionary." But "it has to be faced and facing it will bring to light beliefs that have too long been kept in the dark." "The drawing of lines that is now going on will not only serve to clear up confusion in our educational estate but will tend to breathe life into the dead bones of philosophy."

In these words Mr. Dewey establishes a spirit in which discussion can be fruitfully carried on. But he goes even further in the attempt at mutual understanding. He frankly acknowledges a basic, though partial, agreement with his opponents. He "disagrees radically" with their reasons and "equally radically" with "the remedy which is urged." But he asserts as strongly as do they that "the present system (if it may be called a system) is so lacking in unity of aim, material, and method as to be something of a patchwork." "We agree," he says, "that we are uncertain as to where we are going, and where we want to go, and why we are doing what we do." "We agree that an overloaded and congested curriculum needs simplification." "We agree as to the absence of unity."

[First published in *Fortune* 31 (January 1945): 207–8, 210, 212, 214, 217, 219. For Dewey's article to which this is a reply, see pp. 261–75. For Dewey's rejoinder, see pp. 333–36. For further letters, see Appendix 11 and p. 337.]

Now the writing of those words is an invitation to fair and honest disputation. Mr. Dewey, with genuine Socratic irony, accepts as his own the goal at which his opponents are driving. Like them, he finds no joy in patchwork thinking or teaching. He, too, hates incoherence and planlessness. He, too, would like to know what he is doing, where he is going. The two parties in dispute have, then, a common problem. How can the curriculum be simplified? How, without losing the richness and the multiplicity of the modern and the new, can we achieve unity in our thinking and in our teaching? By defining that common issue Mr. Dewey states the problem in terms his opponent can accept. Such a formulation of the basic issue by which our current thinking about education is tormented and confused is a notable achievement, worthy of the man who makes it.

But Mr. Dewey's declaration that his opponents are wrong is quite as sharp—though, I think, not quite so clear—as his statement that they are right. They think, he tells us, that unity can be found by a study of the past. He is certain that it must be found in a study of the present. "We differ profoundly," he says, "from the belief that the evils and defects of our system spring from excessive attention to what is modern in human civilization—science, technology, contemporary social issues and problems." And he launches his attack upon the enemy with the words, "I begin then with the fact that we are now being told that a genuinely liberal education would require return to the models, patterns, and standards that were laid down in Greece some twenty-five hundred years ago, and renewed and put into practice in the best age of feudal medievalism six and seven centuries ago."

Now, as one of Mr. Dewey's opponents, I find unsatisfactory at two points this statement of my position. First, why must I choose between the study of the past and the study of the present? Why not study both? Some years ago, in the Experimental College at the University of Wisconsin, I had a free opportunity to share in the making of a new curriculum. And the line that we there followed was exactly that which, in his abstract formulation of the issue, Mr. Dewey leaves out of account. In the first of our two years we studied the life and thought of Athens in the fifth and fourth centuries B.C. In the second year we plunged ourselves and our students into the "science, technology, contemporary social issues and problems" of the U.S. in the nineteenth and twentieth centuries A.D. We adopted both the programs that Mr. Dewey now presents to us as alternative to each other.

But there is a second difficulty. Mr. Dewey suggests that a study of Greece "would require return to the models, patterns, and standards that were laid down in Greece." Why? Does the study of the past imply that we intend to imitate it? That was certainly not true in the Experimental College. It is not true in St. John's College. Both those institutions have been engaged in the attempt to cultivate, in the minds of teachers and pupils, the processes of critical intelligence. They study Homer, Plato, Euclid, Aquinas, Newton, Shakespeare, Darwin, Marx, Veblen, Freud, not because these great minds were right but in order to find out how right, and wrong, they were, in order to find out what "right" and "wrong" are. One does not, for example, study Ptolemy because he is "superior" to Copernicus. One studies him in the belief that a prior understanding of Ptolemy may contribute to a better understanding of Copernicus. And, that being true, I can find no basis whatever for the assertion that the study of the past implies the acceptance of the standards of the past as superior to our own.

At this point, however, we would do well to follow Mr. Dewey's example by stating frankly our agreement with his position as well as our disagreement with it. In a certain basic sense it is true that all education should be a study of the present. Schools and colleges are called upon to equip young people intellectually for the actual living they have to do here and now. Our pupils are individuals before whom lie ten, twenty, thirty, forty, fifty years of activity in the midst of the changing American scene. What, then, do they need to know, what methods of thinking do they need to acquire, in order that the living of those years may be well done? The justification—as well as the condemnation—of any teaching is to be found in its effect upon the subsequent daily experience of the person taught. Do they know what they are doing, why and where they are going? If so, the school, or some other agency, has achieved the purpose of education. If not, then no matter how much the pupils may know, education, for them, has failed. The goal of teaching is an understanding of the present. With respect to that statement there is, so far as I know, no disagreement whatever between Mr. Dewey and those whom he criticizes.

But there is a second question on which Mr. Dewey and his opponents do not agree. Granted that the goal of teaching is an understanding of the present, we must still ask how that goal may best be reached. And this inquiry into the method of teaching, though of course interdependent with the determination of the goal, is not identical with it. By ignoring that difference Mr. Dewey seems to me to misinterpret his opponents. Their answer to one question he takes to be an answer to another. Because of that mistake he and many of his adherents regard as reactionaries fellow teachers who are quite as ardent as themselves in the fight for democracy. The major question that now unites, as well as divides, the teachers of America is not, "Shall we go forward or backward in the struggle for freedom and equality?" The question is, "How shall we go forward?"

If we turn from Mr. Dewey's general accusation to his more detailed attacks it is, I think, essential that we select, as a proving ground for the argument, some concrete college program that is now going on and that is therefore open to firsthand observation. Mr. Dewey asserts that if a college devotes itself to a study of the past, certain consequences will follow. But it is well known that St. John's College, for a number of years, has deliberately engaged in a study of the past. Have the predicted consequences followed? If so, Mr. Dewey's argument is validated. If not, it is refuted. The question here involved is one of fact. And though the facts are, in the nature of the case, tinged with opinion, they are, I think, sufficiently objective to give warrant for the acceptance or the rejection of Mr. Dewey's contentions.

The first charge is an exceedingly serious one. If it is valid, then St. John's should be urged to reform its methods or to close its doors. Mr. Dewey tells us that those who study the past lose sight of the work of the sciences and their transforming influence in our contemporary culture. "The reactionary movement," he says, "is dangerous (or would be if it made serious headway) because it ignores and in effect denies the principle of experimental inquiry and firsthand observation that is the lifeblood of the entire advance made in the sciences—an advance so marvelous that the progress in knowledge made in uncounted previous millenniums is almost nothing in comparison." Is that charge justified? Does St. John's ignore science? Quite the contrary is true. No other liberal college in the country even approaches St. John's in the intensity and persistence of its endeavor to build up acquaintance with and understanding of the methods and results of scientific inquiry. From most of our colleges students can graduate with little or no acquaintance with work in science, with little or no realization of the fact that "experimental inquiry and firsthand observation" have created a new world in which older forms of thought and action are out of place and inefficient. But at St. John's, on the other hand, one-half of the entire time of the student is given to that task. The makers of the St. John's curriculum have seen with unusual clarity that unless one knows what science is and does, one does not understand the world or the society in which we live. They have therefore "required" that every student shall devote one-half of the entire course of study to the learning of science and of mathematics as the "language" upon which advances in scientific achievement are seen to depend. In the face of that fact Mr. Dewey's charge cannot be justified.

At this point it may be worth while to correct a popular picture of life at St. John's upon which some estimates of its work seem to be based. It is often spoken of as the college where students read "One Hundred Great Books." And the impression given by that phrase is that young, untutored American boys spend some part of their days and nights in perusing and glibly discussing the writings of the creative minds of our culture, which even our most able and sophisticated scholars find it difficult to understand. Now there are, of course, serious and fundamental questions about the direct use of the great books for teaching purposes. The St. John's plan is, I admit, startling in its audacity. I cannot, in this paper, discuss the merits of that audacity. May I simply register in passing my conviction that the direct reading in sequence of the intellectual sources of our culture is, for teaching purposes, vastly more valuable than are the secondhand expositions of those sources ordinarily provided by our colleges in textbooks and lectures and books of reference.

But the St. John's student does not merely read and discuss great books. His daily schedule is very much like that which prevails in most of our colleges. He has regular classes for which to prepare one by one. And the quantity and quality of his preparation are closely, and even savagely, tested. On the five mornings of each week from Monday to Friday there are required tutorials in mathematics, with from five to ten students present. On the same mornings are five tutorials in language. On one or two afternoons of each week there is a long session in the scientific laboratory. The seminars meet on two evenings for discussion of the great books. One evening there is a public lecture followed by a question period. The schedule consists, then, of fourteen or fifteen required meetings. It gives assurance that the studying is not irresponsibly done. From one week's end to the other it is subjected to assignments, to guidance, to correction, to close supervision and criticism.

Now it is within this working schedule that one must see the "scientific" teaching of St. John's if one wishes to determine the validity of Mr. Dewey's attack upon it. If we ask how students can be led into active participation in scientific inquiry, the St. John's answer is to be found in the well-ordered combination of three kinds of teaching: (1) four years of required mathematics, (2) four years of required laboratory practice, (3) four years of required reading of the masters of scientific discovery (approximately one-half of the great-books assignment). Each of these is studied in relation to the others. The mathematics is interpreted as the "language" of an advancing science and technology. The laboratory exhibits, step by step, the growth of knowledge of the processes of nature and the use of these for human purposes. The great books reveal, also step by step, the activities of those creative minds by which progress in knowledge has been achieved. No one who has had active touch with that plan of teaching could make the charge that a college which thus studies the past "ignores and in effect denies the principle of experimental inquiry and firsthand observation." He might question the wisdom of the teaching method that has been followed. But he could not criticize its purpose, its intention. As one who has for a number of years watched with a critical eye the self-critical development of the St. John's program, I have no hesitation in saying that its success in introducing its pupils into the scientific fields overtops its achievement in the humanities. St. John's, as I read the record, has given a fifty-fifty chance, an even division of effort, to these two sides of human understanding. But the sciences and technologies are today, in America, easier to teach than are the humanities. As Mr. Dewey has told us, the former is the field where knowledge advances by leaps and bounds. The latter is the field in which we do not know what we do, where we go, or why we are going. Euclid is not so hard to grasp as is Plato. It is easier to make weapons of war than to make a human society from which the use of those weapons would be excluded. In view of the temptations, the illusions, the vices of a contemporary American society, my fear is that St. John's has gone too far in a direction in which Mr. Dewey declares that it has not gone at all.

Our attempt to repel Mr. Dewey's first attack brings us, I fear, under the fire of his second onslaught. We have distinguished the "humanities" from the "sciences and technologies." This distinction Mr. Dewey views with strong suspicion, if not with active condemnation. There are, he thinks, lurking beneath it most of the errors of those who, fearful of the risks of an actual present, seek security in the authority of ancient beliefs and dogmas.

This distinction, which he suspects, Mr. Dewey finds to be made by his opponents in many varying forms. They separate liberal education from vocational training. They regard the humanities as spiritual, while scientific inquiry and industrial invention are said to be material. The liberal and spiritual are rated as higher in moral status, while the material and the practical are either lower or have no moral status at all. Values are distinguished from facts. Literary education is exalted above training for the practical and the useful. In these and other forms, Mr. Dewey tells us, a deep cleavage runs through traditional thinking about education.

Mr. Dewey's reaction to this dualism is not easy to interpret. At times he seems to deny the assertions of difference that it makes. There is no difference, he seems to say, between the spiritual and the material, between the liberal and the vocational, between values and facts. And yet that cannot be his intended meaning. He himself has always made the distinction and has based his thinking upon it. For example, in the article we are now discussing it underlies all that he is saying. He has told us, in words already quoted, that, in the modern world, we have accomplished in the sciences "an advance so marvelous that the progress in uncounted previous millenniums is almost nothing in comparison." But he has also told us that, in the same modern age but in another field, "we are uncertain as to where we are going, and where we want to go, and why we are doing what we do." What possible meanings can those two statements have unless we distinguish two fields of understanding to which they severally apply? In one of those fields knowledge advances by leaps and bounds. In the other, we fumble and fail. It is one thing to know "how to do." It is a wholly different, though related, thing to know "what to do." It is one thing to become the richest and most powerful nation in the world. It is a very different, and vastly more difficult, thing to acquire the sensitiveness and intelligence that would enable the U.S. to use its power and riches with high devotion to the common good of humanity. For an American teacher to deny the validity of that distinction would be to make all our teaching "a tale told by an idiot." Mr. Dewey is not doing that.

What, then, is Mr. Dewey's attack upon "dualism"? The intellectual crime he rightly abhors and condemns is not that of *distinguishing* fact and value. It is that of *separating* them. This unholy divorce can originate from either side. In the field of fact one finds too often the investigators, the "scholars" who, under the banner of knowledge for its own sake, build up huge systems of accurate, systematic, and nonsignificant information. In the field of value are too many "dreamers" who, without seeking dependable knowledge of ways and means, spin out of their own heads theories as to what the world should be. The fact finders and the wishful thinkers—those are the dualists who, on the one hand, make knowledge meaningless, and, on the other, make virtue visionary. Against both these eccentricities Mr. Dewey has, throughout his career, waged valiant warfare in the cause of organic unity. That has been, perhaps, his greatest contribution to the theory and practice of teaching.

But, for the purposes of this paper, the sting of Mr. Dewey's argument lies in his suggestion that students of the past are peculiarly prone to the separating of fact and value in many ways that he and we alike condemn. Can that charge be substantiated? I do not think so. My own impression is that the countercharge has greater validity. In the contemporary scene, the fact finders are, I think, more sorely tempted to ignore values than are the value seekers to ignore facts. Our business at present, however, is not to make an attack but to repel one. What, then, shall we say in answer to the charge that those who are now engaged in "the present campaign of assault upon what is modern and new" have torn values out of their factual setting, that they "think" values rather than "investigate" them?

Mr. Dewey finds, resulting from the value-fact separation, two disastrous consequences. First, it leads, he says, to the adoption of "fixed" and "static" ideas of value, to an authoritarian dogmatism about matters of morals. Second, it tends to make liberal education "aristocratic," a privilege of the upper classes, radically different in kind from that vocational training which is regarded as suitable for the masses of the people. Can those charges be fairly made against the type of education that St. John's College represents? I am certain that neither in theory nor in fact can either of them be substantiated in this case.

Why should the study of the past, as carried on at St. John's College, lead to dogmatism? When, in the Experimental College, we turned to ancient Athens to read what Homer, Euripides, Thucydides, and Plato had said about judgments of value, it did not mean that in our opinion those writers had, for all time, fixed standards of value that we must accept as unchanged and unchangeable. There was not a student or a teacher in the college who would not have laughed at that suggestion. And, in the same way, when St. John's College turns to Homer and Plato to find a beginning for its study of the humanities, to Euclid and Archimedes to find a beginning for its study of the sciences and technologies, it is not looking to those writers for "the last words" on those subjects. It is looking for "first words." Its entire scheme of education is built upon the basic postulate that, from the time of the Greeks until the present, the knowledge and wisdom of men have been growing, that, with many losses as well as gains, they are still growing. And the intention of the curriculum is that the student shall follow that growth in order that he may be better equipped to play his part in the intellectual and moral activities of his own time and country.

As he follows the sequence of ideas the pupil will be confronted, not with one "static" set of dogmatic beliefs, but with all the fundamental conflicts that run through our culture. He will find Protagoras at war with Plato, Kant at war with Hume, Rousseau at war with Locke, Veblen at war with Adam Smith. And he must try to understand both sides of these controversies. He is asked, first of all, not to believe, but to think, as a precondition of justifiable belief. How that program could commit St. John's to the acceptance from the past of "fixed" and "static" ideas, I do not know. Such acceptance would seem to me more nearly a contradiction of the program than a deduction from it.

Second, if we say that a given type of liberal education is "non-vocational," the statement needs sharp definition. It is one thing to say that liberal teaching must be deeply concerned with the vocations of men. It is an altogether different thing to say that the liberal learning of each pupil must be centered upon the specific vocation of that pupil. The first of these statements is, I think, both true and exceedingly significant. The second seems to me both false and disastrous in its educational implications. I can say here only a brief word about each of them.

If we assume that liberal teaching intends to equip a student to understand the human situation, who can doubt that a major part of its interest must go to the trades and professions of men? One need not be a Marxist to recognize that men must earn their livings. And, further, as their agricultural, industrial, and financial activities change, so do their social institutions, their beliefs, their joys and sorrows. No one can understand the modern age or any other age unless he understands, both in idea and fact, the sciences and technologies by which the life of that age is sustained and determined. Such knowledge, may I add, is not, in a democracy, the privilege of an upper-class few. It is the necessary intellectual equipment of every citizen of a free society. Such study of the vocations of men is not vocational. It is liberal.

But, as against this, the plan of building the liberal education of each pupil around his own vocation, while it has appeal to immediate individual interest, is open to many objections. It tends to leave the student ignorant of all vocations other than his own. For the common understanding that is the primary aim of genuine liberal teaching it substitutes a multitude of specialized understandings that have no real communication with one another. But, worst of all, it cuts away the moral foundations of liberal education by finding its significance not in its own effectiveness but in its connection with the private, vocational interest of the pupil. The full discussion of this point would take us deep into the examination of the basic theories of human nature and of education. May I here say only that, in my opinion, St. John's College is making a magnificent contribution to liberal education by its unqualified refusal to yield, as nearly all our colleges have done, to the pressures of the vocational demand. A liberal college tries to understand and to teach how men make their livings. It does not teach any one individual how to make his living.

Mr. Dewey's article seems to me exceedingly important because it gives promise that mutual understanding may replace misunderstanding in our discussions of college education. He offers common ground on which both he and his opponents may take their stand. They are dissatisfied with contemporary education. So, too, is he. They deplore that we have, at present, no philosophy. He makes the same complaint. "I come back," he says, "to the fact that we are living in a mixed and divided life. We are pulled in opposite directions. We have not as yet a philosophy that is modern in other than a chronological sense. We do not have as yet an educational or any other social institution that is not a mixture of opposed elements. Division between methods and conclusions in natural science and those prevailing in morals and religion is a serious matter, from whatever angle it may be regarded. It means a society that is not unified in its most important concerns." No assailant of the modern and the new could ask for a more forthright expression of his attack than that statement gives. Mr. Dewey and his "opponents" have a common belief and a common purpose. As against those who believe that philosophical understanding of the contemporary world is neither possible nor desirable they together believe it to be both necessary and worth working for. I am not suggesting that, as they may work together, the two groups will reach the same philosophy. I am only saying that they will be engaged in the same inquiry, will be discussing the same problem.

For the furthering of that common enterprise I venture to make a suggestion. I wish that Mr. Dewey and his colleagues would not speak of those who differ from them as "challenging liberal thought." May I say in all friendliness that I think they harm the causes for which they fight by claiming too much of proprietorship over them. We, too, love liberal thinking. Why should we be outlawed? Why are we accused of conspiracy, of being agents of the American Association of Manufacturers, or even of the Nazi party? I, for one, do not "challenge liberal thought." I do challenge Mr. Dewey's analysis of it. I cannot accept the pragmatic interpretation of the modern and the new.

But that does not mean that my heart is fixed upon the past rather than upon the future. To many of us Mr. Dewey's account of "the scientific method" is very unsatisfactory, especially as it bears upon the difference between values and facts. But surely our opposition to a theory of science should not be taken to mean that we are hostile to science itself. I find Mr. Dewey's interpretation of democracy misleading and incomplete. But that criticism does not indicate my lack of interest in democracy. And, finally, if we find that an intellectual colleague has taken a view of American institutions different from our own, that need not mean that he is un-American. I hope the time has come when, with Mr. Dewey leading the way, American students of education will realize that together they have tragically serious and sober work to do. We have common problems to tackle. We can and should deal with them in terms of mutual respect and friendly cooperation.

Appendix 11
Meiklejohn Replies to Dewey

To the Editors:

I am very sorry that Mr. Dewey finds me to have "misconceived" his "plain meaning." And it is at least equally disconcerting to find that he has, in the same way, misconceived mine.

It is, of course, possible that one of us—or both—may have been more successful in speaking to the general reader than in speaking to his opponent. In view of that possibility I am allowing my original statement to stand without further explanation.

However, the joint failure of Mr. Dewey and myself to secure effective communication seems to call for two observations. First, each of us is bound to recognize that, if he had made his meaning "plain" to the other, it would not have been "misconceived" by him. And, second, our failure in spite of good intentions may serve to remind us that we are dealing with a problem so difficult that men were unclear and perplexed about it long before we came on the scene and that other men will, presumably, be unclear and perplexed about it long after we are gone. Together, as students of education, we have been searching for models, patterns, and standards of behavior. It is a long, hard, and as yet unfinished undertaking.

ALEXANDER MEIKLEJOHN

[First published in *Fortune* 31 (March 1945): 14. For Dewey's earlier article, see pp. 261–75. For Meiklejohn's reply, see Appendix 10. For Dewey's rejoinder, see pp. 333–36. For Dewey's reply to this letter, see p. 337.]

Appendix 12
Comments by John L. Childs
on Dr. Dewey's Letter

I should like to state at the outset that I am in accord with much that Dr. Dewey has to say about the Russian situation. His letter performs the useful service of reminding us of certain stubborn realities which we should not ignore in our present enthusiasm for the heroic and effective manner in which the Russians have withstood the thrust of Hitler's armed hordes. My difficulty with Dr. Dewey's statement relates to its possible implication that all we have in common with Russia is a common enemy, and hence our cooperation should end once that enemy—Hitler—has been defeated. Russia under Stalin is a totalitarian state, and, according to Dr. Dewey, "totalitarianism and democracy will not mix." It is this conclusion which gives me concern.

I begin with a summary of my agreements with Dr. Dewey, because it is from the standpoint of these agreements that I desire to explore the problem of our post-war relations with Soviet Russia. We both believe that:

1. The Stalinist regime is a dictatorship, and the participation of Russia in the struggle of the democratic countries against Hitlerism does not alter this primary fact. As Dr. Dewey indicates, it was Russian national interest, and not love for Britain and America which led Stalin to resist the Hitler onslaught.

2. Stalin came to power in Russia only after a bitter struggle with a number of the outstanding leaders of the original revolutionary movement. His ruthless suppression of these former comrades constitutes one of the tragic chapters of human history. As Ambassador Davies suggests it is highly probable that Ger-

[First published in *Frontiers of Democracy* 8 (15 March 1942): 181–82. For Dewey's letter to which this is a reply, see pp. 338–41. For a further letter by Dewey, see pp. 342–44.]

man agents were at work in Russia, as elsewhere, during the decade of the 'thirties. But his book, *Mission to Moscow*, offers little evidence to support his hypothesis that the Russian trials and purges are not to be viewed as part of the struggle of Stalin to eliminate his political rivals, but rather as the effort of a far-sighted statesman who was merely doing his patriotic duty in thus getting rid of fifth-columnists and traitors. Dr. Dewey is correct in emphasizing that we do not strengthen the cause of democracy by slurring tyrannical actions of this sort.

3. The present Stalinist regime is a cultural as well as a political dictatorship. Freedom of thought and expression are not enjoyed by even scientific and professional leaders, to say nothing of the ordinary worker and citizen. Our regard for the magnificent resistance of Russia should not prompt us to justify the present Stalinist practice of putting all cultural and scientific workers into a party uniform, and of making them conform to an orthodox, political line.

4. The present Communist Party in the United States has given abundant evidence that its first loyalty and interest is Moscow, not American democracy. Its present uncritical support of any program that is alleged to be in the interest of the war is on a par with its earlier persistent effort to sabotage the American defense program in that recent strange period when Hitler and Stalin were friendly collaborators. No amount of appreciation of the present inspired resistance of the Russian armies and people should prompt us to condone the practices of this American communist group so long as it continues to act as the subservient tool of the Kremlin. Its revolutionary democratic aim does not, and cannot, justify the kind of means it has stooped to employ.

On all of these important points Dr. Dewey and I are in accord. The question I want to raise is, assuming that we ultimately defeat the Axis powers, what do the foregoing considerations imply for the relations of the United States and Soviet Russia during the post-war period? This is a difficult problem, and momentous consequences are involved in whatever decision we make with regard to it.

Although the chief attention of Dr. Dewey's statement is directed to another issue, the implication of some of his remarks seems to be that America's partnership with Russia is one of expediency to last only for the duration of the present war. In spite of the many difficulties involved, I am inclined to think that we now should so move as to make it possible to continue cooperation with Russia in the period of post-war reconstruction.

A number of considerations lead me to recommend this policy. In the first place, if the United Nations win, the four great national powers at the end of the war will be Britain, China, Russia and the United States. In our interdependent world we cannot each hope to go our own independent way. If we isolate Russia because of the authoritarian and totalitarian character of her government, we shall further deepen old attitudes of suspicion and hostility. Undoubtedly, the fear that all of the other nations of the earth were conspiring to destroy her, has been one of the factors that has induced Soviet Russia to embrace the military and totalitarian pattern. Either we shall through a policy of collective security remove these old fears and rivalries or we shall run the risk of starting all over again that chain of events which will ultimately lead to war. The stark fact seems to be that no attempt to organize the world for abundance, peace, and security has any chance to succeed unless it includes Russia as one of the cooperating partners in the enterprise.

In the second place, Russia is a country which because of the size of her territory, the wealth and diversity of her natural resources, and the extent of her population is not coerced by internal necessities to pursue an aggressive foreign and military policy. In this respect her situation is somewhat similar to our own. In addition, Russia confronts the still unfinished task of developing her own industrial plant, and of working out her own domestic program of reconstruction. To succeed in these huge tasks she requires security and peace, and her record down to Munich demonstrates that she was more eager for opportunity to go ahead with her own internal program, than to aggrandize herself at the expense of her neighbors. We should capitalize these tendencies in the Russian situation for world peace.

In this connection it is not too much to hope that even her present political leaders may recognize that the program of the Third International has failed miserably, and that it is in the interest of Russia as well as the rest of the world to abandon this effort to penetrate foreign countries with conspiratorial groups controlled from the Kremlin. Certainly the cause both of the workers and of socialization throughout the world stands to gain and not to lose by the repudiation of this disruptive political practice.

In the third place, although Russia is now a totalitarian state under a dictatorial government, this is not all that needs to be said about her. Russia is also a country which for generations had been left in the ignorance of peasantry under the combined autocratic rule of Tsar and Orthodox Church. Many things have happened in Russia during the last twenty years which all friends of human freedom and dignity must deplore, but some of these certainly must be charged to the backward situation which the Soviet revolution inherited from the previous regime. Even under the wisest and best leadership Russia could not have achieved all of the transformations in this short period which we prize under the name of civil and cultural freedom. Moreover, not all of the occurrences in Russia have been bad by any means. Her present unexpected national military strength shows that important technological, industrial, and social developments have also taken place. It is still too early to say that in the long run these economic, technological, and social changes may not prove to be more characteristic than certain autocratic political developments.

We would also do well to remember that the capitalist democracies of Britain and the United States now operate under very un-ideal economic and political systems. Our own country falls far short of the democratic conception, and if we are to re-enact the democratic way of life under the changed conditions of industrial society we shall have to undertake drastic institutional reconstruction. Undoubtedly our situation is in some respects far superior to that of Russia and China, but such advantages as we enjoy should not lead us to try to play a lone hand. Even an Anglo-American effort to organize the world apart from the co-operation of both Russia and China seems to me doomed in advance to failure. Somehow we must find the way in which "imperialist" Britain, "totalitarian" Russia, "disorganized" China, and "capitalist" America can cooperate to develop a regional and world order. The task is indeed difficult, but the alternative is even more forbidding.

Finally, as an experimentalist in philosophy and social outlook, Dr. Dewey is aware that the objective terms in any situation do not in and of themselves uniquely dictate our response to that situation. This cardinal experimental principle applied to the present problem means that we have to take due account of the effects which any national policy we adopt will have on the Russian attitude and response. As Dr. Dewey has so often emphasized, in human affairs conditions are seldom so predetermined that our mode of response to them cannot influence eventual outcomes. In sum, the kind of Russia we shall have to deal with will, in part, be determined by the manner in which we now treat her. In my opinion, an open-eyed policy of sincere cooperation with Russia in both the war and the post-war period will achieve more for the cause of democracy than a policy which seeks to isolate Russia once the war is over. The sooner all liberals discard the program of segregation the better for all concerned.

I am not at all sure that Dr. Dewey would disagree with what is here proposed. His letter was primarily a protest against the tendency of certain liberals to whitewash Stalin's past record, and to attempt to form once again a united front with the Communist party in the United States. In order to advocate a policy of honest cooperation with Russia we do not have to ignore the features in her national system which make such cooperation difficult, nor do we have to encourage the Stalinists within our own country to suppose that they can easily return to the old role of underground manipulation of political and labor movements. Certainly not with the support of those liberals who can learn from experience.

Unfortunately, we all must live and work amid conditions far less democratic and ideal than we might wish. But no experimentalist believes this coercive necessity is anything more than a challenge to his intelligence and his democratic purpose to see what can be done to re-make these conditions. As I confront the possibilities, I believe a policy of cooperation with Soviet Russia promises more for democracy than one which seeks to ignore or segregate her from the affairs of the post-war world.

Appendix 13
Mission to Moscow Film Viewed as Historical Realism

The author of the following letter is director of the Iranian Institute and School for Asiatic Studies, organizer and director of the Committee for National Morale. He has been in Russia fourteen times, traveling extensively in the country. He was associate director of the International Exhibition of Iranian Art at Leningrad and the International Congress of Iranian Art in Leningrad and Moscow in 1935.

To the Editor of the *New York Times:*

The film *Mission to Moscow,* which was acclaimed by the New York press as brilliant, informing, a timely presentation of an important subject, is primarily political. The bitter debate that for more than twenty years revolved around the character and policies of the Soviet Union has fortunately been dying down, thanks to Russia's immense progress in the last decade and the magnificence of her battle against Germany, which has demonstrated a power and unanimity that have astonished most of the world and refuted the majority of Russia's critics. But now the film has been made the occasion for a revival of angry invective.

In a letter in the *Times* last Sunday, Professor Dewey repeats the arguments which marked his original attack on Ambassador Davies and his book in the *New York Times* of Jan. 18, 1942— arguments which have not gained in validity by their iteration or by the passage of time.

A biographical note informs the reader that John Dewey and Miss Suzanne La Follette, joint signers of the letter, served respectively as chairman and secretary of the International Com-

[First published in *New York Times,* 16 May 1943, p. 12. For letter by Dewey and Suzanne La Follette to which this is a reply, see pp. 345–50. For rejoinder by Dewey and La Follette, see pp. 351–53. For a second letter by Pope, see Appendix 14; for a final response by Dewey and La Follette, see pp. 354–55.]

mission of Inquiry into the Moscow trials. This, Professor Dewey says, "conclusively disproved" much of the Moscow testimony and its condemnation of the Moscow trials "was endorsed by intelligent world opinion."

The commission was without status, competence or authority. It was conducted in a thoroughly amateurish and somewhat ludicrous fashion. Carleton Beals, the one independent member of the original commission, declared the inquiry "was a fraud" and resigned in protest over the obvious partisanship and ineptitude of the entire proceedings. The volume which the commission published was without documents.

The film controverts the conclusions of the commission. Professor Dewey actually says that "the film is a major defeat for the democratic cause." He charges that the producers "have assailed the very foundations of freedom." He says the film is "anti-British, anti-Congress, anti-democratic, anti-truth," and gives us fair warning that a few more such films "uncritically accepted . . . and Americans will be deadened to all moral values." This is indeed crying havoc with a vengeance and Hitler would certainly be relieved to know that our plight is so desperate.

In an admirable statement the film critic of the *Times*, Bosley Crowther, on May 9 laid down the requirements for a political film and urged the necessity for scrupulous honesty. But the Dewey-La Follette letter makes unreasonable and unrealistic demands that render films on political subjects practically impossible, apparently requiring that a film on a controversial subject be thoroughly intellectual, orderly, and with comprehensive coverage of the problems involved, with qualifications, addenda and other paraphernalia of scholarship.

Professor Dewey and others are scandalized that the three treason trials are telescoped, but three separate trials would destroy the unity and tempo of the picture. The critics use a derisive question-begging epithet for the trial scene—"synthetic," they call it, as if it were a sort of artificial and inferior substitute. Of course it is synthetic; for a film representation of a trial that took days has to be a synthesis to be intelligible. All the defendants were part of the movement, and it was artistically justifiable, as it was the moral fact, to represent them together. The essential question is whether there was a guilty plot against the state. In the opinion of the best informed there was.

Dr. Dewey and Miss La Follette notwithstanding, it is historically and evidentially insignificant whether Mr. Davies had been
personally introduced to Radek, Bukharin and Yagoda. It is elementary practice in fictional technique, of which cinema technique is a special type, to introduce a character incidentally before his major appearance.

Many of the specific charges against the film are quite unfair.
For example, the assertion that it is a "sinister totalitarian critique of the parliamentary system" is quite absurd, and that its
"whole effort is to discredit the American Congress and at the
same time to represent the Soviet dictatorship as an advanced democracy" is purely imaginary. There is no such intent. The scene
in Congress occupies 100 seconds and reports statements which
represented a substantial section of Congressional opinion. Cannot Congress be cited in a film without polling all its members on
all relevant issues?

Similarly, in the scene in Secretary Hull's office, not an opinion
is represented which was not forcefully expressed by many Con-
gressmen. The statement of one Senator that he had just as good
sources of information as the State Department and his categorical affirmation that there was going to be no war were made
by Senator Borah in August, 1939. The charge that the whole
effort of the film is to "represent the Soviet dictatorship as an advanced democracy" is a pure fabrication.

The critics similarly misread Soviet foreign policy. It would
certainly surprise the Poles to learn that "it was Chamberlain
who came to her defense." They have not forgotten that it was
Chamberlain who refused their urgent demand just before the
war for credit of £25,000,000.

Professor Dewey and Miss La Follette object that the film represents Stalin as having been "driven into Hitler's arms by the
French-British policy of appeasement." Well, he was, and of this
there is an increasing mass of proof. "There is no reference to the
desperate efforts of France and Britain to reach a defensive alliance with Stalin in 1939," says Professor Dewey. How desperate was that attempt? Mr. Maisky, the Soviet Ambassador in
London, requested Lord Halifax or some equally high representative of the government to proceed to Moscow.

But Lord Halifax and other members of his Cabinet were too
busy. So William Strang was sent; an able and honest man, but of

inferior diplomatic status. The English and the French were so "desperate" to reach a conclusion that instead of going to Moscow by plane, as they could have done in twelve hours, they went by boat—which took two weeks.

Zhdanov's comment was justified: "The English and French Governments do not desire the only kind of an agreement that a self-respecting government could enter into. They do not wish a real pact, but only conversations about a pact." Again, he stated "that the Soviet Government had required only sixteen days to prepare their answers to the various British proposals" but that "fifty-nine days were expended in delay and red tape on the part of the British and the French."

The critics have quite misinterpreted the Soviet-German pact which was Russia's bid for time to prepare for war that she knew was inevitable. They seem scandalized that "Uncle Joe" and Molotoff could both play poker when the diplomatic necessities required it. Do the critics really think that the Soviet preparations for war should have been sabotaged by revealing the plans to their destined enemy?

The Dewey-La Follette letter protests that the film creates the impression that the Soviet Union is our ally against Japan and thinks that "nothing could be more dangerous than to mislead the American people into believing that the Soviet Union will turn against Japan the moment Hitler is defeated." Perhaps Professor Dewey will allow this to stand as a prophecy and a test of his understanding of Soviet policy. He suggested last year that Stalin was going to make a separate peace.

He has apparently forgotten that while we were sending hundreds of thousands of tons of precious scrap to Japan, loading her up with oil and bolstering her financial system, while she was engaged in massacre in China, it was Russia which kept China supplied at a cost that she could ill afford; it was Russia who lent China $300,000,000 before we lent her a cent and bargained meanly for what we did send.

Russia's deep sympathy with China's struggles and her very practical aid, which military men believe enabled China to stay in the battle in those first dreadful years, are symbolized in the film, showing Russian doctors and nurses tending Chinese victims. There is no essential misrepresentation here.

Professor Dewey states that Marshal Tukhachevsky had no

trial at all. How does he know? Military courts-martial are not reported for the information of foreign civilians, and there are good reasons to think he was altogether guilty. Military intelligence of all governments knows about the mass of evidence against Marshal Tukhachevsky which the Deuxième Bureau in France uncovered and turned over to the Russian Government. Marshal Tukhachevsky sat next to Mme. Tabouis shortly after he had many conferences with the German General Staff, heaped glowing praises on the Nazis and declared repeatedly of the German Army, "They're already invincible."

Professor Dewey is quite improperly scornful of Ambassador Davies's competence to render judgment on the trials. Yet in the foreword to the report on the Trotsky hearing Professor Dewey recognizes that courtroom experience can be valuable. "It is an established rule, even in legally constituted courts, that the bearing of the witness may be taken into account in weighing the value of the testimony" (p. viii). Ambassador Davies, in his long career as a lawyer of high standing, has had a great deal of courtroom experience. And in Professor Dewey's remark that in the film the confessions at the trial were "obligingly delivered in English, of course, since Mr. Davies knows no Russian" the sarcasm is of a quality that one does not expect of Professor Dewey. Would the critics think it good cinema technique to have a whole section of an American film made for the American public rendered in Russian?

Since the critics find their own judgment worthy of precedence, what of their qualifications? They have had no legal training or courtroom experience, were not present at the trials, and the lack of Russian with which they taunt Ambassador Davies would have applied also to them.

Ambassador Davies's judgment, moreover, has the support of numerous other extremely competent observers. Naturally, a review of the treason trials is a case for a book and not a letter. But it is worth remembering that many astute observers at the trial were convinced that substantial justice was rendered. This is the belief of Walter Duranty, whose reporting of Russian affairs in the *Times* has been one of the outstanding journalistic feats of our time. It was the conviction of Lion Feuchtwanger, acute and subtle observer of human character; a conviction of D. N. Pritt, who speaks Russian fluently, knows Russia and is a trained lawyer. It was the view of Baltrusaltis, the wise and learned Ambassador of Lithuania, who knew the Russian scene as no other foreigner did, used the language as his own tongue, and was present throughout the trials.

Back of all Professor Dewey's criticisms is the belief that Trotsky was innocent of plotting against the Soviet regime, that the Moscow trials were farcical. But the critics ignore the fact that this was not an ordinary civil trial, but a court-martial in a foreign country with an entirely different procedure. They make no acknowledgment of the unanimous testimony of all present that General Ulrich, the presiding judge, was scrupulously fair.

In the mass of confirming evidence, one important confession of Trotsky has been overlooked. In 1931, Emil Ludwig had an interview with Trotsky on the Island of Prinkipo, which he published. Trotsky stated that his own party was "scattered and therefore difficult to estimate"; and, in reply to the question as to when it could come together, he said: "When an opportunity is presented from the outside—perhaps a war or a new European intervention when the weakness of the government would act as a stimulus."

Professor Dewey sees nothing but wickedness and deceit in the Soviet Government. He does indeed praise the magnificent resistance of the Russian people to the German onslaught. But he can hardly be so naive as not to know that the success of their effort is due not merely to their mass courage but also to far-sighted planning, powerful organization, discipline and a spontaneous loyalty, engendered in no small measure by the very government of which he is so contemptuous, whose solid achievements and humane ideal have, after many years given the Russian people a common rallying point.

It is important in the crucial tasks of both war and peace that lie before us that the public mind should not be unduly agitated. A cool objectivity, a looking beyond feuds and controversies, is indispensable if we are to surmount the barriers between us and a decent and recreated life. We have to guard especially against the disbalanced view: the substitution of some detail for the major fact. They serve us ill who darken counsels with their own animosities or import the feuds of others into the political scene.

The major fact now as far as Russia is concerned is her stupendous effort and immeasurable sacrifice for the common welfare of the nations and her will to a collective peace. The fact of her ten million dead—nearly twenty times that of her Allies—the unfathomable suffering, the vast destruction that she has endured, ought to stay reckless and venomous speech. We can never be sufficiently grateful that at immense cost she was the first to destroy the German myth of invincibility and half cripple her military power.

There is no fear that the general public will be misled about either the film or the book, or about Ambassador Davies, if they will see the picture themselves and not be deterred by denunciation. They will see there as the public has already found in the book, the personality of an able and forthright man, courageous, clear-headed and factual, who carried through with high success one of the most difficult diplomatic missions of modern times, who saw the truth and who proved his insight by prophecy that came true; who has done more than any one person to promote friendship and understanding between the two nations.

The American public has already purchased more than 700,000 copies of *Mission to Moscow,* and has by that very act rendered a favorable verdict—a verdict that will be confirmed by the film. If critics of the film are as sincere as they are passionate in their affirmations of democracy, if they really respect the capacity of the common man to render judgment on public servants and political fundamentals, they might with becoming grace acquiesce in the verdict—or else summon against it sober, factual, provable arguments.

ARTHUR UPHAM POPE

Appendix 14
Merit Seen in Moscow Film

To the Editor of the *New York Times:*

The letter from Professor Dewey and Miss La Follette about *Mission to Moscow* in the *New York Times* of May 16 contains misstatements, misunderstandings and misinterpretations that require more space for correction than the *Times* could possibly give, but they will be fully dealt with elsewhere. A few points may be noted here.

Professor Dewey and Miss La Follette cite their participation in the Commission of Inquiry (the term "international" has prudently been dropped) as if that fact guaranteed special knowledge and impartiality, and accuse me of stereotyped repetition of Communist "smears" on their work. I would not know, as I don't read the Communist press. But the most devastating indictment of the commission was published in the *Saturday Evening Post* of June 12, 1937, by Carleton Beals, an original member, who resigned in disgust over the proceedings. The *New York Times* correspondent designated the proceedings as fraudulent. Neither the *Saturday Evening Post* nor the *New York Times* is generally classed as Communist.

It is true that the commission's report, as Professor Dewey says, "bristles with references to documents." But the charge is still valid that according to standards of legal tribunals, or scholarly history it is not convincingly or sufficiently documented to constitute a serious challenge to the essential justice of the Moscow trials.

The Dewey-La Follette letters to the *Times* seek to justify their unqualified condemnation of the film by appealing to a discarded

[First published in *New York Times*, 12 June 1943, p. 12. For earlier letters by Dewey and La Follette, see pp. 345–50 and 351–53. For Pope's first reply, see Appendix 13. For a final response by Dewey and La Follette, see pp. 354–55.]

and invalid literalism, any deviation from which they regard as proof of evil purpose and a deliberate intent to deceive the American public; all, mysteriously enough, in the interest of an unspecified totalitarianism. But condensations, omissions, re-arrangements, symbolizations, divergences from literal facts are all permissible and necessary in a motion picture addressed to the general public so long as the central theme is honestly set forth and the main conclusions justified, which many believe is true of this particular film.

The average man wants to know what the Russian people are like. Are they making progress? Can we cooperate with them in the future? The film says "Yes." He would like to know whether there really was a counterrevolutionary plot on the part of the old Bolshevist-fundamentalists. Did they resent Stalin's hard drive to achieve industrialism and agricultural collectives, in the record time he thought necessary for the nation's safety—"sixty years in ten," as John Whitaker said? Did they resent their loss of power and, as Trotsky did, accuse Stalin of betraying the world revolution? And did they, with their familiar revolutionary arts in which they were so accomplished, try to overturn the present regime?

The picture says they did. "Trotsky practiced all his old arts to bring down his hated enemy," says Sir Bernard Pares. The major-ity of competent witnesses say the same. These answers truthfully represent Mr. Davies's own experience and convictions. Com-pared to these important affirmations, any minor divergence of factual detail between book and film is of slight significance.

Nor did Stalin's playing for time have any analogy with the Munich appeasement, as the critics triumphantly asserted. Ger-many was then rearming twice as fast as England. One year after Munich England was in a relatively much worse position vis-à-vis Germany than she was when that shameful agreement was concluded, while every week that passed after the Soviet-German pact saw Russia increasingly able to defend herself.

Nor is it "objective truth" to publicize the rumor that one mil-lion of Chiang Kai-shek's troops are "kept busy riding herd on the Chinese Communists," while to equate the so-called Com-munist army in China with the Soviet government in Moscow and to imply that Soviet Russia and China are in effect at war is as gross a distortion of the fact as any these critics charge against the film.

Professor Dewey and Miss La Follette suggest I ought to know that a decent re-created life cannot be built on a morass of "historical falsification and deliberate confusion of the people of this world"—something which everybody knows and nobody proposes. Equally universal is the knowledge that the morale of the United Nations cannot be maintained if the citizens of one country feel free to denounce and malign the government, institutions and personnel of an associated nation.

Thanks to Russia, Germany has lost more than three and a half million men, colossal masses of costly matériel and formidable prestige. What if this vast power, destroyed at such a cost, were still intact, still threatening, still to be overcome? Our debt to Russia is immeasurable. Shall it be paid in calumny, misrepresentation and hate? "But we hate only Stalin and the Soviet regime," say the detractors. No such distinction can be made. The Russian people have profound confidence in their government and in Stalin. He is their leader; they want no other.

No one asks Professor Dewey or Miss La Follette to keep silent, as they charge, but every one's freedom of speech is necessarily somewhat curtailed in wartime, and in moments of national stress and peril the common will must be protected from divisive conflicts.

It is particularly unwise and unfair to malign a gallant ally or its chosen leaders on whose courage, endurance and organized effort so much has and still depends. Mutual suspicions are easily engendered to our mutual danger; old animosities are easily heated up again to the delight of our enemies; and the Nazi propaganda machine is ready in many clever and devious ways to assist both operations.

Fear and hatred of Russia have been the greatest weapon in Hitler's powerful psychological arsenal. It represents now his own great hope for prolonging the war. Why should any American aid and abet him?

ARTHUR UPHAM POPE

Appendix 15
A "Fresh Start" in Economics

The Theory of Economic Progress. By
C. E. Ayres. Chapel Hill: The University
of North Carolina Press, 1944.

Reviewed by Henry Hazlitt

This is a strange and yet familiar book. Like a hundred other volumes of recent years, it sets out to destroy "classical" economics. Mr. Ayres, who is Professor of Economics at the University of Texas, begins by assuming that economics is today in "general disrepute" and that what is needed is "a fresh start." He disposes of his predecessors in no timid or retail fashion. The "fatuity" of Boehm-Bawerk's theory of capital and interest, for example, "is so extreme that it would be apparent to the most elementary student," and is so apparent to Mr. Ayres that he doesn't waste three paragraphs in refuting it to his own satisfaction. Gresham's Law that bad money drives out good, cited approvingly in almost every textbook and history of money, is "plainly false"—and Mr. Ayres only needs three rapid sentences to explain why. Gathering momentum, he tells us that "All that was added in the last third of the nineteenth century (to classical value theory) was the resolution of the want-satisfying quality into infinitesimal increments for purposes of mathematical treatment." This gets rid of more than thirty years of thought in fewer than thirty words. But why is Mr. Ayres wasting his time on details? "The absurdities of traditional theory," he concludes sweepingly, "are only too apparent."

What has Mr. Ayres to offer in exchange? It is a new theory of economic value, which he tells us is implicit in the theories of Thorstein Veblen and John Dewey. Mr. Ayres's reasoning on this

[First published in *Saturday Review of Literature* 27 (15 July 1944): 38. For reply by Dewey, see pp. 359–60. For Hazlitt's rejoinder, see Appendix 16.]

point seems to me so dark and confused that I am not certain that I can do it justice; but as nearly as I can make out he is saying that value lies not in our own wishes or desires but in machines.

It is the technological continuum which is, and has always been, the locus of value. . . . "Value" means continuity, literally; and that is its sole meaning. . . . All that man has done and thought and felt has been achieved by the use of tools. The continuity of civilization is the continuity of tools. . . . For every individual and for the community the criterion of value is the continuation of the life-process—keeping the machines running.

Regardless, apparently, of what they turn out. Machines, one gathers, are not to be judged by the extent to which they forward the welfare of humanity, but as ends of their own—or rather as wonderful means to still more wonderful means. Tools exist to make tools to make tools. If we only keep redoubling our efforts we can forget our aim. His theory of progress inevitably recalls the old song, "We don't know where we're going, but we're on our way!"

Mr. Ayres is a man of wide learning, or at least of wide allusions. He has at least dipped into a lot of the "classical" economic volumes of the last decades, and can talk knowingly of painting, music, inventions, folklore, and philosophy. He has taken from Veblen a persistent tone of irony and a love of paradox. He seems constantly delighted by his own cleverness, and is certain that his own outlook is as up-to-date as it can possibly be, while other economists still grope in the mists of outworn superstition. He seems, indeed, less eager to understand economics than to prove that others have not understood it. If he can prove that a present idea in economics resembles a past idea he seems to think that he has proved it must be false—as if truth depended on the calendar, and if two plus two was thought to equal four in the eighteenth century that answer must be wrong now. At times he affects a tone of Olympian detachment and scientific exactness, but will break out suddenly with something vehement, then return to his Olympian mood and complain that "Economic controversy now seems to be rising to a higher pitch of violence than ever before."

Appendix 16
Mr. Hazlitt Replies

Sir: It is "the application of Dewey's theory of valuation to an understanding of the meaning of value in the field of economics," Mr. Ayres declares in his book, "toward which the present discussion is attempting to move." It is not strange that Mr. Dewey should defend the work of his disciple. But it is regrettable that he should think it necessary to make the "serious" and unsubstantiated charge that my review gave a "completely perverted" idea of Mr. Ayres's book.

In interpreting Mr. Ayres's theory of value I was careful to warn the reader that "Mr. Ayres's reasoning on this point seems to me so dark and confused that I am not certain I can do it justice." Neither Mr. Dewey's letter, however, nor a re-reading of the relevant passages, has convinced me that my interpretation actually was unjust, on this or any other point. What are we to make, for example, of this astonishing passage on page 242:

> We sometimes hear it said that the only result of the invention, for example, of airplanes is that people are killing each other on a larger scale than ever before. If such a proposition were true, it would indeed nullify the technological conception of progress [*i.e.,* Mr. Ayres's conception]; for if people are indeed being killed on a larger scale than ever before, this circumstance must eventually operate to the disadvantage of further airplane building and of technological development generally.

One can only gather from this that under the "technological conception" the test of progress is not what happens to human-

[First published in *Saturday Review of Literature* 27 (14 October 1944): 29–30. For Hazlitt's review, see Appendix 15. For Dewey's reply to which this is a rejoinder, see pp. 359–60.]

ity, but what happens to "further airplane building" or to "technological development"!

I assumed in my review that what Mr. Ayres was mainly trying to unfold in his book was a new theory of value. His publishers also assume so. "For the price theory of value," they tell us on the jacket, "the author substitutes a conception of value drawn from technology itself." I tried to state this theory almost entirely in Mr. Ayres's own words. But Mr. Dewey now tells us that the *real* central theory of the book is "that the state of industry at a given time reflects the state of technology of the period, which in turn reflects the state of scientific knowledge. Hence economic progress depends upon technological advances."

I am willing to take Mr. Dewey's word for it. But I must confess that without his help I should hardly have suspected, reading Mr. Ayres's pretentious volume, that its real theory was anything so simple and obvious as this. For to state that industry, technology, and science are interdependent and advance together is to state a mere truism. I can think of no "orthodox" economist of standing who would dispute it. The real question is, of course, what factors, forces, and incentives make possible and promote technological advance? It is at this point that economic analysis would call attention to the determining role played by previous production, saving, and capital accumulation.

It was Boehm-Bawerk who made the greatest contribution on this point of any single economist. It is merely captious for Mr. Dewey to insist that the "fatuity" of which Mr. Ayres accuses Boehm-Bawerk applies not to the latter's theory of capital and interest but merely to an argument in support of the theory. The argument so labeled happens to be central to theory. If it is fatuous the whole of Boehm-Bawerk's theory must be so. On the very next page, for that matter, Mr. Ayres continues: "Not only does the [Boehm-Bawerk] 'round about' *theory* [my italics] confuse industrial facts," etc.

The only fatuity involved, as it happens, applies not to Boehm-Bawerk's argument or theory but to Mr. Ayres's "refutation" of it. As Mr. Dewey has raised the point of misrepresentation and perversion, perhaps this is the place to add what I refrained from saying in my review: that Mr. Ayres himself grossly perverts and misrepresents the views of the great "traditional" economists that he attempts to criticize. Let us charitably attribute this not to deliberate intent, but to a profound lack of understanding of these writers that his prevailing tone of condescension and irony does not conceal.

HENRY HAZLITT

Appendix 17
God and Mathematics

Another attempt to buttress some rarefied sort of philosophical theism is found in *Current Religious Thought,* June '47, where Sir Edmund Whittaker, F.R.S., in an address on the British Broadcasting Corporation, discusses "Mathematics, Matter and the Mind of the Universe." Apparently, "mathematics is altogether independent of the external world: it depends on no experiments and on no assumptions. In itself it gives information not about the material universe but about the structure of our own minds." Sir Edmund then jumps to the conclusion that because the laws of the universe can be expressed mathematically, "there is a mind analogous to our minds in or behind material nature."

Let us see. If "mathematics is altogether independent of the external world" and "depends on no experiments" then it is difficult to imagine how it could ever be applied to the external world. The theory of relativity, involving elaborate mathematical constructions, is not merely a "structure" in the mind of Einstein. It was shown by actual experimentation to be a closer approximation to reality than Newton's laws. The thing which transforms a daring hypothesis, such as relativity, into a universal law, is not just "the structure of our minds" but the verification of this hypothesis by reference to objective reality.

There are two schools of thought on the interpretation of mathematics: the one presented by Sir Edmund is closely allied to the old idealistic philosophy according to which thought alone is real and matter a mere shadow, and God is some immaterial mathematical mind beyond a shadow universe. The other, represented by Hyman Levy in England, and D. J. Struik in the United

[First published in *Humanist* 7 (Autumn 1947): 101. For Dewey's comment, see pp. 376–77.]

States, is that the objective world is real and that our mathematical mental constructions are valid only in so far as they reflect this real world. This is not just an academic controversy. From mathematics as a mental construction "independent of the external world" the road is easy to religion as mental construction "independent of the external world," and finally to religion as a mystical contemplation of immaterial spiritual essences allegedly more real than this sad materialistic world! And so the way is paved to anti-social escapism! It is the task of Humanism to "nip in the bud" this type of thought, even when it originates in the rarefied atmosphere of higher mathematics.

Notes

The following notes, keyed to the page and line numbers of the present edition, explain references to matters not found in standard sources.

97.9   Professor Katharine Gilbert] Gilbert was, at this time, chairman of the department of aesthetics, art, and music at Duke University. In 1947, under the auspices of the U.S. State Department, she surveyed philosophical movements in Italy.

98.29   The Live Animal] The title of the first chapter of Dewey's *Art as Experience* is "The Live Creature."

159.20–21   A distinguished member of this school of contemporary thought] The quotations in this passage have been identified as those of Bertrand Russell.

174.40 The second of the freedoms of the socalled Atlantic charter] This is the second of the "Four Freedoms" that were given in a message to Congress by Franklin Roosevelt on 6 January 1941. The "Atlantic Charter" was drawn up by Winston Churchill and Roosevelt on 14 August 1941.

184.9–10   The brief account] The author of this account was A. Gowan Whyte.

193.2   eight years] The quotation is from Addams's *The Second Twenty Years at Hull-House,* published by Macmillan in 1930.

197.22 UNRRA] United Nations Relief and Rehabilitation Administration, a temporary agency founded in 1943.

241.6   PAC] Congress of Industrial Organizations Political Action Committee.

249.17 plea made in *Labor and Nation*] *Labor and Nation* 4 (November–December 1948): 8–19.

281.3   Senators Murray, Morse, and Pepper] Senators James Edward Murray of Montana, Wayne Morse of Oregon, and Claude Pepper of Florida.

290.7–8   Walter Duranty] Walter Duranty was the Moscow correspondent for the *New York Times* from 1922 to 1941.

291.2   Litvinoff] Russian ambassador to the United States.

291.6–7   French ambassador] Robert Coulondre.

292.16   *Darkness at Noon*] A 1941 novel by Arthur Koestler.

310.24   Dr. Adelbert Ames] In 1960, *The Morning Notes of Adelbert Ames, Jr.*, was published by Rutgers University Press. This book was edited by Hadley Cantril and includes correspondence between Dewey and Ames. Dr. Ames died in 1955.

321.1   Tribute to James Hayden Tufts] A copy of this memorial pamphlet is in Dewey's personal library, John Dewey Papers, Special Collections, Morris Library, Southern Illinois University at Carbondale.

326.2–9   I wish . . . acknowledgment] Funds were collected on the occasion of the retirement of William H. Kilpatrick from Columbia University Teachers College, in 1937, for a portrait of Kilpatrick that was to be presented to the College. Residuals from this collection were used to establish the William H. Kilpatrick Award for Distinguished Service in Philosophy of Education, to be given biennially to a person recommended by a committee especially convened for this purpose. Because of World War II only two men, Kenneth D. Benne and Isaac B. Berkson, had received the award prior to 1947.

At a meeting held on 10 November 1947 in the Horace Mann Auditorium at Teachers College, Boyd H. Bode became the third recipient of the Kilpatrick Award. George S. Counts chaired the meeting, and statements of appreciation of Bode and his work were offered by H. Gordon Hullfish, Kilpatrick, and Dewey.

351.13–14   our report] John Dewey et al., *The Case of Leon Trotsky: Report of Hearings on the Charges Made against Him in the Moscow Trials, by the Preliminary Commission of Inquiry* (New York and London: Harper and Brothers, 1937); *Not Guilty: Report of the Commission of Inquiry into the Charges Made against Leon Trotsky in the Moscow Trials* (New York: Harper and Brothers, 1938).

358.28–29   Odell Waller . . . penalty.] Waller was executed on 2 July 1942. He was twenty-five years old.

361.5   his book] *The Great Transformation* (New York: Farrar and Rinehart, 1944).

371n.1   Conference] A pedagogical conference was held from 20 to 27 March 1944 in Apata, Peru. The pamphlet produced by the Conference included this message from Dewey.

Checklist of Dewey's References

This section gives full publication information for each work cited by Dewey. Books in Dewey's personal library (John Dewey Papers, Special Collections, Morris Library, Southern Illinois University at Carbondale) have been listed whenever possible. When Dewey gave page numbers for a reference, the edition has been identified by locating the citation; for other references, the edition listed here is his most likely source by reason of place or date of publication, general accessibility during the period, or evidence from correspondence and other materials.

Addams, Jane. *Newer Ideals of Peace.* New York: Macmillan Co., 1907.

———. *Peace and Bread in Time of War.* New York: Macmillan Co., 1922.

———. *The Second Twenty Years at Hull-House: September 1909 to September 1929.* New York: Macmillan Co., 1930.

Aiken, Henry. Review of *Ethics and Language,* by Charles L. Stevenson. *Journal of Philosophy* 42 (16 August 1945): 455–70.

Ames, Edward S. Tribute. In *James Hayden Tufts.* Privately printed memorial pamphlet, pp. 15–31. N.p. [1942].

Aristotle. *The Organon, or Logical Treatises, of Aristotle.* 2 vols. Translated by Octavius Freire Owen. London: H. G. Bohn, 1853.

Arnold, Matthew. "Stanzas from the Grande Chartreuse." In *The Poems of Matthew Arnold, 1840 to 1866,* pp. 256–61. Everyman's Library. London: J. M. Dent and Sons; New York: E. P. Dutton and Co., 1908.

Ayres, C. E. *The Theory of Economic Progress.* Chapel Hill: University of North Carolina Press, 1944.

Bacon, Francis. *The New Organon.* In *The Works of Francis Bacon,* edited by James Spedding, Robert Leslie Ellis, and Douglas Devon Heath, 4:39–248. London: Longmans and Co., 1875.

Bell, Daniel. "Adjusting Men to Machines." *Commentary* 3 (January 1947): 79–88.

Benda, Julien. "The Attack on Western Morality." *Commentary* 4 (November 1947): 416–22. [*The Later Works of John Dewey,*

1925–1953, edited by Jo Ann Boydston, 15 : 381–92. Carbondale and Edwardsville: Southern Illinois University Press, 1989.]

Bentley, Arthur F. "Truth, Reality, and Behavioral Fact." *Journal of Philosophy* 40 (1 April 1943): 169–87.

Blanshard, Brand, et al. *Philosophy in American Education: Its Tasks and Opportunities.* New York: Harper and Bros., 1945.

Bode, Boyd H. "Cognitive Experience and Its Object." *Journal of Philosophy, Psychology and Scientific Methods* 2 (23 November 1905): 658–63.

———. "The Concept of Pure Experience." *Philosophical Review* 14 (November 1905): 684–95.

Brotherston, Bruce W. "The Genius of Pragmatic Empiricism." *Journal of Philosophy* 40 (7 and 21 January 1943): 14–21, 29–39.

Brown, J. Douglas, et al. "The Spiritual Basis of Democracy." In *Science, Philosophy and Religion: Second Symposium,* edited by Lyman Bryson and Louis Finkelstein, pp. 251–57. New York: Conference on Science, Philosophy and Religion in Their Relation to the Democratic Way of Life, 1942.

Bryson, Lyman, and Louis Finkelstein, eds. *Science, Philosophy and Religion: Second Symposium.* New York: Conference on Science, Philosophy and Religion in Their Relation to the Democractic Way of Life, 1942.

Chesterton, G. K. *What I Saw in America.* New York: Dodd, Mead and Co., 1922.

Childs, John L. "Comments by John L. Childs on Dr. Dewey's Letter." *Frontiers of Democracy* 8 (15 March 1942): 181–82. [*Later Works* 15 : 487–91.]

Cowles, Edward Spencer. *Don't Be Afraid!* New York: Wilcox and Follette Co., 1941.

Croce, Benedetto. "On the Aesthetics of Dewey." *Journal of Aesthetics and Art Criticism* 6 (March 1948): 203–7. [*Later Works* 15 : 438–44.]

Dallin, David J., and Boris I. Nicolaevsky. *Forced Labor in Soviet Russia.* New Haven: Yale University Press, 1947.

Daniels, Jonathan. "A Native at Large." *Nation* 151 (21 December 1940): 635.

Davies, Joseph E. *Mission to Moscow.* New York: Simon and Schuster, 1941.

Dewey, John. *Art as Experience.* New York: Minton, Balch and Co., 1934. [*Later Works* 10.]

———. *Logic: The Theory of Inquiry.* New York: Henry Holt and Co., 1938. [*Later Works* 12.]

———. "Ethical Subject-Matter and Language." *Journal of Philosophy* 42 (20 December 1945): 701–12. [*Later Works* 15 : 127–40.]

————. "How Is Mind to Be Known?" *Journal of Philosophy* 39 (15 January 1942): 27–33. [*Later Works* 15:29–36.]

————. "Logical Conditions of a Scientific Treatment of Morality." In *Investigations Representing the Departments*. University of Chicago, The Decennial Publications, first series, 3:115–39. Chicago: University of Chicago Press, 1903; *Problems of Men*. New York: Philosophical Library, 1946, pp. 211–49. [*The Middle Works of John Dewey, 1899–1924*, edited by Jo Ann Boydston, 3:3–39. Carbondale and Edwardsville: Southern Illinois University Press, 1978.]

————. "The Objectivism-Subjectivism of Modern Philosophy." *Journal of Philosophy* 38 (25 September 1941): 533–42. [*Later Works* 14:189–200.]

Dewey, John, and James H. Tufts. *Ethics*. New York: Henry Holt and Co., 1908; 1932. [*Middle Works 5*; *Later Works 7*.]

Dewey, John, et al. *The Case of Leon Trotsky. Report of Hearings on the Charges Made against Him in the Moscow Trials, by the Preliminary Commission of Inquiry*. New York and London: Harper and Bros., 1937.

Dewey, John, et al. *Not Guilty: Report of the Commission of Inquiry into the Charges Made against Leon Trotsky in the Moscow Trials*. New York: Harper and Bros., 1938.

Dorner, Alexander. *The Way beyond "Art"—The Work of Herbert Bayer*. New York: Wittenborn, Schultz, 1947.

Dynnik, M. "Contemporary Bourgeois Philosophy in the U.S." *Modern Review* 1 (November 1947): 653–60.

Edman, Irwin. "The Arts of Liberation." In *The Authoritarian Attempt to Capture Education*. Papers from the 2d Conference on The Scientific Spirit and Democratic Faith, pp. 25–29. New York: King's Crown Press, 1945.

Field, Frederick V. "Behind the Chinese Front." *New Masses* 46 (26 January 1943): 21–23.

Finkelstein, Louis, and Lyman Bryson, eds. *Science, Philosophy and Religion: Second Symposium*. New York: Conference on Science, Philosophy and Religion in Their Relation to the Democratic Way of Life, 1942.

Geiger, George R. "Can We Choose between Values?" *Journal of Philosophy* 41 (25 May 1944): 292–98. [*Later Works* 15:445–52.]

Glazer, Nathan. "Government by Manipulation." *Commentary* 2 (July 1946): 81–86.

————. "What Is Sociology's Job?" *Commentary* 3 (February 1947): 181–86.

Goncharov, N. K., and B. P. Yesipov. *I Want to Be Like Stalin*. Translated by George S. Counts and Nucia P. Lodge. New York: John Day Co., 1947.

Hazlitt, Henry. "A Fresh Start in Economics." *Saturday Review of Literature* 27 (5 July 1944): 38. [*Later Works* 15:502–3.]

Hook, Sidney. *Education for Modern Man.* New York: Dial Press, 1946.

———. "Ballyhoo at St. Johns College—Education in Retreat." *New Leader* 27 (27 May 1944): 8–9.

———. "Ballyhoo at St. Johns—II. The 'Great Books' and Progressive Teaching." *New Leader* 27 (3 June 1944): 8–10.

———. "Intelligence and Evil in Human History." *Commentary* 3 (March 1947): 210–21.

———. "The U.S.S.R. Views American Philosophy." *Modern Review* 1 (November 1947): 649–53.

Humanist. "God and Mathematics." *Humanist* 7 (September 1947): 101. [*Later Works* 15:507–8.]

Hume, David. *A Treatise of Human Nature: Being an Attempt to Introduce the Experimental Method of Reasoning into Moral Subject.* Vol. 1, *Of the Understanding.* London: John Noon, 1739.

Hutchins, Robert M. "Toward a Durable Society." *Fortune* 27 (June 1943): 159–60, 194, 196, 198, 201–2, 204, 207.

James, William. *The Letters of William James.* Edited by His Son, Henry James. Vol. 2. Boston: Atlantic Monthly Press, 1920.

———. *Memories and Studies.* New York: Longmans, Green, and Co., 1911.

———. *A Pluralistic Universe.* New York: Longmans, Green, and Co., 1909.

———. *Pragmatism: A New Name for Some Old Ways of Thinking.* New York: Longmans, Green, and Co., 1907.

———. *The Principles of Psychology.* 2 vols. New York: Henry Holt and Co., 1893.

———. *The Will to Believe: And Other Essays in Popular Philosophy.* London: Longmans, Green and Co., 1927.

Kelley, Earl C. *Education for What Is Real.* New York and London: Harper and Bros., 1947.

Krikorian, Yervant H., ed. *Naturalism and the Human Spirit.* New York: Columbia University Press, 1944.

Lewis, Clarence Irving. "Some Logical Considerations Concerning the Mental." *Journal of Philosophy* 38 (24 April 1941): 225–33.

Locke, John. *An Essay concerning Human Understanding.* In *The Works of John Locke,* 10th ed., vols. 1–3. London: J. Johnson, 1801.

———. *Further Considerations concerning Raising the Value of Money.* In *The Works of John Locke,* 5:131–206. London, 1823. Reprint, Berlin: Scientia Verlag Aalen, 1963.

Mackay, Donald Sage. "What Does Mr. Dewey Mean by an 'Indeterminate Situation'?" *Journal of Philosophy* 39 (12 March 1942): 141–48. [*Later Works* 15:393–401.]

Maritain, Jacques. "Contemporary Renewals in Religious Thought." In Maritain et al., *Religion and the Modern World*. Philadelphia: University of Pennsylvania Press, 1941.

Meiklejohn, Alexander. "A Reply to John Dewey." *Fortune* 31 (January 1945): 207–8, 210, 212, 214, 217, 219. [*Later Works* 15:474–85.]

Moore, G. E. *Ethics*. New York: Henry Holt and Co., 1912.

———. *Philosophical Studies*. New York: Harcourt, Brace and Co., 1922.

Morris, Charles W. *Foundations of the Theory of Signs. International Encyclopedia of Unified Science,* edited by Otto Neurath, vol. 1, no. 2. Chicago: University of Chicago Press, July 1938.

———. "Reply to Dewey." *Journal of Philosophy* 43 (28 March 1946): 196. [*Later Works* 15:473.]

Murphy, Arthur E. "Tradition and Traditionalists." In *The Authoritarian Attempt to Capture Education*. Papers from the 2d Conference on The Scientific Spirit and Democratic Faith, pp. 13–24. New York: King's Crown Press, 1945.

Neill, Thomas P. "Democracy's Intellectual 'Fifth Column.'" *Catholic World* 155 (May 1942): 151–55.

Newman, John Henry. *Lectures on Certain Difficulties Felt by Anglicans in Submitting to the Catholic Church*. London: Burns and Lambert, 1850.

New York Times. "Gaynor Appoints Herman Robinson." *New York Times,* 13 January 1910.

Nicolaevsky, Boris I., and David J. Dallin. *Forced Labor in Soviet Russia*. New Haven: Yale University Press, 1947.

Oxford English Dictionary. Oxford: At the Clarendon Press, 1933. [s.vv. "alas"; "intrinsic."]

Peirce, Charles Sanders. *Collected Papers of Charles Sanders Peirce*. Edited by Charles Hartshorne and Paul Weiss. Vols. 1, 2, 3, and 5. Cambridge: Harvard University Press, 1931, 1932, 1933, 1934.

Perry, Ralph Barton. *The Thought and Character of William James*. Vol. 1, *Inheritance and Vocation*. Boston: Little, Brown, and Co., 1935.

Polanyi, Karl. *The Great Transformation*. New York: Farrar and Rinehart, 1944.

———. "Our Obsolete Market Mentality." *Commentary* 3 (February 1947): 109–17.

Pope, Arthur Upham. "Merit Seen in Moscow Film." *New York Times,* 12 June 1943, p. 12. [*Later Works* 15:499–501.]

———. "*Mission to Moscow* Film Viewed as Historical Realism."

New York Times, 16 May 1943, p. 12. [*Later Works* 15:492–98.]

Rice, Philip Blair. "'Objectivity' in Value Judgments." *Journal of Philosophy* 40 (7 January 1943): 5–14. [*Later Works* 15:402–12.]

———. "Quality and Value." *Journal of Philosophy* 40 (24 June 1943): 337–48. [*Later Works* 15:413–25.]

———. "Types of Value Judgments." *Journal of Philosophy* 40 (30 September 1943): 533–43. [*Later Works* 15:426–37.]

Roosevelt, Franklin D. *Atlantic Charter. Congressional Record.* 77th Cong., 1st sess. 1941. Vol. 87, pt. 1, pp. 44–47.

Royce, Josiah. *The Spirit of Modern Philosophy.* Boston: Houghton, Mifflin and Co., 1892.

Russell, Bertrand. *A History of Western Philosophy.* New York: Simon and Schuster, 1945.

Savery, Barnett. "Intrinsic Good." *Journal of Philosophy* 39 (23 April 1942): 234–44.

Schaefer-Simmern, Henry. *The Unfolding of Artistic Activity.* Berkeley and Los Angeles: University of California Press, 1948.

Seligman, Edwin R. A. "Economics: The Discipline of Economics." In *Encyclopaedia of the Social Sciences,* edited by Seligman and Alvin Johnson, 5:344–46. New York: Macmillan Co., 1931.

Sheldon, Wilmon Henry. "Critique of Naturalism." *Journal of Philosophy* 42 (10 May 1945): 253–70. [*Later Works* 15:453–72.]

Smith, T. V. Tribute. In *James Hayden Tufts.* Privately printed memorial pamphlet, pp. 8–14. N.p. [1942].

Stevenson, Charles L. *Ethics and Language.* New Haven: Yale University Press, 1944.

Thompson, Ralph. "Books of the Times." *New York Times,* 29 December 1941, p. 19.

Tufts, James Hayden. *America's Social Morality: Dilemmas of the Changing Mores.* New York: Henry Holt and Co., 1933.

———. *The Real Business of Living.* New York: Henry Holt and Co., 1918.

Tufts, James Hayden, and John Dewey. *Ethics.* New York: Henry Holt and Co., 1908; 1932. [*Middle Works* 5; *Later Works* 7.]

Whyte, A. Gowans. "The Three Humanisms." *Literary Guide and Rationalist Review* 59 (March 1944): 30–31.

Williams, Eric. *Education in the British West Indies.* Port-of-Spain, Trinidad, B.W.I.: Guardian Commercial Printery, 1946.

Windelband, Wilhelm. *A History of Philosophy with Especial Reference to the Formation and Development of Its Problems and Conceptions.* Translated by James H. Tufts. New York: Macmillan and Co., 1893.

Woodward, Frederic. Tribute. In *James Hayden Tufts*. Privately printed memorial pamphlet, pp. 1–7. N.p. [1942].

Yesipov, B. P., and N. K. Goncharov. *I Want to Be Like Stalin*. Translated by George S. Counts and Nucia P. Lodge. New York: John Day Co., 1947.

Index